D1523296

Exemplary Bodies: Constructing the Jew in Russian Culture, since the 1880s

BORDERLINES:
RUSSIAN AND EAST EUROPEAN –
JEWISH STUDIES

ACADEMIC
STUDIES
PRESS

Exemplary Bodies: Constructing the Jew in Russian Culture, since the 1880s

by Henrietta Mondry

Boston
2009

Library of Congress Cataloging-in-Publication Data

Mondry, Henrietta.
Exemplary Bodies : constructing the Jew in Russian culture since the 1880s /
by Henrietta Mondry.
    p. cm.—(Borderlines: Russian and East European Jewish studies)
Includes bibliographical references and index.

ISBN 978-1-934843-39-0 (hardback)

    1. Jews in popular culture—Russia (Federation) 2. Human body in popular culture—
    Russia (Federation) 3. Body image—Social aspects—Russia (Federation) 4. Russian
    literature—History and criticism. 5. Russia (Federation)—Intellectual life. 6. Russia
    (Federation)—Ethnic relations. I. Title.

DS134.83.M66 2009
305.892'4047—dc22
    2009026734

On the cover: Mark Chagall. The Red Jew (a fragment). 1915
Cover design by Ivan Grave

Published by Academic Studies Press in 2009
28 Montfern Avenue
Brighton, MA 02135, USA
press@academicstudiespress.com
www.academicstudiespress.com

"In a moment of tenderness my wife tells me that I look like a Viking, but it is flattery: another Jew, Kirk Douglas, plays Vikings in Hollywood"

Alexander Melikhov. *The Confession of a Jew.* 2004.

Acknowledgements

I am indebted to several colleagues and friends for special support and advice during the work on this book. My first thanks go to the series editors, Harriet Murav and Alice Nakhimovsky for their invaluable comments on the content of the book and numerous points of detail. I am particularly grateful to Igor Nemirovsky for his unfailing support of my work. I greatly appreciate advice given to me by Sander Gilman, Elena Katz, and the late Joseph Sherman at various stages of this project. I acknowledge with gratitude the constant encouragement of my colleagues Alexandra Smith and Evgeny Pavlov. Special thanks are due to Sally Blundell and John Goodliffe for their editorial support in preparation of this book. The Skirball Fellowship at the Oxford Centre for Hebrew and Jewish Studies and the financial support of the University of Canterbury's Oxford Exchange Fellowship helped me to conduct research at Oxford libraries and exchange ideas with colleagues at Oxford University.

A Note on Transliteration

In transliterating Russian, I have used the Library of Congress system, except for personal names commonly appearing in English, such as "Leo Tolstoy" and "Alexander Nevsky." In bibliographical references, however, I have used the conventional transliteration of personal names.

Contents

List of Illustrations

Introduction

How does one recognize a Jew in Russia? What makes a Jew visible in Russia and its successor state, the Soviet Union? According to a famous Russian folk "witticism" a surname is not a real indicator of a person's ethnic origins — one cannot, therefore, trust the identity document that states a person's ethnicity. Such folk wisdom materialized in Russia in the proverb: "You beat a person on his mug, not on his passport," implying that, to recognize a member of a different race, including a Jew, you must look to the physical characteristics written on that person's face. This proverb, used in turn-of-the-century tsarist Russia, was popular in Soviet Russia and is still widely used in Russia today.[2] But are Jews a different race? Do Russian Jews all look like a race apart from their Russian and quasi-Russian neighbors?

The Case of Afanasy Fet

There is an extraordinary case in the history of the Russian literary élite that encapsulates the subject of Jewish origins and the way in which Jewishness was seen to be reflected in the physical body. This case concerns the famous Russian poet Afanasy Fet (1820–1890).[3] Born to a Russian father from the gentry class and a German-born mother whose first husband's surname was Foeth or Voeth, Afanasy Fet was considered by his circle of friends to be Jewish. This circle included such major personalities as Ivan Turgenev and Leo Tolstoy, whose country estates were situated not far from the Fets' property.[4] The mystery surrounding the ethnic origins of Fet's mother (née Carlotta Becker) and his biological father (Foeth or Voeth) has never been resolved, due to the lack of documentary evidence.[5] Previous rumors claimed that the missing documents pertaining to the alleged "Jewish origins" of Fet's mother were buried with Fet in accordance with his wishes.[6] The mystery surrounding this saga did not prevent even the well-known skeptic Ilya

Ehrenburg from accepting this rumor as evidence of Fet's Jewish origins, and in his famous chronicle *People, Years, Life* (1960–1965), he confirmed that Fet was a Jew, repeating the story of the documents in Fet's coffin.[7] Fet's contemporaries liked to discuss the story of Fet's parents—how, during a military campaign, the Russian officer Shenshin met and fell in love with a beautiful Jewess who was married at the time and pregnant with a child by her husband. Shenshin bought her from her husband and took her with him to Russia. There she converted to the Russian Orthodox faith and after a few months gave birth to a child from her marriage in Germany. This child was Afanasy Fet. Yet all the existing evidence points to the falseness of these assumptions about the Jewish origins of Fet's mother. Fet himself traveled to Darmstadt where he met his German family from his mother's side, all the members of whom were Protestant Germans. His contemporaries however, still liked to talk about the beautiful Jewess and Fet's Jewish looks, which he allegedly inherited from his mother and his real father. Even to the present day, Fet is considered to be of Jewish origin by those who, for some reason, find it either useful or convenient.[8]

As was mentioned above, in Russia, a Jew is beaten on his face even if his passport indicates non-Jewishness. Certainly, the case of Fet confirms this cultural belief that a Jew is identifiable due to special "Jewish" external features. Of relevance to this present study is the fact that the claim concerning Fet's supposedly Jewish origins rests only on one piece of "evidence": his appearance. Fet allegedly had "Jewish looks," as seen in the following descriptions:

> "Afanasy Afanasievich's appearance was characteristic [of Jews]." (S. L. Tolstoy, Leo Tolstoy's eldest son [11])[9]

> Fet's Jewish origins "were strongly expressed by his physical appearance." (P. Bartenev, Fet's contemporary [12])

> "My mother used to tell him [Fet] that he looked like a Jew." (N. Puzin, a distant relative [12])

> In the portrait painted by Ilya Repin (1881), Fet's Jewish features are "especially typical" and "catch the eye" (V. Fedina, Fet scholar in 1915 [34]).[10]

> Fet's Jewish looks "can be seen on his portraits and photographs" (Boris Bukhshtab, Fet Soviet scholar [12]).[11]

Leo Tolstoy's wife, Sofia, with whom Fet was in lively correspondence and whom he held in highest esteem, felt sorry for Fet because of his unfortunate "Jewish" appearance.

This situation has puzzled me for a long time for a number of reasons, one of which is being that even the most contemporary Fet scholar, Boris Bukhshtab (1904–1985), a Jew himself, considered it possible to see from Fet's photographs and portraits that he was Jewish. As a product of Russian and Soviet society Bukhshtab could have internalized anti-Jewish prejudices and stereotypes among other beliefs, but did it not occur to this brilliant scholar that the image on a portrait and even a photograph can be manipulated? And that "characteristic features" on a face might be just the product of the painter's will or the photographer's skill?

When I look at one of Fet's earlier portraits I see a handsome young man resembling the famous Italian tenor Luciano Pavarotti. But I have been exposed to a visual culture that provides me with a wide variety of faces and appearances, and it becomes increasingly difficult to classify a person's ethnicity on the basis of his or her looks. I understand that some of Fet's acquaintances had very limited exposure to foreign faces. If they did go to Spain or Italy they would have seen in Fet's face the features of "a noble Spaniard" or "a handsome Italian." Then they might have rethought their typological and aesthetic judgment. Instead, they probably read about beautiful Jewesses and Spanish and Italian women from travelers' notes and romantic literature, written by male authors who, in the tradition of European Orientalism, did not praise the looks of the Spanish, Italian, and Jewish men as much as they praised the looks of the women.[12] Did Fet's friends see many Jews in the Russian countryside where their estates were situated, from which to form an opinion on their supposedly typical appearance? Did they see paintings representing Jewish patriarchs such as Abraham or Moses, or Spanish or Italian men?[13] And even if they did, would those representations be true reflections or just constructs of such "typical" features? But they would have helped Fet's commentators to pass an aesthetic judgment about a particular face. I expect that what happened in their case is exactly what happened in the case of Afanasy Fet himself: the aesthetic ideal that was instilled in all of them embodied the concept that the face of a male Jew could not be beautiful. And they all believed it. Yet the logic behind this assumption is absurd: why cannot such a face look beautiful? Because it is Jewish. It is Jewish because it is not beautiful. But there should be more evidence than that to substantiate this judgment.

Another fascinating aspect of Fet's alleged Jewish looks and origins relates to his own self-perception and staging of the Self. Fet vehemently denied his Jewish origins. Indeed, he tried all his life not only to excel as a poet but also to look and act like a born member of the Russian nobility. Perhaps because he was deprived of the aristocratic rights associated with the surname Shenshin, he spent most of his life in pursuits that were typical of the behavior of a Russian nobleman: he entered the army, he bought land, and he became an exemplary landowner whose practical skills made him a wealthy man. Even his conservative social views can be attributed to this self-styled Russianness. But no matter how precisely he adhered to the behavior of a Russian gentleman, those who knew him interpreted his practicality and his ability to make money as Jewish traits of character. Despite his assumed behavior and crafted sense of self, he continued to be a Jew in the minds of his friends and acquaintances.

Although this assumption was based primarily on Fet's appearance, there is evidence to suggest that his acquaintances believed that his "Jewish" nature was also inscribed on his psyche. Some of his friends, including Ivan Turgenev, who had a special interest in phrenology and craniology, considered him to be quite mad, and emphasized the hereditary nature of his madness: "And he too [like his two mad brothers and a mad sister] has a dark spot on his brain," wrote Turgenev in 1872 (236).[14] Nikolai Chernyshevsky, another author well versed in biological discourses, called Fet "an idiot" (1878) — a term used clinically at the time.[15] Both writers, nevertheless, held Fet's poetic gift in high esteem. Was there a psychological flaw that Fet recognized in himself and yet was incapable of escaping? His mother ended her days in an asylum for the mentally ill, and some of his brothers and a sister followed suit. It appears that in the same way in which Fet could not change his appearance even after he was granted permission from the tsar to change his "foreign" surname to his father's Russian name, Shenshin, he obviously believed that he could not change his psyche. This account of alleged hereditary madness is highly illustrative. Fet describes in his memoirs how Shenshin was a difficult man, with episodes of cruelty and depression.[16] But it was not his father's psychological traits that he regarded as symptomatic of mental illness. His mother had been hospitalized during the last years of her life and was allegedly prone to fits of melancholy and depression. These episodes increased over the years into a fully developed psychological condition. With no medical documents available it is plausible to conclude that the German (or German Jewish) woman who had been brought into a hostile and foreign environment started suffering from fits of anxiety, which the gender-biased doctors diagnosed as a clinical condition. In Fet's own mind there was no doubt that he had inherited his mother's "madness" as a physical manifestation inscribed on his body. During the last moments of his life, in a state of great agitation preceding his heart attack, he allegedly tried to cut himself with a knife that his secretary tried to take away from him.

Fet's lack of ability or desire to consider aspects of his father's character in his own behavior strikes one as astonishing, and attests to the fact that he did not regard madness as a characteristic feature of the Russian gentry. Rather, he felt more comfortable seeing himself as the depository of a hereditary illness that came from his mother's side. Did Fet believe that he was destined to go mad because he had inherited madness as part of his mother's "Jewishness"? If yes, then he believed that there was such a thing as a Jewish body and that nature inscribed on it not only external markers but also internal ones, including madness. After all, Fet was a contemporary of the doctor and criminal anthropologist Cesare Lombroso (1835–1909) who, although a Jew himself, in his highly influential work, *The Man of Genius*, singled out Jews as a people prone to madness, thus promoting a link between race and ethnicity and mental health. Fet's friends, including Tolstoy and Turgenev, were familiar with Lombroso's views on madness in men of genius as well as in Jews — views that may well have served as "scientific evidence" of Fet's derangement, with the "dark spot on his brain". Did Fet (as a Jew) believe that he was mad because of his Jewish origins? Did his friends believe that he was mad because he was a Jew?

The link between Fet's alleged madness and his Jewish origins becomes more overt in discussions about him at the beginning of the twentieth century. As racialist discourse based on pseudo-scientific notions of biological determinism gained momentum in Russia, greater emphasis was put on hereditary characteristics and the link between race and madness. In 1915 the most famous Russian ideologue of the body, Vasily Rozanov, devoted an entire article to new speculations about Fet's origins. He called it "New Research on Fet."[17] The debate centered on the issue of the mysterious and strange nature of this poet. In line with the intellectual trends of the time, authors explained Fet's "madness" (617) by his artistic genius.[18] At the same time, characteristically for contemporary discourse, Fet's strangeness was seen to be firmly grounded in his biological roots. The question asked was, how could Fet, the practical and mercantile man, also be the author of the most mystical lyrics ever written in Russian poetry? Rozanov gave a highly illustrative answer: the paradox, he argued, could be explained by Fet's "dual physiology" (615). He was "a mystic and a seraphim" (616), the author of "seraphic poetry" (517). Such characteristics, Rozanov claimed, were the manifestations of Fet's Jewish nature, which he inherited from his tender and melancholic mother. His practicality, on the other hand, he inherited from his Russian father, Shenshin. By referring to seraphims in relation to Fet, Rozanov thus establishes a direct corporeal genealogy of the Jewish body from the bodies of the Old Testament.

The "case of Fet" continued to develop within the modern discourse of the 1910s to form a phylogenetic set consisting of Jewish appearance, psyche and character. In this regard a new set of questions emerged: Do inherited traits of character apply more to Jews than to others? Is Jewish physiology more powerful than that of non-Jews? Can a Jew escape his/her hereditary script? Can one read the script on the Jew's body and, if so, what are the signs? What kind of behavior results from a typically Jewish psyche and physiology? And can a change of circumstances—geographic, political, economic, and social—alter inherited characteristics in Jews in the same way that it does in other ethnic groups and nationalities? These questions gained special momentum during the seventy years of the Soviet experiment.

The present book applies the questions embodied in "the case of Fet" to a number of authors from the 1880s to the 2000s who made these themes a subject of their work. It demonstrates how the construct of the Jewish body, psyche, and character has been modeled by Russian culture from the times of the Tolstoys and the Fets to the present, and how Russian culture has responded to this construct during this period.[19] I argue here that the Jewish body is the body onto which culture inscribes meaning, and that this body has a surface and inner organs — its psyche is as material and biological as the brain, and it is this that results in a special type of behavior. Both the body's exterior and interior are inscribed with characteristics that aim to define the Jew as the Other. In the same way that Fet saw his own inner world as determined by his (half) Jewish origins, the present book also finds answers to a set of questions relating to the Jews' own perception and expression of the Jewish body, and the strategies employed by Russian Jews to conceal, change, and erase signs of their Jewishness. How has this strategy evolved from Fet's time during the 1880s to the present? And how has emigration and the Diaspora experience affected Jews' perception of their own bodies, their visibility, and their inner selves?

In discussing these questions I argue that Russian discourse on the Jewish body is still underpinned by the concept of race — a concept that defines Jews as a group of people that displays inherent, heritable and predictive characteristics on a biological or quasi-biological basis.[20] Such a discourse continues to gain momentum in post-Soviet Russia due to the rise of Russian self-assertiveness and nationalism. The latest genetic findings show that genetic differences among groups of people with different phenotypic attributes are minor (phenotypes are the joint products of an organism's genes and the environment in which they develop and appear, whereas a genotype is an organism's complete hereditary information or genetic make-up, whether or not every aspect is apparent[21]).[22] Yet in Russia in the twenty-first century there remain, as will be shown further, major proponents of quasi-biological racial science.

Exploring Jewish Recognizability

Recent work on race differences has a strong interdisciplinary character: anthropology and psychology, cognitive philosophy and political history, genetics. Commentators have to take into account the impressive amount of material available on the issue of race differences. People who believe in the primacy of environment and people who believe in the primacy of heredity are looking for common ground, and both parties have agreed to take into account the influence of genes and different environments on the group of individuals representing "race." There is a clear distinction between ethnicity and race and the present book makes use of this distinction: ethnicity refers to a cluster of people who have common cultural traits that distinguish them from those of other people — language, religion, sense of history, food habits, beliefs, and so forth. The concept of race as it emerged in twentieth century sciences focuses on human biogenetic variation;[23] yet this popular concept of race is a cultural invention, fusing together physical features and behavior. In the same way that race as a biological term has been proclaimed a fiction, the existence of the "Jewish race" has also been deemed a myth.[24]

The empirical reality of the question of the recognizability of the Jew in countries such as Poland and Russia has been well described in the book *The Myth of the Jewish Race* (1975) by Raphael Patai and Jennifer Patai Wing. They explain that the only people in these countries who exhibit Mediterranean features are Jews, because Jewish people have retained sufficient Mediterranean features to enable identification in non-Mediterranean settings; hence, a Mediterranean-looking individual was "recognized" as a Jew. ("Similarly, in the same countries, an Indian-looking individual was 'recognized' as a Gypsy" [192].) This explanation has a special appeal to me as it helps to explain why, in my own perception, Afanasy Fet looks like Luciano Pavarotti. But what needs to be stressed in regard to visibility is that "we fail to notice and identify a much larger number of Jews who have taken on traits of the people among whom they live and thus pass unnoticed" (192).[25]

My purpose is to explore the construct of the Jew's physical and ontological body in Russian culture as represented in literature, film and non-literary texts from the 1880s to the present. My premise is that, with the rise of the dominance of biological and racialist discourse in the 1880s, the depiction of Jewish characters in Russian literary and cultural productions underwent a significant change, as these cultural practices started to conceptualize the Jew not only as an archetypal exotic and religious or class Other (as in both Romanticism and Realism),[26] but as a biological Other whose acts, deeds and thoughts were determined by biological and racial differences.[27] This Jew allegedly had definite and distinct physical and psychological characteristics which were genetically determined and which could not be changed by education, acculturation, conversion to Christianity, or change of social status. The stereotype resulting from such perceived racial and biological differences has become a stable archetype that continues to operate in contemporary Russian society and its cultural productions. Sander Gilman and Daniel Boyarin, among others, have demonstrated the emergence of this new construct of the Jew's body in fin-de-siècle Europe — a construct that was informed by the quasi-scientific theories of racialist science and medicine. Scholars of the Jewish body in European cultures have shown that this construct was also accepted as a given by Jewish scientists, doctors, writers, thinkers and prominent public figures, and that even emerging Zionism internalized these stereotypes of the special nature of the Jew's physical body. This body has been construed as both alternative and pathological in line with the turn-of-the-century preoccupation with the notion of degeneration and the physical and psychological pathology of inbred and "tied nations." Jews have been viewed as archetypal examples of almost every kind of pathology associated with such theories. At the same time, they have also been viewed as a racial group, which has survived for almost four thousand years as a unified biological species. This stereotype has become one of the most enduring discursive formations of both the sub-culture of Russian antisemitism and mainstream cultural discourse that exists in Russia to this day.[28]

Recent scholarship on racism in Imperial Russia at the end of the nineteenth and the beginning of the twentieth centuries stresses that during this period racism became widespread among political and cultural élites as well as in popular culture. Laura Engelstein (1992) states that after "workers, peasants, and professionals had jointly engaged in a common political culture and after the privileged groups had secured the measure of political responsibility for themselves that biological determinism already current in the West began to exert a noticeable appeal" (130–131) in Russia.[29] Eli Weinerman (1994) states that when racism emerged in Russia as a pseudo-scientific concept its adherents' main demand was "to stop Russians from mixing with non-Russians, especially Jews" (442).[30] In his opinion these ideas were restricted to narrow circles of nationalist intellectuals. Eugene Avrutin's study on racial categories and politics of difference in Russia at the beginning of the twentieth century (2007) shows that out of all ethnic groups of the Empire Jews defined racial difference.[31] Both political and popular periodicals such as *Novoe vremia* (*New Times*), *Vampir* (*Vampire*) and *Karikaturnyi listok* (*Leaflet with Caricatures*) regularly published caricatures of Jews who were depicted as filthy and dangerous, polluting the streets of Russia and destroying the moral fabric of the society. Cartoons depicted Jews with exaggerated physiognomic features such as large and hooked noses and thick lips.[32] Avrutin concludes that by the beginning of the twentieth century, the negative image of the Jew as a racial Other was firmly entrenched in popular culture. Eric Weitz's recent study (2002) on racial politics in Stalin's Russia demonstrates racialist underpinnings of Soviet ethnic and national purges. It demonstrates that "traces of racial politics crept into Soviet nationalities policies"(3), the state deported entire national groups, and "particular populations were endowed with immutable traits that every member of the group possessed and that were passed from one generation to the next"(3).[33] Of special relevance to my study is Weitz's point that in Stalin's Russia the escalation of ethnic and national purges came alongside the elevation of Russians into "an essentialized, virtually racialized nation" (11) — a point that demonstrates the racialist underpinnings of Soviet Russian nationalism and self-assertiveness. It is against the Russians as a biological group of people that Jews' biological difference has been played out in Russian cultural productions under examination in this book.

My study examines a set of texts and primary sources that are chronologically wider but thematically narrower than the materials studied by these historians on the topic of race in Russia. My intention in analyzing the texts of both Russian and Russian Jewish anthropologists, doctors, writers and film directors is to demonstrate the extent to which the construct of the Jewish body has been internalized by Jewish and non-Jewish writers and artists at the end of the nineteenth-century Russia, and during Soviet and post-Soviet Russia, thus revealing various psychological dynamics operating within the depiction of the Jewish body by Russian and Russian Jewish authors, and the different strategies employed by Russian authors of Jewish origin in dealing with the cultural construct of the Jewish body. In addition, my analysis of the works of both male and female Russian Jewish authors examines complex gender-related mechanisms they employ in their dealings with their own Jewishness.[34] Also included are Russian Jewish authors of the post-Soviet era who moved to Israel in order to depict the complex and the fully representative cultural dynamics in contemporary Russian-language texts. My approach and methodology are underpinned by the work of various body theorists (Lacan, Freud, Deleuze, Grosz) as well as by the work of scholars such as Sander Gilman and Daniel Boyarin, who have developed investigation into the Jewish body as depicted in Western culture.[35] The core idea that underpins the work of the body theorists and cultural historians is that the human body is a site onto which culture inscribes meaning.

This study offers examples of the construction of the Jewish body from anthropological and biological works and prominent authors and film directors, through purveyors of pseudo-scientific fantasy, masquerading as philosophers or scientists, to popular propagandists and agents provocateurs who put their material on the Internet. Although there are other writers whose work could provide suitable material for case studies of the depiction of the Jew's body during the chosen period, I believe each of the authors selected here provides a graphic illustration that typifies political and ideological trends of a particular time, and/or psychological underpinnings of the desire to deal with the characteristics of the Jewish body. All the cases demonstrate aspects of continuity in the representation of the Jewish body, at the same time showing that each author has an individual way of expressing ideas.

Chapter One explores the theme of the Jewish body in early Russian anthropological and biological sciences. By no means exhaustive, it lays a foundation for the themes and issues explored in the following chapters.

Chapter Two marks the first step in this chronological investigation. It examines how Anton Chekhov was exposed as a medical student to the scientific theories that conceptualized pathologies according to race. It analyzes his literary characters in stories written during the 1880s as marked by physical and psychological peculiarities viewed as typically Jewish. It also shows how Chekhov negotiated his own physical pathology — tuberculosis — in the context of race and ethnicity.

Chapter Three shows how Vasily Rozanov, although a contemporary of Chekhov, emerged as the first and most influential "theorist" of the Jewish physical and ontological body at the turn of the century. Rozanov embraced Western "findings" in regard to racial differences pertaining to the Jewish body and combined them with his own interpretation of Jewish bodies as determined by race and religion. He created a link between the body of the Creator (Adonai) and that of his creation (Adon) both of which he visualized as a physical, sexed body sharing the same features. The Jew's body thus became a transgressive body that crosses boundaries between male and female sex and gender, between human and divine body, and violates sexual prohibitions.

Moving into the second decade of the twentieth century, Chapter Four provides a reading of two of Ilya Ehrenburg's picaresque characters from his modernist texts of the 1920s, demonstrating his authorial position vis-à-vis Jewish essentialism. It also gives a close reading of Lazik Roitschwantz as a caricatured character to whom Ehrenburg ascribes all the staple features of the antisemitic folk image of the male Jew. In 1962 Ehrenburg had to interfere in the case of a Jewish man accused of ritual blood letting in Georgia: an example both of a stable superstition in Russian culture and of the political exploitation of antisemitic beliefs by the authorities.

Chapter Five covers the years from the 1930s to the 1950s and concentrates on the construct of the male Jew's body in Stalinist culture in the period marked first by the rhetoric of "reforging" (*perekovka*) in the 1930s, then by the exposure of Jews as ultimate traitors to the Soviet economy in the 1950s. It studies the imagery of Jewish males in Solomon Mikhoels's film *Seekers of Happiness* (1936) and in Valentin Ivanov's novel *The Yellow Metal* (1956), both of which include Jewish characters who are involved in illicit economic activities.

Various studies of the image of the Jew in Russian literature between the 1950s and the 1980s have shown how this image has been stripped of any specific ethnic characteristics.[36] Such "deracination" was said to occur alongside the ban on Jewish themes in Russian textbooks in relation to both the pre-revolutionary period of Russian history and Soviet history, including the theme of pogroms and the Holocaust. Chapter Six demonstrates that, contrary to this belief, the notion of Jews' specific and often pathological nature did not disappear from antisemitic discourse but resurfaced in fiction and film, as well as in political texts. This chapter looks at Ivan Shevtsov's novel *Love and Hatred* (1970) as well as a number of political texts that present the notion of such a stereotype during the anti-Zionist campaign that preceded and followed the 1967 Six Day Arab-Israeli War.

Chapter Seven reveals how, in the decade of the 1980s, the lifting of censorship brought about by Glasnost led to a resurgence of antisemitic material and with it the re-emergence of stereotypes, many of which are encapsulated in the construct of the male Jewish body as that of an oversexed (and yet, paradoxically, not virile) Other. This body was depicted as dangerous and alien to the collective Russian body, its lascivious nature and hyperbolized sexual lust threatening the racial purity of the Russian people. Vasily Belov's controversial novel *The Best Is Yet To Come* (1987) is examined as a text that encapsulates the construct of the Jew under the new political regime. This chapter also shows how the image of the Jews as "the people of the body" found its representation in the Glasnost film *Ladies' Taylor* by Leonid Gorovetz (1990).

Chapter Eight traces the importation of the construct of the Jew's body by a Jewish writer who emigrated to Israel in the 1990s. It demonstrates how the Russian Israeli woman writer Dina Rubina (b. 1953) negotiates her ethnic identity through the construction of her own ethnic body following emigration from Russia. Although a surface reading of her texts reveals her immigration to Israel to be a liberating experience, a deeper reading exposes more ambivalence and hesitation about her Jewish Self as her fantasies incorporate a wish for Spanish rather than Jewish genetic origins. Her own body thus becomes the site onto which she projects her fantasy in flesh through her literary texts.

Chapter Nine extends the examination of the cultural construct of the racial difference of the Jewish body by writers living in Israel through an investigation of Alexander Goldstein's post-modernist prose. Goldstein (1957–2006) emigrated to Israel in 1990, but his work won him several prestigious literary awards in Russia. His complicated prose is saturated with reflections on the theory of the body out of which he constructed his own body politics. This body is gendered and sexed, and is informed by the textual and semantic fragments of the cultural history of the Jew's racialized body.

Chapter Ten returns to literary work written in Russia in the present decade to show how economic wars against prominent oligarchs of Jewish origin have been fought as racial wars. It examines the caricatures of the prominent contemporary personalities Boris Berezovsky and Vladimir Gusinsky in Alexander Prokhanov's best-selling novel *Mr. Hexogen* (2002).

Chapter Eleven continues to examine the post-Soviet construct of the Jew's body, turning not to literary texts but to non-fictional quasi-scientific discourse. It shows the phenomenal success and popularity of the work of the self-declared Russian antisemite Grigory Klimov (1918–2007). It shows how Klimov uses, abuses, and misuses the Russian intellectual heritage of the past in his construction of the Jew. This chapter also examines the construct of the Jew's racial body in the work of Vladimir Avdeev, whose work represents a return to the racial sciences of the past with the Jew's body as the most common example of the raced body. As such it provides evidence for the rise of Russian nationalism and xenophobia in today's Russia.

The Conclusion shows what has changed in the construct of the Jewish body and what has remained stable; it demonstrates the ongoing development of new variants and versions, new assemblages and conglomerates which Russian culture continues to produce and reveals how the culture recycles and reinvents old stereotypes and endows them with contemporary meaning and the sense of today.

Notes

1   V. V. Rozanov. Literaturnye novinki. *O pisatel'stve i pisateliakh. Sobranie sochinenii.* Ed. A. Nikoliukin. Moscow: Respublika. 1995. 166–175. 175. Rozanov uses the word passport for the identity document as it has been used in Russian culture up to the present. Unless otherwise stated all translations are by me.

2   Vasily Rozanov used a version of this proverb in his article on Gogol in 1909. See V. V. Rozanov. Magicheskaia stranitsa u Gogolia. *O pisatel'stve i pisateliakh.* Moscow: Respublika. 1995. 383–421. 413. On the Soviet and post-Soviet period see Aleksandr Melikhov. *Ispoved' evreia.* Moscow and St. Petersburg: Limbus Press. 2004.

3   Philosopher and poet Vladimir Soloviev called Fet "a genius" and put him on the level of Pushkin and Tiutchev: "Russian poetry... has diamonds of Pushkin, pearls of Tiutchev, emeralds and rubies of Fet." See V. Soloviev. *Pis'ma Vl. S. Solovieva.* Vol. 1. St. Petersburg. 1908. 226.

4   Leo Tolstoy held Fet in high esteem and treasured his friendship. See Boris Ia. Bukhshtab. *A. A. Fet. Ocherk zhizni i tvorchestva.* Leningrad: Nauka. 1990. On Tolstoy and the Jewish theme see George Lieberman. "The Jewish Experience in Russian Literature as Reflected in the Writings of Leo Tolstoy." *Proceedings of the 8th World Congress of Jewish Studies.* Jerusalem: World Union of Jewish Studies. 1982. 135–140.

5   See Boris Ia. Bukhshtab. *A. A. Fet. Ocherk zhizni i tvorchestva.* Leningrad: Nauka. 1990.

6   V. S. Fedina. *A. A. Fet (Shenshin): Materialy k kharakteristike.* Petrograd. 1915.

7   Ehrenburg writes that Fet's father was a Hamburg Jew.

8   For a discussion see Maxim Shrayer who included Fet in the anthology of Russian Jewish literature: Maxim Shrayer. *An Anthology of Jewish-Russian Literature: Two Centuries of Dual Identity in Prose and Poetry.* Vol. 1. New York: M. E. Sharpe. 2007. 20–26.

9   Quoted in Bukhshtab. Op. cit.

10   Quoted in Fedina. Op. cit.

11   Quoted in Bukhshtab. Op. cit.

12   A typical example of this depiction is found in Fet's contemporary, V. P. Botkin's *Letters about Spain* (1857). See V. P. Botkin. *Pis'ma ob Ispanii.* Leningrad: Nauka. 1976.

13   See Ivan Goncharov's 1874 article on the depiction of Biblical characters in Russian paintings and in Western art. I. Goncharov. "Khristos v pustyne": Kartina g. Kramskogo. *Sobranie sochinenii.* Moscow: Pravda, Ogoniok. 1952. Vol. 8. 220–231.

14   See I. S. Turgenev. *Polnoe sobranie sochinenii i pisem v 28 tomakh.* Moscow and Leningrad: Nauka. Vol. 9. 1960–1968. 236.

15   N. G. Chernyshevskii. Pis'mo 1878 g. *Polnoe sobranie sochinenii v 15 tomakh.* Vol. 4. Moscow: 1939–1953. 508. On his biological views see Irina Paperno. *Chernyshevsky and the Age of Realism.* Stanford, CA: Stanford University Press. 1988.

16   See A. A. Fet. Vospominaniia. Moscow: Pravda. 1983. On the theme of madness in Fet's poetry and its polemical aspects see Susan Layton. "A Hidden Polemic with Leo Tolstoy: Afanasy Fet's Lyric 'Mine was the madness he wanted...'". *The Russian Review,* 66. April 2007. 220–237.

17   V. V. Rozanov. Novoe issledovanie o Fete. *O pisatel'stve i pisateliakh.* Moscow: Respublika. 1995. 614–619.

18   Rozanov refers to the article by D. Darskii. O Fete. *Russkaia mysl'.* No. 8. 1915.

19   It is ironic that Andrei Belyi in his antisemitic article "Shtempelevannaia kul'tura" (1909) includes Fet in the Russian cultural canon next to Pushkin, Tolstoy and Dostoevsky—the canon that represents the Russian culture that contemporary international Jewry allegedly destroys by creating a consumer culture. Andrei Belyi. Shtempelevannaia kul'tura. Ed. G. S. Zelenina. *Evrei i zhidy.* Moscow and Jerusalem: Mosty kul'tury, Gesharim. 2005. 365–376.

20   See Raphael Patai and Jennifer Patai Wing. *The Myth of the Jewish Race.* New York: Charles

Scribner's Sons. 1975.

[21] See Michael Levin. *Why Race Matters. Race Differences and What They Mean.* Westport, CT: Praeger. 1997.

[22] D. Unander. *Shattering the Myth of Race: Genetic Realities and Biblical Truth.* Valley Forge, PA: Judson Press. 2000.

[23] See Audrey Smedley and Brian Smedley. Race as Biology is Fiction, Racism as a Social Problem is Real. (Anthropological and Historical Perspectives on the Social Construction of Race). *American Psychologist.* Vol. 60. No 1. 2005. 16–26.

[24] Patai and Patai Wing, Smedley and Smedley. Op. cit.

[25] Patai and Patai Wing quote Juan Comas, Racial Myth in *Race and Science.* New York: Columbia University Press. 1961. 38.

[26] See John D. Klier. *Russia Gathers Her Jews: The Origins of the "Jewish Question" in Russia, 1772–1825.* DeKalb: Northern Illinois University Press. 1986; John D. Klier. *Imperial Russia's Jewish Question, 1855–1881.* Cambridge UK: Cambridge University Press. 1995.

[27] For the latest exposé of the image of the Jew in the age of realism see Elena Katz. *Neither With Them Nor Without Them: The Russian Writer and the Jew in the Age of Realism.* Syracuse: Syracuse University Press. 2008. For a good summary of the typology of Jews in Russian romanticism and realism see Mikhail Edel'shtein. Istoriia odnogo stereotipa. Ed. G. S. Zelenina. *Evrei i zhidy v russkoi klassike.* Moscow and Jerusalem: Mosty kul'tury. Gesharim. 2005. 384–391.

[28] On the latest scholarship on the concept of antisemitism in the European context see *Rethinking European Jewish History.* Ed. Jeremy Cohen and Moshe Rosman. Oxford: The Littman Library of Jewish Civilization. 2008.

[29] Laura Engelstein. *The Keys to Happiness: Sex and the Search for Modernity in Fin-de-Siecle Russia.* Ithaca NY: Cornell University Press. 1992.

[30] Eli Weinerman. Racism, Racial Prejudice, and the Jews in Late Imperial Russia. *Ethnic Racial Studies.* Vol. 17. No 3, July 1994. 442–495.

[31] Eugene Avrutin. Racial Categories and the Politics of (Jewish) Difference in Late Imperial Russia. *Kritika: Explorations in Russian and Eurasian History* 8. No. 1. 2007. 13–40.

[32] See *Vampir*, No. 6. 1906; *Karikaturnyi listok.* No. 4. 1906; *Novoe vremia.* No. 10599. 4 September 4, 1905.

[33] Eric Weitz. Racial Politics Without the Concept of Race: Reevaluating Soviet Ethnic and National Purges. *Slavic Review.* Vol. 61. No. 1. Spring 2002. 1–29. See the discussion of this article in the same volume.

[34] On Jewish identity in Russian Jewish literature see Alice Stone Nakhimovsky. *Russian Jewish Literature and Identity: Jabotinsky, Babel, Grossman, Galich, Roziner, Markish.* Baltimore: The Johns Hopkins University Press. 1992.

[35] Jacques Lacan. *The Four Fundamental Concepts of Psycho-Analysis.* Ed. Jacques-Alain Miller, trans. Alan Sheridan. New York: W.W. Norton. 1978. Sigmund Freud. On the Mechanism of Paranoia in *The Standard Edition of the Complete Works of Sigmund Freud*, Vol. 12, Trans. James Strachey London: The Hogarth Press. 1958, 59–80. Sander L. Gilman. *The Jew's Body.* London: Routledge. 1991. Elizabeth Grosz. *Volatile Bodies: Toward a Corporeal Feminism.* Bloomington: Indiana University Press. 1994. Daniel Boyarin. *Unheroic Conduct: The Rise of Heterosexuality and the Invention of the Jewish Man.* Berkeley: University of California Press. 1997. George Mosse. *Nationalism and Sexuality.* New York: Howard Fertig. 1985.

[36] Jakub Blum and Vera Rich. *The Image of the Jew in Soviet Literature: The Post-Stalin Period.* London: Institute for Jewish Affairs. 1984.

Afanasy Fet. Photograph in the 1860s.

Afanasy Fet. Photograph from 1891.

Afanasy Fet. Drawing by E. S. Selivacheva (1884),
superimposed on Fet's handwriting.

Ilya Repin's portrait of Afanasy Fet (1881) which served for commentators as evidence of his "Jewish" appearance.

Chapter 1

Russian Anthropological and Biological Sciences and the Jewish "Race," 1860s–1930

> "If, in order to make a broad study of various problems of biology and pathology, an ethnic and national organism is necessary for 'experimental' purposes, there is none more useful than the Jewish"
> V. I. Binshtok. *Problems of the Biology and Pathology of Jews.* 1926.[1]

Russian anthropological science flourished from the middle of the nineteenth century. Because the majority of Russian scientists were educated in Germany and France, and had read literature published in German, French and English, it tended to follow in the footsteps of Western anthropological and biological sciences.[2] It quickly accepted the notion that Jews were the most exemplary representatives of a physical and psychological typology that was determined by race.[3] The father of Russian racial anthropology, Stepan Vasilievich Eshevsky (1829–1865), for example, after graduating from Moscow University, embarked on a European research tour where he met with various historians and scientists. On his return he prepared a series of lectures on the history of the world from a racial perspective. He later published these lectures in the book *O znachenii ras v istorii* (*On the Significance of Races in History*).[4] Referring to the classification of races by Johann Friedrich Blumenbach, James Cowles Prichard and Arthur de Gobineau,[5] Eshevsky devotes a whole passage to the Jewish race as he pursues the argument of the unchangeability of races in history:

> Polygenists stress that racial typology does not change with the influence of conditions of surrounding nature. Is it necessary to quote an example of the Jewish tribe [plemia] which always and everywhere preserves its unique characteristics which have remained unchanged for thousands of years while Jews lived among other foreign peoples, in foreign climates and under the most varied climatic conditions, under the yoke of the most cruel and tough

29

circumstances? Among the Jews one meets today on the streets of London, one can recognize from the first glance the direct descendents of the people whose visual images you have observed on the tombs of the Egyptian pharaoh, held in the collection of the British Museum. (13)

As early as the 1880s Russian medical students were exposed to the theories of racial determinism and genetic pathology, and Russian intellectuals embraced Western racialist discourse with its accent on Jews as a typical exhibit of racial difference. The years 1881–1882 saw the first mass pogroms, which shook the Pale of Settlement, as well as the emergence of political antisemitism in Russia that was starting to influence public opinion from the pages of the Russian press.[6] This was the time of the mass circulation of printed and pictorial material depicting the physical appearance of Jews; in parallel with the textual formulations of anti-Jewish arguments these images became part of the construct of the antisemitic stereotype. Jews as a racial Other, whose physical differences were engraved by nature on their bodies and faces and whose psychological and moral characteristics were tattooed on their inner "soul," became a stable stereotype of Russian society and culture.

The Russian historian, Nikolai Ivanovich Karaev (1850–1931), in his essay "Rasy i natsional'nosti s psikhologicheskoi tochki zreniia" ("Races and Nations from the Psychological Point of View" [1876]),[7] chose Jews as an example of a race whose psychological make-up is linked to their monotheism. Karaev followed in the footsteps of Ernest Renan, who linked the monotheism of Jews to their desert surroundings, maintaining that their lack of achievement in the representational arts was explained by the poverty of this landscape.[8]

With the rise in popularity of Cesare Lombroso's work on criminal anthropology in Russia, the link between race and criminal predisposition was firmly established in a number of works by Russian authors, both scientists and lawmakers. As we have seen, in spite of Lombroso's own Jewish origins, he considered Jews prone to neurotic conditions; his work came to be used widely as a source of antisemitic references in Russian racial discourse. The most prominent follower of Lombroso's anthropological method in Russia was Ivan Alekseevich Sikorsky (1842–1919), who endeavored to establish a link between the physical features and the criminal psychological make-up of various races and nations. Sikorsky published his major work *Dannye iz antropologii* (*Data from Anthropology*)[9] in 1902. In this work he maintains that the anthropomorphic method of anthropology is of value to psychology, as it is through physiology that one can read human psychology and even the human soul. He devotes a whole chapter to a number of common generalizations about the psychology and physical constitution of Jews. Physically, they are

[s]maller in height than other people, with poorly developed chests; they have a high childbirth rate, higher life expectancy and lower mortality; due to this peculiarity Jews constantly grow in number, in spite of the unfavorable conditions in which this race is found everywhere. One of the most noticeable features of the Jewish people is their high adaptability to various climatic conditions, which was mentioned earlier. (260)

Sikorsky draws parallels between the permanency of Jews' physical features and their psychological constitution, identifying a "moral simplicity" (*nravstvennyi simplitsizm* [262]) as their main feature. This "moral simplicity" is explained as an inability to show a wide range of emotions, thus resulting in their alleged one-sidedness and grotesqueness of character. Thus, the sense of pride within Jews manifests itself in vanity, the sense of sorrow in tears and a "general expansivity of emotions" (262): "The essence of such shades and variations is manifested by the substitution of multiple feelings by only one emotion: either the strongest one, or the most elementary" (262). In this way Sikorsky develops the idea of the primitiveness of the Jewish people in comparison with their Aryan counterparts; his idea of "moral simplicity" is firmly grounded in his belief in the inferiority of Jews on a hierarchical scale of races. In line with the European scientific tradition, in which scientific arguments were combined with theological and religious beliefs, Sikorsky uses examples from the Old Testament to substantiate his ideas on the elemental nature of the Jewish character. He quotes Ernest Renan's views on the phenomenon of prophets in Jewish history as confirmation of the moral simplicity of the Jews — without these prophets, he argues, Jews were incapable of making moral judgments on their own; they needed prophets to "awaken and purify feelings, and to lead to the development and growth of those feelings" (263) as neither the Jewish masses nor the Jewish kings or high priests were capable of high or delicate moral feelings.

It is a logical outcome that, on the basis of such views, Sikorsky arrived at the idea of the ethical deficiency of Jews due to their inability to make correct moral judgments. The culmination of these views was reached in 1913 when Sikorsky was a professor at Kiev University at the time of the trial of Mendel Beilis, a Jewish man accused of the ritual murder of a teenage Christian boy. Sikorsky was invited to the trial as a medical expert on matters relating to criminal psychology. He maintained that Jews were predisposed to sadism due to the special psychological characteristics of their race. His views on Jewish blood libel were substantiated by the biological and theological arguments that had been widely disseminated through the publication of his pamphlet "Ekspertiza po delu ob ubiistve Andriushi Iushchinskogo" ("Expert Opinion on the Andriusha Iushchinskii Murder Case"), published in St. Petersburg in 1913.[10]

Sander Gilman has demonstrated that this view of the special diseased nature of the Jewish body, as manifested through both physical and mental illness, was common in European medical discourses.[11] This belief was certainly adopted by Russian scientists. The medical scientist P. A. Minakov, in "Znachenie antropologii v meditsine" ("On the Significance of Anthropology in Medicine" [1902]) refers to Jean-Martin Charcot's views on the propensity of Jews to mental illness, in advancing the idea of the predisposition of certain races to certain diseases:

> The data that exists on the Jews' physical and mental illnesses convinces us that one can not explain the frequency of certain diseases by such external factors as special everyday life conditions, nor by marriages among close relatives. Even if certain conditions of Jewish life cannot be excluded from etiological reasons for their illnesses, they do not play the dominating role, and one has to see first of all the racial peculiarity of Jews as the reason for their psychopathology and mental illnesses. Tsimssen, Blanchard and especially Charcot note that no other race provides us with such wide material in psychopathology as the Jewish race. The statistical data from various European countries shows that mental illnesses among Jews are four to six times higher than among other races. Of all the forms of psychopathology it seems that mania is the most common mental illness among the Jews. (379)[12]

The Jewish body emerges in Russian science as a racially alien body, but it is nevertheless a racially pure body. Russian anthropologists were divided on the question of whether racial purity was a positive or a negative category. Jews were granted both positive and negative physical and mental characteristics; their intellectual brightness and high energy, and their ability to acclimatize to— and take part in— the economic life of the country of their residency, were all viewed with ambivalence and served as explanations for their adaptability and survival. However, in spite of this adaptability to various economic, climatic and cultural surroundings, their separateness was viewed as a deliberate strategy of their own choosing. This detachment explains the anxieties expressed by Russian anthropologists and physicians concerning Jews as members of their society.

It is obvious that, as objects of anthropological research, Jews were to remain separate from investigators representing a superior race. In the work of Russian anthropologists, Russians were endowed with superior racial characteristics, and there are no cases describing racial mixings between

Russians and Jews. Whenever there *is* a description of racial intermixing between Russians and non-Russians in the span of Russian history, such contacts are described as examples of the absorption of Siberian races by Russians, with minimum effect on the Russian race. One such example is found in the work of Anatoly Petrovich Bogdanov (1834–1896) who, in his *Antropologicheskaia fizionomika* (*Anthropological Physiognomics* [1878]),[13] explains that the Russian race could not have been contaminated by Siberian races because it was Russian men who married Siberian women, whereas the opposite situation — Russian women marrying Siberian men — simply is not to be found in the history of Russian expansion into Asia. Natural selection, he argues, works against the physically ugly men of the Asian races as Russian women do not find them attractive as sexual partners, and the same laws of nature make Asian women prefer Russian men to Asian men because of the natural beauty and virility of the Russian male. The work of some Russian anthropologists thus describes Russian people as both white and racially superior.

In writing on the racial exclusivity of the Jewish people, Eshevsky in *O znachenii ras v istorii* concludes that wherever Jews have preserved their religion they have also preserved the purity of their blood. Yet Eshevsky also explains that among Jews one finds variation in the color of hair and eyes, from red hair to dark, and from blue eyes to brown. Although he does not compromise the blood purity argument, he does have to make a concession, and he does so by explaining these changes as a result of various climatic conditions. Nevertheless, he maintains that, in spite of these variations in the color of eyes and hair, Jews are physically recognizable as a racial type due to more permanent taxonomic racial characteristics such as the shape of their skulls. In a 1903 study, another anthropologist, Aleksei Ivanovsky, concluded that, whereas it is difficult to distinguish one ethnic group of the Russian Empire from another on the basis of a particular physical trait, when it comes to Jews the situation is different: "Jews form a complete and totally isolated anthropological group that is not related to any other group" (107).[14]

The views expressed by Russian anthropologists illustrate that, in turn-of-the century Russian medical and anthropological discourse, the Jew's body was regarded as an alien one that needed to be kept at a distance to prevent it from infecting and contaminating the Russian members of the body politic. The high birth rate among Jews, combined with their social mobility and penetration into the educated classes of society, was seen to cause two major threats: the contamination of the purity of the Russian body through sexual contact and the intellectual impact that Jews could have on social and political institutions (the fear of seeing Jews in power has been well documented as an established driving force of anti-Jewish politics during the reign of the last two Russian tsars).[15]

Of special interest is the response by Russian scientists of Jewish origin to the phylogenetic arguments advanced by Western and Russian scientists regarding specificities of the Jewish body and psyche.[16] To what extent did Jewish representatives of the medical profession accept or reject hereditary arguments about Jewish illnesses, physical and especially psychological, in the context of Russia's heightened interest in the subject of degeneration and psychic illnesses at the turn of the century?[17] This nervous period at the end of the nineteenth century was thought to trigger nervous diseases, especially among those people, like Jews, who were believed to have a natural disposition toward such ailments. An illustration of Russian Jewish opinion on psychopathology among Jews can be found in an article by the Jewish psychiatrist Dr. S. A. Trivus, which was published in the Russian language Jewish monthly journal *Voskhod* (*Dawn*) in 1900. The article, "Mass Psychoses in Jewish History: The Sabbatean Movement," was the published version of a lecture delivered by Trivus to the Historical Ethnographic Committee of the Society for the Dissemination of Enlightenment among Jews (Istoriko-etnograficheskaia komissiia obshchestva rasprostraneniia prosveshcheniia mezhdu evreiami).[18] The article focuses on the case of the famous self-proclaimed Jewish messiah of the seventeenth century, Shabbatai Zevi (1626–1676), and the mass movement of his followers. The Sabbatean movement was one of the most striking examples in relatively modern European history of the messianic movement among Jews, spreading across the Ottoman Empire and the Ashkenazic lands, including Holland, Germany and parts of Poland and Russia.

In his article, Trivus treats Sabbateanism as an example of mass psychosis and the case of Shabbatai Zevi as an illustration of clinical psychopathy. His evaluation of psychosis relies on the work of all major scientific authorities of the nineteenth century, and his list of medical and anthropological authors is in itself testimony to what constituted the reading canon of the time: Cesare Lombroso, Richard von Krafft-Ebing, Charcot, Sikorsky. Of particular relevance is Trivus' approach to aspects of biology and ethnicity, and what he regarded as the culture-specific underpinnings of psychopathology. He navigates carefully between the two modes. On the one hand he establishes rather firmly a view of the universality of mass psychoses among peoples, independent of their race or creed, putting more emphasis on their cultural and religious beliefs. He refers, for example, to instances of witch hunts in medieval Europe and instances of mass hysteria (*klikushestvo*) among Russian villagers in the eighteenth and nineteenth centuries. But Trivus also quotes the opinions of scientists who stress that Jews are particularly disposed to various forms of nervous breakdown. In doing so, he channels his arguments away from the notion of the biologically inherited nature of psychoses, advancing instead an argument regarding the decisive factor of persecution and anti-Jewish violence as formative in the morphology of Jewish mental health and psychological behavior. He puts emphasis on circumstances and culture rather than on biology and inheritability. Because the notion of the messiah is central to Biblical Judaism, Shabbatai Zevi's personal psychosis manifested itself in the delusion of being a messiah. Although Trivus does not doubt that Zevi himself was a clinical case, he shows that his followers were affected by mass psychosis due to the especially harsh circumstances for Jews at the time. As a Jew, Dr. Trivus is thus anxious to promote a universalist approach to mental illness and to get away from biological determinism linked to race and ethnicity.

With the rise in the popularity of eugenics in the 1920s, racialist discourse gained new momentum. This movement was fully embraced by Soviet doctors and biologists.[19] In 1926 the publishing house Practical Medicine issued a collection of articles devoted entirely, as its title attests, to *Problems of the Biology and Pathology of Jews* (*Voprosy biologii i patologii evreev*).[20] It was edited by a group of four professors and doctors of medicine and contained twelve articles written by Soviet doctors and biologists examining the etiologies of various illnesses and pathologies among different groups of Jewish people. Their findings were based on the results of a number of studies carried out in various Jewish communities in Russia relating to tuberculosis, mental illness, and the unusually high number of gifted people among Jews. It appears that in the 1920s Jewish people were considered to be a unique object of study, especially in light of the new trends in eugenics and anthropology, and the introduction to the book provides a striking example of the way in which the Jewish body, with its unique biological characteristics, was treated as a scientific specimen. The introduction explains the aims of the planned series of "Scientific volumes":

> *Problems of the Biology and Pathology of Jews* is of general scientific interest. If, in order to make a broad study of various problems of biology and pathology, an ethnic and national organism is necessary for "experimental" purposes, there is none more useful than the Jewish. Questions of demography, statistics, anthropology, anthropometrics, matters of race hygiene and eugenics, questions of physical constitution, hereditary, immunity, various aspects of social biology and pathology: all these can be graphically studied by using the body of the Jewish nation. The particular experimental interest presented by this national organism is determined by the fact that it can be studied during its long history;

first as a territorial and later as an extra-territorial people, in conditions of very broad Diaspora and migration, and, more importantly, in difficult socio-biological conditions; sociobiological strata, role of social conditions in the biological constitution of a national ethnic organism can be studied precisely on the Jewish national body. It has already been shown that, in its constitution, the Jewish organism manifests biological extremes: on the one hand it shows a physical degradation bordering on degeneration; on the other, in certain cases it reveals an extraordinary physical stability, a hardiness, a biological immunity (3).[21]

Dr. Binshtok, the author of this introduction, includes in the list of paradoxes to be studied: the high degree of tubercular infection among Jewish populations, but the low mortality rate from tuberculosis among the same groups; immunity to a number of highly infectious diseases; the high number of endocrine pathologies; nervousness; and the "general disharmony between the somatic and the psychiatric spheres" (3). This list is of special relevance to the present study because it encapsulates those biological characteristics of the Jewish body which, as will be demonstrated, both form and inform the stereotype of the Jewish body in Russian culture.

Another characteristic, regularly featured on lists of the stereotypical "pathologies" of the Jewish body, is that of interbreeding and incest. Levirate marriages have often been viewed as manifestations of incestuous practices among Jews. This question of inbreeding is raised in one of the articles in *Problems of the Biology and Pathology of Jews* in which the author argues that in recent science there has been a significant change in attitudes toward the practice.[22] Thus it is no longer automatically assumed that marriages between close relatives produce pathological offspring. On the contrary, it is now believed that two strong and healthy individuals will produce a strong and healthy progeny, and the fact that the two individuals may be closely related is of no consequence. The author explains this shift in attitude by referring to recent trends in eugenics that put due emphasis on the transmission of abilities and talents to the next generation. He quotes the opinion of a prominent Russian scientist who had suggested that the fact that Gogol and Chekhov did not have any children was a great loss to the human race: better to have another genius like Gogol, even with mental problems, and another writer like Chekhov, even with tuberculosis, than two physically healthy, but ordinary people.[23]

The 1926 volume of *Problems of the Biology and Pathology of Jews* quotes statistics from the 1880s to the 1920s, using scientific data from the same period. It pays tribute to trends in eugenics and, in line with its theoretical sources, is overtly hereditarian and racist.[24] The next two volumes under the same title, published in 1930, represent a significant shift away from the racialist paradigm of 1926 to a more social framework in the way they explain the etiology of illness and the physical state of the Jewish organism. The first chapter in Volume 3, No. 2, (1930) sets out this new paradigm. It overtly attacks racist science and formulates a new "Soviet" approach to issues of biology and pathology:

> The aim of this research is to study the relationship between the state of health of the *déclassé* Jewish population and its ability to contribute to the work output. This approach is correct not only from the point of view of social hygiene, but also from the point of view of a class understanding of social health issues. In the Soviet Union the principal class is proletariat, and Soviet social hygiene has to develop measures which will help to build socialism.
>
> Many competent anthropologists maintain that, like other civilized races and peoples, the Jews consist of many different racial elements, and that religion is the only element that makes up Jewry. So it is pointless to apply such zoological measurements as those exemplified by the eugenicist views of Galton Lenz. There is a fundamental contradiction between the socio-hygienic and the "racial-biological" approach.
>
> It should be pointed out that it is scientifically dubious to study aspects of racial biology and hygiene, because the very existence of the so-called "pure races" among peoples is dubious (5–6).[25]

Although Volume 3, No. 1, (1930) contains an article quoting verbatim Dr. Binshtok's definition of the Jewish organism as "exemplary," most contributions to the 1930 volumes stress the role of socioeconomic conditions in the biology of a nation.[26] This difference in approach between the volumes of 1926 and 1930 can be explained by the strengthening and unification of the ideological paradigm of the Soviet Union. Medical science was by now in the service of the state, and the 1930s were characterized by a change in Stalin's nationalities policies from the "indigenization" of the 1920s to a hostile attitude toward nationalism and manifestations of ethnicity. Differences in race and ethnicity were played down, with emphasis placed instead on class distinctions. The new goal was to improve the physical stamina of the Jewish people, who were regarded as physically weaker than the Slavic population because of the social and economic conditions in which they lived. The majority of Jews were viewed as "*déclassé*," and the aim of social medicine was to improve their physical constitution by engaging them in physical work in order that they might join the two working classes of Soviet society: the proletariat and the peasantry. A number of studies were devoted to the physical constitution of various agrarian Jewish communities, which were designed to prove that Jews from these communities had stronger physical constitutions than their "*déclassé*" counterparts (tailors, furriers, shoemakers, and petty traders). Thus, in order to improve their health and their physical and mental constitution, Jews had to become members of the proletariat or peasantry.[27]

This official script, which privileged social change in matters of biology, nevertheless coexisted with the ongoing view that Jews constituted a race apart and that their difference was defined by their biology and pathology. Such double standards in relation to the "Jewish organism" continued to exist as part of Soviet discourse relating to Jews and representations of Jews, despite the racial model being watered down by the rhetoric of class differences.[28] This view existed as a silent phantom, which could be sometimes explicated overtly or implied through various codes. With the end of censorship and the collapse of the Soviet state in the 1990s these racist concepts of the Jewish physical body re-emerged and began to be disseminated in various forms of discourse, both popular and quasi-scientific.

The main proponent of racial theories in Russia today is Vladimir Avdeev, author of *Rasologiia: Nauka o nasledstvennykh kachestvakh liudei* (*Raceology: the Science of Inherited Characteristics of People* [2005]) and editor of several volumes authored by nineteenth- and twentieth-century Russian biologists, physicians, historians, anthropologists and ethnographers on the topic of race. The following statement by Avdeev contains a succinct formula used by today's right-wing political and cultural personalities who theorize their views on the role of racial and ethnic characteristics of various nationalities in politics: "There exists a rule ancient as the world itself: if you want to check the certainty of a scientific theory, apply it to the Jews, and everything will fall into its place, everything will become clear" (303).[29] The Jewish body is thus viewed as an explanatory one as the author delineates the scientific nature of experiments conducted on this body. As such, the Jewish body is presented as particularly suited for laboratory experiments, just as it was in the hands of Nazi doctors in the concentration camps. Avdeev is an open follower and admirer of those German scientists who articulated racial theories on the inferiority of the Jewish race and the superiority of Aryans. The explanatory function of the Jewish body is considered to be its most valued function, and it is in this capacity that this body is presented to the Russian reader today by authors such as Avdeev — authors who, as it will be shown later in this book, follow in the footsteps of a racist science, which they resurrect from the past and disseminate.

The next chapter looks at the way Anton Chekhov distilled views on the biology of the Jewish body through the representation of Jewish characters in his fiction.

Notes

[1] V. I. Binshtok. O zadachakh nauchnykh sbornikov "Voprosy biologii i patologii evreev". *Voprosy biologii i patologii evreev.* Eds. Dr. V. I. Binshtok, Dr. A. M. Bramson, Prof. G. I. Dembo and Prof. M. M. Gran. Leningrad: Prakticheskaia meditsina. 1926. 3–6. 3.

[2] On ethnicity in Imperial Russia see *Russian Modernity: Politics, Knowledge, Practices.* Eds. David L. Hoffmann and Yanni Kotsonis. New York: St. Martin's Press. 2000.

[3] On the topic of race and the Jews in Imperial Russia see Eli Weinerman. Racism, Racial Prejudice, and the Jews in Late Imperial Russia. *Ethnic Racial Studies*, Vol. 17. No. 3. July 1994. 442–495. Eugene Avrutin. Racial Categories and the Politics of (Jewish) Difference in Late Imperial Russia. *Kritika: Explorations in Russian and Eurasian History.* Vol. 8. No. 1. 2007. 13–40.

[4] S. V. Eshevskii. O znachenii ras v istorii. *Russkaia rasovaia teoriia do 1917 goda.* Ed. V. B. Avdeev. Moscow: Feri-V. 2004. 55–110.

[5] On the original essays by J. F. Blumenbach. "On the Native Varieties of Human Species" (1796) and J. C. Prichard's "The Natural History of Man" (1848) see *Race: the Origins of An Idea, 1760–1850.* Ed. and introd. H. E. Augstein. Bristol: Thoemess Press. 1996. 58–68 and 204–213. Arthur de Gobineau. The Inequality of Human Races. *The Idea of Race.* Ed. and introd. Robert Bernasconi and Tommy L. Lott. Indianapolis: Hackett Publishing Company. 2000. 45–54.

[6] See John D. Klier and Shlomo Lambroza, Eds. *Pogroms: Anti-Jewish Violence in Modern Russian History.* Cambridge UK: Cambridge University Press. 1993; John D. Klier. Tradtional Russian Religious Antisemitism: A Useful Concept or a Barrier to Understanding? *Jewish Quaterly* 174. Summer 1999. 29–34.

[7] N. I. Karaev. Rasy i natsional'nosti s psikhologicheskoi tochki zreniia. *Russkaia rasovaia teoriia do 1917 goda.* Ed. V. B. Avdeev. Moscow: Feri-V. 2004. 207–218.

[8] On modern consensus on "aniconisity" of Judaism and racist arguments around this concept in European thought see Kalman Bland. *The Artless Jew: Medieval and Modern Affirmations and Denials of the Visual.* Princeton NJ: Princeton University Press. 2000.

[9] I. A. Sikorskii. Dannye iz antropologii. *Russkaia rasovaia teoriia do 1917 goda.* Ed. V. B. Avdeev. Moscow: Feri-V. 2004. 229–266.

[10] Ibid. 325–336.

[11] Sander L. Gilman. *The Jew's Body.* London: Routledge. 1991.

[12] P. A. Minakov. Znachenie antropologii v meditsine. *Russkaia rasovaia teoriia do 1917 goda.* Ed. V. B. Avdeev. Moscow: Feri-V. 2004. 373–384.

[13] A. P. Bogdanov. Antropologicheskaia fizionomika. *Russkaia rasovaia teoriia do 1917 goda.* Ed. V. B. Avdeev. Moscow: Feri-V. 2004. 111–144.

[14] A. A. Ivanovskii. Opyt antropologicheskoi klassifikatsii naseleniia Rossii. *Russkii antropologicheskii zhurnal.* No.3/4. 1903. 103–115. Ivanovskii used such characteristics for his typology as color of eyes and hair, height, size of head, cranial measurements, length of face, shape and size of nose, width of chest, size of arms and size of legs.

[15] Benjamin Nathans. *Beyond the Pale: The Jewish Encounter with Late Imperial Russia.* Berkeley: University of California Press. 2002.

[16] On opposing views of two Russian Jewish anthropologists A. D. El'kind and S. Vaisenberg (1867–1928) on Jews and race see Marina Mogil'ner. Evreiskaia antropologiia v Rossii v kontekste evropeiskikh rasovykh issledovanii (XIX–XX vv.). *Istoriia i kul'tura rossiiskogo i vostochnoevropeiskogo evreistva: Novye istochniki, novye podkhody.* Moscow: Dom evreiskoi knigi. 2004. 116–137.

Chapter 1

[17] On Western European Jewish doctors' attitude toward the race see John Efron. *Defenders of the Race: Jewish Doctors and Race Science in Fin-de-siècle Europe.* New Haven: Yale University Press. 1994.

[18] S. A. Trivus. Massovye psikhozy v evreiskoi istorii. — Sabbatianstvo. *Voskhod.* Vol. 7. (July) 1900. 79–101.

[19] Mark B. Adams. "Eugenics in Russia, 1900–1940". *The Wellborn Science: Eugenics in Germany, France, Brazil and Russia.* Ed. Mark B. Adams. Oxford: Oxford University Press. 1990. 160–187.

[20] *Voprosy biologii i patologii evreev.* Eds. Dr. V. I. Binshtok, Dr. A. M. Bramson, Prof. G. I. Dembo and Prof. M. M. Gran. Leningrad: Prakticheskaia meditsina. 1926.

[21] V. I. Binshtok. O zadachakh nauchnykh sbornikov "Voprosy biologii i patologii evreev". *Voprosy biologii i patologii evreev.* Eds. Dr. V. I. Binshtok, Dr. A. M. Bramson, Prof. G. I. Dembo and Prof. M. M. Gran. Leningrad: Prakticheskaia meditsina. 1926. 3–6.

[22] V. I. Binshtok. K voprosu ob odarennosti evreev. *Voprosy biologii i patologii evreev.* Eds. Dr. V. I. Binshtok, Dr. A. M. Bramson, Prof. G. I. Dembo and Prof. M. M. Gran. Leningrad: Prakticheskaia meditsina. 1926. 7–30.

[23] Binshtok quotes Prof. N. K. Kol'tsov. *Uluchshenie chelovecheskoi prirody.* Petrograd: izd-vo Vremia.1923.

[24] The volume contains abstracts of various publications by physicians and biologists in Europe, the United Kingdom and the United States devoted to the matters of race, Jews and the state of their health and physical characteristics. Abstracts are in German and Russian.

[25] S. R. Dikhtiar. Deklassirovannoe evreistvo g. Minska. *Voprosy biologii i patologii evreev.* Vol. 3. No. 2. Eds. Dr. V. I. Binshtok, Dr. A. M. Bramson, Prof. G. I. Dembo and Prof. M. M. Gran. Leningrad: Izd-vo Evreiskogo Istoriko-Etnograficheskogo Obshchestva. 1930.

[26] V. M. Koganskii. Patologiia endokrinnoi sistemy u evreev. *Voprosy biologii i patologii evreev.* Vol. 3. No. 1. Eds. Dr. V. I. Binshtok, Dr. A. M. Bramson, Prof. G. I. Dembo and Prof. M. M. Gran. Leningrad: Izd-vo Evreiskogo Istoriko-Etnograficheskogo Obshchestva. 1930. 3–19.

[27] M. M. Gran. Blizhaishie zadachi nauchno-issledovatel'skikh rabot v sviazi s perekhodom evreev k zemledeliiu. *Voprosy biologii i patologii evreev.* Eds. Dr. V. I. Binshtok, Dr. A. M. Bramson, Prof. G. I. Dembo and Prof. M. M. Gran. Leningrad: Prakticheskaia meditsina. 1926. 95–102.

[28] On genetics and biology in the USSR see Valerii Soifer. *Vlast' i nauka: istoriia razgroma genetiki v SSSR.*Tenafly: New York. 1989.

[29] V. Avdeev. *Rasologiia: nauka o nasledtvennykh kachestvakh liudei.* Biblioteka rasovoi mysli. Moscow: Belye Al'vy. 2005.

Chapter 2

Stereotypes of Pathology: The Medicalization of the Jewish Body by Anton Chekhov, 1880s

> "Don't you go marrying Jewesses, psychopaths, or blue-stockings..."
>
> Anton Chekhov. "Ivanov." 1887.[1]

The Jewish stereotypes in Anton Chekhov's writing owe their origin not so much to the anti-Jewish typology found in the Russian literary tradition or in the political rhetoric disseminated in the right wing press,[2] but rather to the views of Jewish people as expressed in the medical and scientific discourses of his time. It is Chekhov the doctor, and Chekhov the man of science, who is the author of his Jewish characters, and the differences and pathological variations that mark these characters, can be regarded as products of Chekhov's knowledge of scientific literature. As they appear in Chekhov's writings, Jews are marked by biological variances that set their bodies and psyches apart, variances that mark them as the bodies of the Other. As a materialist, Chekhov did not separate the psychological sphere from the physiological,[3] and it is the pathology of the Jewish body as inseparable from the mind in his characters that is the subject of this chapter.

As a medical student at Moscow University Chekhov was familiar with antisemitic stereotypes disseminated in Russia during the 1880s. During the anti-Jewish pogroms of 1881 he wrote a letter to a Jewish fellow student in which he expresses his awareness of both anti-Jewish violence and the image of Jews as a discursive construct. In a jocular tone he writes, "May you have bad dreams about the slaughter in Kiev and Elizavetgrad, about the Judeophobe Liutostansky and the newspaper staff of *Novoe vremia*" (10).[4] This little known letter shows that Chekhov understood the role of literature and the press in the formation and dissemination of such antisemitic stereotypes as those propagated by Ippolit Liutostansky (1835–1915) whose infamous fabrication *Talmud i evrei* (*Talmud and the Jews*) (1879) maintained that Jews derive their genealogy from Satan, that they conspire against Christians and that they use Christian blood in baking *matzot*.[5] There is significant irony in Chekhov's reference to the newspaper *Novoe vremia* as a center of antisemitic propaganda, as he soon started publishing in this newspaper and became a friend of its editor, A. Suvorin, known for his active political antisemitism. But in dealing with Jewish characters in his own writing Chekhov did not follow the path of political and religious antisemitism; instead he chose the domain that was closer to his professional interests — that of medical and scientific discourse.

That Chekhov's Jewish characters depart markedly from the traditional depiction of Jews in Russian literature was noted by the Jewish reviewer S. G. Frug in commenting on Chekhov's stories "Perekati-pole" ("Tumbleweed" [1887]), "Tina" ("Mire" [1886]), and "The Steppe" (1888) when all these works appeared in a collected volume of short stories in 1889.[6] Frug stressed that the Jews in Chekhov's stories not only differ from their literary predecessors, but they also show no likeness to real Jews in contemporary Russian society. In these three stories Chekhov's Jewish characters are seen as grotesque to the point of "psychopathy" (Frug 33) and it is this feature, which can be called the medicalization of the Jew, that sets Chekhov's Jewish characters apart from their literary kin in Russian literature.

The stories containing Jewish characters—"Tina," "The Steppe," "Tumbleweed," and the play *Ivanov*, (1886–1889) — were all written at the beginning of Chekhov's medical career, soon after his graduation from Moscow University as a medical practitioner in 1884. As an undergraduate student and the successful writer of short stories, Chekhov had previously considered a career as a scientist. In 1883 he planned to write a research thesis entitled "Istoriia polovogo avtoriteta" ("History of Sexual Authority") which was inspired by his reading of Darwin's *The Origins of Species* in Russian translation (1871). Chekhov intended this dissertation to combine aspects of zoology, anthropology and the history of science and medicine. In the plans for this thesis he shows a degree of biological determinism combined with a general belief in evolution: "There is no need to interfere with nature — it is not advisable... One has to help nature the way nature helps people, creating heads of Newton, heads which are almost reaching the perfection of a perfect organism" (14).[7] In the same year that he wrote "Tina" he reread Darwin, confessing his love for the great evolutionist and declaring his work to be an ultimate "roskosh'" (luxury [4]).[8]

During the years that Chekhov was training as a doctor, the medical faculty had a strong professorial staff including such respected names as K. A. Timiriazev and S. P. Botkin.[9] These were first-rate scholars with a reputation for disseminating the latest scientific literature produced in the West. The mid-1880s was a time when the fin-de-siècle culture, with its interest in race, gender, and sexuality, had already been formed. The reigning theory of anthropology was Lombroso's biological determinism; Jean Martin Charcot had already conducted and described his experiments with hypnosis as a treatment for hysterics, and his most able student, Sigmund Freud, was involved in scientific experiments that would later be described in the 1890s.[10] Von Krafft-Ebing's work on psychopathology was also well known in Russia, not only through his publications but also through his guest lectures during the 1870s.[11] All of this work was characterized by the underlying assumption that there existed visible differences between races that were manifested in various biological features.[12] In particular, fin-de-siècle science defined the Jewish physique in racial terms, and promoted the idea that Jews as a group shared certain external features and characteristics as well as certain diseases. *The Russian Ethnographic Dictionary* (1880) describes the Jewish body as being prone to both inherited and acquired diseases, a propensity that formed a circular relationship of inescapability, as even illnesses caused by lifestyle could be passed from one generation to another:

> As for the appearance of the Jews, one should note that their frailty and the weakness of their body strength result not only from historical causes, but also from many of the conditions of their lifestyle that depend on them alone... Various diseases stem from this [lifestyle], such as haemorrhoids, scrofula, consumption, and eye problems, which the Jews transmit by inheritance to their descendants (391–392).[13]

The Jewish body was certainly regarded as an anomalous one in Russian science. In an 1886 work known to Chekhov, Professor Botkin maintained that Jews were exceptional in their resilience to tuberculosis which, in his view, should affect Jews in larger numbers than it actually did.[14] It was such presumed biological features and characteristics of the Jewish body, both external and internal, that were accentuated by Chekhov in his representations of Jews. Whereas scholars have long recognized the presence of medical and scientific theories in stories like "The Attack of Nerves" ("Pripadok"), "The Duel" ("Duel"), "Black Monk" ("Chernyi monakh") and the play *Ivanov*, they have failed to notice this link between his Jewish characters and biological theories of the day. The accepted view is that Chekhov rejected those theories that placed the role of genetic inheritance above the power of human will and improved environment. Common, too, is the view that Chekhov especially rejected views on degeneration, both in his conversations with his biologist friends and in his work;[15] yet there is ample evidence that Chekhov was indebted to the theories of hereditariness in a more significant way than is commonly admitted.[16] Donald Rayfield points out that in Chekhov's opinion Jews could not be fully admitted to Russian life in the same way that women could never reach the genius of man,[17] thus suggesting a conflation of prejudice to race and gender that is in itself extremely symptomatic of the biological views of the turn of the century.[18] Mark Swift has recently demonstrated that Chekhov was influenced by the model of "congenital psychopathic constitutions"[19] as propounded by Professor S. S. Korsakov, whose psychiatric textbook *Kurs psikhiatrii* (*A Course of Psychiatry* [1893]) was found in Chekhov's library.

In Chekhov's play *Ivanov* the most important feature of Sarra, the rich Jewess, is her illness; indeed, her whole role in this play is defined by her position as a terminally ill person. Her tubercular body with its "pale face" and "sunken chest" (64) drives Ivanov to despair, and her predicted death stirs up a range of contradictory emotions and contributes to his eventual suicide.[20] Although noted by commentators, Sarra's illness has not been interpreted as a specifically Jewish feature (commentators have had difficulty in interpreting Sarra as a stereotype of a Jewish woman, and have regarded her instead as an expression of Chekhov's remorse at creating a highly unsympathetic Jewish woman in "Tina"). Similarly in "Tumbleweed," the Jewish convert Isaak (Andrei Ivanovich) is marked by consumption and a serious nervous disorder; indeed, his whole being is characterized as "abnormal" ("nenormal'nost'") [285]).[21] Through a careful reading of the depiction of the Jewish body in Chekhov's cognate texts in the 1880s, it is possible to see that unhealthy bodies as evident in the ailing health of both Sarra and Isaak are markers of their Jewishness. This Jewish essence clearly remains unchanged following their conversion to Christianity — further proof that the Jewish organism is marked by race.[22]

Anomalous Bodies: Jews as Mad Birds, Fat Turkeys and Multi-Headed Hydras

Chekhov's most fully developed Jewish characters can be found in "The Steppe" and "Tina." The former work brought Chekhov a level of success that affirmed his place in Russian literature as a major talent. The tale's ethnographic aspects were particularly praised. At this time the *povest'*, or long story, was viewed as a genre that was based on the depiction of real life people and situations in the tradition of the sketches that were so in vogue in the 1880s.[23] In Chekhov's own evaluation of "The Steppe," he stresses that it consists of a succession of episodes of independent value, constitutive of separate stories that have little to do with one another.[24] One of these episodes is devoted to the description of a Jewish family of innkeepers. This occupation was very common among Jews who lived within the Pale of Settlement. Yet this ordinariness, taken as a typical depiction of a typical situation, is misleading — the family is not shown to sell liquor; indeed, only tea is offered to the visitors. The stereotypes Chekhov employs in this story are only superficially related to the realist tradition of the representation of Jews in Russian literature.[25] A closer examination reveals that such depictions were informed by the scientific understandings of the day. Chekhov reveals the medical sub-layer in "The Steppe" in his explanation of the planned suicide of his protagonist Egorushka. His notes demonstrate that he understood an etiology of suicide to be a combination of physical and psychological features, with each of these two sets of characteristics construed as both hereditary and acquired. In relation to "The Steppe," Chekhov was working with such categories as "Slavic melancholy," "nervousness," and "early sexual maturity" (194), all of which are presented as congenital features of a people which, together with external factors (harsh climate, poverty, political oppression), contribute to a Russian predisposition to certain pathological models of behavior. The link between the ethnic group and its characteristic physical and mental diseases was affirmed and established.[26]

Certainly Darwinist theories did not exclude the depiction of Jews as anomalous to the evolutionary process. The reader knows that anthropological science in the 1880s singled out Jews as a group outside the normal process of development due to their unique isolationist lifestyle and mentality. The views of Jews as depicted in the science of the 1880s were summed up by the anthropologist Richard Andree: "No other race but the Jews can be traced with such certainty backward for thousands of years, and no other race displays such a constancy of form, no race resisted the effects of time as much as Jews" (23).[27] The Jewish body was thus viewed as an atavistic, one in which archaic and rudimentary features survived by escaping the evolutionary process of change. Paradoxically, with this view there coexisted an opposite view of the mutability of the Jews — whereas the Jewish body was both atavistic and capable of deceit by appearance, it was also regarded as a sample body of primitive mankind that had remained essentially unchanged and untouched by the process of evolution.

In "The Steppe" the whole Jewish family is primarily a biological entity. The members of the family — the two brothers, the wife of the elder brother and their children — all exhibit congenital and hereditary features. The two brothers show inherited characteristics from their parents, and the young children in turn show signs of a pathology that is both hereditary and acquired due to the unhealthy lifestyle of Jewish people. Among these signs of pathology are physical problems, indefinite sexualities and psychological disorders, including madness.

The two brothers, the first two Jewish characters Chekhov presents, carry Old Testament names — Moisei Moiseevich and Solomon Moiseevich.[28] Whereas one is depicted as an ordinary innkeeper, the other is shown as a strange fellow and his brother's exact opposite. Moisei Moiseevich is tall, Solomon Moiseevich is short; Moisei Moiseevich is polite, Solomon Moiseevich is rude; Moisei Moiseevich is respectful, Solomon Moiseevich is arrogant. This juxtaposition creates a comic effect (indebted to the comic devices Gogol used to depict his characters Ivan Ivanovich and Ivan Nikiforovich and also explored by Chekhov in "Tolstyi i tonkii"),[29] but an analysis of what makes these characters so comical reveals stereotypes of race under which hide stereotypes of pathology.

Moisei's appearance receives a detailed description; his costume signifies his ethnicity and his physical features attest to his state of ill health. His complexion is very pale — in the medical discourses of the nineteenth century a Jew's complexion was a marker of his diseased body. Whether swarthy or pallid, both types of extraordinary complexion distinguished the Jew not only racially but also as physically sick. And Moisei has a high voice ("tonkii, pevuchii golos" [35]) — as we are told, he "bursts into laughter in a high pitched voice" ("zalilsia tonkim smekhom" [40]). His voice even has falsetto qualities — he can go two notes higher than his usually high voice ("dvumia notami vyshe" [40]). Such a voice is yet another marker of the male Jew's pathological body and a sign of his femininity.

Sander Gilman has demonstrated that Jews come out as "gender benders" in racialist turn-of-the-century scientific discourse, and the timbre of their voice is linked to this diseased physiology. The link between the nasal and larynx membranes and genitalia was accepted as fact in turn-of-the-century medicine,—a view based on the parallel development of the genitalia, nose, and larynx in embryos. Krafft-Ebing quotes an 1884 article by John Mackenzie, published in the *Journal of Medical Science*, in which there is a description of the parallel swelling of the nasal/larynx tissue and women's sexual organs during menstruation (48). Similarly, McKenzie's article claims that nasal bleeding could either replace or increase with uterine bleeding. At the same time, Freud and Fliess established the view that men's nasal bleeding is equivalent to menstruation. Through this link between nasal tissues and genitalia the masculinity of Jewish men was undermined not only by the folk belief which claimed that Jewish masculinity was impaired by circumcision, but also by turn-of-the-century medical science. Medical scientists' views on the nosology of Jews echoed older anthropological beliefs, such as those of Jewish ethnologist Adolf Jellinek who stated that Jews belonged to a feminine race, using as physiological evidence the high voice of Jewish males: "Let me note that bass voices are much rarer than baritone among the Jews" (43).[30] Moisei Moiseevich's thin voice thus becomes a marker of his racial and biological difference. When his brother Solomon is introduced, his nose becomes the locus of his racial difference: predictably, he has a long "birdlike nose" (35) — a substitute for his circumcised penis. Certainly the hooked nose was a staple feature in caricatures of Jews in newspapers and journals such as *Razvlechenie* in which Chekhov's friends published their work.

In addition to the nose, Chekhov the scientist found a less vulgar feature for his protagonist. This feature is Solomon's eternal smile. In his semiotic reading of Chekhov's language, Douglas Clayton shows that a smile in his work is not normally a sign of happiness, but rather a grimace that might conceal psychological trauma.[31] And indeed, in Solomon's frozen smile we find the smile of an idiot, so indicating a mental condition attested to by the brother Moisei who claims that he is quite out of his mind ("ne v svoem ume" [46]). Moisei confirms his diagnosis by the gesture of turning his finger against the side of his head. Solomon is also ironically referred to as Solomon the Wise ("Solomon premudryi" [44]) — an antonymical epithet meant to show that, in his mental qualities, he is the exact opposite of his Biblical predecessor:

> Putting a tray on the table he looked mockingly ["nasmeshlivo"] sidewards and continued to smile strangely. Now, in the light from the lamp, it was possible to see his smile; it was very complex and expressed a lot of feeling, but the prevailing feeling in it was an obvious contempt. It was as if he was thinking about something funny and silly, could not stand someone and loathed that someone, was happy about something and was waiting for the right moment to attack with mockery and then to start rolling with laughter. His long nose, his fat lips, his bulging eyes seemed to be tense from the desire to burst into laughter (37).[32]

Lombroso's *The Man of Genius*, translated into Russian in 1885 in "Influence of Race and Heredity," presents statistical examples ("Jews, again, offer us an eloquent example" [133]) of the differences between Jews and non-Jews in a list of 100,000 celebrities. Although this survey pointed to a greater incidence of creative genius among Jews, Lombroso also claims that "[Jews] have not accomplished their ethnic evolution, as they show by the obstinacy with which they cling to their ancient beliefs" (136). Commenting on the statistics of madness, he quotes the 1871 findings of the German scholar Mayr according to which, when comparing 10,000 Jews with 10,000 Christians in German-speaking lands, there were about three times more cases of madness ("lunatics" [136]) among Jews than non-Jews.

Lombroso characterized Jewish creativity as radical, quoting Jesus Christ and Karl Marx as examples of people who revolutionized religion and politics. In Chekhov's work, Solomon's mania is that of a nihilist, who burns all his inherited money in a gesture best described as a combination of madness and social radicalism. And indeed, Solomon's frozen smile, depicted as a paralytic grimace, is not the only clinical marker of madness. He is also characterized as a hater of Jews whom he loathes for their greed and love of money. His madness thus manifests itself in political and religious radicalism. He is a rebel in his own family. He burns in a single gesture the bag of cash that comprises all his inheritance. This act is reminiscent of the famous gesture of Nastasia Filippovna in Dostoevsky's novel *The Idiot*, in which the heroine throws a packet containing a large fortune into the fireplace — an act interpreted as confirmation not only of her eccentricity but also of her suspected clinical madness.

Solomon is depicted paradoxically as both a Jew and a caricature of a Jew (he used to act as an impersonator of Jews at the annual market). His ability to parody the Jewish body and accent is a result of his self-confessed hatred of Jews, but even his self-hatred does not save him from being seen by others as a quintessential Jew. He is thus depicted both as somebody who can mutate and, at the same time, as someone who cannot escape his own Jewish essentiality. The Jewish body is thus presented as one that can imitate but at the same time paradoxically always remains the same. It is this body that is marked by racial difference:

> ...Solomon in a voice toneless and husky from a hatred that was choking him, burring and hurriedly, started talking about the Jews; first he spoke correctly, in Russian, then adopted the tone of the Jewish storytellers and started talking as if at a sideshow, with an exaggerated Jewish accent. (45)

These two qualities of the Jewish body — to be able to mimic and yet to remain the same — were well explored in nineteenth-century science, and Jews were used as examples of both immutability and mutability. Robert Knox, in one of the best known mid-century studies on race, expressed the opinion that a Jew can never be mistaken for another race no matter how assimilated he is, whereas French historian Anatole Leroy-Beaulieu, in his attack on antisemitism (1893), states that "there is in every Jew a secret power of metamorphosis which has often amazed me. He has the remarkable faculty of taking on a new skin, without at bottom ceasing to be a Jew" (17).[33]

The biological approach to the Jewish protagonists in "The Steppe" is further evident in Chekhov's treatment of the children of Moisei Moiseevich and his wife, Roza. In spite of Roza's large size, the children she bears are sick and pale. In order to meet the children, the narrator takes his reader into the bedroom, where the whole space is taken up by a large bed. This intimate space is a place where children are conceived and born. Moisei invites the Russian orphan Egorushka into the bedroom in order to allow his guests to have a business talk downstairs. In the private space of the bedroom Egorushka is warmly treated by Roza who feeds the boy with sweet cookies — food that Egorushka, who is used to much better food, later gives to the dog. The whole scene is intended as a comic episode, employing a number of well-established stereotypes of Jews of nineteenth-century literature from Dickens to Gogol: the bed linen is predictably unclean, Roza's Russian is full of grammatical mistakes, and the sound of the Jewish language is compared to doggerel: Roza speaks like "a turkey" ("tu-tu-tu-tu" [43]) and her husband Moisei makes bird-like sounds such as "gal-gal-gal-gal" (evoking the word *galka*—a jackdaw, hence galdet'—to make a noise like a jackdaw).

The scene is built on recognizable devices in the tradition of *natural'naia shkola*,[34] however there is one element that serves as its most distinguishing feature: the portrayal of the children of the Jewish couple. For comic effect, the children are concealed under the blanket. When they first appear, their heads on their long pale necks emerge one by one. When all four heads are visible, the narrator remarks that one could imagine that a hydra with a hundred heads was hiding under the blanket. The image of the hydra is markedly different from the semantics of such words as bird and turkey, which Chekhov uses in his description of both the brothers and Roza. Although a comparison of Jewish heroes with plucked chickens, turkeys and other poultry had already been used in the work of Gogol and Dostoevsky (the Jew Yankel in "Taras Bulba" and Isai Bumshtein in "Notes from the House of the Dead"),[35] in an association clearly employed as a comic device, the case with the image of the hydra is different.[36] Whereas comparison with domesticated birds that cannot fly away to freedom stands as a metaphor for the pathetic and weak physique of the Jewish body, the image of a mythological creature that is part human, part animal clearly comes from a different semantic field. This image is no longer funny, but rather scary: "Esli by Egorushka obladal bogatoi fantaziei to mog by podumat' chto pod odeialom lezhala stoglavaia gidra" ("If Egorushka had had a rich imagination he might have thought that under the blanket there lay a hydra with a hundred heads" [43]). This has totally different connotations: it is a real monster that is being imagined hidden under the blanket and, although a monster from primeval times is a mythological creature, its mythological origins do not exclude the possibility of its existence in prehistoric reality. After all, Dostoevsky's hero from "A Ridiculous Man's Dream" (1877) was nostalgic for Arcadian times when the gods descended from heaven and had sexual contact with humans. It was during those prehistoric times that hybrid creatures like the Hydra and the Centaurs were born as a result of such interspecies contact.[37] The Jew's body was viewed as the only surviving body genetically linked to the times when divine beings were believed to have cohabited with the daughters of men — physical contacts described in the Bible in Genesis 6: 1–4 (J).[38] Chekhov, who as a boy sang in the church choir and who went to a school with the obligatory daily drill of Bible lessons, could well have been familiar with these stories. His pious family bought religious literature written for simple folk that inevitably contained apocryphal stories about the origins of evil spirits and evil creatures. The mythological Hydra was the offspring of the union between the composite woman-serpent creature and the human male.[39] Is it surprising that the body that defies evolution shows signs of atavism? If there can be two-headed Siamese twins born in the nineteenth century to Thai parents, why can't a multi-headed freak of nature be born to a Jewish couple? Where little Egorushka needed to use his imagination, the grown up Dr. Chekhov had "scientific" evidence to rely upon.

For centuries the archaic and freakish nature of the Jewish body was associated in European beliefs with the special smell of the Jew — *foetor Judaicus* — and the Jews in the "The Steppe" also emit a special smell, an odor permeating the apartment and stemming from the bedroom: "the smell of something sour and musty, which was far thicker here [in the bedroom]" (43) and producing a nauseating effect on the Russian Egorushka. This anthropologically alien smell clearly evokes the *foetor Judaicus*, the smell attributed to the Jews not only in folk beliefs but also in the medical literature of the 1880s. Gilman reminds us that in 1880 the German scientist Gustav Jaeger considered *foetor Judaicus* to be a special feature of the Jewish body, a feature that marked Jews as racially different.[40]

The fact that Chekhov employed both folk beliefs and scientific views in his depiction of Jewish characters is especially evident in the case of Solomon's body. His frozen smile is a detail that serves as a medical illustration of his madness, visible to the narrator, Dr. Chekhov, but his strange appearance is viewed differently by the dozing child, Egorushka. When described through the eyes of the Russian boy, Solomon's body has an uncanny resemblance to the devil. His figure resembles an "unclean spirit" ("nechistaia sila" [45]) that appears in one's dreams. This "unclean spirit" is the same Satan as seen in numerous pictorial representations of the Jews as devils — images with which many a Russian boy from a pious provincial family, like Egorushka or Chekhov himself, was well familiar.

The mature Dr. Chekhov, however, leaves this image to be entertained by the little boy, and derives seemingly much more pleasure in depicting his Jewish characters as a combination of anthropological-biological stereotypes integrated with the stereotypes from folk beliefs and superstitions.[41] The subtitle of the *povest'* "The Steppe" is "The History of a Journey" and indeed, it is during one's travels that a voyager encounters exotic biological species.[42] As a source for quasi-ethnographic fantasies, the steppe has, from medieval times, occupied a special place in Russian culture in defining the difference between the Orthodox Slavs and the godless Others.[43] In the eschatological geography that identified the steppe with the land of Gog and Magog, this region was believed to be inhabited by exotic creatures such as the Dog-headed people (Cynocephali) among whom were Ishmaelites and Israelites, with little distinction made between them. Chekhov could continue this tradition in folk ethnography, developing his own quasi-ethnological depiction of the strange Jewish family. Thus it is only fitting that in his story entitled "The Steppe" the Jewish family should be defined in biological and racial terms, Chekhov employing congenital characteristics combined with mytho-poetic features to create anomalous bodies and psyches that bear the features of those pathologies defined as peculiarly Jewish.

The Body with No Bounds:
A Jewess's Excessive Mind and Body

In "Tina," the plot develops mainly in the heroine's bedroom and it is in the bedroom that the Jew's secret is concealed. The secret chamber, the Jew's intimate space, is thus put under surveillance. It is here that the special smell of the Jew, the *foetor Judaicus*, once more reveals itself with a strength that is suffocating, exciting, and asphyxiating. This time the smell is emitted by flowers and the body of the Jewish woman, Susanna—her bed linen, dresses and most notably her numerous shoes. The smell is undeniable, sickening, all pervasive, and has little in common with the precisely identified smell of the perfume (bought in a Japanese shop) that Chekhov's protagonist Gurov finds in the hotel room of the blonde and blue-eyed woman from the Russian province — "Dama s sobachkoi" ("The Lady with a Lapdog" [1899]). The smell which both repulses and attracts the young Russian officer in the snow white shirt on his visit to the rich Jewess is inescapably *foetor Judaicus*, but it is not only a marker of her Jewish body, it is also a sign of her diseased psyche, her own olfactory mania. Addiction to smells was classified in Krafft-Ebing's *Psychopathia Sexualis* (1886) as a form of sexual pathology. It is this mania which, as will be shown later, prompted Rozanov to write his infamous book *The Olfactory and Tactile Attitude of the Jews to Blood* (1913–1914) in which he claims that Jews get intoxicated by the smell of blood due to the atavistic cells of their brains.[44] Similarly in "Tina," smell acts as a marker of the Jewish woman's psychopathology. And indeed, she is not only immediately identified by the *poruchik* as "strange" ("Kakaia strannaia!"), but she is also diagnosed as "a psychopath of some sort" ("psikhopatka kakaia-to" [479]). And psychopathy, it must be remembered, was classified in S. S. Korsakov's textbook as a hereditary illness.

Susanna's shoes also emit a smell — again, this is not only the *foetor Judaicus* but also a form of fetishism. The sheer number of shoes suggests a mania of greed and compulsion that further pathologizes her. Indeed, her shoes are a double fetish, for they attract attention and arouse the young man. According to Freud, the smell of hair and feet is a contributing factor to the fetishist qualities of these parts of the body. Anthropologically, evolution diminished human sensitivity to these qualities, unlike in the development of the animal world, and, as an avid reader of Darwin, Chekhov could not have been unaware of the role of smell in erotic sexual selection. Freud wrote:

> Both the feet and the hair are objects with a strong smell which have been exalted into fetishes after the olfactory sensation has become unpleasurable and been abandoned. Accordingly, in the perversion that corresponds to foot-fetishism, it is only dirty and evil-smelling feet that become sexual objects. Another factor that helps towards explaining the fetishist preference for the foot is to be found among the sexual theories of children: the foot represents a woman's penis, the absence of which is deeply felt.[45]

The presence of the Jewish woman's shoes valorizes the theme of legs and feet and this valorization underscores the fact that she is a woman with legs, a phallic woman. Legs, we might remember, were concealed by women's long dresses in Victorian fashion, and shoes became metonymic replacements for women's legs and feet. Susanna is described by the Russian officer as a "monstrous creature" ("chudovishche" [488]), but this description might be more than a characterization of her immorality. Her many shoes may testify to her concealed anomalies: she might have many legs, just as the children under the blanket in the Jewish bedroom in "The Steppe" were taken for a hydra with many heads. If they were anomalies, testimony of evolution gone very wrong and betraying fantasized features of prehistoric times, then Susanna too could conceal under her bed the key to the secret of her anomalous body in the form of many legs.

In the 1880s Freud, as a young scientist, was conducting experiments on eels. The bisexuality of these creatures was viewed as rudimentary proof of the hermaphrodism of ancient bodies before separation into the two sexes took place. Jews were also regarded as rudimentary bodies, whose sexuality was not only ambivalent but also bivalent. Not only were they seen as prone to homosexuality, but their bodies could also be viewed as atavistic with anomalous genitalia. In his *Psychopathia Sexualis* Krafft-Ebing propounded the latest phylogenetic thinking among scientists of the 1880s in his explanation of ambivalent sexuality as a rudimentary form of hermaphroditism.

To parallel her implied hermaphrodism, Susanna's shoes, a metonym for her genitalia (Chekhov was a keen reader of Gogol and could not have missed the concealed erotic meaning of Bashmachkin's surname), are both blunt-ended and pointed: "From under the bed looked out the blunt and sharp noses of the long line of various shoes" ("Iz-pod krovati gliadeli tupye i ostrye nosy dlinnogo riada vsevozmozhnykh tufel" [476]). Her shoes are depicted as living organisms, whose "noses" look out from under the bed. She is certainly not a woman who lacks; rather, she is the opposite of the feminized Moisei Moiseevich — she can be both "round and pointed" (479), and can possess genitalia of both shapes. No wonder she has never married.

The expression, "Kakoi u nee odnako dlinnyi iazyk" ("She has a long tongue" [477]) is awkward in its application to the situation it describes. Susanna is making jocular remarks, the appropriate Russian idiom to describe her talk being "ostryi iazyk," "ostra na iazychek" ("sharp-tongued"). She is erect and phallic in figure — "Stroinaia, v dlinnom chernom plat'e, s sil'no zatianutoi, tochno vytochennoi taliei" ("Slender, in a long black dress, with a strongly tightened, perfectly formed waist" [479]); in the physical fight she has with the officer over the check, her body is revealed as "gibkoe" and "uprugoe"("lithe," "elastic" [483])—a description far removed from that of the fat Jewish woman–mother in "The Steppe."

Susanna's body is further compared to that of a grass snake—a phallic symbol in anthropological discourse. This comparison is not to be confused with the image of the snake with glossy "scales" (398) which Chekhov reserved for his description of the sexually active but male-oriented Russian women in his work "The Lady with a Lapdog" (in Russian "uzh," "grass snake," is of masculine gender, whereas "zmeia," meaning "snake," is feminine).[46] Susanna's characterization by the second Russian lover as "a chameleon" (488) is similarly physiologically loaded: as a lizard a chameleon is recognized as phallic in anthropology, and its zoological characteristics are defined by its ability to change color in moments of danger or excitement.[47] Thus the body of a chameleon defies boundaries; it is a mutating body. And, as a mutant, it stands as a trope of trans-sexuality. Susanna is characterized as a chameleon in comparison with and in contrast to Russian women of dubious behavior who are described as witches (as in "Ved'ma" [1886]). If oversexed Russian women are linked to the world of folk beliefs and superstitions, the Jewish woman's sexuality is linked to the riddles of evolution. As a chameleon, Susanna's body emerges as an atavistic one linked to the archaic strata.

Her masculinity is represented through the young officer's comments on the total lack of female house care in her disorganized rooms ("polnoe otsutstvie zhenskikh khoziaistvennykh ruk" [479]). Her notoriously misogynistic response becomes plausible[48] only when seen as a part of the hidden meaning of these signs: "Is it my fault that God gave me such a cover [obolochka]?... I normally love myself very much but when somebody reminds me that I am a woman, I start hating myself" ("Razve ia vinovata, chto bog poslal mne takuiu obolochku?.. Ia sebia ochen' liubliu, no kogda mne nachinaiut napominat,' chto ia zhenshchina, to ia nachinaiu nenavidet' sebia" [478–479]). "Obolochka" is also an anatomical term in Russian denoting a membrane (as in "slizistaia obolochka," a mucous membrane [357]).[49] Chekhov makes Susanna's trans-sexuality quite obvious, knowing only too well that it is precisely their *obolochka*, the physical body, that transsexuals want to dispose of as the object of their hatred. The desire for a body with different sexual organs and secondary characteristics had already been described in psychiatric literature in the 1880s. Krafft-Ebing's *Psychopathia Sexualis* is full of studies describing such cases. Rozanov quotes such studies generously and liberally in his *Liudi lunnogo sveta* in 1909/1911 (one example describes a man who feels that he is physiologically producing feminine genital secretions, thus developing the very membrane which Susanna finds so despicable).

Susanna is a "blednaia nemoch" (literally a sufferer of a "pale illness" or chlorosis [480]), and is thus diagnosed by the officer as "a pale dystrophic": her pale face, pale ears and pale gums are observed with medical precision, as all these features betray the signs of degeneracy which late nineteenth-century science attributed to East European Jews as a result of their unhealthy lifestyle and alleged inbreeding. These physical symptoms of her diseased body are augmented by characteristics of her nervous system: she is, we are told, "hyper-nervous like a turkey" (480). This characterization reflects the contemporary "scientific" view regarding Jews' special predisposition to nervous diseases, a diagnosis that was also explained by an unhealthy lifestyle, specifically a lack of contact with nature due to an over-commitment to business.[50] The stereotypical Jew of the time was a city dweller, and the noisy environment of the new capitalist city was seen to contribute to his or her deficient nervous system. Susanna runs a large business and spends her time indoors. Her improvised indoor garden with its plants and birds held in captivity underscores the distance between her artificial environment and the healthy and wholesome countryside traditionally idealized in Russian culture as the place that produces the healthy bodies and psyches of strong peasant men and women.

Published in *Novoe vremia*, "Tina" thus reflects the combination of biological stereotypes and political antisemitism that was propagated by this newspaper. The pogroms of 1881–1883 were explained by the conservative press as a result of the hatred felt by the local population towards Jews because of their exploitation of peasants and the part they took in the liquor trade and in manufacturing. The fact that Susanna is depicted as an heiress to a vodka manufacturing business factory confirms that Chekhov conformed to the anti-Jewish stereotypes promulgated by the *Novoe vremia*, which systematically published articles accusing Jews of encouraging drunkenness in the Russian peasants (Helen Tolstoy argues that in this story Chekhov's own mercantilism in considering marriage with the wealthy Jewess Evdokiia Efros is exposed and his attitude toward the real life protagonist of Susanna is shown to reflect the hidden attraction Chekhov felt toward strong-willed and independent women[51]).

"The Steppe," on the other hand, was published in *Severnyi vestnik* and Chekhov did not feel obliged to apply political antisemitic stereotypes in his portrayal of Jews. The theme of Jewish love for money is, however, depicted in a way that reflects the political situation surrounding Jews in the 1880s. Whereas one brother is shown as a quasi-revolutionary, another is a man interested in money, but not excessively, just enough to keep the family going.

Chapter 2

Chekhov's Own Ailing Body

In the works discussed here, the Jewish stereotypes that interested Chekhov were mainly biological as opposed to political. When pogroms began in the south of Russia in the spring of 1881, Chekhov expressed his opinion on the reasons for the pogroms in the already quoted letter to his Jewish fellow student, S. Kramarev, who was in Kharkov at the time: "In the place where people keep busy [*delom zaniaty*] there is no time left for beatings, and in Moscow everybody keeps busy"(82).[52] He reveals here an understanding of pogroms as the result of the activities of declassed former peasants, migrant workers without work and a stable income — an understanding that shows no interest in the slanderous accusations of Jews being guilty of exploiting the local population. Although free from the political propaganda disseminated by the Russian press, Chekhov does reveal himself to be influenced by a different type of prejudice — one disseminated in the scientific discourses of his time.

Afflicted with a tubercular body, Chekhov was doubly sensitive to ideas surrounding the etiology of disease, and his alleged trust in the supremacy of hygiene and the beneficial effects of the environment over hereditary predisposition was partly a strategy for personal survival. His trust in science was constantly challenged by the signs of his own weakening body, which served as a reminder of the possible hereditary nature of his own disease which he shared with his uncles and his brother whose condition deteriorated rapidly in the late 1880s.[53] What has been considered as a marker of his art — the mutability and fluidity of his optimistic messages of a bright future for new generations on the one hand, and a pessimism manifested by his inability to depict this bright future convincingly in any concrete form on the other — was a reflection of his struggle between two coexisting medical paradigms: the inescapability of the laws of biological determinism and dialectical improvement due to scientific advancement.[54] In the evolutionary process of the survival of the fittest there was little place left for damaged consumptive bodies. Jews, on the other hand, presented a case for the paradoxical survival of bodies that were viewed as diseased but survived against all the laws of evolution. In the play *Ivanov*, it is Sarra's death from tuberculosis that is prognosticated but it is Ivanov who dies, while Sarra's demise is not depicted at all. Maybe she survives, against all the odds. Jews were thus regarded as an ideal body of the alien Other with whom one could secretly associate oneself but against whom, at the same time, one could project all the fears connected with one's own pathological body. Chekhov ridiculed anomalous and diseased Jewish bodies because they provided him with much needed comic relief. Laughter, as Freud taught his patients (many of whom came from Russia), is the manifestation of a deeply seated fear: ". . . we produce a comic effect, that is, a surplus of energy which has to be discharged in laughter, if we allow these models of thinking to force their way through into consciousness" (644).[55]

Scholars have explained that Chekhov stopped depicting Jewish characters in his later writing inasmuch as he distanced himself from Suvorin and his antisemitic *Novoe vremia*; however, it is in his letters to Suvorin that we find evidence of his continuing interest in Jews and his preoccupation with the issue of biological determinism in relation to health and race.[56] He was seriously ill and recuperating in Yalta when, in a letter to Suvorin in 1894, he passionately insisted on his mistrust of the theories of pathological degeneration in contemporary society as espoused by the German-speaking Jewish physician and writer Max Nordau. Nevertheless, in 1896 he donated Nordau's book *Degeneration* (*O vyrozhdenii*) to the library of his native town, Taganrog, along with a number of books that he clearly considered important.[57] Nordau's book synthesized theories of degeneration based on the Darwinian theory of evolution, and maintained that the fin-de-siécle period exhibited features of degeneration in both art and literature. However, as a physician Nordau believed that the current epoch of degeneration would not be long lived because, as in biology "a morbid variation does not subsist and propagate itself"(15), but becomes sterile and dies out.[58]

Although Nordau was clearly optimistic that a new epoch would evolve, his call for the need to conquer degeneration, and his faith in the power of science, were not well received by Chekhov.[59] Why is this? In Chekhov's reaction to Nordau's book we find the same signs of anxiety about his own body that surfaced in his depictions of the Jewish body in his writing. We know that in 1890 Chekhov expressed his belief in the power of biological inheritance: "As regards to heredity, one has to reconcile oneself with it, since it is unavoidable and necessary. It is necessary because, apart from the bad things, a human inherits from his predecessors also many good things" (137).[60] In the same letter in which he expresses his distaste for Nordau's work he also gives an optimistic account of his own health, which was, in fact, rapidly deteriorating at the time. He wrote that, in spite of some health problems he was experiencing at the time, he nevertheless continued to believe in improvement, "in progress" (49). While musing about the state of his own body and reflecting on his optimistic credo, he also stressed that he had "peasant blood flowing in his veins" (49). By giving this biological detail he involuntarily expressed more trust in hereditariness than he had in abstract "progress." In the Russian medical discourse of the time, to be of peasant stock meant to be healthy — a view influenced by the prevalent populist adulation of the peasantry.[61] By underscoring his own inherited healthy background, Chekhov marked a boundary between his own body and those of the group with degenerative potential: Nordau himself and the Jews he both depicted and represented. Nordau, who was a Zionist, called for the development of a new "muscle Jew," as opposed to the degenerate Jews with pale skins and sunken chests produced in the confines of the ghetto.[62] Like many other Jewish physicians of the time, he followed the dominant scientific belief in regard to the special deformed biology of Jews. But he expanded the notion of degeneration to cultivated classes and maintained that derangement of the nervous system becomes encoded on the very level of the genotype, passing on from one generation to the next all features of cultural declension, which he called degeneration. He turned the discourse of degeneration against those who used it to demonize the Jews. For Nordau the solution is the eventual disappearance of degenerates when humanity will triumph over its exhausted condition.

If Chekhov really believed in the power of progress that could change "bad" hereditary features, why would he call Nordau a "whistler in the wind" ("svistun," 50)? After all, he himself spoke seriously of the "degeneration" ("vyrozhdenie") "of the intellectual class" (74) in 1895, explaining, however, that the process could be helped by changes in lifestyle.[63] Could it be that he did not believe that degenerate Jews with their sickly pale skins and sunken chests — those that he had depicted in his work — could join the path of biological progress? After all, none of his Jewish protagonists show any "good" hereditary features, only the "bad" signs of pathology. To complicate matters further, in the same letter in which he criticizes Nordau's theories, Chekhov confesses his own liking for nervousness ("nervnost," 49) — a condition that in this letter he equated with sophistication, although, as the reader will recall, some of his Jewish literary characters were marked by grotesque nervousness. This same condition, considered to be a typical feature of modernity, was qualified in Nordau's book as a marker of contemporary civilization and a product of modern literature and art. Nordau nominated a figure of the avant-garde artist to replace the Jew as arch-degenerate. Could it be that Chekhov made a connection between "the Jews" and modern artists like himself, the connection that Nordau used in his book as a strategy to displace the antisemitic cliché?[64]

The fact that Max Nordau was a Jew might have motivated Chekhov to separate himself from those conclusions as the product of a Jewish mind. In the same way that the opponents of psychoanalysis labeled it a Jewish science, the opponents of Nordau's theories also viewed them as a result of a specifically Jewish mind or "Jewish race" (9) — so conflating the pathological subject and its production.[65] That Chekhov himself was familiar with such attitudes toward Jewish medical scientists is evidenced by his statement in a letter to Suvorin in 1897 during the plague epidemic. He notes that the only hope to curtail the epidemic is by way of a special vaccination invented by the Jewish bacteriologist V. M. Havkin, but even that act was likely to be doomed because, as Chekhov writes ironically, "unfortunately Havkin is not popular in Russia: 'Christians have to protect themselves from him since he is a Yid'" (141).[66] Here, Chekhov puts an antisemitic credo (to protect Russia from Yids) into quotation marks, thus using authorial irony to expose the antisemitic subculture of the time. He went on to use this Jewish scientist (a pupil of Louis Pasteur) as a fellow traveler in his arguments for positivism against religious obscurantism. Paradoxically, as Chekhov's reaction to Nordau's work attests, he also showed that Jews stood outside the process of progress, remaining immune to the achievements of science even if they themselves are among the scientists who moved it forward.

Chekhov's desire to separate himself from the conclusions of the Jewish physician Nordau on the one hand, and his ability to reveal the mechanism that drives this very rejection on the other, is symptomatic, and reflects a complex relationship that he continued to have with the Jewish body and mind well after he stopped depicting Jewish characters in his fiction. It is quite possible that he stopped depicting Jewish characters in his fiction because he understood the meaning and the implications of the connection between the Jews and modern artists that Nordau made in his book. After all, Nordau defined the artist not merely as the witness of degeneration but also as its source.

Chekhov's interaction with Jews was clearly informed by the stereotypes of pathology produced by turn-of-the-century science and culture. The irony of this employment of stereotypes was that Chekhov's own personality was thoroughly scrutinized within the topic of "normality," as Russian psychiatrists were only too keen to draw parallels between what was perceived as the pathological characters of his fiction — the whole array of apathetic, unmotivated and often suicidal representatives of the Russian intelligentsia — and the writer's own mindset. Chekhov was considered by followers of degeneration theories in Russia as an author whose work typically reflected and contributed to the increasingly unhealthy state of the Russian public and the decline of Russian culture.[67] It is here that the link was established between the decadent degenerate writer and his degenerate creations. This situation serves as powerful proof that stereotypes of pathology formed a dominant discursive formation in fin-de-siècle Russia, and that racial Others and intellectuals were viewed as sharing the same features of difference and pathology.

Notes

1   A. P. Chekhov. Ivanov. *Sobranie sochinenii v dvenadtsati tomakh.* Vol. 9. Moscow: Khudozhestvennaia literatura. 1956. 19–86. 28. Unless otherwise stated all quotations from Chekhov's works are from this edition.
2   See Gabriella Safran. *Rewriting the Jew: Assimilation Narratives in the Russian Empire.* Stanford: Stanford University Press. 2000.
    Savelii Senderovich. O chekhovskoi glubine, ili Iudofobskii rasskaz Chekhova v svete iudaisticheskoi ekzegezy. *Avtor i tekst.* Eds. V. M. Markovich and Vol'f Shmid. St. Petersburg: St. Petersburg University Press. 1996. 306–340.
    Helena Tolstoy. From Susanna to Sarra: Chekhov in 1886–1887. *Slavic Review.* Vol. 50. No. 3. 1991. 590–600.
    E. Kalmanskii. Paradoksy peresechenii: evrei v proizvedeniiakh A. P. Chekhova. *Evrei v Rossii: Istoriia i kul'tura.* Vol. 3. St. Petersburg: Peterburgskii evreiskii universitet. Trudy po iudaike. 1995. 171–186.
    Boris Chernyi. Tema izgnaniia i iskhoda u Chekhova. Ed. Oleg Budnitskii. *Russko-evreiskaia kul'tura.* Moscow: Rosspen. 2006. 191–216. Henrietta Mondry. Ob odnom kripto-evree u A. Chekhova. *New Zealand Slavonic Journal.* Vol. 41. 2007. 43–55.
3   In a letter to Suvorin in 1889 Chekhov wrote: "When one knows how big is the similarity between somatic and mental illnesses, and when one knows that both of these illnesses are treated with the same medicine, one will not want to separate souls from the body" (358). A. P. Chekhov. A. S. Suvorinu. May 7, 1889. *Sobranie sochinenii.* Moscow: Khudozhestvennaia literatura. 1956. Vol. 11. 356–358.
4   A. P. Chekhov. P. S. Kramarevu. May 8, 1881. *Sobranie sochinenii v dvenadtsati tomakh.* Vol. 10. Moscow: Izd-vo Pravda. 1985. 10–11.
5   See Steven G. Marks. *How Russia Shaped the Modern World: From Art to Anti-Semitism, Ballet to Bolshevism.* Princeton: Princeton University Press. 2003.
6   S. G. Frug. V korchme i v buduare. *Voskhod.* October 1889. 21–37.
7   Quoted in V. Romanenko. *Chekhov i nauka.* Khar'kov: Khar'kovskoe knizhnoe izdatel'stvo. 1962.
8   Quoted in I. M. Geizer. *Chekhov i meditsina.* Moscow: Medgiz. 1954.
9   Among the courses that comprised the curriculum at the Medical Faculty of the Moscow University were courses on nervous and psychiatric diseases ("uchenie o nervnykh i dushevnykh bolezniakh"), forensic medicine, and venereal diseases (98). See *Letopis'zhizni i tvorchetsva A .P. Chekhova. 1860–1888.* Vol. 1. Moscow: Nasledie. 2000.
10 Chekhov wrote of his preference for German scientists over French, and noted that he visited a lecture by German anthropologist Rudolf Wirhow around August 1891. See A. P. Chekhov. A. S. Suvorinu. August 16, 1892. *Sobranie sochinenii.* Moscow: Khudozhestvennaia literatura. 1956. Vol. 11. 586–590. On the influence of Lombroso's and Max Nordau's determinist views on Russian psychiatrists, including Chekhov's friend G. I Rossolimo, see Irina Sirotkina. *Diagnosing Literary Genius: A Cultural History of Psychiatry in Russia, 1880–1930.* Baltimore: The Johns Hopkins University Press. 2002.
11 G. S. Vasilenko. Predislovie. R. Krafft-Ebing. *Polovaia psikhopatiia.* Moscow: Respublika. 1996. 3–7.

[12]   Chekhov's interest in biological theories in their most extreme manifestations are reflected in his story "The Duel" (1891) in which a zoologist, fon Koren, serves as a mouthpiece of Lombrosian criminal anthropology and the general extremism in the zoologist's views on the hereditary nature of pathology. Ambivalence and uncertainty in Chekhov's own attitude to fon Koren's views was noticed by a number of contemporaries, and their criticism led to Chekhov making adjustments in the text for the separate edition of the story. See K. D. Muratova. Primechaniia. A. P. Chekhov. *Sobranie sochinenii.* Vol. 6. 1956. 501–502.

[13]   Soboleva. Evrei. *Narody Rossii: etnograficheskie ocherki.* St. Petersburg: Obshchestvennaia pol'za. 1878–1880. Vol. 1. 391–392.

[14]   Chekhov was familiar with this view from an article by his friend V. V. Bilibin in "Oskolki Peterburgskoi zhizni" No 13. 1886. See Senderovich. Op. cit. 316.

[15]   Michael Chekhov claimed that Chekhov rejected degeneration ("vyrozhdenie," 209) in his arguments with the zoologist Dr. V. A. Vagner, the protagonist of fon Koren in "The Duel." See M. P. Chekhov. *Vokrug Chekhova.* Leningrad: Academia. 1933.

[16]   Leonid Grossman wrote of the influence of Zola's views of the hereditary on Chekhov in "Naturalizm Chekhova". *Vestnik Evropy.* No. 7. 1914. 218–247.

[17]   Donald Rayfield. *Anton Chekhov: A Life.* New York: Henry Holt and Co. 1997.

[18]   Sander L. Gilman. *Freud, Race and Gender.* Princeton: Princeton University Press. 1993

[19]   Mark Swift. Chekhov's 'Ariadna': A Portrait of Psychopathy and Sin. *Slavonic and East European Review.* Vol. 86. No. 1. 2008. 26–57.

[20]   A. P. Chekhov. Ivanov. *Sobranie sochinenii.* Vol. 9. 1956. 19–86.

[21]   A. P. Chekhov. Perekati-pole. *Sobranie sochinenii.* Vol. 5. 1956. 275–291.

[22]   In a recent work devoted to the subject of Jews in Russian literature, Gabriella Safran (*Rewriting the Jew: Assimilation Narratives in the Russian Empire.* Stanford: Stanford University Press. 2000) devotes a whole chapter to Chekhov's representation of Jews, with a particular focus on his interest in converted Jews. In an earlier work Savely Senderovich (O chekhovskoi glubine, ili ludofobskii rasskaz Chekhova v svete iudaisticheskoi ekzegezy. *Avtor i tekst.* Eds. V. M. Markovich and Vol'f Shmid. St. Petersburg: St. Petersburg University Press. 1996. 306–340) reads the plot of "Tina" against the religious exegetics of the two subplots encoded in the image of the protagonist Susanna — the first being the apocryphal story of the unjustly accused Susanna by the elders (Chekhov inverts this story by presenting the innocent Biblical Susanna as a seductive wench) and the second being the rivalry between the two religions, Christianity and Judaism, as based on the presence of a picture of Jacob and Esau in Susanna's apartment. This picture portrays the victory of the elder brother who was tricked out of his rightful place of the first born by his younger brother Jacob. The seniority of Christianity over Judaism is established not only on the level of religious exegetics but also on the level of the plot of the story: an immoral Susanna is guilty of tricking Christian men into sexual depravity.

[23]   Gleb Uspensky was the leading master of sketches. On the influence of his work on Chekhov see M. Semanova. Chekhov i Gleb Uspenskii. (K voprosu o tvorchestve Chekhova vos'midesiatykh godov). *Uchenye Zapiski* . Leningrad: Leningradskii Gosudarstvennyi Pedagogicheskii institut. 1959. 3–63.

[24]   See K. D. Muratova. Primechaniia in A. P. Chekhov. *Sobranie sochinenii.* Vol. 6. 1956. 482–486.

[25]   See David Goldstein. *Dostoevsky and the Jews.* Austin: University of Texas Press. 1981. Elena M. Katz. *Neither With Them Nor Without: The Russian Writer and the Jew in the Age of Realism.* Syracuse: Syracuse UP. 2008. Mikhail Edel'shtein. Istoriia odnogo stereotipa. Ed. G. S. Zelenina. *Evrei i zhidy v russkoi klassike.* Moscow and Jerusalem: Gesharim. 2005. 384–391.

[26]   D. V. Grigorovichu. 5 February 1888. *Sobranie sochinenii.* Vol. 11. 1956. 193–195.

[27]   Sander L. Gilman. *Freud, Race and Gender.* Princeton: Princeton University Press. 1993.

[28] In Ashkenazi practice it is not possible for father and son to have the same first name, so "Moisei Moiseevich" is a literary device in the Gogolian tradition.

[29] On Chekhov's humor in the 1880s see S. D. Balukhatyi. *Rannii Chekhov. A. P. Chekhov. Sbornik statei i materialov.* Vol. 1. Literaturnyi muzei Chekhova. Rostov-on-Don: Rostovskoe knizhnoe izdatel'stvo. 1959. 3–95.

[30] Gilman 1993. Op. cit. 43.

[31] Daglas Kleiton. Ulybka Konstantina: k probleme poeticheskogo iazyka Chekhova. *Avtor i tekst.* Ed. V. M. Markovich and Vol'f Shmid. St. Petersburg: St. Petersburg University Press. 1996. 341–354.

[32] A. P. Chekhov. "Step'." *Sobranie sochinenii.* Vol. 6. Moscow: Khudozhestvennaia literatura. 1955. 16–112.

[33] Quoted in Gilman. Op. cit.

[34] Konstantin Leontiev criticized as superfluous the tradition of using sounds and phonemes to imitate sounds of nature and peasant speech. See his *Analiz, stil' i veianie. O romanakh gr. L. N. Tolstogo.* (Reprint) Providence: Brown University Press. 1968.

[35] See Joshua Kunitz. *Russian Literature and the Jew.* New York: Columbia UP. 1929 and Henrietta Mondry [G. Mondri]. *Pisateli-narodniki i evrei.* St. Petersburg: Akademicheskii proekt. 2005.

[36] Douglas Clayton overlooks the difference between the semantics of farm birds and wild birds (such as magpies) in his analysis of Chekhov's poetic language in "The Steppe" and other stories. He states, "It is this kind of 'democracy' which lies at the centre of Chekhov's favorite metaphor comparing a human being with a bird" (351). He, however, stresses that a human being is equated with nature through the usage of such "empty words" as "gal-gal-gal-gal" and "tu-tu-tu-tu". Op. cit. 351.

[37] Chekhov experimented with the plot of the love of an animal and a earthly woman in a jocular way in his "Ryb'ia liubov'" ("Fish's Love," 1892) in which he made a carp fall in love with a woman in the same way as Lermontov's Demon fell in love with Tamara, and a swan fell in love with Leda (99). Although intended as a parody on the plot of such love, it nevertheless serves as a proof of Chekhov's thinking on this topic. "Ryb'ia liubov'." *Sobranie sochinenii.* Vol. 7. 1956. 99–101.

[38] Howard Eilberg-Schwartz. *God's Phallus: And Other Problems for Men and Monotheism.* Boston: Beacon Press. 1994.

[39] J. C. Cooper. *Symbolic and Mythological Animals.* London: The Aquarian Press. 1992.

[40] Gustav Jaeger. *Die Entdeckung der Seele.* Leipzig: Ernst Guenter. 1880. 106–109. On smell see also Jay Geller. The aromatics of Jewish difference; or, Benjamin's Allegory of Aura. *Jews and Other Differences.* Eds. Jonathan Boyarin and Daniel Boyarin. Minneapolis: University of Minnesota Press. 1997. 203–256.

[41] It has been stressed that, at the end of the nineteenth century, scientific discourse on race relied heavily on earlier quasi-theological work as their proof. See Sander. L. Gilman. *The Case of Sigmund Freud: Medicine and Identity at the Fin de Siècle.* Baltimore: Johns Hopkins University Press. 1993.

[42] On the conflation of reality and fantasy in "The Steppe" see Stephen C. Hutchings. *Russian Modernism: The Transfiguration of the Everyday.* Cambridge UK: Cambridge University Press. 1997.

[43] Leonid Chekin. The Godless Ishmaelites: The Image of the Steppe in Eleventh-Thirteenth-Century Rus'. *Russian History.* 19, Nos. 1–4. 1992. 9–28.

[44] Henrietta Mondry. [G. Mondri]. *Rozanov i evrei.* St. Petersburg: Akademicheskii proekt. 2000.

[45] Quoted in Sander Gilman. *The Case of Sigmund Freud.* Op. cit. 135.

[46] A. P. Chekhov. Dama s sobachkoi. *Sobranie sochinenii.* Vol. 8. 1956. 394–411.

[47] Otto Rank. *Art and Artist: Creative Urge and Personality Development.* New York: W.W. Norton. 1989.

Stereotypes of Pathology: the Medicalization of the Jewish Body by Anton Chekhov, 1880s

48 Senderovich underestimates Chekhov's intent in making Susanna misogynous when he states that "the oblique form of these ideas are only implied by Chekhov" and states that these ideas found their full expression in Otto Weininger's *Sex and Character* (1903). Op. cit. 324.
49 *Russko-angliiskii slovar'*. Ed. O. S. Akhmanova et.al. Moscow: Russkii iazyk. 1975. 357.
50 See Sander L. Gilman. *The Visibility of the Jew in the Diaspora: Body Imagery and its Cultural Context*. Syracuse: Syracuse University Press. 1992.
51 Helena Tolstoy. From Susanna to Sarra: Chekhov in 1886–1887. *Slavic Review*. Vol. 50. No. 3. 1991. 590–600.
52 A. P. Chekhov. P. S. Kramarevu. May 8, 1881. *Sobranie sochinenii v dvenadtsati tomakh*. Vol. 10. Moscow: Izd-vo Pravda. 1985. 10–11.
53 On Chekhov's health problems and his self-deception see M. B. Mirskii. *Doktor Chekhov*. Moscow: Nauka. 2003.
54 Leonid Grossman wrote of the tension between optimism and pessimism in Chekhov's art as a consequence of his positivism and materialism. See his "Naturalizm Chekhova". *Vestnik Evropy*. No. 7. 1914. 218–247.
55 Sigmund Freud. *The Interpretation of Dreams*. Trans. and ed. James Strachey. New York. Avon Books. 1998.
56 A. P. Chekhov. A. S. Suvorinu. March 27,1894. *Sobranie sochinenii*. Vol. 12. 1956. 49–50.
57 A. P. Chekhov. P. F. Iordanovu. November 24, 1896. *Sobranie sochinenii*. Vol. 12. 1956. 123–126.
58 Max Nordau. Degeneration. *The Fin de Siècle: A Reader in Cultural History c. 1880–1990*. Eds. Sally Ledger and Roger Luckhurst. Oxford: Oxford University Press. 2000. 13–17.
59 Darwinian theories of evolution provided the basis for notions of racial and cultural degeneration and, as a self-confessed Darwinist, Chekhov should not have found the theory objectionable. See Sally Ledger and Roger Lukhurst, Ed. "Degeneration". *The Fin De Siècle: A Reader in Cultural History, c. 1880–1900*. Oxford: Oxford University Press. 2000.
60 Quoted in V. Romanenko. *Chekhov i nauka*. Op. cit. 137.
61 On the idealisation of peasants' physical and moral health by the Russian doctors see: Laura Engelstein. *The Keys to Happiness: Sex and the Search for Modernity in Fin-de-Siècle Russia*. Ithaca: Cornell University Press. 1992.
62 See Daniel Boyarin. *Unheroic Conduct: The Rise of Heterosexuality and the Invention of the Jewish Man*. Berkeley: University of California Press. 1997.
63 A. P. Chekhov. E. M. Sharovoi. February 28, 1895. *Sobranie sochinenii*. Vol. 12. 73–75.
64 On Nordau's strategy see Jonathan Freedman. Henry James and the Discourses of Antisemitism. *Between "Race" and Culture: Representations of "the Jews" in English and American Literature*. Ed. Bryan Cheyette. Stanford: Stanford University Press. 1996. 62–83.
65 Egmont Hake in his response to Nordau's *Degeneration* wrote: "For characteristics revealed in his work, the observant reader will, no doubt, conclude that Max Nordau belongs to the Jewish race" (9). Egmont Hake. *Regeneration: A Reply to Max Nordau*. Westminster: Archibald Constable. 1895. For a similar response to psychoanalytic theory see Sander Gilman. *The Jew's Body*. London: Routledge. 1991.
66 A. P. Chekhov. A. S. Suvorinu. January 17, 1897. *Sobranie sochinenii*. Vol. 12. 1956. 140–141.
67 Psychiatrists Ivan Sikorsky and Fedor Rybakov considered Chekhov to be part of a group of degenerate artists. See Irina Sirotkina. *Diagnosing Literary Genius: A Cultural History of Psychiatry in Russia, 1880–1930*. Baltimore: The Johns Hopkins University Press. 2002. Professor of psychiatry L.B. Blumenau identified Chekhov's own psychological state with the psychopathology and degeneration of his heroes. See L. B. Blumenau. Nravstvennaia evoluitsia i vyrozhdenie. *Vestnik psikhopatologii, kriminologii i gipnotizma*. St. Petersburg. January 1904.

Chapter 3

Carnal Jews of the Fin-de-Siècle: Vasily Rozanov, the Jewish Body, and Incest

> "The secret of Jewry lies in the fact that there exists what is purely Jewish, pure-blooded Jewish, and around it a 'skin' of other peoples that is judaized with incredible speed. In the world now there is not a single people completely free of Jewish blood, and there is Jewry with blood that is absolutely unmixed. So there are Jews, half-Jews, quarter-Jews, fifth-part Jews, hundredth-part Jews and so on. And every year every people increases its percentage of Jewish blood, i.e. has its original identity diluted"
>
> Pavel Florensky, 1913.[1]
>
> "Evil tongues were saying that [Rozanov] was smitten by his step-daughter and at the same time 'up to his ears' in love with his wife"
>
> Alexandre Benois.[2]

Vasily Rozanov (1856–1919), the controversial turn-of-the-century writer and philosopher, can be regarded as the first ideologue of body politics in Russia in general, and of the Jewish body in particular.[3] Rozanov created his own generic brand of the philosophy of the body, a brand that he termed his "sermon of sex" (132).[4] He chose the Jew's body as an exemplary body, one that could be studied as an exhibit because of its long history of physical survival. He saw this body as rudimentary and archaic, and defined his mission of sex as part of the struggle between Christianity and Judaism: "Further denial of sexuality by Christianity will lead to the increase of Jewry's triumphs. This is why the start of my sermon of sex is 'so timely'"(132).

The twenty-year span of Rozanov's work on human sexuality was marked by alternating periods of attraction to Jews and Judaism and fervent Judeophobia. This protracted schema of acceptance/rejection involved an identification with the exotic Other, the separation of the Self from this Other and the transformation of the Other into an object of loathing and rejection.[5] As a constant theme in Rozanov's work, the subject of incest serves to illustrate these dynamics of this prolific writer's interaction with the issue of the Jewish body and sexuality. Indeed, ideas about incest form a structure around which Rozanov builds his entire politics of Jewish sexuality.[6] This chapter discusses Rozanov's manipulation of incest as a marker of Jewish sexuality, and his fluctuating evaluation of this category of behavior. It puts Rozanov's approach into the context of those theories on incest held by authors contemporary to him, both Jewish (Sigmund Freud and Otto Rank) and non-Jewish (Edward Westermarck), and explores the formative influences underlying Rozanov's quasi-political, subjective views.

In order to understand Rozanov's obsession with Jews it is necessary to consider the general racist mode of Russian fin-de-siècle discourse. Russian philosophers and theologians such as Nikolai Berdiaev (1874–1948) and priest-theologian Father Pavel Florensky (1882–1937), as well as the highly influential adventuress of a theosophical bent, Madam Elena Blavatsky (1831–1891), all articulated racist views on Jews.[7] The writings and teachings of each of these personalities reflected the turn-of-the-century preoccupation with race. Berdiaev saw a link between Karl Marx's Jewish origins and the materialism of his method and the materiality of Jews;[8] Florensky was preoccupied with the eschatological advantages of the Jews as the only chosen people who were guaranteed physical resurrection; and Blavatsky expressed her preferences for Aryan people over Jews, whom she considered to be relics of obsolete root races.[9] The philosopher Vladimir Soloviev (1853–1900) put forward the concept of "sacred corporeality" (45) as a characteristic of Jews in response to the ideas prevalent in popular European culture on the materialism of Jewry.[10] Whereas popular antisemitic myths linked Jewry with a disposition towards material accumulation, and looked for an explanation for this in Judaism, Soloviev "theoreticized" this view with the intention of finding a scientific explanation for the Jewish "national character." He stressed Israel's concern for bodily cleanliness, manifested in the ritual observance of washing and kosher practice, and the metaphysical intensity of Jews' preparation for life beyond the grave in trying to ensure not only clean souls, but also clean flesh: "One may say that the whole religious history of the Jews was directed towards preparing for the God of Israel not only holy spirits, but also holy bodies" (45). In Soloviev's writing Jews become "people of the body".[11]

Rozanov himself was influenced by biological sciences to a much greater extent than these mystically inclined personalities of his day. This is evidenced by his original research interests in the field of natural sciences and philosophy. His first voluminous work *O Ponimanii: opyt issledovaniia prirody, granits i vnutrennego stroeniia nauki kak tsel'nogo znaniia* (*On Understanding: A Study of Nature, Science's Limits and Its Internal Structure as Holistic Knowledge* [1886]) was written as a formal treatise providing an overview of the scientific literature and opinions on the topic of cognition in the physical world, and was an attempt to systematize knowledge of natural phenomena and metaphysics. His interest in academic scientific discourse cannot, therefore, be undermined or disputed.

An overview of Russian biological and anthropological science reveals that in the context of the late nineteenth-century Russian empire with all its numerous nationalities, it was Jews that, *mutatis mutandis,* exemplified the very notion of race. As one researcher points out: "When one talks about the presence of the racist discourse in the politics of the Russian Empire (as well as racism in science and culture), as a rule, one has in mind racial antisemitism of the turn of the nineteenth century, i.e., the notion of 'race' in the Russian context is linked in one way or another to the notion of the 'Jews'" (116).[12] Scientific discourses represented the Jews as a primitive people who had managed to evade the forces of acculturation in their various places of residence and so survive the "civilizing" influence of Christian culture. The parallels drawn between the Jewish body and that of a "tribal savage" meant that, for the purposes of study, Jews in Europe were regarded as valuable examples of a primitive and unrestrained sexuality.[13] As Yosef Hayim Yerushalmi demonstrates in *Freud's Moses* (1991), the association between biology and the "nature" of Jews was so pervasive in European racial science that even Jewish physicians and psychoanalysts such as Freud and Rank felt compelled to address the biological aspects of Jewish "nature" as a serious topic in their work.[14]

In the literature known to Rozanov, the notion of the excessive sexuality of the Jew, signifying a diseased body and psyche, was widely disseminated, particularly in the work of Richard von Krafft-Ebing. Accusations of Jewish involvement in sex crimes and the prostitution trade prompted the belief that this supposed excessive sexuality was a force that must be restrained.[15] Rozanov's politics of the Jewish body, however, were much more complex. He was attracted to the idea of a Jewish sexuality in his search for rudimentary and atavistic phenomena; he held to the belief that Jewish bodies had an inherently mystical quality because, thanks to their ethnic purity, Jews were the surviving remnant of a time when bodies were created in the likeness of the body of God. In his arguments against the hierarchical separation between celestial and earthly bodies, and his belief in the transcendental nature of sex/sexuality (*transtsendentnyi kharakter pola*), as seen in *Brak i khristianstvo* (*Marriage and Christianity*),[16] he maintained that the very essence from which sexual organs ("that place") was made was not of a "phenomenal" but of "supra-natural" (*sverkhestestven*) and even cosmic origin:

Quite often, the thought occurred to me, and still occurs to me, that the very "clod of earth" from which that place is made has a totally different origin from the other parts of the body (this is why, during the *usual, phenomenal time and with the usual eye, we cannot even look at it*) and it is to other parts of the body the same as iron from a *meteorite* is to *ordinary* iron. (*Marriage and Christianity*, 119)

Alongside Rozanov's interest in religion and metaphysics, and his unusual consideration of the Jewish body as a special, metaphysical one, there is also present an anxiety around the contamination of this body that would stand in the way of the Jews' eschatological mission. If, in Rozanov's view, Florensky was right about the Jews' eschatological mission (that Jews will have literal physical resurrection), then Jews as the chosen people had to remain in their original physical form until the Day of the Last Judgment.[17] Any contamination of Jews' bodies with non-Jewish blood would therefore spoil the plan of Providence.

Incest and the Jews as a Theme in Scientific Discourse

In his seminal studies on the perception of Jewish sexuality in the work of turn-of-the-century European thinkers, Gilman established that incest is one of the most significant of all the sexual perversities that have been assigned to Jews in (quasi-)scientific discourses. Whereas criminal statistics reveal a very low incidence of incest among Jews, Gilman shows that a belief in the incestuousness of Jews was remarkably persistent in the forensic and anthropological literature of the time. This can be partly explained by the fact that Jewish levirate marriages, (i.e., the marriage between a man and the widow of his dead brother who has died childless),[18] as well as marriages between first cousins, were viewed as examples of brother-sister incest. Michael Satlow discusses the part played by Jewish marriage practices in the perpetuation of fantasies about Jewish tendencies toward incest in European discourse.[19] In Russia, the belief in brother-sister incest among Jews was further reinforced by the Russian lexis for male and female cousins— *dvoiurodnyi brat* (secondary brother) and *dvoiurodnaia sestra* (secondary sister). Edward Westermarck, in his voluminous *History of Human Marriage* (1891), regards levirate marriages among Jews as a means of preserving racial boundaries and incest as a marker of Jewish ethno-psychology, partly on the basis of the presence of incest stories in the Old Testament.[20] Whether an inherited predisposition signaling the atavism of the Jewish body or a manifestation of psychoneuroses, the supposed tendency to incest among the Jews was taken, at this time, to be a strong indicator of a pathological and racially coded Jewish sexuality.

The ideological association of Jews with incest gained new momentum with the emergence of the Vienna school of psychoanalysis, which considered incest as a kernel of unconscious drives. According to Gilman the fact that the psychoanalytical movement was perceived by some as a Jewish peculiarity was due, in part, to the popular association of the Jews with consanguineous marriages.[21] Freud was aware of this perception of psychoanalysis, and Yerushalmi has shown that Freud's special "courtship" of Jung was largely a strategy to maintain an important non-Jewish member of the psychoanalytical movement as an ally.[22] Ironically, when Jung defected from Freud, he was quick to accuse Freud of an incestuous love for his "sister," Minna Bernays, who was in fact Freud's sister-in-law.[23] The idea that psychoanalysis was a Jewish movement also sprang from the perception that the Jewish psyche was "special," and Freud's oedipal theory was seen as yet another aberration of the Jewish mind.[24] Partly in response to this phenomenon, Otto Rank's extensive study, *The Incest Theme in Literature and Legend* (1906/1912), was aimed at showing the universal nature of unconscious desires for sibling unity and copulation with parents.[25] In this book the Old Testament story of Lot and his daughters features alongside incest plots from the myths and legends of most of the ancient and modern nations. Interestingly for my purposes, Rank cites a story catalogued in a German collection of fairy tales, dated 1850, about a Russian king who has an incestuous love relation with his daughter.[26]

In his twenty-year preoccupation with Jewish sexuality Rozanov repeatedly makes use of the Lot story, the *Song of Songs*, and the marriage of Abraham and Sarah as examples of Jewish father–daughter and sibling incest. What makes Rozanov's work on incest so different from that seen in other contemporary discourses is his enthusiastic evaluation of this phenomenon.[27] If Freud shocked his Victorian contemporaries by unraveling matters relating to children's sexuality, and by making incestuous fantasies part of both unconscious desires and conscious day-dreaming (as in "Family Romances" [1909]), Rozanov went even further. Freud, in *Three Essays* (1905), had proposed that the erection of "barriers against incest" was a necessary "cultural demand" of human progress,[28] but Rozanov reversed this thinking, maintaining that incestuous drives were good *because* they were characteristic of the privileged sensuous cultures of the past and a marker of the body and psyche of ancient peoples, namely the Egyptians and the

Hebrews. As he constructed them, contemporary Jews, who had survived as a race due to the maintenance of racial purity, were the only truly ancient bodies still extant, with all the associated hereditary drives. Where Freud was trying to destigmatize Jewish sexuality by showing the universal nature of incestuous motives, Rozanov reaffirmed the notion of a racially peculiar Jewish sexuality. Where Freud had abandoned phylogenetic arguments, Rozanov fixated them on the Jewish people.[29]

The Sexual Otherness of Jews

It is in *Iudaizm* (*Judaism* [1903]) that Rozanov first argues that Jewish sexuality is a distinctive type, explicable by the special nature of the Jewish body and psyche. His Jew is marked by the stamp of physiological and archaic Otherness; his visibility among the European nations is a result of his physical features:

> When at times we look attentively at the small figure of a Jew, this always tiny, often hunchbacked, limitlessly tired small figure, we think: "he looks as if he came from the other world." In any case, we can think such thoughts only about the Jews, not about other nations.[30]

Among antique and contemporary nations alike, the Jew is made out to be the sole carrier of special, atavistic, supernatural features. But Rozanov's atavistic Jew is not a generic Agasfer, the *juif errant* figure of the European romantic tradition. Jews' secret knowledge is, according to Rozanov, quite specific, and is revealed by his particular sexuality of which incest is the key feature. Alluding to Old Testament stories, Rozanov reminds his readers that Sarah was Abraham's "sister," "if not from the same womb [*edinoutrobnaia*], then of the same *blood* [*edinokrovnaia*]" (*Judaism* 117). The word "blood" is significant here, marking the Jewish nation as one built on consanguineous, incestuous genealogies. Rozanov identifies the topography of this "otherworldliness" (*potusvetnost'*) of Jews in the place names Sodom and Gomorrah where, according to him, Jews entered the territory of "either light, or darkness", the territory "beyond" the norms of this world (117, 118). In the language of post-Nietzschean Russian modernism, the territory of "beyond" means beyond the moral values of good and evil. In Rozanov's taxonomies, this moral beyond is where sexual taboos are transgressed.

In his construction of Jewish sexuality in *Judaism*, it is notable that Rozanov makes indiscriminate use of both Jewish sources and slanderous antisemitic interpretations of these sources. Among the texts Rozanov uses are *The Talmud* in the Russian translation of N. Pereferkovich and the antisemitic works of Russian Jewish converts to Christianity, such as Semen Tseikhanshtein's "Avtobiografiia pravoslavnogo evreiia" ("An Autobiography of a Russian Christian Orthodox Jew" [1850]), and *Talmud i evrei* (*Talmud and the Jews*) (1879) by Ippolit Liutostansky. From these sources, Rozanov constructs the Jewish body as oversexed in a Weiningerian way, forged through the rituals of circumcision and mikvah, which give genitalia a metaphysical significance in Jewish culture. In the collective nature of the mikvah bathings, Rozanov finds fuel for his fantasy of the communal character of Jewish sexuality, a sexuality aroused by physical closeness in the sharing of the bath. On the basis of Tseikhanshtein's commentary, which describes Sabbath meals as filled with the sensuous aromas of food and wine, Rozanov eroticizes the atmosphere of Sabbath and parallels its shared celebration with the physical, communal closeness of Jewish bodies during mikvah. Jews emerge from Rozanov's text with collectively excited libidinal drives that are satisfied in the simultaneous copulation of the whole Jewish nation during the night of Sabbath:

> The secret mystery of mikvah consists in the mysterious mutual touching of the *skin* of every Jew and Jewess to *everyone* and *everybody*. Everyone in a very unique and special way joins in (they even take a sip [of water]!) with the rest of the communal body of all of the local Jewry, since it would be impossible to join the body of the whole [Jewish] world, but it would be good if it was the body of the whole [Jewish] world! Sabbath is the day of mysterious mutual touches, entered through the mikvah. (*Judaism* 133)

The image of a collective Jewish body forms a trope for collective coitus. Rozanov perpetuates the fiction that incest is a prevailing feature of Jewish sexuality. Boundaries are being transgressed by incestuous sexual arousal both within individual families and within the larger collective family of the Jewish nation.

The motif of a special type of Jewish incestuousness is particularly marked in Rozanov's piece entitled "Magicheskaia stranitsa u Gogolia" ("Gogol's Magical Page" [1909]), the subject of which is Nikolai Gogol's tale, *A Terrible Vengeance* (1835), the story of a wizard's love for his own daughter.[31] In Gogol's work the wizard's ethnicity is vaguely Orientalized but left undefined, but in Rozanov's text the wizard is identified as a crypto-Jew, largely on the basis of his incestuous desires.[32] Rozanov claims that Gogol's story is the Russian/Ukrainian equivalent of the story of Lot and his daughters but, notably, his own evaluation of the Lot motif is affirmative. As in the earlier *Judaism*, Jews are here depicted as an "atavistic" (404) people who preserve all the instinctive drives of the Ancients. The archaization of Jews is evident even in his choice of epigraph—an extract from Clement of Alexandria's *Stromati* that makes reference to incestuous practices among the Magi. Rozanov alludes to Egyptian, Persian and Jewish customs, and places them on a single Orientalist continuum; for instance, he cites the marriage between Isis and Osiris of Ancient Egypt as an example of brother-sister love, before presenting the story of Adam and Eve as the Jewish equivalent along with the following extract from the *Song of Songs*: "Nevesta moia/ Sestra moia/ Laski tvoi/ Slashche vina" (My bride / My sister / Your caresses / Are sweeter than wine [393]). Throughout this piece Rozanov manipulates his data to build the phylogenetic argument that incestuous desire is transmitted from one generation to another within one racial group of people. Again, because only the Jews, among all the ancient nations that he names, have survived as a racial group with definite ethnic boundaries, only they have inherited this atavistic feature.

In order to illuminate Rozanov's subjectivity, we can compare this approach to that of Otto Rank in *The Incest Theme*, where in the chapter "Incest in Historical Times: Tradition, Customs and Law" he discusses the same data. For Rank, marriages in Ancient Persia between blood relatives, or between Isis and Osiris in Egyptian mythology, as well as sibling marriages and marriages between parents and children in Ptolomean Egypt, are historical evidence of the absence of neuroses and repression in ancient civilizations due to the lack of oedipal hatred. Like Rozanov, Rank mentions the surviving custom of a bride being addressed as "sister," but here the *Song of Songs* appears alongside examples from other cultures: "the custom of addressing the marriage partner with the term designating the originally permitted, related sexual object (sister, cousin, etc.)... is observed in many cultures (cf. the Egyptians, the Bataks, and the Arabs; the *Song of Solomon*)."[33] For Rank, the existence of such a custom does not represent any endorsement of incest in these cultures, but rather illustrates the strength of incest prohibition.

In Rozanov's understanding, the Jewish nation had maintained archaic incestuous desires, and in this capacity should be regarded by Russians as exemplary. Not only does Rozanov exoticize Jewish sexuality, he also praises levirate marriages. In an article dating from 1903 he challenges the Russian law that criminalized marriages between first cousins, citing Queen Victoria and Prince Albert as an example of a happy and successful marriage of that type.[34] In 1909 we find Rozanov re-addressing this theme in "Gogol's Magical Page," lauding the advantages of blood marriages among Jews over the marital prohibitions among Christians. Within the context of contemporary debates on the moral status of the Russian family, the Jewish family is here seen as having definite psychological advantages:

> Everybody who knows those cold, hostile, envious feelings around inheritance in the relations between brothers, brothers and sisters among *Christians* will understand the great change made by this law among the Jews: "A husband loves a healthy wife/ A brother loves a rich sister." Such is the nature of our [Russian] relationships that a brother who always overspends on women finds a refuge in his sister's purse when she marries a rich man, and he thus exploits both his sister and his brother-in-law. This kind of relationship developed habitually: as a result of sexual habits, which play an all consuming part in human life, [Russian] sisters in their own right are not interesting to their brothers, brothers and their children are of no interest to brother or sister... As a result of the law among the Jews, all child-rearing is directed towards the family, rather than away from it, and the children multiply without leaving the family boundaries. It is sufficient for a father and mother to marry their daughter to an outsider, or even to the mother's brother; this daughter will give birth to many daughters who will marry. Procreation is guaranteed if there is a husband, wife and one of their brothers; from this the whole nation can emerge ("Gogol's Magical Page" 388).

Rozanov's quasi-sociological musings on the differences between Russian and Jewish families is not confined to the topic of Jewish marital laws. His creative imagination takes him further, and from marriages that he deduces are permitted by the Talmud he moves on to the sphere of sibling and father-daughter incest. In this extension of the discussion, Jews are even said to transgress the incest prohibitions of the Talmud as a result of their special capacity to be excited and intoxicated by near blood relatives:

> But with Jews, the whole of their blood is aroused towards consanguinity; with the strange whisper of Talmud about uncles and their nieces, it is all directed here, not only towards nieces and uncles, but mainly towards brothers and sisters and, further, towards the whole circle of relatives... The nearer to this border, the more *sacred*: but it is frightening *to transgress* this border — it is a terrible sin, death, one worth dying for. But... the human soul always goes further than the physical matter, and the heat of the Jew's soul, always so phallic, transgresses even further, much further than it is taught in the Bible and explained in "Talmuds" which extend the soul: The sugar of my daughter is allowed, but my sugar — not... ("Gogol's Magical Page" 393).

In the same text, Rozanov criticizes Christ for his politics of breaking family ties, and blames Christianity for the current crisis in the Russian family. The warmth and closeness of the Jewish family is explained by the "magic" effects of close blood ties, and the erotic aura of the Jewish family is juxtaposed to the cold and ascetic relations of the Christian one (415). The psychologically viable Jewish family is held up as an example to the adulterous and immoral Russian family.

Westermarck and Freud on Incest

Rozanov's construction of the Jewish family as especially close is particularly interesting when read alongside Westermarck's influential model of incest prohibition.[35] Westermarck's approach to the phenomenon of incest is the opposite to that of Freud (and Rank), having as its core the concept of biological incest aversion. He maintains that there is a "remarkable absence of erotic feelings between persons living very closely together from childhood" and that for such persons "sexual indifference is combined with the positive feeling of aversion when the act is thought of."[36] In contrast, for Freud, any love, including sympathies among friends and love among family members, is linked with libidinal forces.[37] In his view, for example, the sensations experienced by a breastfeeding mother are erotic to a degree, just as the child's suckling is of a sexual nature. Whereas for Freud this idea was held to apply universally, for Rozanov it was specific to Jewish culture. Indeed, although Rozanov held Westermarck's model of biological incest aversion to be true for the Christian/Russian family, he turned it on its head in relation to the Jewish family. Far from impairing erotic desire, he thought that the special closeness among Jewish family members stimulated it. The key to his argument is, of course, the supposed archaic nature of such desire. According to Rozanov, the Jews had culturally, psychologically, and physiologically preserved this ancient desire, and other cultures should make it their goal to nurture and revive such passions.

In the *Introductory Lectures on Psychoanalysis* (1916), in the chapter entitled "Archaic and Infantile Features," Freud enters into a debate with the Westermarckian and general biological model of incest aversion. Like Rozanov, Freud regards incest prohibition as proof that incestuous desire is both common and strong. The very title of his chapter creates a nexus between the archaic and the infantile, but, unlike Rozanov, Freud treats incest prohibition as something imposed by culture and education. He views positively the cultural, civilizing model of the superego, and places incest within the boundaries of the archaic/infantile, which is repressed. He disagrees with Westermarck's views, asserting that they understate the power of incestuous drives and the need for forceful cultural prohibitions. Westermarck's argument for the existence and efficacy of universal safety mechanisms — in the biological and social aversions to incest — is reduced by Freud *ad absurdum*:

> [A]n avoidance of incest would be secured automatically, and it would not be clear why such severe prohibitions were called for, which would point rather to the presence of a strong desire for it. Psychoanalytic researches have shown unmistakably that the choice of an incestuous love-object is, on the contrary, the first and invariable one.[38]

In the same chapter, Freud speaks of the arrogance that leads humans to think they are wholly separate from animals, maintaining that, of those features that are treated as "perverse," a "disregard of barriers between species, and incest (the prohibition against seeking sexual satisfaction from near-blood relations)... has not existed from the beginning; barriers were only gradually erected in the course of development and education" (245). In another chapter, "The Development of Libido," he makes it clear that psychoanalytic theory does not treat primitive people as an exception in the mechanisms of incest prohibition: "Among the primitive people living today, among savages, the prohibitions against incest are even very much stricter than among ourselves" (378). In his model, as in Rank's work, racist arguments are absent. If a regression to incest occurs in an adult individual, it is a matter of neuroses and psychopathology, and not a marker of psychoethnicity.

It has been noted that Freud's and Rank's Jewishness played a role in their gradual rejection of phylogenetic arguments in matters of psychopathology and interpretations of sexuality.[39] Rank maintained that, "Psychoanalysis corrected the immoderate overvaluation of hereditary and phylogenetic influence," and he goes on to remind his readers that this overvaluation became fundamental to Jung's model, with its "untimely introduction of the phylogenetic point of view into analysis."[40] Rank also criticizes Jung's attempt to explain the phenomena of individual psychology by means of "uninterrupted ethnological material" (192). We know that the extreme side of Jung's phylogenetic ethno-psychology culminated in his becoming a Nazi sympathizer.[41] And as we also know, the view of ethnicity as a marker of psychological difference has proven in Jewish history to be particularly controversial and dangerous.[42] Freud's persistent strategy of safeguarding psychoanalysis from being labeled as a Jewish movement becomes even more understandable in the light of the Rozanov case. Taken on its own, Rozanov's statement that "moral prohibitions [on incest] are one thing, but matters of character — something totally different" ("Gogol's Magical

Page" 419) is not particularly problematic. However, what is problematic is both his construction of a unified type of Jewish body and psyche, and his fabrication of a causal link between the so-called atavistic nature of Jewish people and their alleged propensity for incest.

Rozanov's admiration for Jewish sexualities, indeed for Jewish "incestualities," quickly turned to hatred when political developments turned Russians into the alleged victims of Jewish peculiarities. The archaic and atavistic can easily be reassessed as perverse, and Freud's "barriers of disgust" imposed by "culture and education" can be re-erected overnight. In Rozanov's case, this disgust was a product of Russian Christian culture, and Jews, with their perverse and anomalous sexualities, became the objects of his loathing.

Incest as a Culture-Specific Phenomenon

In the period between 1911 and the Russian Revolution of 1917, Rozanov continued to refer in his texts to anomalous Jewish sexuality. The Beilis Affair almost coincided with the murder of Pyotr Stolypin by the Jewish revolutionary Dmitrii Bogrov.[43] Rozanov penned several articles during the Beilis Affair (1911–1913) that were later collected in the book *The Olfactory and Tactile Attitude of the Jews to Blood* (1913–1914) in which he launches an attack on the perverted, anomalous Jews who, he claims, are driven by their atavistic natures to commit sadistic murder.[44] He makes mention of the "archaic, atavistic brain cells" (337) that have survived only among the Jews and which are "unconsciously" responsible for their pathological behavior.

Rozanov depicts Beilis as a sadist and Jews as racially different from the rest of humanity with latent, biologically inherited criminality.[45] As scholars have shown, Rozanov sincerely believed that Beilis's murder of the Christian boy was a manifestation of his latent criminality and that his actions were in response to an atavistic call of which Beilis himself was not even conscious.[46] Certainly at times when Russia's political reputation was at stake (as in the case of the Beilis Affair) or when the Jews had a prominent presence in democratic and revolutionary movements, Rozanov turned his attention to Jewish bodies, thus bringing them into the public eye to be stigmatized and exposed as sexually perverted, atavistic and dangerously anomalous.[47]

Jewish incestuousness remains a theme much elaborated upon in his work of this period, where we see the rhetoric of a Russian patriot interspersed with wild fantasies about forms of sexual transgression among Jews in which the evil Jewish Other is accused of violating several of the sexual prohibitions written in the book of Leviticus. Here are samples of Rozanov's aphorisms from *Mimoletnoe* (*What is Transient* [1914]), written after the defeat of the right-wing press in the Beilis Affair:

> ...and I shall guide you, you "wonderful Endymions," through the stench and the blood — I shall shove you into Sodom as though it were your native land, for in *Genesis XIII* it is written: "and Lot chose for himself (when he separated from Abraham, so that the flocks and the herds of the nephew and the uncle should not be mixed) *the valley of Jordan, where stood the cities of Sodom and Gomorrah...*" I shall show you that this is not an "allegory," not "a matter of chance," because I've no doubt you well remember how "your father" appeared to your mentor in the sodomite way, *modo sodomico...*
>
> The Jews approach the Russians with this sodomite smile of a bisexual being, with the soft step of a sodomite, and say: "What a talented nation you are," "what broad hearts you have," and beneath this is heard merely — "give me, empty person, everything you can," "yield to me in everything, person without talent."
>
> But the Jews, who had an "understanding of everything," introduced into the mode of circumcision, as a necessary part — this *actus sodomicus*, which while performed with the baby does not seem as anything special, but obliquely shows the meaning of the first coitus, towards the accomplishment of which the whole of Israel is being summoned upon.[48]

Rozanov at once both captures and distorts the logic of Leviticus 18 and 20, — grouping together such trangressions as incest, homosexuality, adultery, and inter-species sex, — and assigns multiple forms of forbidden behavior to Jews. In the first of the above aphorisms he creates a cluster of accounts of homosexuality and father-daughter incest (the story of Lot in Sodom), and makes homosexuality and father-son incest converge. In the second he presents Jews as bisexual beings open to sexual encounters with both men and women and, in addition, implies that promiscuous adultery is part and parcel of the smiling "approach" of these transgressive creatures. In the third statement he again groups a number of sexual violations: homosexuality and pedophile contact by fellatio between an adult male and a male infant — which he says occurs "obliquely" in the ritual of circumcision — converge with an act that crosses boundaries between human and non-human (divine) beings, and incest between a son and his divine father. It is clear from *Mimoletnoe* that Rozanov picked up the several themes that constitute forbidden sexual practices in Leviticus and made a full and creative use of what anthropologist Francoise Heritier recently called "the subterranean and obscure progression of associative thought" in Leviticus 18 and 20, where verses on forms of incest alternate with verses on other sexual offenses, and made multiple clusters of all these forms of sexual transgression.[49]

Two years after *Mimoletnoe*, in 1916, Rozanov published *Poslednie list'ia* (*Last Leaves*).[50] Here the theme of Jewish communal coitus during Sabbath, which we have already encountered in *Judaism*, is discussed again, and it is apparent that in the intervening years the theme had acquired some evaluative ambivalence. Rozanov's musings about Jewish sexuality are by now rid of the quasi-political rhetoric of the time of the Stolypin murder and the Beilis Affair. His new fantasies are built around the same elements as before, but their evaluative tone betrays his personal needs. His subjective, voyeuristic gaze returns his own projected desires:

> On my way from Sakharna to Petrograd in early August I went through Rybnitsa ("a shtetl"). An indescribable sight. What struck me most of all was the absence of any light, and all the doors were open. Not half open, but fully open. And I recalled from the Talmud, and immediately it dawned on me, that Yids have a form of *khlystovshchina*. (*Last Leaves* 37)

> The mystery of Israel, its deepest secret, is, without doubt, the group sin — "all on top of one another" ("sval'nyi grekh"). But this had happened in such a mysterious way that "all on top of one another" is performed in the name of "Our One and Only Jehovah" (*Last Leaves* 146).

Rozanov's references to "*khlystovshchina*" and "*sval'nyi grekh*," both euphemisms for the alleged group sex rites of the Russian *khlysty* sect, are of particular significance. In 1914 he had authored a quasi-ethnographical study of the Russian mystical sects of the *khlysty* and the *skoptsy* in which he denied the existence of group sex "celebrations."[51] The strategy, only two years later, of exploiting the widely held belief that group sex did take place among the *khlysts*, so that he could establish a link between the sexual transgressions of Russian sectarians and Jews, points to his insistent need to project sexual fantasies onto the Jewish body. We know that it was a fashion among Russian intellectuals in the 1900s to "recreate" ancient group sex rites, and Rozanov was a keen participant at such events, including Viacheslav Ivanov's "Wednesday parties" and orgiastic dance parties visited by Rasputin.[52] In addition, in his arranged meetings with Rasputin, Rozanov questioned the Siberian sex mystic on "group rejoicings."[53] In the light of these biographical facts, Rozanov's attempts to develop a parallel between Russian and Jewish sexual practices may be seen as an indication of his own personal need to create links between Russian (i.e., his own) and Jewish bodies.[54]

Underlying Rozanov's fantasies about Jewish sexuality is his belief in the "metaphysical" connection between God's body and the human — primarily

Jewish — body. For Rozanov, the ritual of circumcision is the manifestation of this metaphysical link. Whereas in 1914, in *What is Transient*, circumcision is described as an oblique act of sodomy perpetrated on a child by a Jewish man, in *Last Leaves* it is presented as an *actus sodomicus* between the Jewish God and the circumcised Jew. Significantly for the typology of Jewish sexuality in antisemitic discourses, Jews in Rozanov emerge as "gender benders" and, by the logic of analogy, the Jewish God is also assigned an indefinite sexuality:

> Scholars, approaching pedagogy "sideways," have completely forgotten what circumcision is. Thus Gladkov (67 years old, wrote "Old Testamental History"), told me at the door, when we were parting: — I, V.V., do not agree that circumcision is God given, because I do not understand: what does God need it for??!! I almost collapsed. My soul was crying, "HELP." Indeed, what does God need it for??? What does He *need(!)* it for? — God, what *did* you *need it for*??!! — *"Needed."* Not only needed, but it is the only thing that God really had a need for. And He did not ask Abraham for anything other than that, like when parents give their daughter in marriage; then they ask (or think): "does he have THAT..."
>
> God, my God, must one believe that circumcision was agreed upon between Abraham-the-groom and God-the-bride?...
>
> And I will renounce any idea, apart from this one, that "the naked bridegroom, Abraham, having been chased by Bride-Jehovah God for a long time", said:
>
> — Well, all right.
>
> And... from that time onwards Yids say that "only" they know God: but they never say what this "knowing" is. (*Last Leaves* 39–40)

Rozanov sees this multiple transgression of sexual barriers between species (heavenly and earthly, physical and metaphysical) as proof of the Jews' secret knowledge of the mystical value and "goodness" of sexual transgressions. By this logic, all forms of sexual prohibition in the book of Leviticus are proof of the special nature of Jewish sexuality. In Rozanov's thinking, the mere existence of prohibition means that transgressions have taken place:

> In Talmud — it is very strange to read (and exciting), how priests chose for sacrifice virginal male and female animals. The very word "he-, she-animal" must have excited Jews... In their thoughts when "choosing their victims" they must have become virtual sodomites, and spiritual sodomism is, no doubt, the main nervous stem of ancient Israel. In "Talmud"... as in "Leviticus," forms of punishment are mentioned for Judea's males and females for "sleeping with animals." One has to point out that the law not only threatens, it also reminds.

"Where there is law, there is crime." And it lures... Ah, God! What is there to explain. "Every breath glorifies God's name." (*Last Leaves* 53)

Howard Eilberg-Schwartz's monograph *God's Phallus and Other Problems for Men and Monotheism* is devoted to the problems of God's sexuality and the sexuality of Israelite men, exploring the implications for Jewish males of God's maleness, or of God having a sexed body. God's possession of a phallus leads to the feminization of Jewish men, who are part of the collective concept of Israel as the bride of God. Eilberg-Schwartz shows that, in various episodes in the Bible, the male gaze has to be averted from the body of God. He interprets these stories as the culture of ancient Israel putting prohibitions on homoerotic desire and father-son incest, so the story of Noah's sons walking backwards in order to cover their father's naked body while averting their eyes is read as a story of the prohibition of father-son incest and a means of ensuring that heterosexual desire remains the norm. He shows that the focus on heterosexual incest led to the question of how the social prohibition on incest between sons and fathers came to be overlooked. He reminds us that Freud developed a theory on how homosexual incest came to be prohibited. Eilberg-Schwartz quotes Freud:

> [A] child has polymorphous sexuality that is only organized along heterosexual lines by forces of the Oedipus complex. In the passive version of this complex, the son wishes in some sense to become a woman so that he can be the object of his father's desires. But his narcissistic attachment to his penis makes him repudiate these wishes and identify, not with his mother, but with his father. (*God's Phallus* 92)

Eilberg-Schwartz sees the story of Noah and his sons as a myth that symbolically expresses and institutionalizes heterosexual desire as the norm. In Eilberg-Schwartz's study the topic of sexual relations between men and God—also a favorite theme of Rozanov — is given attention. He focuses on the Old Testament story in which God visits Lot in the form of two angels, and the men of Sodom and Gomorrah come seeking them, demanding, "Bring them to us, that we may know them" (Genesis 19). As Eilberg-Schwartz notes, it is well understood that the biblical term "to know" frequently connotes sexual intimacy (Gen. 4:1, 8, 17, 19:5, 24:16, 25, 38:26) and, therefore, "from the narrator's (and hence the reader's) standpoint, the men of Sodom desire to have intimacy with divine men" (95). In addition, he stresses that the story is not only about the abhorrent nature of homosexual rape, but also about men seeking intimacy with divine beings: "This desire reverses another hierarchy, that between heaven and earth" (95).

As a keen reader of the Old Testament, Rozanov noticed these ambiguities and tensions in the text and spun them into an exotic fantasy of the transgressive sexualities of the Jews. Although his intuition in finding ambiguities and gaps in Biblical texts is undeniable, the politics of his interpretation is skewed: what the culture of ancient Israel prohibits and restricts, Rozanov turns into a prescription for permission and permissiveness. In the context of this chapter it is important to note that the Biblical stories featuring topics of potential homosexual encounters function as attempts to avert homosexual desire as well as to prohibit father-son incest, whether it be the story of Noah and his sons, or the men of Sodom and the divine men, or the story of God turning away from Moses. All these stories, as well as the story of Lot and his daughters, are part of a strategy to keep the integrity of the Israelite lineage. In the ancient Israelite imagination, as Eilberg-Schwartz says, "male-male sexual acts were considered alien and hence were linked to the stereotyping of its proximate others, the Canaanites," and, "The same strategy is used to defame the Moabites and Ammonites, who are descended from the incestuous union of Lot and his daughters (Gen 19: 30–38), which repeats in significant ways the story of Noah and his son Ham" — who did not turn away from his father's nakedness (*God's Phallus* 93–94). As a result of this strategy Israel is depicted in the Bible as one of the few genealogical lines untainted by sexual perversions. Needless to say, Rozanov turns this tactic on its head and uses the story to tarnish the Jews because he ignores the distinction between the various nations and ethnic groups of the Old Testament.

In line with his essentialist approach to the Jewish body, he had to accept Jewish sexuality holistically, with all its transgressions: incest in fact became a Jewish culture-specific phenomenon. Freud and Rank viewed the prohibitions against incest and other forms of sexual transgression as proof of the existence of universal desires that must be subject to prohibition. They also viewed various religions, myths, and the fear of God the Father as projections of a repressed fear of punishment for oedipal desire.[55] Similarly, Freud did not treat circumcision as a phenomenon specific to Judaism; rather he saw it (and the castration complex linked to it) as a universal remnant of the ancient threat of castration by a punishing and jealous father.[56] In contrast, Rozanov posits Jewish culture as God-given, and on this basis makes a claim for a special Jewish immunity to the "barriers of disgust" that other cultures have put up in order to avoid incest and other sexual taboos. In advancing these phylogenetic arguments, Rozanov assigns to the Jews a special type of knowledge, intuitive or mystical, that may not even be clear to Jews themselves:

> In the meantime, in the *Song of Songs*, it is vividly expressed that the one lying in the dark speaks of someone whose ear is not close by, but is somewhere *afar*, and she calls him from *afar* "he."
> Such a mode of speech is possible only as an inner one, as a whisper, because there is no one there over the shoulder.
> Nobody has noticed this before, not a single one of all the commentators. Even the great rabbi Akiba, even if he knew, was silent about it. (*Last Leaves* 71)

In this fantasy of extraterrestrial coitus, barriers are dismantled between physical and metaphysical bodies. In this passage, "he" is not the King Solomon who, in "Gogol's Magical Page," was identified as the brother of his bride. To the notion of sibling incest found in that earlier interpretation, Rozanov now adds supernatural and cosmological dimensions. Within Rozanov's phylogenetic world, only Jewish bodies are privileged to be open to such encounters with the divine body. In understanding the subjective forces underlying Rozanov's interpretation, it is significant that he claims to be the first commentator to have made this important discovery, or at least the first to speak of it. This was not the first time he had compared himself with the famous Rabbi Akiba, martyred by the Romans; in *Sakharna* (1913–1914)[57] Rozanov and the great Jewish sage are interchangeable:

> In short, the rabbi Akiba was the "Rozanov of the first century A.D.," the same sort of ignoramus, the same sort of genius, the same sort of sage and poet, and "Rozanov" is the "Rabbi Akiba of the twentieth-century," also "the shepherd and ignoramus," who knows all things. And he now deigns to blurt out Akiba's secret, for now it seems, that "everything is coming to an end" and "nothing is necessary" (239).

This claim is made in the context of the Beilis Affair, and Akiba's secret relates specifically to the mysteries of Jewish rituals, including the allegation that Jews used Christian blood for ritual purposes — the blood libel. But in *Last Leaves*, the knowledge to which Rozanov lays claim relates particularly to the mysteries of Jewish sexuality. In both references to the Jewish sage, Rozanov assigns himself special powers of insight into the mysteries of Jewishness, its collective body and sexualities, and in both cases there is a strong desire to penetrate the secrets of Judaism and to link himself with the Jewish collective body.

Rozanov's apparent search for a personal connection to the Jews can be explained by his belief in the special, privileged and chosen nature of Jewish bodies as the only bodies to be resurrected physically. His desire to be part of the collective Jewish body becomes particularly transparent in the last year of his life, when his fears about personal salvation are laid bare beneath his construction of the exotic Other.

The Mysterious Relation Between a Russian and a Jewish Soul

In 1912 Rozanov told his Jewish correspondent, Mikhail Gershenzon, the reasons for his change in attitude toward Jews. He states that it was the involvement of Jews in Stolypin's murder that had caused his change of heart; their taking part in terrorist acts had shown that they were capable of godless behavior. Rozanov's reference to political events here is, quite simply, a red herring. His political responses, although they map out the trajectory of his Judeophilia/phobia, are not the only cause of his changing approach. However, Rozanov's letter to Gershenzon is of interest as a confession of his faith in, and fear of, the Jewish God:

> I am in an anti-Jewish mood (whether they killed Stolypin or not, but they felt they had the right to kill Russians just for the sake of it), and (forgive me) I have the same feeling as Moses did, when he saw an Egyptian kill a Jew. I feel pain, I am even frightened (of Jehovah), but this is a fact and where am I to hide it?[58]

Rozanov's sincerity in expressing his fear of "Jehovah" is confirmed by events in his life. When his son died in World War I, Rozanov took this as proof of the omnipotence of the Jewish God, seeing this death as a punishment for his anti-Jewish writing during the Beilis Affair. In "Address to the Jews" in his last book, *Apokalipsis Nashego Vremeni* (*Apocalypse of our Time* [1918]), in which he orders that all his anti-Jewish books be destroyed, he writes, "I learned that the God of Israel is alive — is alive and continues to punish, and I became horrified."[59] Significantly, in the same text Rozanov mentions "some kind of mysterious relation between a Russian and a Jewish soul" (185). The lexical choice is most illustrative, as *rodstvo* (relation) means being of the same hereditary stock or in a relationship of kinship.

In *Apocalypse of our Time* Rozanov returns to the incest themes of the Bible, but now the story of Lot is interpreted as proof of the exemplary honesty of the Jews, who did not hide such occurrences in their history. He retells the Rybnitsa sabbath "story," but his earlier (1916) ambivalence here gives way to idealization and an admiration of the "happening." Whereas the Sabbath at Rybnitsa was once said to be covered by deep darkness, in its 1918 reworking the Jewish village is symbolically lit by wondrous light:

> The whole of Rybnitsa was lit with lights... "Here it is, the Sacred Night of the Orient," I thought. "Here it is, all in the fire of passions, where the Heaven is fiery, where the Heaven came down onto Earth, where a tree brings fruit

twelve times a year (Apocalypse), where a grandmother, daughter, grandson, grandfather, son, lots of sons, daughters, granddaughters, and male neighbors, female neighbors — all of them having taken the blessed mikvah — all of them during the same night, the same hour and almost the same minutes are joined under the cupola of the heaven, are lit by the evening dawn and by the first morning stars" (*Apocalypse of our Time* 77–78).

In this fantasy of the all-encompassing simultaneous coitus of multiple members of one great Jewish family, the event is presented as a mystical rite. Earthly bodies metamorphose into heavenly bodies, and the barriers between the physical and the metaphysical are removed. But, most importantly for understanding the etiology of Rozanov's fantasy, this passage is preceded by reminiscences of his own childhood sexuality during which he recalls that, as a five-year-old boy, he was aroused by secretly observing a woman in her early forties and her teenaged daughter undressing. This voyeuristic experience relates to bath-house visits with his mother, and he confesses to being attracted to women's stomachs, including the "wrinkled stomach" of his mother (76).[60] Typically, he frames his personal sensations in terms of incest archetypes: "In essence, it is all motherhood, and a man's, boy's, child's instinct to unite with 'the mother.' Here is Oedipus, husband and an Adonis" (76).

There is one more case that serves to illustrate Rozanov's alignment of his own sexuality with the Jews' incestual quest. In letters dictated not long before his death, dated January 10 and 17, 1919, Rozanov asks Jews to forgive his sins against them and asks his stepdaughter to forgive his "great sins against her."[61] Rozanov's contemporaries liked to gossip about his much-advertised affection for his stepdaughter. Alexandre Benois, for example, elaborates on the rumors that he was in love simultaneously with both his wife and his stepdaughter from his wife's first marriage, but for the purpose of this chapter it is not important whether he had relations with her or even imagined himself in love with her.[62] Rather, what is important is that it again allows him to imagine in himself a likeness to Jewish bodies (as in the case of Rabbi Akiva). His belief in the special, exclusive nature of Jewish bodies with their metaphysical, incestuous sexuality ultimately manifested itself in his desire for a commonality with these bodies, both in (physical) life and in (metaphysical) death. In the end the politics of his own personal body, based on narcissistic interests of self-preservation, proved to be more powerful than the national politics of Russia.

The last chapter in this book will demonstrate that Rozanov's views on the pathology of the Jew's body are quoted by proponents of racial theories and members of the Black Hundred in Russia today.[63] However, Rozanov's obsession with Jews had very little to do with the feelings of a Russian patriot. Instead, Rozanov is interesting as an example of a self-invented and self-styled crypto-Jew in the cultural formation of Russian modernism — a man who attributed to himself all the fantasized attributes of Jewish "perversions." But his influence on the construct of the Jewish body in Russian culture is enormous.

Notes

1   Pavel Florenskii. Evrei i sud'ba khristian (Pis'mo V. V. Rozanovu). *Sakharna. Sobranie sochinenii*. Ed. A. Nikoliukin. Moscow: Respublika. 1998. 361–368. 364.

2   Aleksandr Benua. Religiozno-filosofskoe obshchestvo. *V. V. Rozanov. Pro et Contra*, Vol. 1. Ed. D. K. Burlaka. St. Petersburg: Izdatel'stvo Russkogo Khristianskogo gumanitarnogo instituta [RKhGI]. 1995. 132–142. 139.

3   On Rozanov and the Jews see E. Kurganov and H. Mondry [G. Mondri]. *Vasilii Rozanov i evrei*. St. Petersburg: Akademicheskii proekt. 2000.

4   V. V. Rozanov. *Opavshie list'ia*. Munich: Neimanis. 1970. 132.

5   On Rozanov's interest in the exotic Jewish body of the Jewish journalist Uri Kovner see Harriet Murav. *Identity Theft: The Jew in Russia and the Case of Avraam Uri Kovner*. Stanford: Stanford University Press. 2003.

6   On incest as a charge against evil Others in rabbinic literature see Michael L. Satlow. *Tasting the Dish: Rabbinic Rhetorics of Sexuality*. Atlanta: Scholars Press. 1996.

7   See Vadim Rossman. *Russian Intellectual Antisemitism in the Post-Communist Era*. Lincoln: University of Nebraska Press. 2002.

8   Berdiaev wrote: "Socialism emerged on the Judaic soil. It is a secularized form of ancient-Hebrew chiliasm with its hopes for the sensual, earthly delight of Israel. And it is no coincidence that Karl Marx was a Jew." See Nikolai Berdiaev. *Mirosozertsanie Dostoevskogo*. Paris: YMCA-Press. 1968. 141.

9   Maria Carlson. Fashionable Occultism: Spiritualism, Theosophy, Freemasonry, and Hermeticism in Fin-de-Siècle Russia. Ed. Bernice Glatzer Rosenthal. *The Occult in Russian and Soviet Culture*. Ithaca: Cornell University Press. 1997. 135–152.

10 V. S. Soloviev. "Evreistvo i khristianskii vopros". *Taina Izrailia*. St. Petersburg: Sofiia. 1993. 31–79.

11 Compare Howard Eilberg-Schwartz. *People of the Body: Jews and Judaism From an Embodied Perspective*. Albany: SUNY Press. 1992.

12 Marina Mogil'ner. Evreiskaia antropologiia v Rossii v kontekste evropeiskikh rasovykh issledovanii (XIX–XX vv). Ed. Oleg Budnitskii. *Istoriia i kul'tura rossiiskogo i vostochnoevropeiskogo evreistva: Novye istochniki, novye podkhody*. Moscow: Dom evreiskoi knigi. 2004. 116–137.

13 Sander L. Gilman. *Freud, Race and Gender*. Princeton: Princeton University Press. 1993.

14 See Yosef Hayim Yerushalmi. *Freud's Moses: Judaism Terminable and Interminable*. New Haven: Yale University Press. 1991. For the part played by biological scientism in the establishment of scientific racialism in the nineteenth century, see Tzvetan Todorov. *Nous et les autres: La reflexion française sur la diversité humaine*. Paris: Seuil. 1989.

15 See Laura Engelstein. *The Keys to Happiness: Sex and the Search for Modernity in Fin-de-Siècle Russia*. Ithaca: Cornell University Press. 1992.

[16] V. V. Rozanov. Brak i Khristianstvo. *V mire neiasnogo i nereshennogo. Sobranie sochinenii.* Ed. A. Nikoliukin. Moscow: Respublika. 1995. 107–339.

[17] Despite all the violent antisemitic utterances in his letter-tract to Rozanov, Florensky still acknowledged that physical resurrection in the flesh is in store for the Jews alone: "The whole of Israel shall be saved. *Not* "ecclesiastical" Israel, as church seminaries comfort themselves, alas—*not* ecclesiastical. The Apostle Paul clearly speaks of 'those akin to each other *in the flesh*' and confirms the *irrevocability* of all the earlier promises about being the chosen race. As for us, we are merely '*what we are* 'by the way. While Israel is the pivot of world history." (366–367) — V. V. Rozanov. Oboniatel'noe i osiazatel'noe otnoshenie evreev k krovi. *Sakharna. Sobranie sochinenii* Ed. A. Nikoliukin. Moscow: Respublika. 1998. 276–413.

[18] Definition from the Glossary of the 1952–1961 printing of the *Soncino Talmud*, at http://www. come-and-hear.com/tglossary.html#LEVIRATE Accessed 27 September 2004.

[19] Satlow. *Tasting the Dish.* Op. cit.

[20] Sander L. Gilman. Freud and the Sexologists: A Second Reading. *Reading Freud's Readings.* Ed. Sander L. Gilman et al. New York: SUNY Press. 1994. 47–76. On Westermarck's popularity in Russia during the modernist period, see Eric Naiman. *Sex in Public: The Incarnation of Early Soviet Ideology.* Princeton: Princeton University Press. 1997.

[21] Gilman. Freud and the Sexologists.

[22] Yosef Hayim Yerushalmi. *Freud's Moses: Judaism Terminable and Interminable.* New Haven: Yale University Press. 1991.

[23] Gilman. Freud and the Sexologists. 36.

[24] Sander L. Gilman. *Freud, Race and Gender.* Princeton: Princeton University Press. 1993.

[25] Otto Rank. *The Incest Theme in Literature and Legend (Fundamentals of the Psychology of Literary Creations)*, trans. Gregory C. Richter. Baltimore: The Johns Hopkins University Press. 1992.

[26] Rank in his *The Incest Theme* cites Friedrich von der Hagen's 1850 collection *Gesamtabetteuer* and the story "The Russian King's Daughter" and also mentions the highly fashionable novel by M. Artsybashev. *Sanin* (1907), which deals with sibling incest. See pp. 313 and 557.

[27] In 1903 the Russian code of law defined incest as intercourse "between blood relations in direct descent, siblings, and a small circle of in-laws," and acknowledged the need to punish those guilty of offenses as defined by the church. See Laura Engelstein. *The Keys to Happiness: Sex and the Search for Modernity in Fin-de-Siècle Russia.* Ithaca: Cornell University Press. 1992. 46. Engelstein also notes that, as a means of rejecting bourgeois moral codes, incest was a fashionable topic in Russian fin-de-siècle literature.

[28] Sigmund Freud. *Three Essays on the Theory of Sexuality.* The Penguin Freud Library. Vol. 7. London: Penguin books. 1991. 148.

[29] On the lapses by Freud and Rank into phylogenetic arguments, see Yerushalmi. *Freud's Moses.*

[30] V. V. Rozanov. Iudaizm. *Taina Izrailia.* St. Petersburg: Sofiia. 1993. 105–227. 115.

[31] V. V. Rozanov. Magicheskaia stranitsa u Gogolia. *O pisatel'stve i pisateliakh. Sobranie sochinenii.* Ed. A. Nikoliukin. Moscow: Respublika. 1995. 383–421.

[32] On Rozanov's manipulation of Gogol's sexuality see Henrietta Mondry. Vasily Rozanov and Sexual Anomalies of Gogol and the Jews. *Wiener Slawistischer Almanach.* No. 48. 2001. 53–77.

[33] Otto Rank. *The Incest Theme.* 350.

[34] V. V. Rozanov. Dary Tsertsery (Shekhiny). *Vo dvore iazychnikov. Sobranie sochinenii.* Ed. A. Nikoliukin. Moscow: Respublika. 1999. 254–264.

[35] Edward Westermarck. *The History of Human Marriage.* 5th Ed. 3 Vols. London: Macmillan. 1925.

[36] Westermarck. *The History of Human Marriage.* Vol. 2. 192.

[37] Sigmund Freud. Instincts and Their Vicissitudes. *On Metapsychology: The Theory of Psychoanalysis.* The Penguin Freud library. Vol. 2. London: Penguin books. 1991. 105–138.

Chapter 3

[38] Sigmund Freud. *Introductory Lectures on Psychoanalysis.* The Penguin Freud Library. Vol.1. London: Penguin books. 1991. 247.

[39] Gilman. Freud and the Sexologists.

[40] Otto Rank. *The Trauma of Birth.* New York: Dover Publications. 1993. 191.

[41] Yerushalmi. *Freud's Moses.*

[42] See Daniel Boyarin. *Unheroic Conduct: The Rise of Heterosexuality and the Invention of the Jewish Man.* Berkeley: University of California Press. 1997.

[43] See Aleksandr Solzhenitsyn. *Dvesti let vmeste (1795–1995).* Vol. 1. Moscow: Russkii put'. 2001.

[44] On ritual murder and blood accusations see Jonathan Frankel. *The Damascus Affair: 'Ritual Murder,' Politics and the Jews in 1840.* New York: Cambridge University Press. 1997. Caroline Walker Bynum. *Theology and Practice in Late Medieval Northern Germany and Beyond.* Philadelphia: University of Pennsylvania Press. 2007.

[45] V. V. Rozanov. Oboniatel'noe i osiazatel'noe otnoshenie evreev k krovi. *Sakharna. Sobranie sochinenii.* Ed. A. Nikoliukin. Moscow: Respublika. 1998. 276–413.

[46] See Harriet Murav. The Beilis Murder Trial and the Culture of Apocalypse. *Cardozo Studies in Law and Literature.* Vol. 12. No. 2. 2000. 243–263. Also see Engelstein. *The Keys to Happiness.*

[47] For a discussion of Christianity's projection onto the Jews of the idea of blood's sacredness, resulting in the belief in the Jewish blood libel, see Alan Dundes. *The Blood Libel Legend: A Case Book in Anti-Semitic Folklore.* Madison: University of Wisconsin Press. 1991. On so-called "scientific" theories about Jews, see Sander L. Gilman. *Difference and Pathology: Stereotypes of Sexuality, Race and Madness.* Ithaca: Cornell University Press. 1985.

[48] V. V. Rozanov. *Mimoletnoe. Sobranie sochinenii.* Ed. A. Nikoliukin . Moscow: Respublika. 1997. 209, 259, 474, respectively.

[49] Francoise Heritier. *Two Sisters and Their Mother. An Anthropology of Incest,* trans. Jeanine Herman. New York: Zone Books. 1999. 66.

[50] V. V. Rozanov. *Poslednie list'ia. Sobranie sochinenni.* Ed. A. Nikoliukin. Moscow: Respublika. 2000.

[51] V. V. Rozanov. *Apokalipticheskaia sekta (Khlysty i skoptsy).* St. Petersburg. 1914.

[52] See Zinaida Gippius. Zadumchivyi strannik. *V. V. Rozanov: Pro et Contra.* Vol. 2. Ed. D. K. Burlaka. St. Petersburg: RKhGI. 1995. 143–185.

[53] See Edvard Radzinsky. *Rasputin: The Last Word.* St. Leonard: Allen and Unwin. 2000. 306–307; also V. V. Rozanov. Pis'ma k E. Gollerbakhu. *Izbrannoe .* Munich: A. Neimanis. 1970. 515–564.

[54] See Aleksandr Etkind. *Khlyst: sekty, literatura i revoliutsiia.* Moscow: Novoe literaturnoe obozrenie. 1998.

[55] On Rank's deviation from the interpretation of myths as projective phenomena, and the irony in his later coming close to Jung's astral explanations, see Peter L. Rudnytsky's Introductory essay, in Otto Rank. *The Incest Theme.* XII–XXXV.

[56] In 1933 Freud stated that there was a time in history when castration was performed by jealous fathers, and that "hints at this punishment must regularly find a phylogenetic reinforcement in [a boy]. It is our suspicion that during the human family's primeval period castration used actually to be carried out by a jealous and cruel father upon growing boys, and circumcision, which so frequently plays a part in puberty rites among primitive peoples, is a clearly recognizable relic of it." Sigmund Freud. *New Introductory Lectures on Psychoanalysis.* The Penguin Freud library. Standard Edition. Vol. 2. London: Penguin books. 1991. 117.

[57] V. V. Rozanov. *Sakharna. Sobranie sochinenii.* Ed. A. Nikoliukin. Moscow: Respublika. 1998.

[58] Perepiska V. V. Rozanova i M. O. Gershenzona, 1908–1918. *Novyi Mir.* No. 3. 1991. 215–242. 227 (letter dated January 1912).

59 V. V. Rozanov. *Apokalipsis nashego vremeni. Sobranie sochinenii.* Ed. A. Nikoliukin. Moscow: Respublika. 2000. 185. Rozanov also cites the murder of the arch antisemite M. O. Menshikov by the Bolsheviks as an act of God. Once more, his interpretation of political events appears to conceal the real reason for his fears.

60 Rozanov called his wife Butiagina "mamochka" in all of his texts.

61 V. V. Rozanov. Pis'ma 1917–1919 godov. *Literaturnaia ucheba* No. 1. 1990. 70–88. 85.

62 Benua. Religiozo-filosofskoe obshchestvo. Op. cit. 139.

63 Quotations from Rozanov's anti-Jewish books are regularly published by the Black Hundred newspaper *Chernaia sotnia.* See Aleksandr Men' i delo Beilisa, in a special issue of *Chernaia sotnia.* No 9/11. 1995.

Chapter 4

Ilya Ehrenburg and His Picaresque Jewish Bodies of the 1920s

> "Beneath his fresh shirt of a communist *kulturtreger*, Ehrenburg managed to preserve 'an old body.' He managed to remain 'a stinking Jew.' I reiterate, we are talking here not about the so called 'moral impurity,' but about elementary (Jewish) corpophilia — the love of the body"
>
> Boris Paramonov. 1993. 87–88.[1]

Ilya Ehrenburg (1891–1967) was a Russian writer of Jewish descent who lived a long and dangerous life. As a young man he survived the tsarist police, as a Soviet patriotic journalist he survived the bullets and bombs of the Russian-German front during World War II, and as a Jew he survived Stalin's reign of terror. Although he lived almost half of his life in Europe, he survived Stalin's campaign against the cosmopolitans. And although he was a member of the Jewish Anti-fascist Committee, most of whose members were killed by Stalin or died in gulags, he stayed alive long enough to witness Khrushchev's debunking of Stalin's rule as a cult of personality.[2] Indeed, it was Ehrenburg who coined the term "The Thaw," which was the title of his 1954 novel, to characterize the new political trend in Soviet society after Stalin's death and the new democratic ideas on which the generation of the men of the sixties, the *shestidesiatniki*, was raised.[3] And it was Ehrenburg who openly stated that he would consider himself a Jew for as long as the last antisemite was still alive.[4] He made this statement in the 1960s at a time when Soviet discourse had pronounced the building of the internationalist Soviet nation to be complete. His statement attests to the possibility of Jewishness as an optional condition — something that you could consider yourself to be, something that could be changed. It suggests that Jewishness is not necessarily inherited, that it is not a genetic category, but rather an attitude toward an historical past held by a group of people united by religion and a cultural belief system. This concept of Jewishness as articulated by Ehrenburg is of utmost polemical importance, because it presents a challenging conclusion at the end of a life that was lived during periods marked by the triumph of racist theories and resulting in the Holocaust. Ehrenburg knew perhaps better than any other Jewish personality of the atrocities committed both by German troops and Nazi collaborators from the local population against the Jews during the Nazi occupation of Russia. As one of the most prominent war correspondents, Ehrenburg never disguised his Jewishness by taking a pseudonym or hiding behind a surname that could not be identified as Jewish. As such he was Jew Number One on the Nazi hit list.[5] The Nazi leadership was familiar with Ehrenburg's fiery articles in newspapers and radio speeches disseminated or broadcast at the Front, and it considered him to be a major enemy. The fact that Ehrenburg was Jewish was used by the Nazi propagandists as an explanation for his supposedly biased reporting of the events at the Front and in occupied territories. Of particular relevance to this investigation is the fact that Russian Jewish soldiers and civilians, as well as members of the local population who witnessed Nazi atrocities against the Jews, wrote to Ehrenburg because they saw him as the only person powerful enough to convey their messages and to give a true account of the events unfolding. The result of this process was an accumulation of witnesses accounts that Ehrenburg and Vasily Grossman edited and endeavored to publish as a book in the Soviet Union—a book that was released only after the fall of the USSR under the title *Chernaia kniga russkogo evreistva* (*The [Complete] Black Book of Russian Jewry*).[6] This book contains witnesses' accounts of how Jews in occupied territories had been murdered by Nazis and betrayed by the local population. Just as the fact that Jews were killed because they were Jews — a nation defined by ethnic and racial unity — is central to the history of Jewry in World War II, so it is to *The Black Book of Russian Jewry*. And just as the Jews' physical body was viewed as the marker of Jewishness throughout the war, such physical identification was fundamental to Ehrenburg's own perception of Jews.

Ehrenburg witnessed physical violence against Russian Jews throughout the years of the Civil War, during which he fled the country fearing for his own life. As he reminisced in his autobiographical *Liudu, gody, zhizn'* (*People, Years, Life*) in 1966, "During the Civil War I became a witness to a pogrom against Jews, which was organized by the White Army. A few months after that a drunken White Army officer wanted to throw me into the sea from the ship on which I was escaping. He shouted: 'Beat the Yids, save Russia!'" (451).[7] Clearly Ehrenburg's much-quoted statement about his intention to keep proclaiming himself a Jew until such a time as antisemitism had disappeared from the face of the world has to be taken in the context of such experiences by Russian and European Jewry in the first half of the twentieth century. The Jew's body is central to this experience.

Ehrenburg is relevant to the theme of this book for a number of reasons: as a man born at the end of the nineteenth century, whose formative years coincided with antisemitic pogroms and the Beilis Affair, he serves both as an historical witness to the epoch and a man who absorbed all the political and ethnic stereotypes of the Jew at the time of heightened political crises and outrageously racist antisemitic policies. At a time when economic stereotypes of Jews were acceptable to the majority of the Russian Jewish youth of his generation who shared the revolutionary and socialist sentiments of the epoch, Ehrenburg could not avoid internalizing some of the ethnic stereotypes of the Jews. It is this latter theme that is of special interest to this investigation. Ehrenburg wrote during the period following the October Revolution — arguably, his most productive and certainly most experimental work was written in the 1920s. His work thus gives voice to a period that functions as a link between pre- and post-Revolutionary antisemitic and Jewish-related discourse. This chapter analyzes Ehrenburg's writing of this period with special focus on the theme of the Jewish body. Ehrenburg also serves as a link between the pre-and post-World War II periods, as well as between Stalinist and post-Stalinist Russia. This chapter will cover chronologically the theme of the Jew's body in Ehrenburg's two major novels of the 1920s: *The Extraordinary Adventures of Julio Jurenito and His Disciples* (*Neobychainye pokhozhdeniia Khulio Khurenito* [1921]) and *The Stormy Life of Lasik Roitschwantz (Burnaia zhizn' Lazika Roitshvanetsa* [1928]). It will also make references to his later work.[8]

Julio Jurenito and the Jewish Body

The Extraordinary Adventures of Julio Jurenito and His Disciples, the novel that brought Ehrenburg international fame, contains an eponymous character of supposedly Mexican origin. This character, Jurenito, whom Ehrenburg calls his Teacher (*Uchitel'*, sometimes translated into English as "Master") acts as the great Provocateur, a debunker of all ideologies and logical and philosophical systems. Jurenito is a cynic; he has limitless talents, knows a dozen European, Asian and American indigenous languages, and is capable of feeling at home in all civilized societies. Although Ehrenburg points out that Jurenito was born into the Catholic faith, some commentators regard him as a crypto-Jew.[9] Of particular interest in this regard is evidence of Ehrenburg's interest in aspects of body discourse — when he describes Julio

Jurenito after his death as his much-missed mentor, he centers his attention on aspects of Julio's physicality. These aspects have an uncanny resemblance to aspects of Rozanov's body politics: namely bodily aromas and bodily secretions in combination with an emphasis on home and homeliness. Such descriptions must have been of programmatic importance to Ehrenburg as he assigns them a place on the first page of his novel in the Introduction, signed with his full name:

> Let my words be as warm as his [Teacher's] hairy arms, inhabited and homely as his jacket reeking of the smells of tobacco and of his sweat, the jacket on which little Negro Aisha used to cry, and let my words be as trembling from pain and rage as his upper lip during bouts of nervous twitching (35).[10]

And:

> I remember how Teacher, pointing to the seed of the maple tree, told me: "Yours is more effective, since it flies not only into space, but also into time" (36).

Not only are all the ingredients of Rozanov's philosophy of sexuality present in this Introduction (semen "seed," sweat, smell — bodily secretions), but even the author's attitude toward the reader is reminiscent of Rozanov's famous opening of his *Solitaria* in which he describes leaves flying in the wind and expresses a totally new attitude towards the reader — a new form of relationship in which the author can tell the reader to go to hell and vice versa: "The reader can tell me without ceremony: Go to hell. O.K, you can go to hell too…" (3).[11] Ehrenburg's Introduction ends with a similar attitude toward the reader — one that suggests that he wrote his work not for his contemporaries but for people of a future formation, a future not of this world: "So, it is not for spiritual heights, not for those exclusive few among my contemporaries I write, but I write for the coming times, for the land which will be ploughed not by an earthly tool, the land on which not his children but my brothers will play in idiotic bliss" (36). It is clear that in this attempt to write an avant-garde piece of prose Ehrenburg shows signs of familiarity with one of the most scandalous writers and thinkers of his time — Vasily Rozanov. This acquaintance with Rozanov's work is particularly relevant to the argument that Ehrenburg regarded the physical body as ontological; the fact that he was familiar with Rozanov's work certainly adds a polemical dimension to his representation of the Jew's body.

Every reader of Ehrenburg's remarkable story would remember the episode in which the autobiographical narrator describes his first encounter with Jurenito: in this surreal, almost hallucinatory scene, the narrator takes Jurenito to be a devil. Ehrenburg is convinced that Jurenito's black frock

hides a long tail, and he perceives a pair of horns above his forehead. When
Jurenito takes off his hat these horns disappear, giving way to "thick curly
hair, like that of a Negro" (39). Ehrenburg thus builds an aura of crypto-
Jewishness around Jurenito with the help of a language of signs that mark his
physical body in the tradition of images of Jews in European literature and
culture. [12] Jurenito's racial alterity is constructed by such markers as blackness
and features resembling those of the Devil. Considered to be racially linked
to black races by nineteenth-century racial sciences, such markers linking
Jews to the Devil have been a staple of European superstition since the
Middle Ages. [13] The image of a Jew as a devil hiding a hoof or a tail or a pair
of horns was a popular motif in caricatures of Jews in nineteenth-century
political cartoons in European periodicals. In Russia this pictorial image
culminated in Ippolit Liutostansky's infamous antisemitic book *Talmud and
the Jews* (1879). By the beginning of the twentieth century this caricature
had become a staple of various antisemitic cartoons in the publications of
the Black Hundred, including *Zemshchina*, the pages of which never ceased
demonizing Jews as political enemies of the Russian monarchy and state.
The early twentieth century antisemitic conspiracy theory *The Protocols of
the Elders of Zion* equated Jews with Satan, and this image of a Jew's body
prevailed during the Russo-Japanese war and the first Russian Revolution
(1905) as well as during the Beilis Affair and the post-Revolutionary Civil
War. It never left the pages of the right wing Russian political émigré press of
the 1920s — the very time that Ehrenburg was writing his novel. It is thus
the recognizable attributes of the Jew's body, assigned to it by the dominant
culture, that Ehrenburg uses as markers of Jurenito's Jewishness — markers
that would have been recognized both by antisemites and by Jews like
himself who had internalized these features of the physical stereotype of
Jews.

Even when Jurenito's mission and occupation are characterized as those
of a Great Provocateur, Ehrenburg uses a dominant metaphor of modernism
— that of the body. In one such instance bourgeois culture, against which
Jurenito fights, is represented by a decaying body: "It is necessary not to
attack it, but to continue to take care of the ulcers which have been spreading
all over its half-decayed body. This date [17 October 1912] was the date of
Jurenito's realization of his own mission — to become a great Provocateur"
(45). Although the belief in degeneration was a dominant belief at the turn
of the century — a degeneration that supposedly affected the aristocratic
bodies of the Russian gentry whose collective body was destroyed by the
October Revolution — in Europe in the 1920s it was the collective body of
bourgeois culture that needed to be finished off. The weapon chosen for this

purpose was its own worst vice: overindulgence in every form of physical pleasure. And Ehrenburg puts a crypto-Jew at the head of this mission. Jews were traditionally regarded as the followers of Biblical prophets who fought for social justice and moral purity. Clearly it seemed only logical that in their midst there would arise a new prophet to put an end to the immorality of bourgeois civilization.

That the date of Jurenito's realization of his great mission coincided with the height of the trials of the Beilis Affair in Kiev in 1912 is telling. Born to a Kiev Jewish family Ehrenburg was twenty years old in 1912, and his interest in the events surrounding this trial had to evoke very personal feelings about this major blood libel accusation against Jews in the twentieth century.

A Jewish Missionary of Sex

The body construct of the dominant culture that Jurenito aimed to bring to an end was the body that had been shaped by Christian culture's ascetic restrictions on human sexuality. Ehrenburg's choice of the word "mission" for Jurenito's project indicates his familiarity with the work of the self-proclaimed "missionary of sex" of the twentieth century — Vasily Rozanov. Certainly Ehrenburg notes that his Teacher had very definite and strong views on the relationship between religion and sexuality, and in his views on sexuality Jurenito emerges as a composite character with aspects of both Sigmund Freud and the Russian theorist of sexuality, Rozanov:

> One other time the Teacher told us about the influence which sexuality has on religion. ...Once in a village near Burgos I saw a shepherd of about twenty years of age, a thick idiot who in a regal gesture castrated himself in front of an icon of St. Mary and an hour later bled to death. He is a "degenerate" like those others who pass various fluids: those who salivate in ecstasy or pour ink onto paper in rapture. And what about sects of fornicators, or transgressing kissers of icons, or old nuns who in the dark of the night clean the statues, and what about old Verlaine who finds his way from an old wrinkled woman to a stone sculpture with the rose in her hand... (59).

Whereas Freud explained the mechanisms of the sublimation of sexual feeling into a state of religious rapture and ecstasy, Rozanov revealed the relationship between sexuality and religion to be quite the opposite — he maintained that sexuality was from God.[14] In Freud's formula God was a projection of human sexuality, but of special relevance for Jurenito is his idea of Christianity, with its cult of asceticism and adoration of the virgin, as a religion that perverts human sexuality. This particular idea was the cornerstone of Rozanov's mission of sexuality and, as a young contemporary of Rozanov, Ehrenburg, like so many Russian writers at the beginning of the twentieth century, was informed by Rozanov's revolutionary attack on Christianity and the Church as institutions that distorted generations of people and deprived them of an acceptance of sexuality as a condition favored — and not loathed — by God. Rozanov's book *People of Moonlight* (1909/1911) is devoted to the history of sexuality in paganism, Christianity and Judaism. It describes instances of sexual pathology taken from the work of sexologists Auguste Forel and von Krafft-Ebing that deal specifically with cases of "perversions," including acts of self-molestation, castration and the rape of statues — acts that Rozanov positioned in the historical and cultural contexts of various societies.[15] Ehrenburg's Teacher shapes up to be a man of the body inasmuch as he himself wants to see it liberated from the constraints not only of bourgeois civilization with its institution of legalized prostitution but also from the constraints of Christianity. It is not in vain that his appearance at the café Rotonde is preceded by a scene in which a naked woman sits on the lap of a sweaty Spaniard — a representative of a sexually repressive Catholic culture much criticized by Jurenito for its tradition of the bull fight which he sees as yet another form of compensation for the lack of sexual freedom.[16]

Julio Jurenito can be critical of Christian culture's sexual education because he himself is familiar with other, alternative cultures that do not denigrate the sexed body. These cultures could be Eastern, as Julio knows a few dozen ancient and modern languages and has applied this knowledge to reading a great number of manuscripts. He can also adopt this particularly critical attitude toward Christianity as a result of his "native" knowledge if indeed he is a crypto-Jew (or Ehrenburg himself, the narrator's alter ego). Julio's polemics against the teachings of the apostles, especially Paul's lessons concerning the virtues of celibacy and the sinfulness of marriage and procreation, are powerful and striking attacks against Christianity. Julio associates these teachings with perversion, and his views on "what was meant to be sacred has become a cloaca" (75) sound like a paraphrase of Rozanov's views on this subject.[17] Jurenito glorifies the physical foundations of the family and in doing so echoes the notion of the Jew as held by Rozanov who maintained that Christianity destroyed Judaism's respect for the family. Julio attacks European Christian society and his mission is clearly underpinned by alternative cultures' attitudes toward the physical body. The special interest that he takes in liberating the body from the oppressive burden of Christianity delineates his crypto-Jewishness. He formulates a prophecy of how future societies would shape human sexuality: the period of scientific excess, he believes, would be followed by an all-consuming celebration of this intimate act:

> The Teacher often spoke about an earthly love for a new man... He told us that the path to the celebrations of [love] is long and difficult. It goes through the rejection of love, through the abuse of the body, through coitus regulated by schedule. There will come a time when instead of a kiss a woman will be receiving a test-tube from a man with his sperm. But after this the man or his great son will consolidate atavistic memories and the desire to create the best of the worlds and will become part of a blissful and almighty embrace. (83)

Jurenito is thus a true missionary of sex, and his last image — that which is built on the celebration of an atavistic call — makes him a crypto-Jew in the framework of the perception of Jews as surviving atavistic bodies in twentieth-century Europe, especially in the articulation of Rozanov's ideas about sexuality.

A Racial Body

Ehrenburg's keen interest in the physical body, not only as an object within the study of the history of religion and culture but also as an object of various scientific investigations, manifests itself in this novel (and in his later works) through various references to contemporary biological science. It is clear to Ehrenburg that science is not only interested in the physical body per se, but that it classifies bodies according to racial and ethnic characteristics. Although Ehrenburg uses many comic devices in his novel, and parodies a quasi-science that studies "degeneration" or "*vyrozhdenie*" (70), he nevertheless makes it clear that there are plenty of scientists who collect and classify anthropological material according to the principles of racism. He mentions a Danish psychologist, False, whose name is a caricature of the falseness of his presumptions. In choosing a scientist from a Scandinavian country Ehrenburg, who wrote this novel in Belgium after being deported from France, also shows his familiarity with the fashions of the time: racialist sciences found a keen following in Germanic and Scandinavian countries and in the figure of False he shows that he was well familiar with this trend and that he found it necessary to parody it in his novel.[18]

But the rise of racial hatred during World War I took place on both warring sides, and Ehrenburg demonstrates and caricatures a range of biological pretensions of xenophobia. He humorously describes an article published in a French provincial newspaper that maintained that Germans could be identified by their peculiar smell. Ehrenburg's reaction to this article was that of a person who was conditioned by the persecution of his own people, Jews: he starts to inhale the smell emitted by his own body. Although he fails to capture any specific smell he panics because of the fear that other people might be able to distinguish him as an alien due to the specific smell of his body. This episode shows not only that Ehrenburg was aware of the quasi-scientific nature of contemporary xenophobia, but that he was also familiar with the notion that Jews could be identified by a specific smell that they allegedly emit: the notorious *foetor Judaicus*, aptly dubbed by Jay Geller as "the aromatics of Jewish difference."[19]

In a different episode, Ehrenburg further explores and ridicules the notion proffered by racist science that ethnic origins could be identified by scientific methods of analysis of a physical body. This time it is the contents of blood that is the subject of scientific investigation. When a Jewish French patriot, with the German surname Zilbershtein, is suspected of being a World War I German spy, racial identification by blood is presented as an accepted scientific method: "Leave your passport alone! A tiny prick of your small finger, and a drop of blood goes under the microscope. There in the lab it becomes immediately clear what kind of blood it is — honest or Prussian. Scientists discovered a method of identification" (163). Ehrenburg's authorial irony shows that, during military times, being Jewish meant being an enemy: during the French-German War a Yiddish-speaking Jew is suspected of being a German-speaking spy.

It is possible, however, to put this Jewish person's blood under the microscope to identify him as a racial Other. This time it is not religious affiliation, not the Mosaic faith, but race that is deemed to be a marker of the body of the Other. Aryan scientists from Germanic lands are specifically targeted in Ehrenburg's novel for their keen advancement in racist science: one of Jurenito's disciples, the Negro Aisha, is saved by German captives only because biological scientists take a keen interest in him as an object for scientific investigation:

> Aisha was mercilessly beaten up but they decided not to shoot him only because they started taking photographs of him and showing him to various Dutch and Swedes as an example of cruelty and barbarism. They politely brought him out into a courtyard and explained something to gentlemen in top-hats, and when those important visitors left they threw him into the cellar, kicking him and shouting at him (176).

Ehrenburg is aware of the dangers of the notion of racial contamination which underpins racist desires to preserve blood purity, and he declares his personal position as antagonistic to purism of any form. He sees anything that has to do with physical cleanness and purity in the context of prejudice:

> From my childhood I have a humped posture, I seldom look up at the sky, only when I hear the noise of an aircraft or when I decide whether I should put on a rain coat or not. All the time I look down at my feet—that is, at dirty, soiled snow paddles, cigarette ends, spit. (171)

Polemical by intention, the novel raises issues of racial and ethnic intolerance and persecution, and contains some strikingly prophetic pronouncements about future genocide and the ethnic cleansing of Jewish bodies. Various commentators have found it possible to see these visions as premonitions of the Holocaust. This theme forms the basis of Chapter 11, entitled "Teacher's Prophecies About the Destinies of the Jewish People." In this chapter Jurenito gives a concise history of the racial persecutions of Jews, and makes a prophecy that the twentieth century will exceed all previous times in the persecutions of Jews. Jurenito devises a striking statement which he circulates on advertising pamphlets:

> *Soon there will take place grand shows on*
> The destruction of the Jewish people
> In Budapest, Kiev, Algiers
> And many other places. (108)

The program includes, in addition to the public's favorite traditional pogroms restored to suit the style of the epoch:

> Burning the Jews, burying them alive, the spraying of fields with Jewish blood, and also new forms of "evacuation," "cleansing from suspicious characters," etc., etc.
> We invite cardinals, bishops, archimandrites, English lords, Romanian boyars, Russian liberals, French journalists, members of the Hohenzollern family, Greeks of all social backgrounds and all others wishing to come.
> The time and place will be announced later.
> Free entry (108)

This chapter also contains a "short excursion into history" (109) which highlights the most cruel instances of the mass extermination of Jews through the centuries. All cases are underpinned by a logical paradox (or irrational beliefs) that motivates the persecution of Jews. In each of these cases Jews find themselves between the archetypal rock and a hard place: in one example, when Jewish blood would be scattered over fields in Egypt as a sacrificial rite aimed at bringing rain during times of severe drought, there were opponents to this belief who maintained that, although it was expedient to kill a few Jews, to use Jewish blood in large volumes was not helpful because of its poisonous qualities. Soil fertilized with Jewish blood would deliver not wheat but the potentially toxic plant henbane.

Although Jurenito shows that Jews were considered by the whole of mankind at all times and in all places as a people in a breed of their own, he does not oppose this view. On the contrary, Jurenito not only confirms the uniqueness of the Jews, he also celebrates this uniqueness. What makes Jews unique in Jurenito's view, however, is their special mentality, their special set of values and, at the core of their way of thinking, a passionate concern for all forms of justice. When asked by his Russian disciple, Alexei Spiridonovich Tishin, "Teacher, are not Jews the same people as us?" (110) Jurenito gives a short answer: "Of course not!" (110). He illustrates his point by making all his disciples give either an affirmative answer, "Yes," or a critical and negating answer, "No." Out of all seven disciples only the Jewish narrator, Ehrenburg himself, comes up with the answer "No," thus rejecting the comfort and compromise implicit in the affirmative answer for the sake of his struggle for justice. This response by Ehrenburg, or "our Jew" as Jurenito dubs him, echoes Jurenito's own "Of course not!" thus establishing kinship between the two characters of the Teacher and his Jewish disciple. Jurenito goes on to give a speech about how important Jews are for humankind, referring to them as "the great medicine of the world" (113). In his speech he refers to the story of Christ: Jews delivered this "red-haired boy" (112) to the world in the naïve hope that the time had come to put an end to tribal and ethnic differences: "What they did not understand, however, was that the child which they delivered to the world would be turned by this world into somebody who would continue to promulgate racial and social segregation, and would subvert the concept of justice by order and expediency" (112). In Jurenito's evaluation Christianity as an institution established itself in rivalry to Judaism and had subsequently abandoned the Judaic prophets' quest for justice. What is striking in Jurenito's teachings is that the Jews came up with the concept of racial and ethnic equality, whereas Christianity abandoned this concept. The result of such a notion was, of course, the survival of the concept of the Jew's body.

Ehrenburg ends this chapter with a striking episode: Jurenito kisses Ehrenburg the Jew on his forehead. There will be another instance in the novel when Jurenito will make the same gesture. In the meeting with a head of the proletarian state, a veiled image of Vladimir Lenin, Jurenito also kisses him on the forehead. This act is a strong literary allusion to Dostoevsky's famous character from *The Brothers Karamazov*, the Grand Inquisitor, who kissed Christ in an act of tragic recognition of the Catholic Church's abandoning the principles of his teaching. Coming from Julio Jurenito, this gesture can be interpreted as an anointment of a disciple by a true prophet, where both the prophet and the disciple are faithful to the principles of the Old Testament prophets. The fact that Jurenito has seven disciples — as opposed to the twelve apostles in the New Testament — is a sign of the Old Testament coding of this story: seven is a number sacred to Judaism.[20]

In this novel Ehrenburg also shows that the idea of blood libel had acquired new political dimensions during the time of revolutionary upheavals, and his description of this accusation against the leader of the international revolution Leon Trotsky is particularly telling:

> The story published by a journalist of the Madrid newspaper *Buenos Dies* [tells] how during the interview Trotsky with particular greed devours small cutlets made out of the flesh of bourgeois toddlers (208).

Ehrenburg reveals the extent to which, in the 1910s and 1920s, the theme of blood and flesh was associated with Jews. The conflation between revolutionaries and Jews had already prompted physical aggression against the Jewish body, and the motto of the soldiers and officers of the White Army was identical to that of the bandits: when a White Army officer proclaims himself to be a Christian he goes on to maintain that the command "Do not kill" does not refer "to Bolsheviks and Jews who have to be killed like mad dogs" (229). This comparison of Jews with defective "mad dogs" once more valorizes the theme of the Jew's body as contaminated and therefore dangerous.

Ehrenburg the narrator, who ends up with his Teacher in post-Revolutionary Russia, worries about his own safety as he believes his facial features, in particular his mouth, are indicative of Jewishness. It comes as no surprise that Jurenito himself is questioned by the mob on his ethnicity, and is taken for a Jew on the basis of his appearance. A Jew's physical body thus clearly remains the marker of Jewishness, and all other attributes, such as citizenship and nationality as shown in their passports, become superfluous in the eyes of a mob that recognizes a Jew according to his or her physicality. In a tradition of the picaresque novel, it is Ehrenburg's ability to swear in Russian that convinces the mob that he might be one of them and thus saves his life. Ehrenburg describes how, in Russian émigré circles, stories of Bolsheviks/Jews in Soviet Russia eating a traditional Russian cabbage soup (*shchi*) made out of the fingers of small children were disseminated by a distinguished academic. The degenerate, bloodthirsty Jew driven by his atavistic nature — such was the stable image of the Jew among both the learned Russian élite and the illiterate classes. Ehrenburg the Jew has to negotiate between these two groups with one stable cultural archetype — the Jew's body.

Lazik Roitschwantz—Before World War II and After

Another Ehrenburg novel written in the 1920s — *Burnaia zhizn' Lazika Roitshvanetsa* (*The Stormy Life of Lasik Roitschwantz* [1928]) — focuses on another picaresque character as immediately identifiable by his surname as Julio was by his first name. Scandalous and provocative, "Xulio" in Russian has a phonetic etymological link to "xui' and "xuli" — swear words denoting "prick" and "what the fuck?" Roitschwantz has a Yiddish etymology — *schwantz* is a slang term for penis in Yiddish and *Roit* means red. It is thus the penis that serves as a metonym and a metaphor for a Jewish man — a significant way to emphasize the symbolic importance of the male procreative organ in Judaism; circumcised, the penis of a Jewish man serves as a symbol of his covenant with the God of Abraham and Isaac. It is also a marker of the Jewish male body in a hostile culture where it becomes a stigma and an object of abuse. As will be discussed later in the chapter, the circumcised penis has been singled out by non-Jews as a sign of the de-masculinization of Jewish men and has thus become the main symbol of prejudice and the driving force for persecution.

And indeed, as a caricature, Lazik Roitschwantz is an embodied parody: although Ehrenburg is familiar with such stereotypes of the Jewish male body, Roitschwantz's body is treated as an exhibit of racial and ethnic qualities and is ridiculed on the basis of its physical characteristics. Ehrenburg finds it possible to adopt a light and humorous attitude toward the physical body of Lazik. This may be due to the fact that the period of numerous pogroms and abuses of Jewish bodies during World War I, the October Revolution, and the Civil War was over, by the time this book came to be written. It is precisely this period of calm that might explain the light-hearted treatment of the adventures of his unfortunate Jewish hero. Ehrenburg wrote two stories, "A Schifs-card" (1922) and "An Old Furrier" (1928), in which he described victims of pogroms in the Pale of Settlement during the Civil War. These stories reveal that he was only too familiar with the kind of physical abuse that Jewish men, women, and children suffered at the hands of *pogromshchiks*. He himself was in several dangerous situations during the Civil War, when he was singled out as a Jew for his "Semitic" appearance by members of the mob. The manner in which he depicts Lazik in the novel is a variant of the wanderings of a small Jew displaced by political upheavals. Although it is quite clear that Ehrenburg's own fears had been very real during the time of the Civil War, some ten years later he appeared to find it possible to derive some comic relief from his personal experience through the creation of a "funny" little Jew. When he created Lazik he fancied comparing him to the famous literary hero of the Czech writer Jaroslav Hashek, "the good soldier Schweik," who survived World War I.[21] Yet this was not the case after the Holocaust. After World War II Ehrenburg was no longer capable of such a light-hearted depiction of a Jew's physical body: he claimed that all the Laziks of the western provinces of Russia had been eradicated by the Nazis and that he could no longer read the novel himself.[22] This obvious change of attitude toward his hero can be explained by his feelings of remorse over the lightheartedness which, as a young man, he had adopted toward the little Jew Lazik. It shows that he intended him as a caricature, an object of ridicule — the physically weak body of a little man from the Pale of Settlement who could not find his place in the new world. It also points to the fact that Ehrenburg as a writer was only too familiar with the stereotypes of a Jewish man's body, and that he used these stereotypes in an irresponsible manner in his depiction of Lazik. A wiser and older Ehrenburg, who had lived through the Holocaust, soon realized that any perpetuation of such stereotypes was inherently dangerous and, as the creator of Lazik Roitschwantz, he had taken part in the dissemination of such stereotypes through literary discourse.

Certainly, nineteenth-century Russian literature had frequently adopted the notion of the little hero: classical examples of such a hero are Pushkin's Postmaster, Gogol's Akakii Akakievich in *The Overcoat* and Dostoevsky's Makar Devushkin in *Poor Folk*.[23] Although Pushkin's and Dostoevsky's depictions of the little man who has no right to happiness in his private life because of the low social status he occupies in the society of Russia under Nicolas I are sympathetic, Gogol's more biting and less sympathetic caricature is written in the mode of social and psychological satire.[24] Ehrenburg's Lazik can be viewed as a Jewish counterpart of this trope of the little man. As such, he is familiar to Jewish culture through oral topos, anecdotes and stories: such a little Jewish man is known in Yiddish as a *schlimazel* — a kind of idiot who cannot make things right no matter how good his intentions. *Schlimazel* is a humorous character in Jewish culture, and works as an example of the Jewish sense of humor: it recognizes that there is a bit of an idiot in everyone, but that there are also unfortunate characters who, no matter how hard they try, will never be able "to make it" socially or financially. Because *schlimazels* mean no harm and do no harm they are treated sympathetically and serve as an object of restorative laughter. Sholom Aleichem's timeless Tevye the milkman is probably the best-known example of such a character, even though he is given the status of a serious hero by the tragic circumstances at the end of his life. Thrown out of his shtetl, Tevye rises to the level of a tragic character who has to gather strength in order to start a new life away from persecution. Although he is not the most representative of such heroes, I use Tevye as an example because he is the most widely known of the characters linked to the *schlimazel* motif in Yiddish culture.

The Little Jew as a Little Hero of Russian Literature

If in the case of Tevye the milkman his inability to father a male child (he has seven daughters), as well as his love for cows' milk and his almost meat-free diet, stands as a metaphor for his effeminateness, then it is to be expected that Ehrenburg would employ a similar methodology — a gender marker as a comic device and a characteristic of his little hero Lazik. Although the terms "little man" or "little hero" as used in Russian literary criticism refer to the low social status of the hero, there is also a definite gender code in this term. And indeed, Dostoevsky's Makar Devushkin's surname indicates not only his celibacy, but also his indefinite gender, and the sexuality of Gogol's little men has attracted significant scholarly attention.[25] Ehrenburg, who regards himself as a Russian writer, continues this tradition in showing his equivalent of a Jewish little hero, and makes him literally a small man.

Like many of the literary predecessors of the little man in Russian literature, Lazik is not successful in his amorous pursuits: he is rejected by the object of his admiration. If the little men of Gogol and Dostoevsky (Popryshchin from *The Diary of a Madman*, Devushkin from *Poor Folk* and Golyadkin from *The Double*) were silently in love with heroines from further up the social ladder, and thus unattainable by these modest city clerks, then in his characterization of Lazik Ehrenburg uses the same motif. A tailor by profession, Lazik stands on a low level of the social ladder in the hierarchy of the Pale of Settlement. Appropriately for a Jew from provincial Gomel, he is in love with a young Jewish woman from the same town, Fenia Gershenovitch. But Fenia is the daughter of the local cantor, or synagogue singer, a position regarded as prestigious by the Jewish communities in the Pale. Although she is the daughter of such a high-ranking member of the Jewish community, the young woman has been liberated from social prejudices by the October Revolution, and she sings in the local club, Red Victory. But, rather than Lazik's social status preventing Fenia, or as he calls her lovingly "Fenichka," from reciprocating his feelings, it is his appearance:

> Lazik's surname, to tell the truth, was not the obstacle for Fenichka: she had liberated views. It was Lazik's height which she could not accept. What should the cantor's daughter do now? Should she dream of the career of Mary Pickford and dance a foxtrot — this dance that does not have political consciousness? With Lazik?.. I will not hide the fact that Lazik's head reached the level of her underarms. True, Lazik tried to walk on his tiptoes in order to be taller, but only acquired corns on his feet as a result of this effort. How should he express his turbulent feelings to her? Kiss her on her cheek during a walk in a dark alley? But even if he jumped up he would not be able to reach her cheek (936).[26]

Lazik thus emerges as a *schlimazel* not because of his psychological make-up, but because of his physical body. He is afflicted with a body that genealogically makes him a loser: it is a site onto which his culture has projected certain values and, as a man's body, it is deemed to be an object of ridicule. This body has been marked both for lack of success and a plentitude of failure. Yet it is the dominant Christian culture that has created the value systems for the physical body, and that has affected the Jewish culture. Lazik, who received a proper religious Jewish education and who studies the Torah and Talmud, is familiar with these "cultural" differences. Daniel Boyarin, in his important work *Unheroic Conduct: The Rise of Heterosexuality and the Invention of the Jewish Man,* demonstrated to what extent the image of the puny Jew's male body has been a construct of the Christian European society, and how this construct was internalized by more learned representatives of Jewish communities in the eighteenth and nineteenth centuries. This internalization culminated in the Zionist concept of the "muscular Jew," a phrase coined, as already discussed, by Max Nordau. The reader will recall that it was Nordau who devised the concept of degeneration and who viewed the small stature of Diaspora Jews as a result of the lifestyle and the limited genealogical pool in ghettos and the Pale of Settlement. What is clear to Boyarin, however, is that Jews placed more value on wisdom and diligent study than on the size of the physical body, and often distinguished themselves by being the opposite of the big and villainous neighbors, the *goyim*. It is important to note that Russian proverbs attest to the value system of the physical body which often privileges small over big: "Mal zolotnik, da dorog" ("A gold nugget is small but precious") and "Bol'shoi, da durnoi" ("Big but stupid") — these sayings clearly mark large as superfluous and unnecessary, and small as smart. Certainly, the polemical privileging of small physical size by the Yiddish culture has been noted by a number of representatives of this culture. In the memoirs of the nineteenth-century Jewish writer Abram Paperna (1840–1919) the writer ironically notes that in order to be liked by the Jewish communities in the western provinces, one had to be puny and crippled.[27] Although the Russian and Jewish folk beliefs did not in fact differ so much in their placement of a value on the physical size of the body, Jewish culture created a violent and physically mighty image of the oppressor, juxtaposing itself to this image of power by cherishing an alternative ideal: small and learned, privileging inner strength that comes from wisdom over the brutal strength of the *goyim*.

Lazik with his Jewish education has an ideal of a masculinity that is in line with the values of old Judaic texts: he bases his arguments to defend himself in Fenichka's eyes on Biblical sources. In order to convince her that his small physical size is acceptable and even preferable, he intends to remind her that King David was small but much more important than that "big wooden pole," Goliath (937). Lazik draws another example from nature and folk wisdom: a nightingale is smaller than a turkey but has a far more beautiful voice. To make Lazik's statements even more ironic, Ehrenburg grounds them in Soviet realia: Lazik states that, in politics, it is "the organized minority that takes control."

Jewish Genealogy and Conception

It is clear that Ehrenburg depicts the physical body as a cultural construct. The idea that a Jew's features are not necessarily a product of race (although we must note that Ehrenburg himself liked to refer to his own lips as those of a Semite — thick and full) is encoded in Lazik's genealogy. We learn from Lazik the story of the marriage of his parents. Told in the picaresque tradition, the story reveals that Lazik was conceived by his parents in extraordinary circumstances that combined mystery and mysticism. As a *schlimazel* he was born to two members of the Gomel Jewish community who were extremely poor. The actual story of their marriage is linked to Jewish occultism and superstition: at the time of a cholera epidemic leaders of the local Jewish community decided to conduct a wedding in the cemetery in order to please the spirits of ancestors by offering them a staged entertainment in the form of a wedding.[28] Because the leaders were cowardly, they chose the poorest members of the community for the ceremony: Lazik's father, Motel Roitschwantz, and his mother, a poor girl. Both were physically handicapped: Motel was a hunchback and the girl was lame.[29] Although this *schlimazel* aspect of Lazik's background is supposed to provide comic relief, it has a deeper meaning in relation to genealogy and inherited features. If both his parents were physically handicapped, then it is a relief that Lazik did not inherit any of their handicaps: he is neither hunchback nor lame. What is "funny" in this story is, of course, the moral that Lazik's situation could have been much worse: he could have been a cripple, or even a double cripple with two impairments, had he inherited them from his parents. So one has to laugh and rejoice at such a positive outcome and the "happy ending" of this story: as with various folk stories of persecuted people like Jews, the moral is that things could have been much worse. The "funny" side of Lazik's physical appearance is thus the optimistic outcome and the irony embodied in it: yes, he is small and puny, but some Jews are even uglier than he. This combination of conflicting opinions forms the basis of the *schlimazel* construction.

There is a Talmudic anthropological subtext in Lazik's physical body vis-à-vis his parents' bodies. The Talmud is not only mentioned in the novel as a book that Lazik refers to, but Ehrenburg himself referred to it as a point of reference for his novel. He mentioned that he explored the notion of Talmudic logic.[30] He also mentioned that he used in the novel Hasidic stories and beliefs. In the novel the marriage of Lazik's parents is clearly one such story that retells one of the superstitions and beliefs of East European Jewry: to ward off cholera one must first measure the perimeter of the cemetery in order to seal its territory. Ehrenburg reveals the logic of inversion that operates in this marriage in the cemetery: on the surface he explains it by the intention to please the dead, but on a deeper anthropological level marriage as a rite celebrates life — the fact that the marriage ceremony takes place in the cemetery demonstrates that life is stronger than death and so reinforces its victory over death.

Degeneration

Ehrenburg introduces the motif of (quasi-)scientific theories in relation to Lazik's inherited characteristics in a comic mode. Lazik gets into trouble for his habit of sighing loudly — he makes a loud sighing noise in public when he is reading a proclamation. A woman ("citizen Puke") who hears him reports Lazik to the police and accuses him of making a mocking comment on the contents of the proclamation. This episode illustrates the atmosphere during the time of revolutionary terror when people informed on one another. The picaresque and comic part of this episode is that sighing is depicted as a marker of Lazik's Jewishness — a cultural habit and gesture, an involuntary physical reaction, a part of his body language. Lazik has already sighed in the narrative on a number of occasions, and the reader understands the absurdity of the accusation that Lazik made a particular sound as a comment on the revolutionary contents of the proclamation. Lazik is brought before the tribunal, and his lawyer — a Jew with the surname Landau — tries to defend him and thus avoid a six-month prison sentence. He bases his defense on the notion that a sigh is a biological feature of Lazik's physical body, a defense underpinned by scientific theorizing that is both ironic and serious:

> Contemporary science knows of cases of hearing hallucinations, of acoustic mirages, so to speak. Thus Arabs can see oases in the deserts. A prisoner hears a nightingale sing. I do not want to cast a shadow over the citizen Puke, but I am going to apply a strict scientific analysis to her words. Of course Lazik Roitschwantz is a degenerate. I insist that he must be examined by a group of medical experts. That phenomenon that he calls "sighs" is a pathological phenomenon. It is possible that we are dealing here with hereditary matter. According to eugenics a marriage which is conducted in a cemetery can produce pathological progeny. We must judge Lazik only in the context of his genealogy. We must blame the Jewish bourgeoisie who created Talmudic schools and other means to enslave the proletariat, such as offensive marriage ceremonies in the cemeteries. As the members of the victorious class we must let this poor worker go free (944).

Ehrenburg thus deals with features of Lazik's body on a number of levels. On the level of general views of hereditary characteristics, the fact that Lazik did not inherit his parents' physical deformities means that not all physical features are transferable from one generation to another. But these issues are grounded in the debates around the racialized body. Lazik, who has in his genealogy a marriage arranged in accordance with Jewish superstitions, can be viewed as a product of the Jewish occult and mysticism. The fact that he does not have a hunch back and is not lame may be seen as the result of the divine interference. On the (quasi-)scientific level, Lazik's body is viewed as determined by race: a pseudo-science like "eugenics" (944) teaches that racial characteristics have a hereditary nature. Ehrenburg creates here a comic effect by showing how phylogenetic arguments are intertwined with arguments based on class ideology, but his interest in the physical body as a racial body is quite obvious. Whatever the cause for the various characteristics of Lazik's body, the effect is represented by a Jew's body which is classified as pathological and degenerative. Ehrenburg here reveals his familiarity with the discursive formation of modernism — the pathologization of the Jew's body.

Size Matters: Sex and Gender

As we have seen, amongst the physical features that the dominant culture ascribes to the male Jew is smallness. This issue of the small size of a Jew's body — short, puny — is an inverted metonym for the size of a Jew's penis. Because Jewish males are circumcised, it has been believed among gentiles that the size of their penis is affected; that it is shorter and smaller than a gentile's penis. This belief was noted by Freud, who saw in the perception of the impaired sexuality of the male Jew the unconscious impulse of antisemitism in Europe. In his investigation known as the case study of "Little Hans" (1909), Freud showed that a circumcised penis represented a trope of a castrated penis and therefore invoked fears of castration among gentiles.[31] This in turn led to disgust and a feeling of superiority among gentiles toward Jewish men. Sander Gilman showed the other side of the dual structure of gentiles' attitude towards sexuality of Jews vis-à-vis their own sexuality and there will be many examples of this dynamic in this book. Jewish men as racial Others have also been viewed as sexually predatory and lascivious, therefore posing a danger to gentile women. The reader knows that in Russia this view of Jewish males as oversexed culminated as a subtext in the case of Mendel Beilis during his trial for ritual murder: what was implied was that not only was there blood libel among Jews but that Jewish males were sexual perverts. In fact, the Beilis Affair features in Ehrenburg's text, albeit in an ironic mode. It functions to valorize the theme of the *schlimazel*: when Lazik is imprisoned for sighing in public he shares a cell with another Jew, a trickster and adventurer. He mentions Beilis as a Jew who was acquitted because "the whole of America stood up in his defense" (951), implying that, in the case of Lazik and other Jews like himself, there is no hope for criminal justice at the hands of the local authorities. Although highly ironic, this reference to the Beilis Affair nevertheless serves as a reminder that for Jews

Chapter 4

there could be no justice in the post-Revolutionary legal system because it had inherited the antisemitic attitudes of tsarist Russia. The fact that Lazik could be imprisoned on political charges for making a loud sigh serves as a metaphor for the racial persecution of Jews in a society that had not cured itself of antisemitism.

Ehrenburg's Lazik embodies the paradox of an undersexed and oversexed male Jew: he is puny and short, and he chooses women who are much taller and bigger than he is. He does not succeed in attracting Fenia because of the link she makes between "size" and "sex":

> How do you think I can kiss such a pathetic pigmy as you are?... In order to become my partner the man needs to have sexuality. And you do not have any sex at all. You walked with me ten times in the park and it did not dawn on you that you could shamelessly kiss me (962).

Although Ehrenburg plays with the awkward usage of the Russian language by his Jewish heroes and heroines, the resulting ambiguity of Fenia's awkward phrase "you do not have any sex at all" (*A u vas net nikakogo pola* [962]) can be read as implying not only that Lazik has no potent sexual drive but also that Lazik is neither a man nor a woman. The trope evoked here is that of Jewish male pathology — the man who lacks his "sex" becomes more like a woman. Lazik's implied sexual passivity stands as an emblem of the non-normativity of the Jewish male's gender and sexuality.

This passivity of the Jewish male becomes apparent in the scene of the seduction of Lazik by a large, overweight Russian woman of peasant stock, one Niusia, whom he later marries.[32] When in one of his *perepetia* Lazik ends up as a respected poet in Moscow with an apartment at his disposal, he becomes a victim of this Russian woman. Lazik's relationship with her represents both a serious and a comic side to his smallness. On the one hand, he attracts a non-Jewish woman and in this reaffirms the gentile view of a Jewish man being hungry for a gentile woman while at the same time creating a competition for gentile men due to his unruly sexual appetites. On the other hand, Lazik is taken for a ride by this big Russian woman who uses him and beats him up after she has taken his property from him. This stands as confirmation of his inability to satisfy her sexually. And indeed, Niusia does not mince words when she tells him why she wants a divorce: "I have had enough of wasting time with you every night, you little flea" (1006). Lazik's sexuality is thus exposed as not potent and therefore not really threatening to a gentile man. Ehrenburg here exposes both stereotypes of the male Jew body and so finds it possible to have a good laugh on account of poor Lazik. With his "excessively short height and thin voice like the squeak of a mouse" (1000) Lazik is hardly the epitome of the gentile construct of Jewish gender and sexuality — at least vis-à-vis the Russian stereotype of size and sexuality. When a Russian antisemitic gentleman stands next to Lazik, Lazik reaches only to his knees — a highly symbolic image indeed. As a tailor, his specialty is that of making male trousers, yet another paradoxical metaphor linking Lazik and the male body. He excels in the art of cutting male trousers, and the fact that he *cuts* trousers, rather than making or sewing them, is again highly symbolic. As a man with a pair of scissors in his hand he serves as the creator of attire that covers men's genitals while at the same time, in the Gogolian tradition, he can be viewed as a castrating agent. Scholars have noticed that Gogol's Jewish tailor in "Ivan Fedorovitch Shpon'ka and his Auntie" (1832) serves as both a castrating agent and somebody who is interested in homosexual relations with his customers.[33] Lazik's profession aligns him with Shpon'ka tailor and, like him, he spends his professional life working his way around the private parts of his male clients. Furthermore, the etymology of his first name — Lazik — is also suspect and is revealed by Ehrenburg on a number of occasions to be associated with sex and sexuality. Although Lazik is a Russian diminutive of the Jewish name Laser, or Lazer in Russian, it is also phonetically related to the verb "lazit'/lezt'" — "to get into" — which is part of the idiomatic expression "lazit'/lezt' v zadnitsu" — "to get into the backside." There are certain refrains in the novel: "*Ia skazal sebe, lez', Lazik, i ia lezu*" ("I told myself, get in, Lazik, and I make my way in" [966]) and "*Lez', Lazik, lez'!*" ("Get inside, Lazik, get inside!" [1004]) that make the symbolic subtext of his name quite explicit. Lazik clearly has to struggle in life, and therefore has to grab any opportunity when it comes along, worming his way in as an outcast and a minority figure in society. This position is further accentuated by the symbolic associations between his occupation and homoerotic sexual practices.

In line with the dual model of the undersexed-oversexed Jew, however, Lazik can be a successful lover in a heterosexual relationship. When in Prussia, he becomes the object of passion for the wife of his tormentor, a German doctor. Enormous in size, she is attracted by Lazik's smallness. Driven by her maternal and libidinal instincts, she becomes Lazik's mistress and engages in what the narrator describes as sexual bliss. In this way Jewish male sexuality is reinforced as treacherous and dangerous to the gentile male, and Lazik is shown to be perfectly capable of "getting into" a vagina. His motivation to get involved with the wife of a doctor is dictated by the instinct of survival — as a true picaresque hero, he manages to take revenge over his tormentor by seducing his wife. The doctor deliberately denies Lazik food in order to use him as an example of a human deprived of fatty acids and vitamins. In his revenge, Lazik thus finds his way *out* of a situation by finding his way *into* the body of his captor's wife. Gentile fears of the sexual powers of Jewish men are also reflected in this picaresque plot. Lazik is truly a "Lazik" in that he will find a "lazeika," a "way out," of any situation due to his special will to live and his ability to survive — attributes Ehrenburg ascribes to his Jewish hero.

The Mutability of the Jewish Body

Another characteristic of Lazik's physical body that needs to be explored, pertains to the idea of the mutability of the Jewish body. The paradox of the Jew's body as perceived in European racist discourses relates to the duality of constancy and mutability. On one hand, Jews are racially visible because they inherit certain racial characteristics; on the other hand, they pose a threat to society because they change their physical characteristics in new climatic and geographical environments.[34] Ehrenburg tackles this paradox by ridiculing this view. As the novel's structure is based on the tradition of the picaresque narrative, Ehrenburg relates Lazik's adventures as he changes his location: from his home town of Gomel in the Pale of Settlement he moves first to Moscow, then Poland, Germany, England and, finally, to Palestine. He is recognized by every antisemite in Russia as a Jew, but as soon as he starts moving to the West his racial and ethnic identity becomes strangely fluid. When captured by Polish police he is identified as a Pole of Mosaic law because of the geopolitical situation of his home town. Before the partitioning of Poland, Gomel was part of Poland, and once he reaches that country he is no longer treated as a Russian Jew, but as a Polish Jew. When he arrives in Prussia he becomes recognizable as a Jew from Eastern Europe, an Ostjude. It is due to Lazik's abnormally small body that the German doctor Drekenkopf ("Shit-head" in Yiddish) uses him as an exhibit for scientific and educational purposes in the window of his clinic in Koenigsberg. Here he is presented as an eleven-year-old child who did not get enough vitamin A and subsequently did not achieve normal size. Although the doctor uses this presentation as a way to sell cod liver oil, which is rich in vitamin A, Lazik's racial identity is central to the German doctor's choosing him as an exhibit. What is so disturbing about this passage is the fact that the German doctor conducts scientific experiments on poor Lazik's body: he does not feed him, he makes him lose weight and thus become a creature of indefinite age. Moreover, he insists that Lazik exhibit hysterical behavior such as beating himself on the chest and pulling out his hair — all perceived acts taken from Jewish ritual prayer. Lazik's body is thus abused and modified, with the aim of showing not only physical signs of malformation but also mental abnormality. He is treated as a monster, and would be turned into a monster by the German doctor's scientific experiments if it were not for his ability to survive. (As a result of his seduction by the doctor's wife she supplies him with plenty of food and thus saves his life.) I call this episode disturbing because, although it predates the mass scientific experiments on Jews in the concentration camps of Nazi Germany and occupied territories, it finds a correlation with scientific views of the Jew's body as exemplary objects for experimentation and study at that time. Together with Ehrenburg's prophecies made in *The Extraordinary Adventures of Julio Jurenito and His Disciples*, this episode stands as a disturbing prediction of the abuse of Jews' bodies during the Shoah.

In Berlin Lazik is taken for a Mongol. In this instance Ehrenburg valorizes the racial aspects of the German's perception of the appearance of foreigners. The person who finds Lazik's appearance of interest is a movie producer, and this professional interest in his physical features underlines the emphasis on the external characteristics of the ethnic Other. Ehrenburg's authorial irony manifests itself in this episode, which ridicules the notion of racial characteristics on the one hand but reinforces the stereotype on the other. What is at stake here is the dual model of a stereotype: whether constant or mutable, the physical features of the Jews are always under scrutiny in a racist society and as a consequence of the duality of a racialist model of the Other, a Jew can only find himself between a rock and a hard place:

> What a find! I can see immediately that you are a Russian and a Bolshevik. You led the Tartar hordes behind you. This mystery in your gaze... The squeak of carriages at night... You have a Mongolian profile. The quick movement of a Cossack warrior. The photogenicity of your eyelashes. I will pay you five thousand marks. You will play the lead part in my new picture "The Song of Machine–guns and Lips" (1032).

Although taken to be a representative of a dominant culture, ironically for a member of an ethnic community in the service of the antisemitic tsarist government, Lazik cannot "act" as a villain. He falls off his horse, breaks his nose, and gets expelled by the film director for his physical awkwardness. The fact that Ehrenburg makes Lazik fall on to his nose is highly symbolic: taken for the typical nose of a Mongol, his nose turns out to be his weakest point physically. The bleeding nose of a Jew stands yet again as one more metonymic indicator of the physical ineptness of the Jewish male. Nosebleeds in both Galenic and Hippocratic medicine were considered to be a sign of a bodily discharge in line with female menstruation.[35] A broken nose is a marker of weakness. Cossack males break the noses of others — their own noses do not bleed. Lazik's passivity once more exposes him as a Jew.

The topos of the Jew's nose as a marker of his/her visibility in the Diaspora (in Gilman's terminology) is further reinforced in the hilarious episode in which Lazik is being recruited by an extravagantly rich young Frenchman. In this episode, which occurs in Paris, Ehrenburg continues to expose the paradox of the Jewish nose, demonstrating the absurdity of the very notion of a Jewish nose while at the same time showing the power of the mythologies attached to the human nose. A rich eccentric, Louis Con, accidentally bumps into Lazik at the very moment when his nose is bleeding. The young French socialite decides to take Lazik as his pet, as he needs someone to replace his mongoose which has recently died. Lazik thus immediately takes the place of an exotic animal in Paris society. His patron is interested in all things Eastern, and Lazik for him is "a Russian" and a "Bolshevik." Because he comes from the East he is also asked whether by any chance he is a Buddhist. This is a charming example of French Orientalism, with Lazik as a representative of the vaguely understood "East" and a symbol of the Oriental Other, which Ehrenburg exposes in humorous terms.[36]

The Frenchman decides to convert Lazik to Catholicism, but instead of the religious ritual of baptism into the Church poor Lazik is made to undergo a quasi-surgical procedure on his nose. His patron resorts to this method in order to reform him because, as he says, "This Lilliputian has a bad temperament" (1088). Lazik finds himself drugged in the quasi-medical surroundings of a cosmetic salon, where the medical nurse performs a special type of massage on his nose. Ehrenburg sets the scene in humorous mode, but in spite if its hilarious tone the sinister connotations surrounding Lazik's nose are evident:

> What do you want from my appendage [*pridatok*]?.. It is not wrinkled. All the wrinkles are on my forehead! Stop it! It is not made of wax.
> — Do not worry. It is a very easy operation. I now proceed to shorten your nose. (1089)

This dialogue has surreal qualities inasmuch as nothing is what it seems on the surface: a nose is not a nose but a penis, and the massage is not a massage but a surgical operation, "a circumcision." The allusion to the wax nose and the very scenario of a man in the hands of a beautician is a literary reference to Gogol's hero Kovalev who lost his nose during the shaving session with his barber in the famous story "The Nose," which functions as an inter-textual interpretation of the real meaning of an operation on the male nose — that of circumcision/castration. Clearly the wrinkled appendage is a euphemism here for genitals, and the analogy between the nose and penis is firmly established.

Through this humorous analogy between the nose and the penis the centrality of the ethnicity of both of these organs is played out explicitly:

> Lazik tumbled out of the medical armchair. Rolling on the floor in his hospital gown he screamed out:
> —You will not get away with it! My nose is not a pair of trousers, and I protest completely and announce a total boycott. It does not harm anybody so that you need to cut it down. I did not shove [pikhal] you with my nose, and I did not shove anybody for that matter. They shoved me. What if I want it to be long? I have shortened my surname [into Rot, H. M.] but it is superstructure. Maybe I will return to my country one day. Nobody will recognize me with the short nose, neither Pfeifer, nor Fenichka Gershanovich. Even this madam Puke will not recognize me. I do not give away my personality and dignity! (1089)

With "*Pikhat*" being a euphemism for "*ebat'*," to fuck, and with the ambiguity of the pronoun "it" instead of "nose," there is hardly any doubt that nose and penis are conflatable entities. Of note here is Ehrenburg's authorial sympathy for Lazik — when Lazik insists that he will not give away his personality and dignity he uses the word "*lichnost'*," which means both individuality or personality and human dignity. Ehrenburg makes Lazik akin to all those "little heroes" of Russian literature who have been socially abused by the system. Lazik, however, in addition to being a victim of social circumstances, is also a victim of racism. This is what makes him into a Jewish little hero of Russian literature.

For his French patron Lazik is both a curio and a replacement for the deceased mongoose, and he is treated in the same way that domestic animals are treated: he undergoes a procedure of vivisection. Pet mongooses were castrated at this time, in the same way that cats and dogs have been and still are castrated in "civilized" European societies.[37] In tampering with Lazik's nose by making it shorter the double analogy is reinforced between Lazik and an animal and the (Jew's) nose and his penis.

Chapter 4

Lazik's Body and the Abused Body of Jesus Christ

Another example of Ehrenburg's interest in the visibility of Jews and Jewish physicality is evident in a striking episode in Rome. As a true picaresque hero Lazik changes his locales but he never reaches the "eternal city." He does, however, make an imaginary trip to Rome through the telling of a story about a Jew called Laser ("Lazer" in Russian) who lived in ancient Rome. Lazik chooses Rome for a number of reasons, including the fact that the city is saturated with religious icons and physical representations of Christ whom Lazik perceives as yet another abused Jew. Always hungry and driven to cheat in order to obtain food, Lazik imagines Christ as somebody who, like himself, is forced to work hard in order to get even a single piece of bread. In Lazik's story Christ is made to perform exactly the same job as Lazik's imagined predecessor who lived in Rome at the time of Christ: to run around like a horse with a heavy load. In one striking scene Jesus Christ is first depicted as Lazik — Laser's double — and then as somebody whose physical features are different from those of Lazik's — that is, Laser's. Significantly for our argument, those facial features are the eyes and the nose — the perceived markers of Jewish visibility in the Diaspora and of Jewish ethnic difference. By making Jesus' appearance first identical to that of Lazik and then different, Ehrenburg exposes the dual model of the perception of the Jew's body in Europe: Jews are all alike and yet they mutate and are different. By showing the physical difference between the two Jews, Ehrenburg challenges the very notion of Semitic features, while also reinforcing Lazik's quest for dignity and individuality. There is only one thing that is constant and unchangeable about Jews — their victimization by the Western world. Although the West wants to see Jewish bodies as a constant and immutable relic of the past, the only thing that does not change is the persecution of the Jews:

> Suddenly he sees that another naked Jew is running along the road, and that this Jew is not him, Laser, but somebody else. What are these bizarre visions? Is it not the case that all Jews bought themselves out of this running activity? He is looking closely at this second Jew and is even more surprised: 'He looks like me, also just skin and bones, and sweat runs down in buckets, and he is all covered in blood, and his beard shakes so that it is obvious that he is almost dead. But it seems that his eyes are not like mine, and his nose is of a different cut. It means that he is not me, but a different Jew. But who can it be... (1043)

"The dead Jew" (1045) with whom Lazik-Laser has an imaginary conversation is Jesus who, when making an appearance in Catholic Rome, is made to perform dirty jobs and is beaten as a slave. The Pope himself issues the order to beat him up as a dirty Jew guilty of crucifying "God." This surreal fantasy shows that if Christ were to be born again in one of the most Catholic countries in the world he would not be accepted as God because of his Jewish ethnicity. The Jew-Christ would thus be crucified by Christians as many times as he would appear in front of the Christian authorities. This powerful episode, based on a literary analogy with Dostoevsky's "The Legend of the Grant Inquisitor" from the novel *The Brothers Karamazov,* presents a Jewish modification of what would happen to Christ in the Christian world if he were to come again in his guise of the champion of the poor. In Dostoevsky's version the Grand Inquisitor sends Christ back because the Catholic Church no longer needs his humility and humbleness. It has become an institution of political power and has long departed from the original principles of Christ's teachings. Significantly, in *The Brothers Karamazov* Christ appears in medieval Spain during the time of the Inquisition, when the fires of autos-da-fé were burning, but Dostoevsky does not make the Jewish theme explicit in his story — it is not clear from the narrative who exactly are the victims of the Inquisition's persecution.[38] Ehrenburg's story, by contrast, makes it crystal clear what would happen to Christ-the-Jew if he were to make a physical appearance in the Vatican. As in Lazik's narrative, he would be physically abused by Christians as a Jew. In Lazik's account of his meeting with Jesus, Lazik-Laser and Jesus find a common language as two poor Jews — a tailor and a carpenter — and are united by class. There are rich Jews in Rome but they have nothing in common with the two Jewish paupers. In this way Ehrenburg reworks the narrative of commonality by ethnic origin into a class narrative. Lazik presents a hypothetical scenario that gives a comic relief to the present day misery of poor Jews — including himself and his interlocutor. Lazik tells the story of Lazer and Jesus while in prison in Berlin, and his interlocutor is another Jew who has been put into prison for certain shady activities. Lazik concludes his story of Jesus in Rome by speculating on the unpredictability of the future. He says that nobody knows what will happen the next day, and who knows — maybe his Jewish friend will become a Pope, and Lazik will become a Rothschild. But this fantasy is not something that Lazik wishes to see happen to them: "If this was to happen to us we would forget all the tears and become ordinary swine" (1046). This comic scenario shows that a Jew can buy his way into a good life and power either with money or by conversion. The price that is paid for this however is too high because he will cease to be a moral human being. Behind the class-conscious moral of the story is concealed the pride of being born a Jew.

A Jew's Body in Palestine: Lazik's Dry Bones

After the *perepetia* Lazik finally arrives in Palestine. There is an autobiographical albeit anachronistic element in Lazik's "repatriation" to Palestine. In 1940, when France surrendered and Russia and Germany were allies, Ehrenburg contacted a Jewish agency in Paris with an inquiry about immigrating to Palestine. Nothing came of it, but Ehrenburg's biographer, Joshua Rubenstein, draws direct parallels between the haunted state in which Ehrenburg found himself in Europe and his hero Lazik: "Like his creation Lasik Roitschwantz Ehrenburg seemed unable to find a safe place in Europe — and like Lasik he considered leaving for Palestine" (182).[39] Ehrenburg was physically ill during this time — he could not eat for eight months, he lost about forty pounds, and resumed eating only after he made the cathartic decision to go back to Moscow.

Lazik did not return home to his country: he went to Palestine and died in the Holy Land. In Palestine he was just the same *schlimazel*, a poor Jew who had to starve because rich Jews did not accept him as their kin. Social and economic differences between Jews in the Land of Israel made Lazik into a second-rate citizen and he died from hunger and physical exhaustion. Ehrenburg's sympathy for Lazik is expressed in the way he dies — he collapses from exhaustion on to the tomb of Rachel in Jerusalem and falls into a deep sleep. He dies with the blissful smile of a child on his face, after telling a Hasidic story of how a little boy made God listen to the prayers of sinful Jews on Yom Kippur by blowing a whistle. God was deaf to the prayers of sinful Jews from Gomel and Berdichev, but opened His ears to the sound of a child's music. The story serves as a parable of Lazik's own childishness. He falls into an eternal sleep with a smile on his face that is described as childlike, and he dies as a child on the maternal grave of the Jewish matriarch Rachel. The Hasidic story of God listening to the child on Yom Kippur and making decisions on the basis of a child's innocent play can also be viewed as a sign of God finally taking Lazik into His protection.[40] Lazik dies in the Holy Land, and in the Holy place, on the tomb of Rachel, which guarantees his passage into the afterlife. On the level of the picaresque plot of the novel Lazik, whose formation is linked to a Jewish cemetery, dies in a cemetery. His conception was associated with Jewish mysticism and superstition, according to which death can be tricked by performing a wedding in its domain. His end also takes place at the cemetery, but the cemetery of a righteous woman who gave the birth to the nation of Israel.[41] It can be argued that the tomb of the woman who gave a genealogical beginning to the Israelites thus becomes the place for Lazik's birth and rebirth into a new life. It is not in vain that he dies with the Hasidic tale of events relating to Yom Kippur, with its links to the notion of the Last Judgment. Lazik's death is like a sleep from which he will wake up in the company of Rachel, the mother of Jews. The Jew's physical body, in spite of all the suffering during life, is nevertheless the only body whose resurrection is guaranteed.

Although depicted as a comic and picaresque hero, Lazik embodies a number of very serious problems and paradoxes that challenged Ehrenburg's modernist contemporaries: nature and metaphysics, biology and genealogy; religion and atheism. These paradoxes and contradictions are played out on the Jewish body. So, if the scenario of abuse has been inscribed onto Lazik's body, it is not so much because of alleged racial characteristics, but because of the inscription that culture(s) made on the Jewish body. After the Shoah, Ehrenburg must have realized that the Russian Jewish culture into which he was born internalized features ascribed to it by the hostile dominant culture, and that the dominant culture itself projected onto the Jew's physical body its own insecurities and prejudices. We know that when, in the 1960s, Ehrenburg was reminded that this novel of the adventures of Lazik had not been published in the USSR, he said that he no longer wished for it to be published. He stated that the reason for this was that the world of Gomel Jews like Lazik had been destroyed by World War II and that all the Laziks of the Pale of Settlement had been wiped from the face of the earth. It is quite clear that Ehrenburg no longer approved of his own ironic attitude toward his hero. In his final work, *People, Years, Life* (1966), he made it apparent that he did not have any confidence in contemporary Soviet society because it lacked maturity and was not yet ready to read with sympathy and compassion the novel's satirical descriptions of Lazik: "I did not include this book in the complete edition of my collected volumes, not because I consider it to be weak and not because I denounce it, but because I consider the publication of the many satirical pages which this book contains premature in the light of Nazi atrocities against the Jews" (451).[42]

In *People, Years, Life* Ehrenburg makes it clear that his attitude towards Jews was dominated by the Jewish experience of the Holocaust. He quotes a passage from a famous article written by the Polish Jewish poet Julian Tuwim entitled "We — the Polish Jews." Tuwin wrote this article on the first anniversary of the Warsaw Ghetto uprising, when he learned that his mother had been killed by the Nazis. After reading it, Ehrenburg recalled that he "could no longer speak to anyone for a long time" (Rubenstein, 204). This essay has never appeared in Russian translation, and Ehrenburg translated it himself before quoting it in *People, Years, Life*. One part of it relates to the topic of Jewish blood, and it is this part which, according to Rubenstein, had an impact on Ehrenburg:

> There are two kinds of blood: the blood that flows inside the veins and the blood that flows out of them. The first is the sap of the body... The other kind of blood is that which the ringleader of international fascism pumps out of humanity in order to prove the superiority of his blood over mine (Quoted in Rubenstein, 205).

It is clear why this article had such a strong emotional effect on Ehrenburg. He lived through the years of the Beilis Affair, the pogroms of the Civil War, and the mass exterminations of Jews during the Holocaust. In 1962 he took a very firm and proactive position against a case of blood libel in Georgia when a Jewish man was accused of inflicting wounds on a Georgian boy in order to suck his blood out,[43] and Georgian militiamen arrested the man and held him in prison. Ehrenburg learned about this case from the letter of a Russian woman who alerted him to the episode. He wrote to the Secretary of the Central Committee of the Communist Party and, thanks to his interference, the man was acquitted. That a Soviet Jew could be persecuted for blood libel in the 1960s must have had a devastating effect on Ehrenburg. When he wrote his parodic novel *The Extraordinary Adventures of Julio Jurenito and His Disciples* he described the history of mass persecution of Jews, including the shedding of Jewish blood by enemies and the accusations against Jews of ritual murder. Tuwim's article put the history of Jewish blood in a concise and accurate perspective: when it comes to blood of the Jews it is the blood that flows out of the veins, it is never just the "sap of the body." Like Tuwim, Ehrenburg understood that blood was deemed cheaper when it came from a Jew's body.

In contemporary Russian culture Ehrenburg is perceived as a Jew with a special interest in the body. Evidence of this perception can be found in the quotation from Boris Paramonov which is the epigraph for this chapter. It demonstrates that a link is made between a Jew and his/her body in that a Jew is interested in the ontological and physical body, and that the dominant culture, when evaluating a Jew, focuses on his/her physical body, even if the Jew happens to be a representative of an intellectual profession. When Paramonov coins a special term to describe Ehrenburg's interest in the physical body, he comes up with the quasi-medical term *"korpofiliia"* — "corpophilia." This word is constructed on an analogy with "necrophilia" — a pathological condition. It also relates to "coprophilia" — preoccupation with faces. There is little doubt that the excessive love of the body ascribed to Ehrenburg involves a certain degree of pathology. His interest in the physical body is excessive because he is a Jew, and his own body as that of a Jew is a genealogical body with all the inherited characteristics of a racial body.

Notes

[1] Boris Paramonov. *Portret evreia.* St. Petersburg: Izd-vo Grzhebina. 1993. 87–88.

[2] On Ehrenburg's political risks see Ilya Altman. The History and Fate of the *Black Book* and *The Unknown Black Book.* Ed. Joshua Rubenstein and Ilya Altman. *The Unknown Black Book: The Holocaust in the German Occupied Territories.* Bloomington: Indiana University Press. 2008. XIX–XXXIX.

[3] For a short literary biography of Ehrenburg see Helen Segall. Il'ia Grigor'evich Erenburg. *Russian Prose Writers Between the World Wars.* Dictionary of Literary Biography. 2003. Detroit: Thompson, Gale. 56–77.

[4] See Efraim Sicher. *Jews in Russian Literature After the October Revolution.* Cambridge: Cambridge University Press. 1995.

[5] Anatol Goldberg. *Ilya Ehrenburg: Revolutionary, Novelist, Poet, War Correspondent, Propagandist: The Extraordinary Epic of a Russian Survivor.* New York: Viking. 1984.

[6] See Ilya Ehrenburg and Vasily Grosssman, Eds. Translated and edited by David Patterson. *The Complete Black Book of Russian Jewry.* New Brunswick NJ: Transaction Publishers. 2003.

[7] See Il'ia Erenburg. *Liudi, gody, zhizn'.* Books five and six. Moscow: Sovetskii pisatel'. 1966.

[8] Boris Paramonov raises the question of body in Ehrenburg and uses Rozanov as the author who viewed Jewishness from the point of view of the clan, genealogy and body. Boris Paramonov. *Portret evreia.* St. Petersburg: Izd-vo Grzhebina. 1993.

[9] V. Kantor. Metafizika evreiskogo 'net' v romane Il'i Erenburga "Khulio Khurenito." Ed. Oleg Budnitskii et al. *Russko-evreiskaia kul'tura.* Vol. 2. Moscow: Rosspen. 2006. 345–372.

[10] I. Erenburg. Neobychhainye pokhozhdeniia Khulio Khurenito i ego uchenikov. *Neobychainye pokhozhdeniia.* St. Petersburg: Kristall. 2001. 33–256.

[11] V. V. Rozanov, *Uedinennoe.* Moscow: Sovremennik. 1991.

[12] Of relevance to "curly black hair" as an indicator of a Jewish raced body is the famous description by Karl Marx of his political rival, Ferdinand Lassalle, as the "Jewish nigger." See Francis Wheen. *Karl Marx: A Life.* London: Fourth Estate. 1999.

[13] Joshua Trachtenberg. *The Devil and the Jew: The Medieval Conception of the Jew and Its Relation to Modern Antisemitism.* New Haven: Yale University Press. 1943.

[14] See Andrei Siniavskii. *"Opavshie list'ia" Vasiliia Vasilievicha Rozanova.* Moscow: Zakharov. 1999.

[15] Henrietta Mondry. Beyond the Boundary: Vasilii Rozanov and the Animal Body. *Slavic and East European Journal.* Vol. 43. No. 4. 1999. 651–674.

[16] In regard to Jurenito's Catholic education it has to be noted that it does not hinder his crypto-Jewishness: Ehrenburg as a young man briefly entertained the idea of becoming a Catholic monk. As a Mexican, Jurenito could have been a *converso* or *marrano*—a member of the Jewish community in Mexico in existence from the fifteenth century as a result of their flight from persecution in Spain. Although some commentators believe that Ehrenburg made Jurenito a Mexican citizen as a tribute to Diego Rivera, others agree that there is no subtext pointing to Rivera in this character. See Anatol Goldberg. Op. cit.

[17] See V. V. Rozanov. V chem raznitsa drevnego i novogo mirov. *Vo dvore iazychnikov.* Moscow: Respublika. 1999. 231–236.

[18] For a history of eugenics and racial science in Scandinavia see Nils Roll-Hansen. Eugenic Practice and Genetic Science in Scandinavia and Germany. *Scandinavian Journal of History.* Vol. 26, issue 1. 2001. 75–82; Nils Roll-Hansen and Gunnar Broberg. *Eugenics And the Welfare State: Sterilization Policy in Demark, Sweden, Norway, and Finland.* Uppsala Studies in History of Science. Uppsala University Press. 2005.

[19] Jay Geller. The Aromatics of Jewish Difference; or Benjamin's Allegory of Aura. Eds. Jonathan and Daniel Boyarin. *Jews and Other Differences.* Minneapolis: University of Minnesota Press. 1997. 203–256.

[20] Number seven is a sacred number both in the Torah and in Cabbalistic tradition: God created seven divine attributes, seven days in a week etc. See Z'ev ben Shimon Halevi. *Kabbalah: Tradition of Hidden Knowledge.* London: Thames and Hudson. 1991.

[21] On smallness of the body size of a Jewish male in the context of military service see Iokhanan Petrovskii-Shtern. *Evrei v Russkoi armii, 1827–1914.* Moscow: Novoe literaturnoe obozrenie. 2003.

[22] Il'ia Erenburg. *Liudi, gody, zhizn'. Books five and six.* Moscow: Sovetskii pisatel'. 1966.

[23] For a recent view of "the little man" see Mikhail Epshtein. Malen'kii chelovek v futliare: sindrom Bashmachkina i Belikova. *Voprosy literatury.* No. 6. 2005. 193–203.

[24] Simon Karlinsky. *The Sexual Labyrinth of Nikolai Gogol.* Cambridge, MA: Harvard University Press. 1976.

[25] See Joe Andrew. *Narrative and Desire in Russian Literature, 1822–49.* New York: St Martin's Press. 1993. Joe Andrew. *Narrative, Space and Gender in Russian Fiction: 1846–1903.* Amsterdam: Rodopi. 2007.

[26] I. Erenburg. Burnaia zhizn' Lazika Roitshvanetsa. *Neobychainye pokhozhdeniia.* St. Petersburg: Kristall. 2001. 931–1127.

[27] A. I. Paperna. Iz Nikolaevskoi epokhi. Ed. V. E. Kel'ner. *Evrei v Rossii: XIX vek.* Moscow: Novoe literaturnoe obozrenie. 2000. 27–177.

[28] On this custom practiced as a *mitzvah* at the times of danger by Jewish communities in the Pale see *Journey to a Nineteenth-Century Schtetl: The Memoirs of Yekhezekel Kotik.* Ed. and introd. David Assaf. Detroit: Wayne State University Press. 2002.

[29] Here we see a parodic allusion to the Dostoevskian world of Khromonozhka, the lame girl from his novel *The Possessed* who marries the prince of darkness, Stavrogin.

[30] See B. Frezinskii. Fenomen Il'i Erenburga (tysiacha deviat'sot dvadtsatye gody). Il'ia Erenburg. *Neobychainye pokhozhdeniia.* St. Petersburg: Kristall. 2001. 5–33.

[31] Sigmund Freud. Analysis of a Phobia in a Five-Year-Old Boy. *The Standard Edition of the Complete Psychological Works of Sigmund Freud,* Ed. J. Strachey, trans. J. Strachey with Anna Freud. London: Hogarth Press. 1955–74. Vol. 10. 5–49. 36.

[32] On the Soviet discourse on gender and sexuality in the 1920s see Eric Naiman. *Sex in Public: The Incarnation of Early Soviet Ideology.* Princeton: Princeton University Press. 1999.

[33] Daniel Rancour-Laferrière. *Out from under Gogol's Overcoat: A Psychoanalytic Study.* Ann Arbor: Ardis. 1982.

[34] In his study of the picaresque novel Alexander Parker significantly stresses that a picaresque hero is normally a delinquent. See Alexander A. Parker: *Literature and the Delinquent: The Picaresque Novel in Spain and Europe, 1599–1753.* Edinburgh: Edinburgh University Press. 1967.

[35] There will be a further discussion of this notion in the book. For a bibliographic source see Gianna Pomata. Menstruating Men: Similarity and Difference of the Sexes in Early Modern Medicine. Ed. Valeria Finucci and Kevin Brownlee. *Generation and Degeneration: Tropes of Reproduction in Literature and History from Antiquity to Early Modern Europe.* Durham: Duke University Press. 109–152. 138.

[36] Of relevance is the fragment from the Russian émigré writer Remizov whom the French in Paris in the 1920s took for a Chinese person on the basis of his perceived 'Mongolian'

features. See Aleksei Remizov. *Vzvikhrennaia Rus'*. St. Petersburg: Akademiia Nauk. 2003.

[37]   On the link between gender and animal vivisection see *Animal Welfare and Anti-Vivisection 1870–1910: Nineteenth-Century Women's Mission*. Ed. Susan Hamilton. Routledge. 2004.

[38]   For the clearest explanation of the Legend of the Grand Inquisitor see Konstantin Mochulsky. *Dostoevsky: His Life and Works*. Princeton: Princeton University Press. 1971.

[39]   Joshua Rubenstein. *Tangled Loyalties: The Life and Times of Ilya Ehrenburg*. New York: Basic Books. 1996.

[40]   Ehrenburg said that he used Hasidic and Talmudic stories as an inspiration for this novel. He read Hasidic stories as narrated by Martin Buber in German at the time of his work on the novel. He also wrote that the novel depicts contemporary life from a Talmudic point of view. See B. Frezinskii. Fenomen Il'i Erenburga (tysiacha deviat'sot dvadtsatye gody). Il'ia Erenburg. *Neobychainye pokhozhdeniia*. St. Petersburg: Kristall. 2001. 5–33.

[41]   According to a legend known among the Jews of the Pale Rachel stood out of the grave to defend the group of Jews led to exile when they were passing her tomb. See Sholom Aleichem's "Iosele the Nightingale" (1890).

[42]   Il'ia Erenburg. *Liudi, gody, zhizn'*. Books five and six. Moscow: Sovetskii pisatel'. 1966.

[43]   *Sovetskie evrei pishut Il'e Erenburgu. 1943–1966*. Ed. Mordekhai Altshuler et. al. Jerusalem: The Centre for Research and Documentation of East European Jewry. The Hebrew University of Jerusalem. 1993.

Ehrenburg's portrait by Adolf Hoffmeister (1927)

The White Army propaganda poster (1919) depicting Leon Trotsky with the psysical features attributed to the Jew: thick black hair, thick lips, hooked nose, animal paws dripping with the blood of Russian victims.

Chapter 5

Criminal Bodies and Love of *The Yellow Metal*: The Jewish Male and Stalinist Culture, 1930s-1950s

> "State security organs in the USSR and the Peoples' Democracies cut off the blood-stained tentacles of the Joint, an international Jewish bourgeois nationalist organization"
>
> *Pravda.* February 14, 1953.

This chapter examines the developments in the typology of the Jewish body in the discourse of the 1930s-1950s.[1] This period involved the construct of the corrupt and corrupting male Jew's body, his material greed and lust for life turning him into a subversive figure in Soviet society. But this greed and lustful nature were viewed not only as a remnant of a bourgeois past, but also as a direct result of his race. This should not be an unexpected development, as it was in the late 1930s that the official policy on nationalities changed from "indigenization" to consolidation into one nation — a policy that involved accusations of "bourgeois nationalism" among ethnic minorities.[2] It was stated in Chapter 1 that Soviet biological science reacted to this change, but explanations of various aspects of the biology and pathology of Jews vacillated between racial and social paradigms. The 1930 volume (Number Two) of *Problems of the Biology and Pathology of Jews*, for example, contains a review of Dr. R. Wassermann's *Betrachtunzen uber die Kriminalitat der Juden. Schriften fur Wirtschaft und Statistik* (*Problems of Criminality among Jews. Papers in Economics and Statistics* [1928]). The reviewer notes that Dr. Wassermann "did not make categorical statements against the racial etiology of the specificity of crimes, maintaining that it has its role, although it is not easily explained by statistic analysis" (216).[3] According to Wassermann's findings, Jews in Germany, Austria, Hungary and Holland commit crimes of swindling and fraud (including the forgery of documents). Although Wassermann's conclusions are drawn on dated statistics from 1898–1904, his findings were nevertheless disseminated in Russia as late as in the 1930s.

Scholars of the body politics of Stalinist Russia in the 1930s have pointed out that the cultural and public discourse of the time was marked by the rhetoric of "reforging" (*perekovka*) human beings. In spite of this culture's Marxist emphasis on the supremacy of the economic and social environment for human formation, this concept of reforging was paradoxically linked to the notion of biological change within an organism.[4] For a number of writers and artists, the reforging concept was underpinned by a biological quest to create better and stronger bodies with a healthier psychological make-up. Some Russian writers and artists expressed their sincere belief in the possibility of such an experiment, Mikhail Zoshchenko's work being the best known example of this endeavor.[5] Admittedly, his experiments were directed not only at describing other individuals but also at his own personal struggle to reforge himself into a more physically healthy and psychologically stable individual. Various Jewish writers, such as children's book writer Lev Kassil', made similar attempts to demonstrate the success of such a reforging of the body and soul as exhibited in many Russian and Jewish characters in the writing of the 1930s.[6] What is relevant to the focus of the present argument is the fact that the human body's biological essence was viewed as a product of the forces of nature against which remedies had to be found. As Zoshchenko's diaries attest, Max Nordau's turn-of-the-century concept of degeneration continued to be influential among the generation of the 1930s, and the question of overcoming degeneration was of great importance to this generation.[7]

This chapter looks at how this notion of a body in need of reforging — the Jew's body — was applied in two works of the 1930s and 1950s. It first looks at the film *Seekers of Happiness* (1936), made with the famous veteran of the Yiddish Theatre Solomon Mikhoels (b. Vovsi) as consultant. It then examines the construct of the criminal subversiveness of Jews who were presented as the ultimate traitors to the Soviet economy in the 1950s, as encapsulated in the little known novel *The Yellow Metal* (1956) by an obscure writer, Valentin Ivanov. This novel is dedicated to members of the Soviet militia and its crime investigation unit. Uniting these two narratives is the representation of subversive Jews through their involvement in illicit dealings in gold. In both works the Jewish criminals are arrested and punished. The 1930s narrative expresses enthusiasm for the notion of corporeal reforging, but it also shows signs of biological determinism as applied to the Jewish male. The 1950s narrative changes the optimistic script of the positive reforging of criminals by emphasising the hereditary aspects of criminality, which in turn are linked to ethnicity and race.

Chapter 5

A Documented Case of the Reforging
of a Jewish Criminal

When Zoshchenko wrote an essay about the re-forging experience of former criminals from the Gulag forced to work on the construction of the Belomor Canal, he chose the story of a former Jewish criminal, Abram Isaakovich Rottenberg: "Istoriia odnoi perekovki" ("A History of One Reforging" [1931–1934]) included in *The History of the Construction of the Stalin Belomor-Baltic Canal, 1931–1934*. A thief and a swindler, Rottenberg was sentenced to hard labor and sent to work on the famous Belomor Canal in the early 1930s.[8] Although some commentators maintain that Zoshchenko presents Rottenberg as a "social enemy," a victim of past indulgences, it can also be argued that he implies that Rottenberg's criminality was linked to his race. Among the indicators of the theme of biological determinism is Rottenberg's own reference to Cesare Lombroso whom he dubs a "bourgeois professor" (495) and against whose theories he presents as evidence his own experience as a former criminal who had changed into an honest laborer.[9] After only two years of labor on the construction of the Canal, Rottenberg becomes a convinced proletarian and the recipient of a special honor for exceeding the requested work output by 180 percent. This 40-year-old man was involved in criminal behavior from his childhood, and had worked in the underworld in many of the world's capital cities: Istanbul, London, even Jaffa in Palestine. Zoshchenko insists that he "changed his psyche and re-educated his consciousness" (524) as the result of the regulations laid down by the authorities. But Zoshchenko adds a significant clause to this conclusion: he stresses that he can vouch for Rottenberg's full rehabilitation and can guarantee his good behavior only within the conditions of the socialist economy. This means that if Rottenberg were to find himself back in a capitalist society his behavior would revert to its old ways. Zoshchenko thus leaves open the possibility of criminal regression and, if read as more than simply lip service to the Stalinist regime in a book dedicated to Stalin's venture, the Gulag, this conclusion can be seen to have a degree of biological determinism in it. By suggesting that no total or unconditional cure is possible, Zoshchenko is contradicting his own affirmations concerning the possibility of change in the human psyche. The question that emerges as a result of this contradiction is whether Rottenberg's regression is made possible because he is a Jew. Does ethnicity play a part in "psyche change"? And, if so, to what degree?

That Zoshchenko believed in a race-related genetic script can be substantiated by his interpretation of his own psychological illness, depression, as linked to his own ethnicity, that of a Ukrainian. In his diaries

Zoshchenko refers to the famous Russian writer of Ukrainian origin, Nikolai Gogol, as an example of the ethnicity-related nature of depression. According to Zoshchenko, Gogol was afflicted by the same "Ukrainian" psychological problems, such as depression, as was Zoshchenko himself. He wrote that this commonality was based on their shared Ukrainian origins ("*khokhlatskoe proiskhozhdenie*" [94]) and "could be the result of the same blood which we have in common" (94).[10] The link between one's nature and race is thus established, and it exemplifies the belief that the process of reforging, or *perekovka,* included a race component that was intrinsic to a biological organism in need of transfiguration. The element of biological determinism in racial and ethnic characteristics, however, which is undeniably present in Zoshchenko's unpublished diaries, casts doubt on the possibility of a wholly positive result in the reforging of an individual. Of specific relevance to this investigation is the fact that this doubt is centered around the issue of hereditary characteristics that are associated with ethnicity and race. This implies a fundamental question: Can representatives of all ethnicities be re-forged? Zoshchenko's writing serves as a preamble to what will follow in the rest of the chapter: the exposure of the link between the criminal leanings of ethnic Jews and other non-Russians, and their ethnic essence.

In his concluding remarks in *The History of the Construction of the Stalin Belomor-Baltic Canal, 1931–1934* the editor, Maxim Gorkii, states that class differences would be erased in the not-too-distant future and that, as a result, class struggle would disappear. This struggle, he wrote, would be replaced by the struggle against nature. Gorkii implied that this struggle against nature, including human nature, was going to be more complicated than the class struggle. In the concluding remarks preceding Gorkii's words the name of "the bourgeois scientist Lombroso" (593) is mentioned a number of times as the target of the polemics initiated by the reformed criminals themselves. The targeting of Lombrosian theories of biological determinism from the 1930s underscores the pathos of the discourse, which was aimed at conquering human nature while also showing the vulnerability of this very discourse. Gorkii congratulates the Party and Comrade Stalin for the successful completion of the Belomor Canal and the reforging of former criminals. Significantly for the context of his speech he dubs Stalin "an iron man" (596), implying that Stalin is an exception in that his metal body and psyche do not need to be rebuilt because they are made of non-corruptible material. This argument, connected with the role of the Gulag in the completion of the project of the Belomor Canal, is based on an analogy between nature and its elements (waterways, lakes, permafrost, sub-zero temperatures) and human nature: both can be conquered and changed. *The History of the Construction of the*

Stalin Belomor-Baltic Canal contains numerous accounts of the re-forging of members of national minorities (*"natsmeny"* [395]) and stresses that these representatives of Central Asia and the Caucasus had been successfully reformed during the process of engagement with the Gulag authorities and other reformed members of the camp. In this context the case of Rottenberg is intended to represent a case of the reforging of a Jew. At the end of the book Gorkii issues a call to writers to base their future work on these new "facts" (596). This chapter will demonstrate how a screenwriter and a writer addressed the theme of the criminal and his/her nature as applied to Jews and other minorities in works from the 1930s and the 1950s.

Pinya's Body in *Seekers of Happiness*

The film *Seekers of Happiness*, directed by Vladimir Korsh-Sablin,[11] focuses on the experience of Jewish settlers in the Jewish Autonomous Region of Birobidzhan.[12] (Solomon Mikhoels [1890–1948] was a consultant.) It was released in 1936, soon after *The History of the Contruction of the Stalin Belomor–Baltic Canal*, including Zoshchenko's essay, was published. Among the group of new Jewish settlers arriving in Birobidzhan there is one negative character, Pinya. Pinya's negative characteristics are expressed via his body, and they are constructed as features that could be recognized by the viewer as "typically" Jewish.[13] His physical features make him appear rather repulsive, and on the scale of physical size as determined by the other characters, both Jewish and non-Jewish, Pinya stands out as particularly short and puny. Not only is he smaller than the other men, but he is also smaller than the women. His skin is covered in sweat, and his shiny bald head has a greasy appearance. This overall impression becomes a metaphor for Pinya's equally unclean soul. Out of the whole group of Jews he is the only one who speaks with a foreign accent — presumably Yiddish. The least positive about the decision taken by his family to settle in Birobidzhan, he becomes more enthusiastic only when he is told that the place has deposits of gold. He is married to a beautiful Jewish woman, Basya, whose physique is the very opposite of Pinya's. Whereas he is unmanly in his smallness, she is taller and stronger than he — more like the non-Jewish peasant women who work on the collective farm. The physical size and build of these strong peasant women were epitomized in the famous sculpture "Worker and Collective Farm Woman" by Vera Mukhina, exhibited in 1937 in the Soviet

Pavilion at the Paris World Exhibition, which still stands today in Moscow's Exhibition of Economic Achievements (VDNKh).[14] Pinya's stature stands as a metaphor for his insubstantial physical abilities, including a lack of sexual potency: not only does he avoid any physical labor, but his wife's obvious physical repulsion toward him betrays his lack of sexual prowess. This is further reinforced by Basya's instant attraction to a physically stronger male. Although a Jew, this Jewish man is Russified and acculturated; he speaks Russian without an accent or any foreign intonation, and is, ideologically, a Soviet man devoted to his country body and soul. Pinya's body, in contrast, is defined by characteristics that repulse his wife and that can be interpreted as signs of degeneration: undersized height, puny build, faulty speech apparatus — all of which are presented as inborn features of a Jew's body. In its smallness Pinya's body is a feminine one with compromised sexuality, and although he might not have a large appetite for his wife, this does not mean that he does not have homosexual tendencies. And if such tendencies are not explicitly expressed in the film, they can be latent. He is smaller than all the women in the film, including the old women, and he is a loner, thus suggesting he has something to hide.

What excites Pinya is gold. Although the motif of Jews' attraction to gold has been a stable stereotype of Jews in European fiction and folklore for centuries, due to the association between Jews and such professions as money-lending and the pawning of silver and gold items, the theme of gold in Stalin's Russia acquired new, political connotations. As a strategic metal, gold was made by the Soviets into an ideological currency, securing the survival of the socialist state in the 1920s and saving it against the imperialist world's alleged united efforts to starve the young country into collapse and submission. Stalin's attention to Russia's rich mineral resources, gold and platinum in particular, is well documented — his strategic encouragement of geological search led to the discovery of diamonds in Yakutia in the 1950s, which made a significant contribution to the economic well-being of the country (a special study devoted to the mineral resources of Birobidzan was published in 1936).[15]

Although in the film Pinya's gold odyssey becomes a tragicomic farce — he mistakenly believes fools' gold, a mineral resembling gold in its glittering appearance, to be alluvial gold — he nevertheless commits a serious offense by trying to cross the border and end up on the Chinese shore of the Amur river. He also almost kills his brother-in-law, who stops him from pocketing the "gold" rather than giving it to the authorities. What strikes the viewer of the film is the director's decision, presumably with Mikhoels's blessing, to make Pinya act as if he is in a trancelike state. From the moment he hears about the gold deposits in Birobidzhan, he seems to be led by instinct, acting in a somewhat somnambular state rather like Frankenstein in the film versions of the 1930s, as if some outer force was leading him to behave in the way he does.[16] Digging for gold, striking his brother-in-law with a spade, trying to bribe the boatman to take him to the Chinese shore — all these actions are performed as if by an automaton. He acts not so much of his own free will but as if under the control of a directing force. It is as if his genetic script makes him do the things he does. Possibly the strategy of both the film's director and consultant was to show the audience that the man was acting like this because he had not been exposed to any ideological education (Pinya is a "foreign" Jew, probably Polish), and therefore was susceptible to codes instilled in him by centuries of oppression. From this perspective Pinya is acting as a result of his environment and circumstances. But it is equally possible to read in this automaton-like behavior the realization of a biological script, of inherited behavior. And, although this film shows one negative Jew among a whole commune of positive Jewish characters, in line with the Russian folk wisdom "*v sem'e ne bez uroda*" ("any family is allowed to have one misfit, or monster"), Pinya is not just a misfit but a full-blown monster, both physically and psychologically. Whereas the film's authors deal with the stereotypes of the "bad" Jew as dictated by his class differences, namely his bourgeois selfishness and love of money, the actor chosen to play this role has physical characteristics that become part of the stereotype and caricature of the Jew's male body.

Research into the representation of the human body in Stalinist culture has pointed out that in the literature and art of that period it became a metaphor for the Soviet Union.[17] Starting in the 1930s, Stalin's Soviet Union was obsessed with the protection of the country's borders from the imagined intruding enemy as well as from the enemy within who wanted to escape after having committed a subversive act. In parallel to this political situation, the human body was described as a phenomenon with definite boundaries. In the same way that the USSR's borders were sealed from penetration by foreign elements, the human body was depicted as a strong and firm physical entity, hence the metal metaphors applied to it.[18] Of course, Stalin's own pseudonym indicated that his body, made as it was of steel, was neither corruptible nor porous, and therefore unsusceptible to outside influences from natural, political, or ideological influences. In this respect Pinya's attempt to cross the border with China with his bottle of alluvial "gold" is the act of a regressive body in the context of Stalinist mythology of the body and country. The fact that Pinya does not have children further emphasizes the notion that his non-procreative body does not deserve to have any future:

there is no place for the progeny of his biological type in the future society of this country. His external physical characteristics were viewed by biological scientists as a result of "degeneration" which, in application to the Jews of the Russian empire, were often regarded as indicative of interbreeding (short, small, pale, bald, incapable of hard physical work). Now that the Jews had been moved from the ghettoes of the Pale of Settlement into the new territory, Birobidzhan, they were exposed to a wider variety of ethnic groups, and through intermarriage a new breed of Soviet human being would presumably develop. From this point of view the marriage between a Jewish girl and a Russian man in the film is highly symbolic: they are attracted physically to each other and as two biological entities coming from extremely diverse territorial and ethnic backgrounds they are shown to experience a libidinal attraction to one another. What is implied is that, out of a unit comprising diverse ethnic species, a new breed of human being will emerge, a breed free of any sign of degeneration. Both the Jewish girl and the Russian man have statuesque builds; strong and tall, they are physically suited to each other. The viewer can rest assured that out of their union a strong child, both physically and psychologically healthy, will be born. Presumably, then, the way to overcome a proliferation of Pinyas is to embrace intermarriage and so escape the phylogenetic script of degeneration. As has been noted, in the Stalinist culture of the 1930s the typology of the body with borders, the sealed body, made an allowance for the transfiguration of borders in order to create the "right" kind of body, its physical form suitable for the new challenges facing the Soviet nation.[19] The film ends with Pinya's arrest and the wedding between the Jewish woman and the Russian man, during which folk dances and songs are performed in Russian and Yiddish. The wedding scene is symbolic: what will follow is a wedding night and a new dawn with happy, healthy children produced, representative of a new generation of physically and morally strong people of Soviet nationality.

This depiction of the Jewish body by the film (and presumably by Mikhoels) is similar to attitudes toward the physical body of the Jew as expressed by other Russian Jewish intellectuals in the 1930s. It has been shown that Lev Kassil's novel for children, *Vratar' Respubliki* (*The Goalkeeper of the Republic*), embodies a Jew's desire to remold the typical Jewish body into one that fits the created construct of corporeality in the Stalinist 1930s: from small into big, from narrow into broad, from weak into strong.[20] This novel was composed between 1932 and 1937 and published in 1939. Like Isaak Babel in his *Red Cavalry*, Kassil is a Jewish author who wanted to remold the stereotype of the Jewish body, thus reflecting his own attempt to fit into the collective of virile men and be accepted by this Russian collective. To remold the stereotype involved remaking the Jewish male's body. The bitter irony of both Babel's and Mikhoels's attempts to remake the Jew's physical body in this way is expressed in the tragedy of their biographies: both of them became victims of Stalin's reign of terror. Babel's participation in the Civil War and Mikhoels's contribution to Russia's victory in World War II as a member of the Jewish Antifascist Committee did not save either of them from becoming victims, and in Mikhoels's case this victimhood is undeniably linked to being Jewish. Certainly it was the Jewish male body of Mikhoels that was abused when struck by a car in a staged automobile accident on the streets of Minsk. It was unmistakably Jewish blood that "flowed out of his veins," in the words of Polish poet Julian Tuwim which resonated in Russian in Ehrenburg's translation.

Valentin Ivanov's *The Yellow Metal* (1956) and the Racial Pathology of the Male Jew

The Yellow Metal, the novel by Valentin Ivanov (1902–1972), contains such blatant xenophobia and ethnic hatred that four months after its publication it was taken out of circulation due to the resolution by Glavlit (Russia's Main Administration for Literary and Publishing Affairs) in April 1957.[21] The reason given for this ruling was that the novel contained "hooliganist attacks against Georgians and other Soviet nationalities" (195).[22] Among those concealed under the expression "other nationalities" were Jews. And indeed, the very title of Ivanov's novel, *The Yellow Metal* rather than gold, is marked by color — color as a category of race. It is well known that Jews have been viewed as Asiatic people (which did not exclude the notion that they were a hybrid people with an admixture of "black blood") and that racist scientists and politicians viewed Jews as members of the "yellow races." This conflation achieved its political peak at the time of the construct of the concept of the "Yellow Peril."[23] In addition, the title is endowed with a definite meaning on the phonetic level: the sound "zh" in "zheltyi" corresponds to the "zh" in "zhyd"—"kike," the derogative nickname of Jews in the Russian language. When Vladimir Korolenko (1853–1921) wanted to ridicule an antisemite in his story *Yom-kipur (Sudnyi den')* (*Yom Kippur, or Day of Atonement* [1890]), he makes him characterize the sounds that Jews make in the synagogue as "zhzh."[24]

Ivanov's novel is saturated with antisemitic conceptions of Jews as a race physically marked as a biological entity. Its narrative revolves around the criminal activities of a group of people representing a whole range of ethnic nationalities of the Soviet Union: Jews, Georgians, Turkish people of Central Asia, and even a national minority of Iranian descent in Azerbaijan. Old Believers fall into the category of enemies of the people, and through their faith are presented as sympathizers with Jews. Together with a few Russians of Siberian origin they form a supply chain covering all stages of illegal gold dealings: from the theft of sand in Siberian alluvial mines to its sale on the borders of Central Asian republics. However, the main protagonists, those whose characters are developed with considerable detail, are Jewish and Georgian. Written in 1956 after Stalin's death and the execution of Beria, the novel brought to the surface a previously hidden hatred of people of "Caucasian nationality."

Even Russians from Siberia are depicted as a special breed and therefore separate from "mainland" Russians. Similarly, Old Believers are depicted as an ethnic group that differs from the Russians not only through its religious beliefs, but also in its ethnicity. The "good" Russians come from Moscow, and are members of the police force (the novel is dedicated to the Soviet police). The rest of the USSR with its vast foreign territories — Siberia, the Far East, the Caucasus and Central Asia — are categorized as suspect due to the assumed subversive nature of its non-Russian population.

Jews are presented as the masterminds behind the entire operation, and in the blatantly racist narrative the typology of the Jew stands out as most prominent. Some of the stereotypes presented are of phylogenetic origin: Jewish males are marked by physical features, that the author links with historical figures from the Old Testament, and Jewish women — unlike their male partners — are presented as oversexed.

One of the most striking physical characteristics with which Ivanov endows the male body of a Jew is a short leg. One of his heroes, Misha Trusengeld, was born with one leg shorter than the other by some four centimeters. Ivanov spends a considerable amount of time referring to this short leg, thus making it clear to the reader that this feature is of special significance. He tells the reader that neither of Misha's parents had this handicap, thus casting suspicion on Misha's mother's fidelity. And indeed, in the light of the frivolous behavior of Jewish married women in the novel, this suspicion functions as a phantom theme. In discussing Misha's short leg the author also alludes to stories from the Old Testament, suggesting that Misha derives his genealogy from those primordial Jews. In this light his short leg becomes a sign of atavism and degeneration. Ivanov's knowledge of the Bible is in itself quite exceptional, and although he uses some of the Old Testament names in a muddled manner, a confusion probably explained by the constraints on Biblical references imposed by the censorship laws of the atheist state, such references betray the author's intention of drawing a genetic line between contemporary Jewry and its forebears of 4000 years ago.

Sander Gilman has demonstrated that the foot of a Jew has been a stable component in the construct of the diseased nature of the Jewish body. A Jew's flat foot also made him an object of ridicule and certainly, because of this alleged handicap, Jews were seen as inadequate for military service. The inborn handicap thus also functioned as a marker of Jews' deviant and tricky behavior, used in a bid to avoid military service. Such apparent lack of patriotism at a time of war further delineated Jewish Otherness. In Ivanov's novel Misha's short leg is seen by his parents as a sign of anointment by the very fact that, because of this handicap, he will not have to join the army or fight in the war. Moreover it makes him eligible for a state pension. Here the stereotype of the devious, parasitic Jew shying away from hard work is entwined with that of the diseased Jew's body. Throughout the text Ivanov refers to Misha's leg with such epithets as "precious short leg" ("*dragotsennaia korotkaia noga*" [96]) and "highly valued" ("*vysokotsennaia noga*" [98]), both of which combine the literal meaning of monetary price with its metaphoric meaning of the leg being a valuable asset to its owner.

The defective leg has yet another important genealogy — it is attributed to the body of the Jew-as-Devil, part of the stereotype of the Jew's body that has existed since the Middle Ages. As was pointed out earlier, in this stereotype a Jew takes his genealogy from the Devil, hiding his hoof in the same way that he conceals a tail or a pair of horns. Ilya Ehrenburg parodied this belief in his description of Julio Jurenito, whereas Ivanov relies on his reader's cultural understanding of a deformed leg as being as much a sign of a Devil as a deformed foot. Popular folk mythology, we must recall, ascribed to Stalin a foot with six toes — a sign that he was the Devil incarnate.

Another male Jewish protagonist in Ivanov's novel is Vladimir Brodkin, Trusengeld's partner in crime who helps him to sell gold to a third party. Brodkin is in his forties. As in the case of the 30-year-old Trusengeld, who is on a pension because of his physical handicap, Brodkin is on a state health pension. This early retirement signifies two stereotypical attributes: the Jew's sick body and his devious use of illness to acquire state support and an easy life. Brodkin's sickness is related to his liver, and the description of his appearance creates an interesting link between his illness and his lifestyle. Grossly overweight, Brodkin's body becomes a signifier of indulgence in gluttony: his rich diet high in fat clearly makes him not only obese but also prone to liver ailments. This link between obesity and rich food had been made clear on various posters that hung in doctors' reception rooms in numerous Soviet clinics and public health centers during this period. These posters normally depicted a fat person and a slender one, each carrying a transparent shopping bag ("*avos'ka*") revealing the kind of food that each carried.[25] The slender person carried modest vegetables such as cabbages and carrots with some dairy products and rye bread, but the fat person's bag contained fatty foods such as salami, smoked fish, rich cakes and chocolates. The subtext of this representation was that the food bought by the overweight consumer was also expensive, falling as it did into the category of delicatessen foods, whereas the "lean" food was not only healthy, but affordable. A class message was thus encoded into this artifact of Soviet health propaganda. Although normally the characters on these posters were two women, the message relied not only on women's vanity; it also sent a class subtext in which a racist implication was concealed, as the stereotype of a Jewish woman as fat was well engraved in Soviet culture.[26] This stereotype finds its representation in Ivanov's novel, where Brodkin's wife is depicted as overweight. A fat Jewess is a stable stereotype in Soviet discourse and, as will be demonstrated later, has been internalized by Jewish writers themselves. For instance, in Yurii Karabchievskii's novel *Zhizn' Aleksandra Zilbera* written in 1974 but published for the first time in 1990 after the Glasnost reforms, this stereotype is rife: "There walked an ordinary fat old Jewish woman of whom there is a million for every thousand" (104).[27]

Brodkin's obesity and diseased liver lead to a loss of sexual potency — the narrator mentions that he no longer visited his wife's bedroom; Madam Brodkin's excessive eating leads to an excessive sexual appetite. Although Ivanov clearly builds this cause-and-effect relationship between excesses of food and excesses of sex in the case of a Jewish woman, his descriptions of Brodkin's appearance are unequivocally racially loaded:

> Brodkin's body was flabby and fat from bad metabolism. Features on his formerly distinguished, handsome face — old family members said that he resembled a famous Zionist "messiah" of the end of the last century — by now had flabbily extended, his mouth sunk in the corners in permanently expressed displeasure (99).

It is significant that the positive aesthetic evaluation of Brodkin's face in his younger days comes from his relatives, thus signifying that the aesthetic ideal of beauty among Jews is different from those of other people. "A famous Zionist 'messiah'" probably refers to Theodor Herzl. The suggestion that Brodkin resembles Herzl is a racially and politically provocative remark:

it is a racist comment not only because of the claim of the physical family resemblance of all Jews, but also because, through the positive aesthetic judgment of Herzl, they show their political admiration for the father of Zionism.

The reader will by now be familiar with the conflation of race and gender in relation to the representation of a Jew's body. It should, therefore, come as no surprise that this anomalous stereotype resurfaces in Ivanov's novel. In a description of Brodkin we are told, "A Tartar gown was open on his flabby, almost woman-like breast which was overgrown with the thick hair of a bear" (110) and earlier, "Brodkin stretched out his hand with hairy fingers" (101). Such descriptions are designed to reflect and inspire feelings of disgust and repulsion by the "healthy" reader toward the abject subject. Brodkin's body is also presented as anomalous because it has remnants of hermaphroditism and because, with its excessive animal-like hair growth, it is atavistic.

Brodkin's wife's body is also put under scrutiny as racialized. It is grossly overweight, as we have seen, and she speaks in "a bass voice" (105) — an indication of the pathology of the Jewish woman's body that mirrors the Jewish male body in anomalous secondary sexual characteristics. If Brodkin is feminine, his wife is androgynously masculine. As we are told, "Overweight, red-faced, loud, crudely sensual, Brodkina thought of herself as being charming" (104).

This oversexed Jewish woman has a sexual relationship with her husband's partner, Trusengeld. What makes this situation particularly piquant is the fact that her husband is aware of this liaison. The lovers spend time together in Brodkina's bedroom while Brodkin himself is at home. While the narrator explains Brodkin's lack of concern over the affair by his cynical understanding that such a relationship is good for business, the notion of the perverted Jew functions as a subtext. And indeed, what the popular culture of the time would have considered to be sexual perversion surfaces again when the narrator mentions Brodkina's secret desire for an eighteen-year-old Jewish man from another *gescheft*-making family. Similarly, the notion of incest is raised in connection with another Jewish woman being married to her cousin: as we have seen, levirate marriages were viewed by the Russians as acts of incest.

Among the stable physical attributes of a Jew's face is the special shape of the eye and the occurrence of bulging eyes — features that invariably find their way into Ivanov's novel. He describes the face of a Jewish woman, Rika Meilinson, as dominated by *"vypuklye glaza"* ("bulging eyes") as well as the inevitable "long narrow nose" (199). This use of bulging eyes as a marker of a Jew's racial difference is evident in a long established "canon" of racist literature. Umberto Eco, in his book on the construction of ugliness in the racial Other (2007), chooses some of these texts as examples of this construct. One such text, written by Dr. Celticus in 1903, describes Jewish eyes as one of the nineteen physical features that characterize a Jew. "The Jewish eye is very particular," writes this author (269), and he goes on to liken it to the eye of a toad. In Giorgio Montadon's fascist racist text "How to Recognize a Jew" (1940), there is a special reference to the eyes of Jews which, he states, are "not deeply set in the sockets." Among other "characteristics of the Jewish type" are "woolly hair... and regarding the body, slightly curved shoulders and flat feet, not to mention rapacious gestures and a slouching gait" (269).[28] In Ivanov's evaluation, Rika's "round bulging eye" makes her face resemble that of a magpie, and in a scene in which a business deal is negotiated Jews are described as gesticulating and shouting in loud voices.

As one can see, Ivanov's depiction of Jewish corporeality is in line with that of the racist and racist canon. Whereas Dr. Celticus also wrote about the lechery of Jews, Ivanov develops the theme of the attraction the "dark races" feel towards Russian women. Clearly, if Jewish women are ugly, then it is no wonder that Jewish men are attracted to Russian women, who are depicted in this novel as pretty and seductive. But Ivanov also has to find an explanation for Russian women's attraction to non-Russian men of the "darker races." Ivanov depicts Georgian men as handsome in build and stature, but the situation with Jewish men is different. Ivanov uses quasi-scientific theories in his identification of a unique biological category, based on a definite racial and gender typology, of Russian women who fall for Georgian and Jewish men, and to whom these men are attracted. These women are voluptuous blondes; they are non-intellectual and greedy by nature. This stereotype expresses a gender prejudice with definite phylogenetic origins. Ivanov employs a physiognomic analysis of such a woman's face, an analysis that can be traced back to nineteenth-century craniology and physiognomics, which found its apogee in the representation of women by the pre-Raphaelites.[29] Of special importance here is the reference to a narrow forehead as a sign of limited intelligence:

> A plump woman who was not more than thirty years old, dressed in a silk dress and wearing shiny shoes on her bare feet, was going towards the exit. It was obvious that she was in good health, because she did not suffer from the oppressive heat of the room. Her face was quite pretty. Her complexion, slightly touched by the sun, was fresh and young, and her nose, slightly turned upwards, looked very coquettish. A curl of her hair, which was naturally blonde, was stuck because of the heat to her forehead — which was neither high nor low, but of a size which belonged to the face of this type, moderately low and tightened by the hair around the temples (25).

This woman, who is part of the gold operation network, attracts the Georgian and the Jew alike, and here again the author's interest in race and gender stereotypes is obvious. Misha Trusengeld's wife is also Russian. She is blonde and voluptuous, vain and shallow in her materialistic desires, and similarly attracted to Misha because of the lifestyle that he can provide. In creating a typology of women who are likely to fall for Jewish and Georgian men, Ivanov makes it clear to his readers that these women are as faulty by nature as the men of the darker races. This selected misogyny would clearly exclude hard-working and honest Russian women who would no doubt prefer their own breed — similarly "normal" Russian men.

The extent to which Ivanov develops a complex racial typology in his novel becomes more evident when looking at his strategy to avoid accusations of spreading racial prejudice by dividing his Jewish characters into "good" and "bad." This strategy operates on the level of the detective plot of the novel, in which the subversive Jewish operators — Trusengeld, Brodkin and Meilinson — are exposed to the Soviet police. When Brodkin comes to Moscow to sell gold, he stays in his sister's apartment. She is the widow of a Jewish war hero who was betrayed to the Nazis by a Ukrainian informant. This Jew, Katzman, spoke fluent German, as he was brought up among the German colonists and passed himself off as a *folksdeutsche,* thus infiltrating the enemy on the orders of the Soviet authorities. Ivanov stresses that his physical appearance was such that he could not be identified as a Jew, and could pass for a German. Ivanov describes this in words that are racially loaded: *"rusyi, dazhe svetlorusyi"* (197), meaning fair-haired in a Russian way, as *"rusyi"* as color is phonetically linked to *"Rus"* and *"Russkii"* — "Russia" and "Russian." Such choice of lexis allows Ivanov to smuggle in a notion of Katzman's European, rather than Semitic or Asian, ethnic origins.

Ivanov's strategy remains racially tinted. In presenting a "good" patriotic Jew he chooses a Jewish man with Aryan physical characteristics. By doing this he creates a separate group consisting of dark Jews, Georgians, and Muslim ethnicities united not only by "bad" tendencies that subvert the socialist state but also by the same vices: greed, lust, and lechery. This group has a common racial characteristic: they are dark-skinned, dark-haired, dark-eyed. Brodkin is described as *"temnyi bogach"* ("a dark rich man" [212]). This typology has an uncanny resemblance to Karl Marx's infamous labeling of his political rival Ferdinand Lassalle as the "Negro Jew."[30] The reader may recall that Ehrenburg's crypto-Jew Julio Jurenito had physical characteristics of the "black races." The good Jew Katzman's appearance receives two evaluations: one by Brodkin, who looks with hatred at his image in the photograph in his sister's apartment, and another by the narrator who praises

Katzman's appearance as that of the Jewish intelligentsia. But the physical features he chooses to describe betray his interest in race: if Brodkin is hairy like a bear, then Katzman's hair is "long and wavy, combed to the back of the head" (197). This interest in the racialized characteristics of human hair is quite striking, as is Ivanov's strategy to de-racinate the "good" Jew.

The two children of Katzman, Brodkin's niece and nephew, find out about Brodkin's gold dealing and decide to report him to the police. The plot of a nephew betraying his uncle to Soviet authorities for hiding illicit material is reminiscent of the true story of Pavlik Morozov, a heroic narrative composed in the 1930s. Pavlik (1918–1932) knew that his *kulak* villagers had hidden grain from government officials, and he reported them to the authorities.[31] Pavlik was subsequently murdered by the *kulaks* and became a state hero of Soviet Russia: schools and streets were named after him all over the country, and children admitted to the Pioneers organization (the first stage before Komsomol, the youth wing of the Communist Party of the Soviet Union) swore their allegiance to the cause through his name.

The manner in which Brodkin is caught and reported to the police has an uncanny resemblance to the Pavlik Morozov incident. Just as rich peasants hid grain in the floor of a grain barn, so Brodkin hides his bag of gold granules under the floor in the bathroom of his sister's Moscow apartment. While hiding the bag he accidentally pricks it with a nail in the floor. Some granules spill out of the bag, and it is this golden sand that Katzman's children find in the bathroom. Ivanov's parallelisms are quite obvious: the physical characteristics of grain and golden granules and the concealment of illicit material under the floor suggest that what grain is for the *kulaks* gold is for Jews.

But the account of a Jewish relative reporting the incident to the authorities has a second dimension, one that operates as a parallel to the plot of ultimate betrayal: that of Christ by Judas Iscariot, who was one of the "clan" when he betrayed a senior member of the group. (It must be remembered that in Russian folk etymology Jews, *iudei,* is a derivative of *Iuda*—Judas.[32]) The incident of Pavlik Morozov has always been read as an anti-story in the non-official cultures of the Soviet Union: loyalty to the family and respect for one's parents were seen as clashing with official state loyalty which put the state above the family. The tension between loyalty to the family and clan and loyalty to the state is fundamental to the Pavlik Morozov narrative, and the story's moral could be interpreted as emphasizing priority of the family over the state, or the other way around, depending on the situation, thus testifying to the schizophrenic nature of Soviet culture.

Although Ivanov praises the two young Katzmans for reporting on their uncle, the Katzmans' act can also be seen as betrayal of their own kind ("*svoikh*" is used often in the novel). In line with this evaluation the deed of the two Katzmans becomes a metaphor for the act of Judas. The message of this metaphor is quite clear: Jews are traitors by nature; they even betray their own kind. And indeed, Ivanov's concluding words about the Brodkin affair hint at the eternal value of the Brodkin story, giving it unmistakable connotations of the eternal struggle between good and evil, with Brodkin representing the powers of evil:

> It is said that one must not grow tired of the continuous repetition of truth. Indeed, Brodkin's sensations are natural for him and are not original at all. The underground rich man from Kotlovo sits among us like an alien body [*chuzherodnoe telo*]. All his intentions are directed against us, and he negates us. He hates us. But is he also ready not only to exploit us but also to trust one of us with his life? Yes, he is. This is not a paradox, but part of reality.
> But in general this topic is old, old, old... (213)

The person who is referred to as "one of us" in this remarkable passage is a Jewish doctor, a surgeon in a Moscow clinic who examines Brodkin's liver and suggests treatment. On the one hand, Brodkin trusts this specialist for his knowledge; on the other, he categorizes him as the type of person who will not take bribes. (Brodkin considers giving the surgeon a platinum [sic!] watch as a present before the operation on his liver, but rejects this idea because he intuitively understands that the doctor, although a Jew, is from a different category of Jew.) Ivanov thus develops a dual typology of Jews in a naïve attempt to present a non-racist image of himself. In reality, as the narrator he raises the question of race by establishing a difference between the Brodkins et al. and the Katzmans, who "work not for the sake of money" (213). Ivanov may write that it is not "physical features" (212) that the Jewish surgeon and Katzman have in common, but, in relegating them to different formations of Jews, he promotes the notion of the "good" Jew, one who is acculturated and assimilated, educated and honest. Ivanov even writes that appearance "is an empty thing; in appearance the surgeon was more like Vladimir Borisovich [Brodkin]. But with his developed intuition Brodkin senses something of the Katzmans in him" (212). The Katzmans are thus alien to the Brodkins. In the passage that follows, however, a statement referring to the color of Brodkin becomes a racial signifier as well as a marker of his association with the realm of evil: "This dark rich man will climb on to the operation table without any hesitation..." (212). In these few words the author suggests that, although Brodkin detests Jews such as the surgeon, he nevertheless will entrust his health to the surgeon's hands.

The reader of the novel in 1956 would have seen in this passage a hint of the "Doctors' Plot," an infamous case and one of Stalin's last "show trials" in which medical doctors were accused of being involved in a plot to poison leading members of the Soviet people.[33] Most of the accused were Jews. This case, one of the biggest anti-Jewish witch hunts of post-war Stalinism, ended only with Stalin's death in 1953. The damage done to Jewish medical professionals was enormous and the belief in the criminality of Jewish doctors never completely disappeared, in part because the very theme of the plot — Jews poisoning Christians — was in itself built on folk superstitions, thus securing the acceptability of the "Doctors' Plot" by the Soviet people. Against this historical background Ivanov's attempt to depict a good Jewish surgeon in a text written between 1954 and 1956[34] serves two purposes: on the surface it complies with the official stance while at the same time it subverts this stance by casting doubt on the official outcome of the campaign. Ivanov's views of a good Jewish doctor (who, after all, is only one doctor) represents two mythologies at once: one being part of the official culture and the other belonging to the unofficial or subterranean subculture of antisemitism.

The secret safe where Brodkin hides his illicit material in the Moscow apartment of his unsuspecting sister is described in astonishing rhetoric in which Brodkin is accused of being of the same breed as fascists, Nazis, and racists. This rhetoric functions as a preventive measure by Ivanov against accusations of racism. As was mentioned earlier, this naïve strategy did not work: so outrageous was the racist rhetoric of his novel that it had to be taken out of circulation. Here is the passage that includes this astonishing attack on the Brodkins and Flimgoltzes which is built on the World War II rhetoric of hatred of the external and internal enemy:

> Here [in this safe] he hid the symbol of the sameness of various souls: his own, that of Flimgoltz, of members of Gestapo, of Flimgoltz's bosses and of others who are the contemporary followers of racism, fascism and Hitlerism, notwithstanding the difference in hair color, color of eyes, skin color and other racial characteristics (202).

Love of gold thus becomes a marker of racism and fascism, and Jews who are prone to this love of gold become equated by this logic with racism and fascism. Jews are thus depicted as natural racists. Ivanov's logic of the reversal of accusation is infantile, implying that it is not "us," the Russians, who hate Jews, but it is Jews who hate Russians. Moreover, such hatred comes "naturally" (213) to Jews because it is part of their nature (213). And a Jew cannot escape the script of congenital heredity.

The detective plot of the novel ends with Brodkin and the other Jews being caught by the police, although they do manage to save their capital because they have hidden it successfully (they send some of the goods abroad to their overseas relatives). They will, therefore, come out of prison, and will continue to be stinking rich. The novel suggests that the Soviet state's legal system is mild and its laws humanitarian, thus allowing criminals like the Brodkins to continue to prosper under the system.

The front page of the book *The Yellow Metal* states that it is a novel. On the back page there is information about Ivanov, entitled "About the author." This information includes a short biography of Ivanov, which states that he took part in the Civil War, worked as a government inspector (*"inspektor-revizor"*), became head of the planning department of a building construction company, and then, from 1951, was "a professional man of letters."[35] But the novel is written in awkward language that lacks the smoothness of a professional writer. These two factors, Ivanov's professional background and the primitive language of his novel, render the book a unique case in regard to its influence on the Soviet reader. Ivanov would have been perceived as a man who had hands-on knowledge of the economic features of his country. The reader would have considered the fact that his narrative is primitive devoid of literary frills as evidence of the true nature of the events it depicts, rather than a product of his imagination. In this way the book would have been viewed not as a novel but rather as a true story written by a professional criminal investigator. The contemporary Soviet reader would have been well aware of the Aesopian language of Russian narratives which tried to conceal from official authorities a politically dubious message. There is no doubt that Ivanov's "novel" would have been read by the sensitive reader as containing all the hidden messages the author intended the reader to understand.

A recent commentator on Ivanov's novel characterized it as indicative of a whole mythology within Russian society that has survived until the present: "Ivanov's novel, with all its political odiousness, is almost the only printed evidence about the unofficial myths of Stalin's times, which had a major influence on the historic memory not only of Soviet, but also of post-Soviet society" (195).[36] To what extent this typology still survives in Russian culture will become more obvious when works written between the 1970s and the present are examined in the following chapters.

Notes

[1] For a comprehensive bibliography of works on Jews in the Soviet period (1917–1991) see N. I. Rutberg and I. N. Pidevich. *Evrei i evreiskii vopros v literature sovetskogo perioda.* Moscow: Grant. 2000.

[2] See Ben Fowkes. *The Disintegration of the Soviet Union: A Study In The Rise And Triumph Of Nationalism.* New York: St. Martin's Press. 1997.

[3] Review by E. K. "Dr. R. Wassermann. *K voprosu o prestupnosti evreev. Betrachtunzen uber die Kriminalitat der Juden. Schriften fur Wirtschaft und Statistik.* Berlin. 1928". Eds. V. I. Binshtok, M. Bramson, G. I. Dembo, M. M. Gran. *Voprosy biologii i patologii evreev.* Vol. 3. No. 2. Leningrad: Izd-vo Evreiskogo Istoriko-Etnograficheskogo Obshchestva. 1930. 216.

[4] On the changing notions of masculinity, sex and gender in Stalinist culture see Lilya Kaganovsky. *How the Soviet Man Was Unmade: Cultural Fantasy and Male Subjectivity Under Stalin.* Pittsburg: University of Pittsburg Press. 2008.

[5] See Irene Masing-Delic. *Abolishing Death: A Salvation Myth of Russian Twentieth-Century Literature.* Stanford: Stanford University Press. 1992.

[6] Keith A. Livers. *Constructing the Stalinist Body: Fictional Representations of Corporeality in the Stalinist 1930s.* Lanham: Lexington Books. 2004.

[7] Mikhail Zoshchenko. Vozvrashchennaia molodost'. *Sobranie sochinenii v trekh tomakh.* Vol. 3. Leningrad: Khudozhestvennaia Literatura. 1987. 5–161. On Zoshchenko's polemics with Max Nordau see Arsenii Gulyga. Razum pobezhdaet (O nauchno-khudozhestvennykh povestiakh Mikhaila Zoshchenko). *Sobranie sochinenii v trekh tomakh.* Leningrad: Khudozhestvennaia Literatura. Vol. 3. 1987. 694–710.

[8] On the construction of the Canal in the context of Stalinist mythmaking see Cynthia A. Ruder. *Making History for Stalin: The Story of the Belomor Canal.* Gainesville: Florida University Press. 1998.

[9] Mikhail Zoshchenko. *Istoriia odnoi perekovki. Belomorsko-Baltiiskii Kanal imeni Stalina. Istoriia stroitel'stva 1931–1934 gg.* Eds. M. Gorkii, L. Averbakh, and S. Firin. Moscow: OGIZ. Gosudarstvennoe izdatel'stvo "Istoriia fabrik i zavodov". 1934. Reprint edition of 1998. 493–527.

[10] Mikhail Zoshchenko. Iz dnevnika. In *Neizdannyi Zoshchenko.* Ed. Vera von Wiren. Ann Arbor: Ardis. 1976. 93–94.

[11] *Iskateli schast'ia.* Dir. Vladimir Korsh-Sablin. Sovetskaia Belarus' Studio. Leningrad. 1936. B&W. 81 minutes.

[12] On Stalin's policy and Birobidzhan see Robert Weinberg. Jews into Peasants? Solving the Jewish Question in Birobidzhan. Ed. Yaacov Ro'i. *Jews and Jewish Life in Russia and the Soviet Union.* London and NY: Routledge. 1995. 87–103.

[13] Pinya is played by the veteran actor of the Yiddish Moscow Theatre, Veniamin Zuskin. On Pinya's Jewish features in the perception of the Jewish generation of the 1930s see Anna Shternshis. *Soviet and Kosher: Jewish Popular Culture in the Soviet Union, 1923–1939.* Bloomington: Indiana University Press. 2006. See a discussion of this film in Miron Chernenko. *Kinematograficheskaia istoriia Sovetskogo evreistva 1934–1941.* Moscow: Evreiskoe nasledie. 2001.

[14] On this sculpture in the context of race in the 1930s see Igor Golomshtok. *Totalitarian Art in the Soviet Union, the Third Reich, Fascist Italy and the People's Republic of China.* London: Collins Harvill. 1990.

[15] I. V. Kamenetskii. *Prirodnye bogatstva Evreiskoi avtonomnoi oblasti.* Moscow: Der Emes. 1936. On industry in Birobidzhan see D. Lerman. *Promyshlennost' Evreiskoi avtonomnoi oblasti.* B.m: TsS OZET. 1936.

[16] See *Frankenstein.* Dir. James Whale. Produced by Universal Studious. 1931.

[17]   Keith A. Livers. *Constructing the Stalinist Body: Fictional Representations of Corporeality in the Stalinist 1930s*. Lanham: Lexington Books. 2004.

[18]   Rolf Hellebust. *Flesh to Metal: Soviet Literature and the Alchemy of Revolution*. Ithaca: Cornell University Press. 2003.

[19]   See Livers. *Constructing the Stalinist Body: Fictional Representations of Corporeality in the Stalinist 1930s*. Lanham: Lexington Books. 2004.

[20]   Keith A. Livers. Op. cit.

[21]   Valentin Ivanov. *Zheltyi metall*. Moscow: Molodaia Gvardiia. 1956. There were 90,000 copies of this novel printed.

[22]   Quoted in Nikolai Mitrokhin. Evrei, gruziny, kulaki i zoloto Strany Sovetov. *Novoe literaturnoe obozrenie*. No. 80/4. 2007. 195–220.

[23]   On the yellow color of the Semitic races in Russian modernism see Mikhail Bezrodnyi. O 'iudoboiazni' Andreia Belogo. *Novoe literaturnoe obozrenie*. No. 28. 1997. 100–125. Also Vadim Rossman. Jewish Conspiracy and Yellow Peril: Antisemitism and Sinophobia in the Nineteenth Century. Jerusalem: The Vidal Sassoon International Centre for the Study of Antisemitism. The Hebrew University of Jerusalem. 2004.

[24]   See Henrietta Mondry [G. Mondri]. *Pisateli-narodniki i evrei*. St. Petersburg: Akademicheskii proekt. 2005.

[25]   See posters in Maria Lafont. *Soviet Posters. The Sergo Grigorian Collection*. London: Prestel. 2007.

[26]   There will be a discussion of stereotypes of the Jewish woman's body later in the book in connection with Dina Rubina's work.

[27]   Yurii Karabchievskii. *Zhizn' Aleksandra Zilbera*. Druzhba narodov. No. 7. 1990. 97–146.

[28]   Ed. Umberto Eco. *On Ugliness*. London: Harvill Secker. 2007.

[29]   Tim Barringer. *Reading The Pre-Raphaelites*. New Haven: Yale University Press. 1999.

[30]   See endnote 12 in Chapter 4.

[31]   Yury Druzhnikov. *Informer 001: The Myth of Pavlik Morozov*. Transaction Publishers. 1996; Catriona Kelly. *Comrade Pavlik: The Rise and Fall of a Soviet Boy Hero*. Granta Books. 2005.

[32]   Olga Belova. *Etnokul'turnye stereotipy v slavianskoi narodnoi traditsii*. Moscow: Indrik. 2005.

[33]   Iakov Etinger. The Doctors' Plot: Stalin's Solution to the Jewish Question. Ed. Yaacov Ro'i. *Jews and Jewish Life in Russia and the Soviet Union*. London: Routledge. 1995. 103–127.

[34]   This information is given on the back cover of the book under the title "*Ob avtore*," "About the author."

[35]   See back page of the 1956 edition.

[36]   Nikolai Mitrokhin. Evrei, gruziny, kulaki i zoloto Strany Sovetov. *Novoe literaturnoe obozrenie*. No. 80/4. 2007. 195–220.

"The bad Jew" Pinya, "the good Jews" Leva and Pinya's wife Basya. Leva and Basya have strong working class physique whereas the "bad Jew" Pinya is puny. Film "Seekers of Happiness" (1936)

"Medical examination in Birobidzhan". Photograph of 1934.
The original photograph is part of the OZET collection in the Museum of
Ethnography in St. Petersburg.

Chapter 6

Sadists' Bodies of the Anti-Zionist Campaign Era: 1960s-1970s

> "The crime investigation department of the Georgian SSR accuses citizen N. N. Bomze as a sadistic Jew who allegedly took blood from the six-year-old Georgian boy"
> from a letter of I. Nikitina to Ilya Ehrenburg. July 27, 1962.[1]

It has been pointed out by various scholars that official Soviet historiography largely ignored the participation of Soviet Jews in World War II and the victimization of Jews in the Holocaust.[2] The Shoah was not officially acknowledged by the Soviet State, and the increasingly hostile attitude of the Soviet Union toward Israel reflected badly on Soviet Jewry.[3] This situation was echoed in the representation of Jews in fiction, in which Jewish characters were often deracinated in line with the official policy and the demands of censorship.[4] Some commentators maintain that this situation continued well into the 1980s, until the advent of Perestroika saw the Jewish theme gradually reappear in Soviet history textbooks and public discourse.[5] Vladlen Izmozik, in his study of Jewry in Soviet textbooks, asserts, "From the early 1960s to the mid 1980s the Jewish theme was almost completely absent" (58). The anti-Zionist campaign of the late 1960s and 1970s, however, was a smokescreen for blatant antisemitic propaganda. Indeed, this period was characterized by the rise of visual antisemitic material, which was circulated in the pages of Soviet newspapers and as illustrations in various political monographs.[6] The most representative example is the book by Trofim Kychko (or Kichko in Russian), *Iudaizm bez prikras* (*Judaism Unvarnished* [1963]) published in Ukrainian by the Ukrainian Academy of Sciences.[7] This book contained anti-Jewish caricatures with strong racial overtones.[8] Although this book was condemned by the Central Committee of the Communist Party soon after its publication, thanks largely to international pressure, on the pages of the daily newspapers the hooked noses and hunchbacked bodies of the Israeli military, and especially the one-eyed face of Moshe Dayan, had an uncanny resemblance to the bloodthirsty figures of Jews as depicted in the antisemitic cartoons of Nazi propaganda.[9] (A selection of drawings from Kychko's book, which categorize the Jew's body as sadistic and perverted, is included later in this chapter.)

The shameful silence about the Holocaust and the lack of statistics on the high representation of Jews in the Soviet Army during World War II was broken by Evgeny Evtushenko in his poem *Babi Yar* (1961) and the subsequent long poem *Bratskaia GES* (Hydro-Electric Brotherhood Station) in which he portrayed, through the figure of the simple worker Izya Kramer, a Jewish man participating in the heroic effort of the Soviet people to build a new hydro-electric power station, thus making his contribution to the growth of the socialist state.[10] Evtushenko's popularity was so strong among the younger generation that the regime had to consider carefully how best to deal with this new social phenomenon. It responded to *Babi Yar* by claiming that the question of the number of Jews who died during World War II should not be separated from the general losses suffered by the Soviet people during the war. Whereas the poem successfully broke the taboo on both political antisemitism and the theme of the Holocaust, the airing of these subjects was again halted by the anti-Zionist propaganda that followed the Six-Day Arab-Israeli war of 1967. This, however, does not refute the fact that images of racialized Jews had crept into works of literature and other texts of the 1960–1980s. As official Soviet political discourse presented Zionism as a racist ideology and practice, it made a weapon out of the theme of race and used this opportunity to make racist remarks against Jews.[11] This meant a renewed focus on the Jewish body.

This chapter demonstrates that although Jews were often represented in literature as "deracinated" characters,[12] beliefs about the peculiar, special and often pathological nature of Jews did not disappear from the antisemitic discourse and are evident in fiction as well as in the political texts of this period. Indeed, the construct of the aggressive and sadistic Jew was a by-product of the anti-Zionist campaign. This chapter looks at Kychko's political text and Shevtsov's novel *Liubov' i nenavist'* (*Love and Hatred* [1970]),[13] both of which develop the theme of the sadistic and aggressive Jew that was disseminated during the political climate of the anti-Zionist campaign that escalated after the Six-Day Arab-Israeli War.[14]

Antisemitic Discourse and the Pictorial Representations of the Male Jew's Body in Kychko's *Judaism Unvarnished*

Kychko's book *Judaism Unvarnished* provides overt evidence of the use of representations of the Jew's physical body as a means of inciting Judeophobic feelings. The book contains several pictorial representations of Jewish bodies in line with its contents.[15] Published in 1963 *Judaism Unvarnished* was such a graphic case of antisemitism that the Central Committee of the Communist Party of the USSR condemned the book in an article in the newspaper *Pravda* in April 1964. The article stated that the book's "erroneous statements and illustrations can offend religious people and can be interpreted as antisemitic" (132).[16] As one commentator notes, it was one of the very few cases where the Party had to distance itself from a piece of antisemitic writing (a few years later the same Communist Party started a major antisemitic campaign under the guise of fighting Zionism).[17]

Kychko's book pays lip service to Marxist views on the importance of social conditions in the formation of nationality (*natsional'nost'*), yet the author's views on Jews are rooted in the biological nature of Jews as a race. Kychko makes frequent statements alluding to Judaism as a religion that is more archaic and primitive than other world religions. He goes as far as to stress that it is the product of forces of nature. In a deliberately obscure statement he even proposes the notion that Judaism is a religion of primitive people, implying that Jews remain driven by primitive instincts. This suggestion is used to explain various patterns of behavior by contemporary Jewry, including their aggressive policy against Arabs and Palestinians, their misogynistic mistreatment of their women (in contrast to the Soviet policy of gender equality), and their persecution of any dissident movement among their own kind. Kychko's main strategy is thus to explain every act conducted by Jews as being rooted in the Judaic belief system, a system that has not changed for some four thousand years since the times of the Torah and the Talmud. One of the outcomes of such a strategy is the image of Jews as being driven by instincts and cultural beliefs that have remained unchanged by the achievements of civilization. Kychko thus presents Jews in much the same way that the racist discourse of the nineteenth century presented them: as a primitive race. As such, they are people of the flesh and of the body, and their religious beliefs and rituals are presented as confirmation of this, as seen in Kychko's explanation of the ritual of circumcision. When describing circumcision he augments his text with illustrations that present

149

Jews as primitive savages. In addition, he makes a quasi-medical argument against circumcision, claiming that it is highly unhygienic. Kychko conceals from his readers the fact that circumcision was viewed by many non-Jews as a desirable medical procedure precisely because of its hygienic advantages. He also conceals contemporary statistics that revealed the low percentage of cervical cancer among Jewish women, a phenomenon that has direct links to circumcised males.[18] Rather, he presents his reader with alternative "data" taken from stable antisemitic folklore and circulated in quasi-scientific literature, and his reference is as telling as the story itself. His source is one "German Dr. Ruest" who is allegedly quoted in a Byelorussian book entitled *Circumcision in the Light of Science* published in 1932, hardly a respectable or up-to-date source of medical expertise.[19] Kychko includes in his book references to syphilis and tuberculosis. Not only were these the two most feared diseases of the nineteenth century but both had been singled out by racialist science at the end of the nineteenth and the beginning of the twentieth centuries as applied to the Jew's body. As noted in Chapter 1, there was some scientific debate in the 1920s and 1930s concerning the risks of tuberculosis. The results of the investigations showed that there was low mortality among Jews from this illness in spite of the fact that the poor Jewish population lived in unsatisfactory sanitary conditions. In the volumes *Problems of the Biology and Pathology of the Jews* (1926, 1928 and 1930) various studies indicated the absence of cases of syphilis among Jews. This was explained by religious rituals and orderly lifestyles among the Jewish population in studied areas of Russia, Ukraine and Byelorussia.[20] Yet Kychko introduces as "scientific evidence" material that is dated, anachronistic and uncorroborated. Particularly alarming and symptomatic of his approach, however, is his recycling of discredited medical material borrowed from sources which form a repository of antisemitic "data" from the Nazi era.

Kychko describes the three stages of the ritual of circumcision as a sadistic act: the foreskin, he writes, is first cut, then ripped off with unclean fingers, then the blood is sucked out of the penis by the *mohel* (the Jewish man who performs the circumcision). After stressing that the *mohels* do not wash their hands well, thus introducing the trope of the dirty Jew, he goes on to provide his "medical information." Referring to a German "Professor of Medicine," (145) he states that there were epidemics of syphilis and tuberculosis among Jewish children in Warsaw and Lvov as a result of male Jewish babies being infected by *mohels* whose mouths contained syphilitic or tubercular particles. A Jew's body is thus explained as a depository of physical pathology and, with the ritual of circumcision functioning as a trope of sadism, this body also harbors a case of mental pathology.

The idea that Jews are sadistic is also conveyed through a set of loose references to the Talmud. Visions of the torture that is awaiting sinners in the afterlife are presented as evidence of the sadism of Judaism and, by proxy, of Jews. As Judaism is presented as a religion resulting from social and "natural" (149) conditions — whatever that means — these visions of the torture of sinners in the afterlife become conflated with the Jews' sadistic predisposition. Kychko takes special pleasure in describing the Jewish hell as a torture room that ironically has as much in common with the product of the popular imagination of Christians as it does with those acts of torture practiced by Christian princes and kings, certainly: "crushed bones" and "burned flesh" proliferate (148).

In the eyes of phylosemites (such as Vladimir Soloviev) and Judeophobes (such as Pavel Florensky), the ultimate corporeality of the Jews is confirmed by their laws of kashrut. Whereas Soloviev explained kashrut as a desire by Jews to preserve their clean bodies as well as their clean souls, the Judophobic tradition deemed kashrut laws to be evidence of the Jews' preoccupation with the physical body on account of their abandonment of the spirit. Kychko follows this latter tradition in his book, juxtaposing a spiritual quest with Jewish concerns about materiality, as seen in his account of their alleged visions of Paradise. Kychko maintains that, apart from a state of spiritual bliss, the Jewish Paradise in the Talmudic version has a strong "sensual" (149) component underpinned by material delights. For instance, the chosen ones "will be eating fat geese and drinking mature wine" (149).

Kychko links the subject of Jewish fixations on materiality and lustfulness with various pathological excesses. In his book Jews are depicted as sexual perverts through the notion of *mohels* sucking blood from a circumcised boy's penis, an act presented as a metaphor for the act of homosexual fellatio. The biblical tale of Ham staring at his drunken father's naked body finds an overtly pornographic pictorial representation in the book: an adult Jewish man directs his gaze at the open groin and anus of a naked man lying in a drunken stupor. This picture has a homoerotic component, as seen in the happy grin on the man's face. Although the explanation under the picture states that it is an illustration of the episode of Ham looking at his father's nakedness, the visual and textual conglomeration functions as an incest plot — it is, after all, a son and a father caught in a compromising situation. It is quite clear that the authors of the text and the illustrations in this book exploit the homoerotic implications of Jewish men's total devotion to their male God as well as the stories of incest as related in the Old Testament. By using this strategy they define the normal collective Self against the pathological racial Other — the body of (Soviet) Slavs against the demonized body of Jews.

Kychko thus conveys the stereotypical idea of the materiality of Jews, and the image of Jews as a people of the body is a prevailing theme in his book. In the historical reality of the 1960s the notion of Jewish materiality and corporeality, in combination with their essential pathology, translates into a blueprint by which Jews could not become normal members of the new Soviet collective. Written in Ukrainian and published by the Ukrainian Academy of Science — part of the structure of the Soviet Academy of Science — this book graphically demonstrates that, among the nations of the Soviet Union, Jews belonged to the lowest stratum. If the structure of progress developed by the Soviet nationalities mimicked Darwinian evolution, then Jews were seen to be among the species that had been left far behind in time. Kychko uses Jewish bodies as exhibits for the rest of the Soviet nationalities, for Ukrainians and other Slavs in particular (the book's bibliography tellingly contains sources in both Russian and Byelorussian).

Shevtsov's *Love and Hatred* and Psychopathic Jewish Men

Ivan Shevtsov's reputation as a rabid antisemite in the manner of the Black Hundred has been well established in scholarly literature — references to his name are found in books and articles devoted to the theme of antisemitism and anti-Zionism in Soviet culture.[21] He acquired this reputation with the publication in 1970 of two novels: *Vo imia otsa i syna* (*In the Name of the Father and the Son*) and *Liubov' i nenavist'* (*Love and Hatred*).[22] The publication of these works was perceived by commentators on the Soviet Union as a watershed in Soviet policy toward expressions of antisemitic views in public discourse. Sovietologists viewed the publication of *Love and Hatred* in such astonishingly large-circulation editions — 200,000 copies — as a sign of change of official policy toward Soviet Jewry.[23] The fact that the novel was published by the powerful publishing house of the Soviet Ministry of Defence, Voenizdat, gave this event an additional political significance. Researchers have stated that the publication of this novel was a line of demarcation between Khrushchev's Russia and Russia under Brezhnev.[24] Unlike Ivanov's *The Yellow Metal* or Kychko's *Judaism Unvarnished*, Shevtsov's book was not taken out of circulation. Admittedly, articles criticizing the novel appeared in 1970 in the newspapers *Pravda*,

Komsomol'skaia Pravda, Literaturnaia gazeta, and the journal *Iunost'*, all raising concern that Shevtsov and his book undermined friendship among the peoples of the Soviet Union. Yet Shevtsov still managed to survive political changes in the Soviet Union. He continued to publish antisemitic novels during Glasnost and continues to write blatantly xenophobic and Judeophobic work in post-Soviet Russia today. The titles of his recent novels, such as *V bor'be s d'iavolom (In a Fight with the Devil* [2003]), suggest that he now "fights" Jews on the mythological level of good and evil, with Jews being the incarnation of the Devil himself.[25] With the return of the occult and superstition, as well as staunch Orthodoxy in contemporary Russian culture, this communist has succeeded in making an easy transition to the new wave of quasi-religious fanaticism and obscurantism. This chapter studies in detail his novel *Love and Hatred* in terms of its representation of Jews' physical bodies in this particular era.

Love and Hatred is divided into three parts: Part 1: At the End of the World; Part 2: Friend; and Part 3: Enemy. Each of these parts has a Jewish male protagonist, who is presented as a criminal. The main character of the novel, who is featured in all three parts, is a Russian man called Andrei Iasenev. Iasenev is presented as an admirable hero, a simple but honest Russian man of humble background who has risen to professional prominence due to hard work, self-discipline and total dedication to "the cause." This complimentary profile is encoded in his surname: *"Iasen'"* means ashtree, considered in Russia to be a humble tree and later made into a symbol of simple and honest Russian people in the cult film *Moskva slezam ne verit* (*Moscow Does Not Believe in Tears* [1979]), with its programmatic song about ash trees taking over Moscow and replacing noble oak trees.[26] Of additional significance is the biological fact that ash-trees seed themselves freely, taking over space in a manner reflected in the following song with its anthropomorphized ash-tree:

> Eto iasen' semenami
> kruzhit val's nad mostovoi.
> Iasen' s vidom derevenskim
> priobshchilsia k tantsam venskim.[27]

> This is the ash tree
> Swirling with its seeds over the pavement.
> The ash tree with its simple looks of a villager
> Has learned Viennese dances.

But etymologically *"iasen'"* also relates to *"iasnyi"* meaning clear, thus suggesting the clear and transparent nature of the Russian hero Iasenev. In Part 1 Iasenev is a young military officer in a submarine division serving in the Russian Arctic North from where he is transferred to Leningrad; in Part 2 he changes his profession to that of a police officer, becoming a member of the Soviet Police Force (the *Militsiia*) in Moscow; and in Part 3 in this new capacity he solves two murder cases in Moscow. In each of the three parts of the novel he crosses paths with Jewish protagonists, and in each case the Jewish characters are involved in serious criminal activities. In Part 1 a Jewish man from Odessa is caught when he tries to board a foreign submarine in the North Sea; in Part 2 a Jewish man is caught and confesses to the murder of a simple taxi driver (it is this incident which inspires Iasenev to change his profession and join the *Militsia*); and in Part 3 another Jewish man commits two sadistic murders — this time it is Iasenev who solves the cases.

The male Jewish protagonist in Part 1 is described through two lenses: the narrative of a Russian woman, Irina, and Iasenev's narrative. Irina is a young woman whom Iasenev has secretly loved since they were both students in Leningrad. She married their mutual friend, another marine officer, Marat Inofatiev. When she divorces Marat and returns to the base to work as a doctor, she finds herself under the spell of a Jewish protagonist, Arkadii Ostapovich Dubavin. There is no direct reference to Dubavin as Jewish, but the reader learns about his ethnic origins when the narrator discloses his real name and patronymic: Arie Osafovich. The narrator uses another code of identification for Dubavin's Jewish ethnicity: Dubavin comes from Odessa, the port city on the Black Sea with a large and important Jewish population. "Odessan" functions as a euphemism for Jewish in Russian culture (as will be discussed later, in Vasily Belov's controversial novel written during Glasnost, the Jewish protagonists have their origins in Odessa).[28] Arie, or Arkadii, Dubavin is described by Irina as a man of considerable sex appeal — he is suave and fits the stereotype of a tall, dark and handsome man. Whereas Iasenev, with his open and honest blue eyes, is unmistakably Slavic in appearance, Arie's looks are exotic. When Irina initially fell in love with Marat, she did so because of his exotic looks. As a native of the Crimea, Marat could be of Tartar or Turkic origin, and his appearance is as foreign and un-Slavic as his temperament: olive-skinned with dark eyes, he is vain and clearly loves the good life. The narrator explains that his temperament suits his native Black Sea more than the North Sea, and he has long ago left the north for better climes. His surname, Inofatiev, is etymologically linked to the Ino-rodets, or Ino-verets—Russian words denoting a non-Russian native of the Russian empire ("Fat-" is phonetically linked to "Fatima" and has as its root Islamic names and surnames). Irina, with her Russian temperament and tastes, however, has left Marat and his alien ways, and has moved from a town on the Black Sea back to a small village in the north. Of importance here is the motif of Russian men losing their women to "exotic" men who come from the Black Sea area: in this narrative Muslim Marat from the Crimea and Jewish Arie from Odessa. Although Irina discloses in her diary that she finds Arie charming and attractive, she does not enter into a sexual relationship with him. Arie Dubavin's behavior toward Irina, however, is portrayed as promiscuous. Having lured her into his apartment for a party, he tries to seduce her after the other guests have left. He is thus shown both as a calculating and dangerous seducer and, at the same time, as a man who does not force himself upon women: Irina is free to leave his apartment.

Demonstrating the Jewish man's sensuality and materiality as seen in his love of good food and attractive women, Dubavin reminds Irina of another man "with an exotic surname" (164) — Boris Peruanskii, whom she knew in Leningrad and who was similarly charming, with a lust for life and for Russian women. He even proposed to Irina but she declined his marriage proposal, the assumption being that she had learned by then not to be fooled by people, presumably after earlier experiences with other "exotic" men. Here Shevtsov develops a typology of Jewish men as carnal and dangerous to the physical safety of Russian women.

Dubavin is shown not only as a seducer of Russian women, but also as a dangerous political enemy of the Soviet Union. He is such a significant figure in espionage, prompting an incident of international importance that a foreign submarine is sent to pick him up and take him away as a traitor of the Soviet Union. But the borders of the country are guarded by the Soviet counterintelligence and the cunning perpetrator is caught and imprisoned. Here the theme of Russia's borders functions in parallel to the theme of the boundaries of the Russian woman's body: the Jew attempts to unseal what is usually sealed from non-Russians and what belongs, by right of ethnic origin, to Russians only. It is not without good reason that Irina now drifts toward Iasenev, finally appreciating his hidden virtues and agreeing to become his wife. Together they decide to move to Leningrad, breaking off their journey to visit Moscow, a place of pilgrimage for any patriotic Russian. It is in Moscow that Iasenev decides to become a member of the police, thanks to an episode again linked to Jewish criminals and a wider Jewish conspiracy.

In Moscow, while talking to a former friend, now a policeman, Iasenev learns that a common friend had committed suicide in an act that is now suspected to be a murder. A talented scientist was found dead with a suicide note, but his friends know that he had made many enemies as a result of his outspoken political views. Among the opinions the scientist challenged was the view that Albert Einstein was the father of the theory of relativity. He also maintained that there was no difference between the Trotskyites and the members of the E.S.R (Socialist Revolutionary Party) in the Russian Revolution; therefore, when the Jewish woman Fanny Kaplan shot Lenin in 1918, she was acting as an agent of Trotsky to help him gain power. Trotsky would have been dangerous for Russia because "Hitler was potentially sitting inside him" (211).

During this conversation, which takes place in the office of the policeman, Iasenev witnesses the interrogation of a Jewish criminal, a murderer. The young Jew, Makliarskii, admits killing a taxi driver because he urgently needed money. The fact that the murderer is a Jew is a strategic device aimed at substantiating the plot of the Jewish conspiracy behind the death of the talented scientist. If murderers are found among Jews it means that Jews are murderers and are capable of killing their political enemies. The line of Jewish genealogy has thus been established: famous men like Einstein and Trotsky are all connected in one gigantic international plot to gain power and influence.

The young man, Makliarskii, is the son of an élite Moscow Jewish family. His father is a professor of law and he himself is a second-year law student at Moscow University. Makliarskii is thus shown to be someone who knows the law and who uses this knowledge cynically to his advantage. He manipulates his evidence and creates a less punishable case for himself — he claims temporary insanity in the knowledge that this can be used by the defense to his considerable advantage.

The details of the murder committed by the young Makliarskii are telling: both the murder weapon and the motive are overtly "Jewish." The weapon is a special instrument made from a spoke taken out of a bicycle wheel and attached to a wooden handle. It is aimed straight at the heart of the victim. A long instrument with a sharp end, which leaves holes in the body, is evocative of the Beilis murder case. Iushchinskii's body was pierced by pricked wounds, which were intended to make the body bleed.[29] In another murder committed by another Jew in Part 3 of Shevtsov's novel the same instrument is used. The motif of madness vis-à-vis the Jewish theme functions on two levels: on one level it suggests that Makliarskii is manipulating the system, whereas on another the sadistic murder that he commits can be seen as a marker of his innate madness — yet another indication of the pathology of Jews.

The motif of the murder is given another, specifically "typical," "ethnic" feature: the murder is made on an impulse, as a result of a momentary decision. The murderer had to pay for an extravagant restaurant dinner. He had shown off and clearly wanted to impress, thus revealing all the characteristics of excess that stand in stark contrast to the self-discipline and modesty of the Russian protagonists. With this emphasis on food and drink, and the excesses of sensuality and indulgence, Shevtsov creates a case for a specific "Jewish" attribute that is evidence of the carnality and materiality of the Jewish male. Makliarskii is driven not only by the instinctive desire for gratification of a spoiled brat — Iasenev describes him as "an overfed male animal" (219) — but also by vanity and selfishness. Makliarskii's physical features reveal this carnality and the primitive nature of the Jewish male, his "square face" (214) and "well developed jaw" (215) signaling a primitive carnivorous essence:

> Here he entered the office of the investigator Strunov, he, this nineteen-year-old man of strong build [*bogatyr'*], overfed, with a square face. His hair was not like Tarzan's — it was reddish in color, cropped like a shepherd's in a musical comedy, his eyes round, empty but alert. An impudent smile on his lips. (214).

What apparently offends Iasenev most is Makliarskii's total disrespect for a simple worker, a humble taxi driver. This naïve attempt to conceal racial hatred in the guise of class hatred fails in the light of the narrator's blatant expressions of biological hatred for Jews, such as: "Is it possible that the life of this overfed wild animal will be spared?" (220). It is at this point that Iasenev joins the Militia and the family settles in Moscow, the capital city clearly in need of protection from the enemy.

Naum Goltser: A Jewish Sadist in the Context of the "Sadistic" Ritual Killers Beilis and Glusker

Jews in Shevtsov's novel are depicted as enemies both within and without. Not only do they conduct illicit deals inside Russia, they are also linked to the international community and serve as its emissaries. Apart from Dubavin and Makliarskii, there is a third Jewish criminal in the novel, Naum Goltser. The son of wealthy parents, Goltser leads an idle life. He is a socialite who has friends among the Moscow élite. As in the case of Makliarskii, Goltser's father was a famous lawyer and a law professor who died leaving enough money "to last a lifetime" (252). Shevtsov depicts Goltser as a pathological murderer, a sadist who murdered his own mother and, later, a young Russian female drug addict. Goltser's murder of his mother remains unsolved because of the clever way in which he organized it. It had all the signs of a sadistic murder — the body was found in her apartment with its stomach cut open, its intestines arranged around the neck, and no money or valuables taken. The police eventually closed the investigation because no motive could be found and because of lack of evidence. In reality, Goltser killed his mother in order to get hold of the inheritance his rich father had left to her. Instead of waiting for his mother to pass on the substantial sum of money to him in due course, Goltser killed her and staged the crime in such a way that he was not suspected.

Goltser's role as a sadist does not stop there. He inflicts physical pain on women who are dependent on his supplies of drugs, as seen in his relationship with a young Russian drug addict whom he sadistically and sexually abuses. He also supplies girls to various important people, virtually running a brothel in his country house outside Moscow and in his Moscow apartment, which his male friends often use as a secret venue for their extramarital relations.

One of Goltser's best friends is Marat Inofatiev, who has become the son-in-law of a government minister. Marat becomes involved with the same drug-addicted girl whom Goltser supplies with morphine. When this girl accidentally learns about Marat's illicit deals Goltser decides he must get rid of her. He lures her to his country *dacha* and murders her. To dispose of the corpse he cuts it into a number of parts, separating the legs and arms from the torso, and deposits them in three different places in Moscow. With the help of investigating officer Iasenev, Goltser is discovered as the murderer, as the girl's blood matches the blood stains on the bed of his country house where the murder took place. When confronted by the investigators, Goltser confesses not only to the murder of the girl but also to that of his mother.

The details of the sadistic murders in this novel are graphic and gruesome. This is highly unusual for socialist realist writing in which depictions of physiological details were generally limited by strict standards of purity. In the case of Goltser's murders, Shevtsov breaks with this accepted tradition of self-censorship and spares the reader no detail, going so far as to describe twice the details of the corpse of Mrs. Goltser — the first time when the corpse is found and the second time, repeated almost verbatim, when Goltser confesses to the murder. The description of the killing clearly suggests ritual murder: certainly the placement of the intestines in a circle around the neck of the corpse is a well-designed and ritualistic act. This scene connotes a ritual performed by primitive people who view the intestines as a microcosm of the world. In this context Goltser's sadism acquires racial connotations, and indeed no detail is spared in presenting Goltser as a typical Jew and his vices as typically Jewish. That Goltser is driven by archaic powers is implied in his participation in orgies: the narrator describes him as "a contemporary Bacchus" (463). He is thus shown to be someone who gets intoxicated by blood and sex. Indeed, in the scene of the murder of the Russian drug addict, he is shown as "experiencing a sexual arousal": "A wild animal and a primitive animal lived side by side in him" (478). His appearance has the same features as Makliarskii's — he too has "strong jaws" — and he uses the same instrument for killing Russian women as Makliarskii did for killing the driver: a home-made weapon made from the spoke of a bicycle wheel with a wooden handle attached. Moreover, he kills the two women in the same way Makliarskii killed the taxi driver — by pushing the spoke straight into the heart with the result that death is instantaneous. And in both cases the corpses are cut up.

The common features of the murders committed independently by Makliarskii and Goltser suggest a certain typology that implies a uniquely Jewish way of killing a victim. And in all three murders in the novel there is an uncanny resemblance to real cases in modern Russian history in which Jews were accused of murder: in Makliarskii's and Goltser's murder-by-sharp-point the reference to the Beilis case is obvious. In the case of the sadistic murder with the gaping stomach and the intestines wrapped around the neck of the corpse there is a more complicated frame of reference, but one that also has precedents in the history of Russian Jewry. One such precedent is the case of Glusker (1909), a Jewish man found guilty of murdering a whole family. Another is the pogrom victims, which the reader will be familiar with from the scenes in Babel's *Red Cavalry* or from accounts such as the infamous Kishenev pogrom of 1903. The first image functions as a means of suggesting continuity in the genetic behavior of Jewish criminals. The similarity with Babel's imagery can be intended as a means to reverse the charge and to present as bandits and sadists not Cossacks and Russians but Jews themselves. Indeed, the words "sadist" and "bandit" are applied in the novel to both Makliarskii and Goltser.

The link to the Beilis Affair materializes, as we have seen, in the use of a sharp object to inflict a body wound. As in the Beilis case, the popular myth of the existence of ritual murder among Jews was connected to rules of kashrut pertaining to the slaughter of animals. The letting of blood from animals was viewed as proof of Jews' sadistic instincts and practices. At the time of the Beilis Affair, Vasily Rozanov wrote an inflammatory article entitled "Stop the Ritual Slaughter of Animals" (1913), drawing a parallel between the way blood was shed from the body of Iushchinskii and the kosher slaughter of animals.[30] He called for a stop to the kosher slaughter of farm animals, maintaining that it was inhumane. But the main rhetorical thrust of his article was to stress the ritual underpinning of the animal slaughter and, by implication, the ritualistic nature of the murder of the Christian boy Iushchinskii. In Shevtsov's novel the notion of a wound made by a spiked object thus functions as a reference to ritual killings by Jews: the method of murder is uncannily known to both Makliarskii and Goltser who, significantly, do not know each other.

There are also significant similarities between the description of Goltser's murder of his mother and the infamous murder case of Glusker. Unlike the Beilis Affair, the Glusker Case is not widely known to students of history, but it stands out as another example of the unjust legal trial of a Jew in the history of Russian Jewry. A Jewish man, Glusker, the foreman in a business run by the Jewish family the Bykhovskys, was accused of murdering this family. He was tried and subsequently hanged. After the execution, various mistakes made by the jury were exposed, and it became clear that the wrong man had been punished. The events of this case were made public by the Russian writer Vladimir Korolenko, known for his courageous writings covering the Kishinev Pogrom and the stance he took during the Beilis Affair.[31] Korolenko's role in exposing the anti-Jewish bias of the Russian legal authorities can be compared to Emile Zola's public role in the Dreyfus Affair in France. The difference is that in the case of the plight of Jews in tsarist Russia at the beginning of the twentieth century, Korolenko had to intervene in a number of cases: he investigated the murder of Jews during the Kishinev pogrom and addressed a crowd of *pogromshchiks* in his native Poltava in 1905, thus preventing a pogrom solely through his powers of persuasion.[32] He wrote about the Glusker Case in 1910 and used all his rhetorical talents in the numerous articles he wrote as a journalist to defend Beilis. It was Korolenko who, in his sketch "Dom No 13" ("House No. 13"), described the results of his personal investigation of the streets in Kishinev where one of the bloodiest pogroms took place. Korolenko exposed unspeakable acts of cruelty by the *pogromshchiks* toward Jews, describing in gruesome detail the acts of physical abuse, beatings, and torture. In his later article "O pogromnykh delakh" ("What Happened in the Pogroms" [1908]) Korolenko described with journalistic precision the history of physical abuse that Jews suffered during the pogroms, including horrific scenes of nails beaten into the heads of the Jews, skulls crushed, and eyes plucked out. Korolenko was thus one of the first Russian writers to depict the scenes of physical violence against the Jewish population during such pogroms. When Glusker was later convicted of murder, Korolenko followed the trial with great attention. In his article "Cherty voennogo pravosudiia" ("The Features of Military Justice" [1910]) he maintained that the accusations leveled against Glusker were based on anti-Jewish prejudice.[33] The fact that the family had been killed sadistically was used as evidence against Glusker, and although Glusker had a perfect alibi he was nevertheless sentenced to death.

Of particular relevance here is that the details of the real-life murder scene bear an astonishing resemblance to Shevtsov's representation of the sadistic murder of Goltser's mother in his novel: inner organs were scattered around the room and the walls were covered with pieces of human brain. Korolenko shows the very logic of the strategy used by the jury against Glusker: whereas it was known that *pogromshchiks* and "Jew-haters" (*"zhidonenavistniki"* [538]) killed their Jewish victims in this particular way, the jury in the case applied this to Glusker, maintaining that as a Jew he was able to do likewise.

Shevtsov's tactics appear to be similar to those of the tsarist court against Glusker. He bases his whole case in the novel on the notion of Jewish sadism, and the details of the murder and the disfigurement of the corpse virtually repeat the descriptions of the Jewish victims, whether from the Glusker case, from the accounts of the victims of anti-Jewish violence in Korolenko's writings, or from Babel's famous stories in *Red Cavalry*. The corpse of a woman with her stomach cut open strikes any reasonably well read person as a scene taken straight out of Babel. Shevtsov's strategy is thus akin to that of the Russian patriots, exposed by Korolenko in his articles for manifesting their patriotic feelings toward Russia by attacking Jews. But in his novel Shevtsov inverts the role of victims and villains in opposition between the Jews and the Russians.

Korolenko has been revered in the Soviet Union mainly as a writer with left-wing leanings, a member of the Russian populists' circle who was persecuted by the tsarist government and exiled to Siberia. Writers such as Shevtsov and Kychko would have had no problem in accessing Korolenko's work — his collected works, including some of his work on Jews, were published in 1955 — and the reworking of material by substituting roles was as a common device, as can be seen in the way Kychko, in *Judaism Unvarnished,* used Korolenko's work. He refers to Korolenko's famous tale "*Sudnyi Den'* (*Yom Kippur: The Day of Atonement*) — a charming story that Korolenko subtitled "A Ukrainian Fairytale" and dedicated to the eradication of hatred between Ukrainians and Jews. The story is based on the Ukrainian belief that during Yom Kippur a sinful Jew is taken away by the Jewish devil, Khapun. In Korolenko's story Khapun ends up taking away a Ukrainian peasant because he, rather than the Jew whom the peasant accuses, is guilty of a number of moral transgressions.[34] Kychko mentions Korolenko's story as an ethnographic text that illustrates the absurdity of Jewish superstitions, thus distorting its meaning: the opposition between the victim and the villain has been inverted and Jews have become the villains.

There is additional importance to the fact that Shevtsov's book was published by the publishing house Voenizdat, which also published material for the army. Korolenko's article in which he addressed the Glusker Case was directed against the Russian military court, which was responsible for passing an incorrect verdict on Glusker. A Russian patriot like Shevtsov could not have failed to notice that the honor of the Russian Army had been undermined. As his political and religious affiliations in post-Soviet Russia in the 2000s reveal, Shevtsov is a proud heir to the tradition of the former Russian Empire. In his novel of 1970, Shevtsov shows Goltser not only as a sadist, but also as an enemy of the state and the Russian people. Not only does he contribute to the destruction of the Russian nation by trading hard drugs, but he is also involved in the dissemination of Zionist material that he receives from foreign agents who come to Moscow. He has applied for a visa and plans to make a trip abroad, with the implication that this trip is intended as an escape not only from prosecution for the sadistic murders he had committed but also from political crimes in which he is implicated. He is intercepted in time by, predictably, the author's alter ego, Iasenev.

Shevtsov's preoccupation with the theme of the danger of "exotic" men betrays an important psychological component of xenophobia: his fear of the sexed Other suggests the sexual insecurity of a man who both loathes and envies the ethnic Other. The preservation of the purity of the Russian woman's body from dark men suggests not only a fear of racial contamination, but also basic sexual anxieties. In this way it is Kychko, Shevtsov, and other writers and personalities to be analyzed in the following chapters, who show that they are driven by basic instincts to no less a degree than their invented protagonists onto whom they project their basic libidinal instincts.

The representation of the sadistic Jew in these two works written during the anti-Zionist campaign demonstrates that this construct extends beyond the confines of the chronology of the campaign itself. The theme of Zionism is a smokescreen behind which the racist essence of the construct of the sadistic Jew is smuggled in. The authors establish a long line of hereditary relationships between Biblical characters and contemporary Jews, and between Trotsky and Jewish men in Moscow in the 1960s and 1970s. Although the Arab-Israeli conflict served as an obvious pretext for resurrecting the typology of the pathologically sadistic Jew, this construct did not go away with the end of that era. Indeed it resurfaced with renewed force in the last years of the Soviet Union and in post-Soviet Russia, when it no longer has to be presented within the context of Zionism. With the removal of censorship in the mid-1980s, the involvement of Jews in the Bolshevik Revolution was acknowledged. This inspired attacks on Jewish revolutionaries who were accused of special sadism toward the Russian people. Trotsky, who was mentioned in passing in Shevtsov's novel, has, since Glasnost times, become an incarnation of this particularly Jewish brand of pathological sadism.[35]

It will be seen from the material analyzed in the following chapters that the construct of the sadistic, bloodthirsty Jew has remained stable despite political changes in Russia, and that, in fact, it becomes more acute, and is evoked more often, during times of instability by those who want to blame political and economic chaos on the Jews.

Notes

[1]   I. Nikitina Il'e Erenburgu. July 27, 1962. Ed. Mordekhai Altshuler et. al. *Sovetskie evrei pishut Il'e Erenburgu, 1943–1966*. Jerusalem: The Centre for Research and Documentation of East-European Jewry. The Hebrew University of Jerusalem. 1993. 431– 435. 431.

[2]   Jakub Blum and Vera Rich. *The Image of the Jew in Soviet Literature: The Post-Stalin Period*. London: Institute for Jewish Affairs. 1984.

[3]   See Ed. Zvi Gitelman. *Bitter Legacy: Confronting the Holocaust in the USSR*. Bloomington: Indiana University Press. 1997. John Klier. Outline of Jewish-Russian History Part II: 1954– 2001. Ed. Maxim Shraeyer *An Anthology of Jewish-Russian Literature*. Vol. 2: 1953–2001. Armonk NY: M. E. Sharpe. 2007. 1199–1206.

[4]   Arlen Blum. *Evreiskii vopros pod sovetskoi tsenzuroi. 1917–1991*. St. Petersburg: Peterburgskii evreiskii universitet. 1996.

[5]   Vladlen Izmozik. Jews in 19th and 20th Century Russian History Textbooks. *Jews in Eastern Europe*. No. 38. Spring and Fall. 1999. 45–73.

[6]   The following items reflect only a small fraction of special propaganda material that continued to be published well into the 1980s: *Yurii Ivanov. Ostorozhno, sionizm! Ocherki po ideologii, organizatsii i praktike sionizma*. Moscow: Politizdat. 1969; *Sionizm-otravlennoe oruzhie imperializma. Dokumenty i materially*. [sbornik] Moscow: Politizdat. 1970; N. Nikitin. Vskormlennye iadom sionizma. *Krasnaia zvezda*. May 23. 1970; L. A. Korneev. *Sionizm — vrag mira i progressa: Material v pomoshch lektoru*. Moscow: Znanie. 1978; Ed. T. A. Karasova. *Sionizm v sisteme imperializma: ocherki istorii i sovremennost'*. Moscow: Nauka. 1988.

[7]   I use this book as an example of Soviet discourse although the book was written in Ukrainian. The title of the book and the name of the author are printed in Russian (Kichko) and Ukrainian (Kychko). Another English translation used for this book is *Judaism Without Embellishment*. T. K. Kychko. *Iudaizm bez prikras*. (In Ukrainian). Kiev: Vidavnitstvo Akademii nauk USSR. 1963.

[8]   On the reception of this book by the various organizations in the West see Isi Leibler. *Soviet Jewry and Human Rights*. A Human Rights Research Publication. 10/6. Melbourne: Human Rights Publications. 1965.

[9]   See Arlen Blum. Op. cit.

[10]   For an explanation of why the Soviet media stopped writing or speaking about Jews during Stalin's pact with Hitler see *Russian Jewry 1917–1967* Ed. Gregor Aronson, Jacob Frumkin et. al. New York. 1969.

[11]   See, for example, L. A. Modzhorian. *Sionizm kak forma rasizma i rasovoi diskriminatsii*. Moscow: Mezhdunarodnye otnosheniia. 1979.

[12]   Alice Nakhimovsky. Review on Jakub Blum and Vera Rich. *The Image of the Jew in Soviet Literature: The Post-Stalin Period*. *Russian Review*. Vol. 45. No. 4. 1986. 437–438.

[13] Ivan Shevtsov. *Liubov' i nenavist'*. Moscow: Voennoe izd-vo Ministerstva oborony SSSR. 1970.

[14] For a political context of antisemitism of this era see Yaacov Ro'i. *The Struggle for the Soviet Jewish Emigration, 1948–1967*. Cambridge UK: Cambridge University Press. 1991.

[15] The name of the artist who drew the illustrations is M. O. Savchenko.

[16] Quoted in Arlen Blum. Op. cit. 132.

[17] See Arlen Blum. Op. cit.

[18] In 1960s' medical literature these statistics were available in Western sources. See Jean Aitken-Sawn and D. Baird. Circumcision and the cancer of the cervix. *British Journal of Cancer*. Vol. 19. No. 2. 1965. 217–226.

[19] Kychko refers to this book: A. Kh. Levin i Chervakov, V. Kh. *Abrazan'e u asviatlen'ni navukovai ekspertizy*. Minsk. 1932.

[20] V. I. Binshtok and S. A. Novosel'skii. Evrei v Leningrade 1900–1924 gg. *Voprosy biologii i patologii evreev*. Eds. V. I. Binshtok, A. M. Bramson, M. M. Gran, G. I. Dembo. Leningrad: Prakticheskaia meditsina. 1926. 30–64.

[21] Yitzhak M. Brudny. *Reinventing Russia: Russian Nationalism and the Soviet State, 1953–1991*. Cambridge, MA: Harvard University Press. 2000.

[22] Ivan Shevtsov. *Vo imia otsa i syna*. Moscow: Moskovskii rabochii. 1970.

[23] See "An Anti-semitic Novel by Juri Kolesnikov in 'Oktiabr'" Radio Liberty dispatch. November 2, 1972. *Open Society Archives*. Accessed February 12, 2008. Reuben Ainsztein. The end of Marxism-Leninism. *New Statement*. London. December 15, 1978. 94–98.

[24] Jakub Blum and Vera Rich. *The Image of the Jew in Soviet Literature: The Post-Stalin Period*. London: Institute for Jewish Affairs. 1984.

[25] Ivan Shevtsov. *V bor'be s D'iavolom*. Moscow: Pravoslavnoe izd-vo Entsiklopediia Russkoi tsivilizatsii. 2003.

[26] Dir. Vladimir Menshov. *Moskva slezam ne verit*. Mosfilm. 1979. 145 min.

[27] D. Dukharev and Yu. Vizbor. "Aleksandra." Tekst pesni. Moskva slezam ne verit. *Cinema for Russian Conversation*. Vol. 1. 2005. 128.

[28] Fedor Dostoevsky called Odessa "the city of the Yids" already in 1878. See his letter of August 29, 1878 quoted in David Goldstein. *Dostoevsky and the Jews*. Austin: University of Texas Press. 1981. 152.

[29] Significantly, the bandits made 13 pricked wounds in Iushchinskii's body to make it look like ritual murder or satanic rites. See A. Tager. *Delo Beilisa i tsarskaia Rossiia*. Moscow: Reprint edition. 1995.

[30] V. V. Rozanov. K prekrashcheniiu ritual'nogo uboia skota. *Sakharna*. Moscow: Respublika. 1998. 307–309.

[31] See Henrietta Mondry [G. Mondri]. *Pisateli-narodniki i evrei*. St. Petersburg: Akademicheskii proekt. 2005.

[32] See Solomon Vermel'. *V. G. Korolenko i evrei. (Vospominaniia, pis'ma)*. Moscow. 1924.

[33] Vladimir Korolenko. O pogromnykh delakh. *Polnoe sobranie sochinenii*. Vol. 9. Petrograd. 1914. 281–297.

[34] Henrietta Mondry. [G. Mondri] *Pisateli-narodniki i evrei*. St. Petersburg: Akademicheskii proekt. 2005.

[35] See Conclusion in this book.

ПЕРША ХІРУРГІЧНА ОПЕРАЦІЯ

Illustration from Kychko's book "The first surgical operation." 1963

І ПОБАЧИВ ХАМ НАГОТУ БАТЬКА СВОГО

Illustration from Kychko's book "Ham saw his father's nakedness." 1963

І ПРОСТЯГ АВРААМ РУКУ СВОЮ

Illustration from Kychko's book "Abraham stretched forth his hand." 1963

ГОСПОДЬ ПОРАЗИВ УСІХ ПЕРВІСТКІВ НА ЗЕМЛІ ЄГИПЕТСЬКІЙ

Illustration from Kychko's book "The Lord slew all the firstborn in the land of Egypt." 1963

В РОКИ ГІТЛЕРІВСЬКОЇ ОКУПАЦІЇ ВЕРХОВОДИ-СІО-
НІСТИ ПРИСЛУЖУВАЛИ ФАШИСТАМ

Illustration from Kychko's book "During the Hitlerites' occupation Zionist
leaders were serving fascists." 1963

Chapter 7

Glasnost and the Uncensored Sexed Body of the Jew

> The castration complex is the deepest root of antisemitism; for even in the nursery little boys hear that a Jew has something cut off his penis — a piece of his penis, they think — and this gives them a right to despise Jews. And there is no stronger unconscious root for the sense of superiority over women.
>
> Sigmund Freud. 1909.[1]

With the advent of the Glasnost reforms the subject of ethnicity gained a particular momentum, becoming one of the dominant themes in public debate. On the wave of this ethnocentricity, which was one of the driving forces behind the disintegration of the former Soviet Union, there returned, in the late 1980s and early 1990s, the theme of Jewish ethnicity. This time both Jewish and non-Jewish authors used the softening of state censorship and its subsequent collapse to express their views on all things Jewish, Russian, or any other ethnicity. In line with the fashion of the day for ethnic themes, the ethnic identity of Jews gained momentum and was invariably expressed by Jewish and non-Jewish authors through the Jew's ethnic body, physical appearance, dress, language, and speech.

This chapter looks at the modification of the peculiar and paradoxical construct of the male Jew's body as a carnal Jew, a Jew whose materiality is expressed in his libidinal drive and lust, both of which invariably lead to corruption. This construct is intrinsically linked to the new post-censorship discourse in Russia that arrived with the reforms of Glasnost. This period was characterized by an increase in expressions of formerly forbidden material, including such topics as sexuality, criminal pathologies — such as sadism — of various kinds, ethnic differences, and family crime. Art and the media responded to, and often exploited, the public's demand for such material, and the market was flooded with semi-pornographic and hard pornographic material depicting devious and criminal behavior. This new art was dubbed *pornukha* and *chernukha* — pornography and dark perversion (*chernyi* refers to the color black) — and included murder, sadistic sex, and every form of pathologic expression of basic instincts.[2] It is under these discursive circumstances that the image of the Jew's body receives its construction, reconstruction and, in line with the culture's newly discovered taste for postmodernism, deconstruction. The construct of the Jew's body is a combination of heightened sexual instinct and lust for Russian women and money.[3] All these instincts find their freedom of expression in the conditions of the Perestroika period, when the government relaxed its controls and Soviet society was imbued with a new sense of anarchy. With a special word coined to characterize this new state — *bespredel,* or a state of things with no limits or bounds — the image of the Jew's body underwent similar reconfigurations. The sexuality and lust of Jews was seen to be limitless; their instinctive greed was deemed to be without boundaries. The Jew thus became the living incarnation of the concept of *bespredel* itself.

Admittedly, the essence of this construct had already existed in fin-de-siècle culture and had found its expression in the work of Vasily Rozanov. It also appeared, as was shown earlier, in the post-Stalin Russia of the 1950s and later in the 1970s, resurfacing again during the Perestroika years and continuing into the present. But never did it receive such overt and explicit expression as it did during the Perestroika years and in post-Soviet Russia. If Ivanov's novel *The Yellow Metal* was taken out of circulation because it contained gross images of ethnic Others, then in the society since Perestroika there have been no such controls imposed, and the proliferation of representations of the grotesque body of the ethnic Other — the Jew, Chechen or other Kavkazets (a person from the Caucasus) — has become unstoppable.[4]

Previously in Soviet culture the construct of a carnal Jewish male hungry for love of Russian women existed both as a vivid image and as a silent phantom. It existed even when it was not part of the official discourse, during the time in which so-called deracinated Jews were appearing on the pages of Russian literature in a form that rendered them indistinguishable from other Soviet people.[5] What is of interest to this investigation, however, is the paradoxical situation in which Jews were not verbally identified as Jews yet were nevertheless, as seen in the previous chapter, recognized by the audience as Jews due to features which, while not verbally articulated as "Jewish" or "Muslim," signified a group that was vaguely Jewish or non-Slavic. Into this latter category fell "people of Caucasian nationality" ("*liudi kavkazskoi natsional'nosti*") — a lexical formation parallel with "people of Jewish nationality" ("*liudi evreiskoi natsional'nosti*") whose darker complexion and dark hair made them a part of a vague group of racial Others with definite moral and economic characteristics, including professions and occupations that earned them considerable money. The cult film *Ivan Vasilievich meniaet professiu* (*Ivan Vasilievich Changes Profession* [1973]) serves as an example of this "code" that was used to depict Jews and other dark non-Slavs: a dentist, tall, dark, and handsome and living in luxury, has extravagant tastes and, as the mild humor of the comedy implies, probably earns his money by having a few private patients.[6] Never does the film make it explicit to what nationality this person belongs; the viewer, however, will think of him as non-Slavic, as Jewish or Armenian or Georgian or belonging to some other nationality from the Caucasus. Why? Because he is depicted as excessively enterprising, not "straight" enough and, of course, because he is too dark in his coloring to be a Slav. The audience thus learns to receive such signals and, in spite of the official culture's perceived attempts to stop sending these signals, the markers survive in society through their circulation in oral culture and their transmission from one generation to another via the microcultures of families and communities. As Perestroika and the decade of the 1990s revealed, ethnic knowledge as a foundation of ethnic identities survived among Jews and other non-Russian nationalities, despite official efforts to erase it. Indeed, antisemitic stereotypes are a part of the larger construct of Otherness against which the Russian Self identifies itself as a monolithic ethnic collective. Russianness thus defined becomes a major feature of Russian nationalist assertiveness in post-Soviet Russia.

This chapter demonstrates the stereotypes of the carnal and material Jew through the examples of a novel and a film: Vasily Belov's novel *Vse vperedi (The Best is Yet to Come* [1987]) and Leonid Gorovetz's film *Ladies' Tailor* (1990).[7] The author of the novel is an ethnic Russian of nationalist orientation, and the director of the film is an ethnic Jew. The novel contains the most explicit attacks on Jewish males by depicting their sexuality as a danger to the very core of Russian society. Gorovetz's film can be regarded as an example of how a Jewish author uses the newly acquired freedom of Glasnost to deal with the alterity of Jews in the dominant cultural discourse. It will be argued that the film represents a Jewish view of Jewish corporeality. Intended to counter antisemitic stereotypes, it attempts to rework these stereotypes by displacing evaluative signs and challenging the dominant culture's binary archetype which privileges spirit over body. But in spite of its attempts to challenge a number of political stereotypes, including those linked to the Jewish character, this film unexpectedly reveals views on Jewish corporeality that confirm the construct of Jews as a people who are associated with distinctive attitudes toward the sexed body. It is these themes that will be the focus of this chapter's investigation.

The Jewish Male as Destroyer of the Russian Family: Vasily Belov's Novel *Vse vperedi*

Belov's novel *The Best is Yet to Come* was the first open outburst against Jews and Judaism to appear in the Soviet Union as a result of the softening of the policy of censorship as part of the Glasnost reforms. The novel was published one year after the Chernobyl disaster of 1986, at a time when the Soviet government and the public were in a state of panic that both triggered the reforms and prompted the Soviet people to start unleashing their hidden fears and frustrations. Before Glasnost Belov had been known to readers as a writer of village prose affiliation — a group of writers that promoted nativist Russian values and endorsed the inborn qualities of simple rural Russian people.[8] Their writing disseminated the rising sentiments of Russian nationalism, and the authorities' approval of this ideological dissemination can be seen as silent support for growing Russian self-assertiveness following the years of Brezhnevite "stagnation" during the 1970s and 1980s. *The Best is Yet to Come,* however, exceeded all the norms of expression of Russian nationalism, effectively launching a new era in the expression of racial hatred and anti-Jewish sentiments in Russian discourse during the time of the collapse of the Soviet Union.[9]

The novel has a definite and well-defined theme devoted to the topic of the disintegration of the Russian family. In interviews Belov has expressed his concern surrounding issues linked to rising divorce rates, alcoholism, infidelity in marriage and the traumatic effect of divorce on children. These issues, he explained, have a considerable impact on the demographic situation in Soviet society which is marked by low birth rates.[10] This demographic crisis facing the Russian population has escalated since the Glasnost period and continues to be a feature of Russian society today. Belov chose to deal with this issue through the introduction of a racial theme: he identifies the enemy as a Jew. The Jew thus becomes an agent of modernity with new weapons of destruction from the West: drugs, sex, consumerism and indulgence in luxury.

The Best is Yet to Come is divided into two parts, each relating the events in the lives of the protagonists a decade apart. The narrative describes the disintegration of the families of the Moscow intelligentsia: in one case because of the sexual promiscuity and alcoholism of a woman; in the other because another woman, left on her own after her husband is imprisoned for causing an accident at work, goes on to marry a Jewish man, an old school friend, who is depicted as a manipulative and devious character.[11] In fact, it is alleged that this Jewish man is also responsible for the moral decline of the alcoholic woman. To add to the piquancy of the situation, the two women are old friends. The novel opens with a highly emblematic scene: the main female protagonist, Liuba Medvedeva, and the Jewish man, Misha Brish, depart for Paris from Moscow's international airport with a group of Russian tourists. And indeed, what can be more emblematic for a Russian Jew in the 1970s than to be associated with a trip to the West? With Jewish immigration to Israel as a subtext, the theme of a departure abroad functions as a marker of Jews as aliens on Russian soil. During their stay in France Misha courts Liuba, who had chosen to marry the Russian man Medvedev a few years earlier because Medvedev, then a promising scientist with good career opportunities, had better prospects than Misha. With her lily-white skin and supple body Liuba is described as seductive in her Russian beauty, and she enjoys the admiring glances of men.

On their return to Russia Misha, who is also a scientist, pursues a successful career while Liuba's husband, Medvedev, not only loses his job but gets imprisoned for not preventing an accident in which one of his workers is killed. At this point, in the second part of the novel, Misha becomes implicated in framing Medvedev in order to gain access to his family: the wife Liuba and the two children, a girl and a boy. Whereas in Part One Belov follows the established code in representing Misha and his two Jewish male friends in Paris as "deracinated" Jews (nothing in their appearance can be read as markers of their ethnicity), in Part Two he uses all the verbal and rhetorical repertory that identifies Misha as a Jew: words such as Jewish, Judaism and antisemitism are all introduced, albeit toward the end of the novel. If in Part One the reader can identify Jewish characters by such codes as "coming from Odessa" and by their quasi-Jewish names and surnames, then in Part Two the Jewish theme becomes the subject of open polemics. The stark contrast between these two parts can be interpreted as Belov's strategy of identifying the political change that has occurred in Soviet society in the intervening ten years, switching as he does from the Aesopian language of Brezhnevite discourse during the years of political stagnation to the new "openness" of the Glasnost period. And in the arena of sexuality and race he takes full advantage of this new openness.

Belov makes it quite clear why the Russian Liuba fell in love with Misha: he is shown to be a good provider who offers stability to her family and takes good care of her and her children. But Belov presents Misha's interest in Medvedev's family as a conspiracy. Misha is accused of "stealing" the family from Medvedev, of taking from this Russian man what is lawfully his. Medvedev's surname is emblematic of Russia — *medved'* is a bear in Russian, an archetype of Russia and the Russian male. A taboo animal in Russian folk beliefs, one of the two roots of this noun — *ved'* — stems from the Indo-European *veda*.[12] Medvedev is thus presented as Vedic, whereas Misha Brish, on the other hand, is presented as the quintessential Jew "with eyes in which through the tearful muddiness gleamed centuries-old anguish" (216). On this level the struggle between Misha Brish and Medvedev over the rights of Medvedev's family becomes emblematic of the struggle over Russia and its future.[13]

So important is it for Misha to take possession of Medvedev's family that he makes sure that when Medvedev comes out of prison, he is not allowed to see his children. He submits reports falsely exposing Medvedev as a drug addict and a churchgoer — a grave offense in the atheist state. Medvedev himself is not aware of this until he is informed of Misha's conniving by his friend, who carries the all–Russian surname of Ivanov. Of special significance is that this Ivanov is a professional psychiatrist who makes it his duty to investigate by private means the actions of Misha. It is thus implied that only a psychiatrist is able to unveil successfully the workings of the Jewish mind.

There are hints in this novel of Misha Brish's alternative sexual orientation. In France Misha is shown to be in the company of two other Jewish men with whom he is in some sort of secret relationship, probably of a sexual nature. When Belov describes Misha's bachelor apartment in Part One he introduces an element of ambiguity about Misha's sexuality: his apartment is extremely neat, as if it was cared for by a woman. When he screams, "his voice becomes like that of a woman" (328). In this light Misha's courting and seduction of Liuba suggests that he might have been using her as a smokescreen in order to openly express his bisexuality. Misha's acts can be interpreted as those of a secret homosexual in the Soviet Union, at a time when homosexuality was considered to be a criminal offence and homosexuals had to conceal their orientation. One way to create such a smokescreen was in fact to get married, in order to conduct homosexual liaisons in secret.[14] From this perspective Jewish males are exposed not only as sexual perverts, but also as devious and treacherous individuals who use the Russian family to conceal their sexual perversion. By being married to a Russian woman, Misha Brish can emerge as a bisexual male as there is no doubt that his wife is having a sexual relationship with him. This bisexuality stands as evidence of the treachery of the Jewish character, a theme frequently articulated in the writing of Vasily Rozanov. As was shown earlier, Rozanov maintained that "Jews seduce Russians" with the distinctive qualities of the "bisexual human being." The ultimate aim of such seduction was the final appropriation of the Russian state. Rozanov exhibited these paranoid tendencies before the Bolshevik Revolution, during a time of great upheaval, when he equated the end of the Russian state with the end of the anthropological formation of the Russian people. Belov's novel exhibits similar paranoid anxieties and his conspiracy theory uses a similar plot: Misha Brish gives his surname to Medvedev's children, thus figuratively "Judaizing" them. The ambivalence of Brish's masculinity makes it possible to presume that he cannot inseminate Russian women in order to produce Jewish progeny, so he has to appropriate another man's Russian children by giving them his surname.

The themes of sexuality, procreation and the future of Russia are the subjects of an angry exchange of accusations in the final dialogue between Ivanov and Misha Brish at the end of the novel. Belov's Jewish protagonist predicts the "extinction" (317) of the Russian nation, an annihilation resulting from endemic alcoholism and the fact that "Russian women refuse to give birth" (317). (Medvedev significantly is opposed to abortion and birth control.) Brish mocks Russian men's national brand of machismo — "*udal*" (216) — as a dubious virtue because of its militaristic character. Brish explains that the Jewish emigration from the Soviet Union is a result of this militarist aggression, with Belov possibly implying that Jews ran away from military service at the time of the war in Afghanistan. Ivanov predicts Misha's own departure to the West and, to complete the image of a Jewish male as an unprincipled traitor, he predicts that he will eventually settle in Munich or America. The implications of this scenario are that, having destroyed the Russian family, the Jew will leave it behind because it is no longer of any use to him. But he has already done his damage by demoralizing Russian women with his ideals of consumerism, materialism and sexual "contamination." As such these "debauched" women will not give birth to healthy children. This scenario remains undeveloped in the novel, although a quarrel between Misha and Liuba suggests that he is ready to walk out on her and leave the country that he now finds very irritating. Ivanov suggests a different scenario, one based on his private investigation of Misha's actions. Misha has allegedly been indoctrinated by anti-Soviet propaganda and so has been making plans to immigrate to the West. Ivanov believes that he will leave with what is now his family, which is by now quasi-Judaized but

Russian in origin. It is this scenario that Ivanov presents to Medvedev and to which he invites him to object. The implication of this development is that Russia does hold the potential for an inspired new generation: the children of the scientific genius Medvedev will inherit his genes and are, therefore, guaranteed to be intelligent and gifted. Yet Jews (Brish) are set to deprive Russia of this future: at the time of this nation's demographic crisis Brish steals what is most dear to it — its children and, ultimately, its future. A Jew thus finds a way to destroy the Russian people by taking away their children.

In this respect it is highly significant that in a dialogue with Medvedev Ivanov speaks of the "degeneration" (203) of the Russian nation as a result of alcoholism. This national degeneration is presented as desirable by American politicians, who see it as a sign of the end of the political struggle between the West and communist Russia. In a particularly grotesque statement Ivanov suggests that American presidents Johnson, Nixon and Kennedy forbade American journalists from writing about alcoholism in the Soviet Union out of a conspiratorial strategy to let Russians die out in a natural way instead of wasting a hydrogen bomb on them! Belov centers his political message around the issues of body politics. His Russian heroes express open disgust at lesbians and homosexuals, divorce, abortion, birth control and even erotic gratification for women. In this context Jews, as agents of change and setters of "Western" trends, take an active part in the destruction of the fabric of the Russian nation. Belov's Russian heroes expressly admire the Russian patriarchal *Domostroi* rules — a set of rules of family conduct dating back to the sixteenth century. The battle is thus fought around the sphere of sexuality and procreation.

Belov deals with the topic of religion in a highly provocative manner, defining differences between monotheistic religions based on racial and ethnic criteria. The book contains blatant racial statements such as, "Islam, for instance, even if it does not force its followers to kill infidels certainly encourages the killings. Not to mention Judaism..." (189). The telling use of "..." can mean anything an antisemite wants to assume. Most importantly, however, it reiterates the notion of the distinctive sadistic nature of Jews and Judaism which has never left the unofficial culture: Kychko's book, discussed earlier is the most vivid illustration of this phenomenon. For a defender of Russian values such as Belov it is important to defend Russian Orthodox Christianity, and in order to define the Russian collective Self he has to juxtapose it to Judaism, the religion out of which Christianity developed. To do so, Ivanov suggests that Christ was not ethnically Jewish, thus implying that Judaism is a religion of the Jews, whereas Christianity is a religion belonging to Russians through their appropriation of the Christ figure as Russian. This took place in the history of Russian Orthodox culture and was most vividly expressed in the faith of peasants who viewed Christ as Russian. The belief found its reflection in various apocryphal materials.[15] Arguments about the Aryan origins of Christ were disseminated in nineteenth-century European discourses on race and religion and culminated in a work by the historian Houston Stuart Chamberlain, who was a member of the influential antisemitic Bayreuth circle.[16] His piece on the Aryan origins of Christ was translated into Russian as *Iavlenie Khrista* (1906) and Rozanov immediately responded to it by publishing two review articles in which he supported the idea that Jesus Christ was not a Semite.[17] As at the end of the nineteenth century, late twentieth-century Russian discourse deliberately conflated the subject of Judaism and Christianity with the subject of ethnic Jewishness and ethnic Russianness. Christ's body was denied Jewish origins, and the body of the contemporary Jew was denied genealogy with Christ. It is clear that such notions about the non-Jewish origins of Christ still remain of paramount importance in Russian thought of this time. With the rise of racist antisemitism, this idea has not only maintained its relevance, but has also been valorized by Russian nationalists.

The presentation of Judaism as a tribal religion is a strategy that allows the separation of Christianity and Judaism while at the same time presenting Jews as a race apart. Brish is often described in a manner in keeping with the latter, which transforms him into a symbolic figure: the eternal wandering Jew, Agasferus, physically marked by such telling signs as his eyes with their "centuries-old" anguish. When Brish falls into a state of rage he is described as being possessed by "a force which is higher than himself" (229). Belov uses the term *"korezhit"* (229) for this fit, meaning to act as if possessed by evil powers, thus implying that the Jew's body is driven by supernatural, or supranatural, forces. This description underscores the subtext of Jewish genealogy as linked to primordial times, and exposes Brish as a creature controlled by the call of instinct. It also implies the pathological nature of a Jew's body, as the term *"korezhit"* in Russian folk culture is applied to the fits of those possessed, usually women *klikushi* who go into convulsions and scream out obscenities, and who are considered to be both mad and touched by the Devil.[17] The Jewish male's body is pathologized through his race, and it is also gendered, thus forming a cluster of prejudices in which race and gender merge.

Medvedev describes Brish as "the one who is ahead" of the others ("*idushchii vperedi*," 193) — hence the link with the novel's title, as "ahead" and "in front" are denoted by the same word in Russian. By using the

Hegelian notion of the triad of thesis, antithesis and synthesis, Medvedev alleges that Misha always rides the "horse" of synthesis. He concludes this clumsy attempt at philosophizing with the image of Misha "riding the third horse" (193), where the third horse is evidently a metaphor for synthesis. When this synthesis becomes a new thesis, Misha changes the horse for a new one, representing yet another new synthesis. The endlessness of this quasi-Hegelian dialectics implies the invincibility of the Brish line, with the image of a Jew riding a horse evoking apocalyptic connotations.[19] In the conversations between Ivanov and Medvedev about eternal evil, Brish becomes an incarnation of evil.

The novel ends with a powerful dialogue between the two Russian men: Ivanov and Medvedev, with Ivanov insisting that Medvedev has to fight Brish and reclaim his children. He also has to make sure that their original surname, Medvedev, is restored. Ivanov calls on Medvedev to abandon his Russian tendency for passivity and suffering, and to fight for his rights over his family. Whereas the likes of Medvedev are presented as passive and forgiving in their Russian way, the likes of Brish "appropriate" and "steal their families"(182), and "take the surnames away from the children" (236) of the Medvedevs. The implication of the act of taking another's surname is encoded in the suggestion that Russian children would be converted into "Jewishness" by means of the new name — as we have seen, Brish makes sure that the children have his surname instead of Medvedev's. Russian children thus become quasi-Jewish children. In this way, the spheres of sexuality and the family are played out in the novel as an anthropological symbol for the importance of preservation against contamination by foreign blood and semen.[20] Belov's message is clear: a Jew's body should not invade the purity of the Russian body.

There is an overt reference to the determinism of Jewish behavior in the society of the country of residence. Toward the end of the novel, when Ivanov discloses Brish's plans to leave Russia, he states that it is not in the power of the Russian community to change Brish. The lexis used is symptomatic: "*Nam ego ne perekolpachit*'" ("We cannot change him" [237]). The word for change, "*perekolpachit*'" is jargon based on the word "*kolpachit*'" meaning to fool somebody. It is implied that Brish has been duped by Western propaganda and that the Russian collective is powerless to reform him. The morphological structure of the *pere-kolpachit*' is identical to the morphology of the *pere-kovat*' (or *pere-delat*') — a term used in the 1930s Stalinist narrative for changing individuals. The prefix "*pere-*" in English is "*re-*" as in "to remake," and in an earlier chapter we saw the optimism behind the state's efforts to reforge the biological nature of the individual as a result of the influence of the social collective. In the case of Rottenberg, Zoshchenko vouchsafed his successful reforging with one significant proviso: as long as Rottenberg stayed in the Soviet Union the experiment was going to be successful. Belov's novel concludes that the Jew's nature cannot be changed. Despite the influence of the Soviet collective, the Jew wants to escape the borders of the country to join a society more suited to his nature. In this way Belov's 1980s script of a Jew's body is based on a phylogenetic argument, and it renders ontogenetic matters superfluous in application to Jews.

In spite of its outrageous anti-Jewish accusations, the novel enjoyed not only republication but also translation into English and publication by the Russian publishing house *Raduga,* specializing in translations.[21] This indicates that the state found funding for this venture, which in turn could be explained by the fact that the novel's rhetoric and pathos had supporters in the high echelons of power in the Soviet Union. Unlike Ivanov's novel *The Yellow Metal,* which was taken out of circulation, or Kychko's book *Judaism Unvarnished,* Belov's novel was not penalized. It was printed in the same number of copies (200,000) as Shevtsov's novel *Love and Hatred.* It thus signaled the arrival of a new era in Russian cultural and political discourse, an era marked by the granting of official status to unofficial subculture. Like Shevtsov's book of the 1970s, Belov's book marked a new period of Russian self-assertiveness. Anti-Jewishness did not have to masquerade any longer as anti-Zionism. In spite of its poor literary qualities, Belov's novel was paradoxically the first marker of this newly acquired freedom to express Russian self-assertiveness and define the Russian Self against the eternal Other, the Jew. The fact that the book was translated into English signified that the challenge it would present to the international community was well calculated, and that the proponents of the new Russian assertiveness did not have to pretend any longer that the opinion of the world community mattered.[22]

Jewish Corporeality in the Film *Ladies' Tailor*

This film is dedicated to the mass slaughter of Jews at Babi Yar in the autumn of 1941, and was the first major production in this genre to retrieve this previously silenced event in Russian history from the category of "blank spots," a term coined during the Glasnost reforms to denote all those episodes that had been silenced by Soviet censorship. Film as a visual art form puts a major emphasis on corporeality: physical appearances, shape, voice, speech, articulation of sounds and gesticulation. So how does the director deal with the issue of the physical body of the Jew?

At the center of the film is the fate of one small family of Jews in Nazi-occupied Kiev. They are given two days to prepare for relocation by the German occupants and the narrative revolves around how each individual member of the family, and a few episodic characters, react to this alleged relocation — a euphemism for the final departure to a mass grave where an estimated 34,000 Jews were massacred in the autumn of 1941. Amidst the tragic preparations for this "relocation," the protagonists' inner worlds are exposed with the economy of cinematic brevity. Do they understand that the Nazis are lying about the "relocation" of Jews? Do they have premonitions about the trap, and, if yes, then what are these premonitions based on? With the Soviet Government's concealment of information about the Nazi onslaught on Jewry in occupied territories, the Jews of Kiev had no prior confirmed knowledge about the eradication of Jews. For the older, more experienced generation of Jews, represented by the ladies' tailor, the knowledge is intuitive, mystical, built on years of persecution as well as the collective memory of the history of the persecution of the Jews. The daughter, who represents the younger generation, is naïve, as a result of the upbringing and education she has received in the Soviet Union.

The old Jew is played by the veteran actor of Soviet drama and cinematography Innokenty Smoktunovsky (1925–1994), a cult figure who played the roles of major tragic characters such as Dostoevsky's Prince Myshkin in *The Idiot* both on stage and in the film and Hamlet in the 1964 film of that name. Smoktunovsky (born Smoktunovich) also played the roles of Russian aristocrats and members of the intelligentsia in Chekhov's plays. With the distinguished appearance of an elegant and well-bred member of the educated classes, Smoktunovsky was a well-loved and respected actor, representing that much-revered aura of nobility that is in stark contrast to the proletarian demeanor of the majority of actors of the Soviet cinema.[23] Smoktunovsky is ethnically Slavic, of Polish descent, and the film's director choosing him to play the role of the old Jew was an interesting strategy. What was the strategy? On the surface the answer appears to be quite straightforward: enlisting a noble "Russian" actor, a Slav, to play the part of a Jew was an attempt to rehabilitate Jews from their long history of unflattering representation and discrimination.[24] But should not such an attempt at representing a central, serious Jewish character be celebrated by using a Jewish actor to play the Jew? Probably not — most likely the director Gorovetz is trying to convey the message that there is no such thing as a different Jewish physicality, which would imply that there is no such thing as a typical Jewish appearance. In this way the ethnicity of the actor becomes irrelevant. This decision to have a Slav play the part of a Jew can in itself be viewed as a strategy to dismantle stereotypes of the Jew's body, but there are more subtle signals that deal with this theme, many of which only a well-read viewer would recognize. Gorovetz clearly wants not only to appeal to a broad audience but also to convey a different message for his more educated viewer. It is this viewer who would understand the film's subtext. The reader will by now be well informed of such topics and may, therefore, be considered a member of the audience to which Gorovetz addresses his ideas.

The choice of the profession of the main character, the ladies' tailor, is highly symbolic for the film's narrative. As a tailor he is in contact with the human body every day — he celebrates the shape of the female body, he adorns it and covers it, while at the same time knowing all its secrets. The tailor is a widower, clearly still in love with his late wife, and is in frequent mental dialogue with his departed beloved. Her qualities — loyalty to the family, industriousness, lack of vanity, and total commitment to her husband and children — are conveyed through his reminiscences. He lives now with the other women of his family: his daughter, granddaughter, and daughter-in-law. The only other male in the family is a baby boy, his grandson by his son who has been conscripted into the Soviet army. The tailor is in his sixties. He wears a long black suit, he is grey-haired, and his long gray beard delineates the noble appearance of a patriarch. He is something of a philosopher, a man with an intense inner life and certain mystical inclinations. In manner, gesture, intonation, even in the tailor's perfectly grammatically correct speech, Smoktunovsky captures the aura of a wise and pleasant old Jewish man very well.

On the eve of the family's "relocation" to Babi Yar, a Russian family arrives at the tailor's apartment: a woman in her fifties, her pregnant daughter and her son. This situation is awkward: even before the departure of the Jewish family their home has been assigned to a Russian family. This family is from old rich bourgeois stock which once had properties and factories in Kiev before the Soviets took them away. As such, according to Hitler's strategy, they viewed German occupation as a way of getting rid of Soviet power. This motif has another layer of meaning for the Russian audience, as it is reminiscent of the Stalinist purges when informants were often given the apartments of the very same families on whom they informed. An example of such behavior is epitomized in Solzhenitsyn's *The Cancer Ward* in which the Rusanov family writes a false report denouncing their innocent neighbor, only to later move into his apartment. But the Russians in the film are a widow and her family who themselves have been victims of Stalin's rule of terror and Soviet expropriation: the family was well-to-do before the Bolshevik Revolution. Gorovetz chooses not to elaborate on how the Russian family ended up being the new occupants of the Jewish family's apartment. Instead, he draws a parallel between the two people of the older generation — the Jew and the Russian woman of good breeding — through their suffering and unjust persecution. The tailor extends his hospitality to the family and offers his bed to the pregnant daughter of the Russian woman, thus symbolically supporting the coming of a new life while his own and that of his family are going to be taken away.

The tailor expresses an eccentric wish — he offers to cut material for a suit for the Russian woman before his departure, suggesting that somebody else will sew it together, and he happens to have a piece of material of excellent quality suitable for the task. The suit thus becomes a gift offering with a deeply symbolic meaning. The tailor explains that he has never had the opportunity to make a properly fitted suit (in Russian terms an "English" suit) for his wife. His desire to make such a suit for the Russian woman suggests that he perceives her as a desirable substitute for his departed wife. And indeed, the process of taking the measurements of the Russian woman becomes a metaphor for an erotic encounter. The scene is choreographed as a dance, with the Jewish tailor working in circles around the Russian woman. He avoids touching her body as the normal measuring procedure would involve, instead delicately positioning his measuring tape against her almost without physical contact. This scene is one of the most memorable in the film due to its perfect kinesthetic qualities and excellent choreography. The synchronicity of the movements of the two bodies suggests that they are both caught in a state of mutual physical attraction: the man's movements are controlled and calculated, conducted with professional knowledge and experience, and the woman's flashed glimpses of skin suggest that she is in a state of sexual arousal. The "dance" thus becomes a metaphor for a sexual encounter which, at the same time, remains unrealized. Clearly there are obstacles that stand in the way of an actual sexual act between these two individuals, but their age is not one of them. The wrong time and place are among the obvious reasons, as well as racial differences. For these two individuals to be together would mean to live in a society that has overcome the prejudices of both cultures. With the Jewish tailor initiating the act it is implied that Jews extend their hand to Slavs. Keeping the male and female body apart as they dance suggests the Hasidic practice of distance and thus becomes a lesson to the audience about the cultural practices of Judaism in relation to sexual behavior.[25] This distance can also imply not only respect for the woman's body but also the maintenance of the boundaries between the Jewish and Russian body, thus introducing the theme of racial difference inscribed by culture onto the human body.

The sexual connotations of the plot, which involves the manufacture of a garment that covers the human body, were famously explored in Gogol's story *The Overcoat*. If Gogol's hero treats his overcoat as a substitute for a non-existent sexual partner ("*Shinel*'" in Russian is a noun of feminine gender) then, in *Ladies' Tailor*, the fitted suit made of an organic material such as pure wool is a metonym for the tight and warm skin that any human body desires to wrap around itself. The woolen fabric was also used as a metonym for a sexed body in the story about Ivan Shpon'ka. The fact that the Jewish tailor chooses to leave a piece of clothing to survive his death is highly symbolic and indicative of the materiality of memory. Jews are the people of the body but, at the same time, the people of the spirit. Perishing as martyrs, the victims of Babi Yar established a line of continuity between Judaism and Christianity.

This film is set in Ukraine, and the cultural genealogy of the motif of the fetishistic value of a piece of clothing, which can be traced to Gogol, has yet another layer of relevance. There is an aspect of polemics and bitter irony in working with Gogolian themes and poetic devices such as metonymy and metaphor. This irony is linked to Gogol's Ukrainian brand of antisemitism which manifested itself in his presentation of stereotypes of Jews in his stories: Gogol's Jews are victims of pogroms staged by the Cossacks. They are depicted as ridiculous characters and a laughing stock of both the Cossacks and Gogol-the-narrator.[26] The historical event at Babi Yar is a culmination of the pogroms against Jews in Ukraine, and it is significant that the only Nazi collaborator in Gorovetz's film is an ethnic Ukrainian[27] as it is known that the Babi Yar massacre was performed with the help of the local police. With cinematographic brevity, the film shows only one such collaborator. Significantly, Germans shoot him and he dies like a dog on the streets of Kiev, so emblematizing what the Slavic nations preferred to forget in the historical reality of 1990 when the film was made — that, for the Nazis, Slavs were only marginally more acceptable than Jews. With the disintegration of the Soviet Union in 1990–1991, various East European nations turned to Germany for economic aid. The argument often used was blasphemous to the victims of Nazism: it was said that these nations would be better off if they had been "colonized" by Germans rather than by the Soviets.[28]

Gorovetz finds a politically diplomatic solution in dealing with the character of the Nazi collaborator: he makes him an epileptic. In this way he implies that only a clinically damaged person could become a Nazi collaborator, thus exposing antisemitism as an illness. On the level of the subtext he also establishes the literary genealogy of this character with another famous epileptic murderer in Russian literature: Smerdiakov in Dostoevsky's *The Brothers Karamazov*. As with Gogol, the Dostoevskian allusion serves as a reminder of the long-established antisemitic tradition in Russian culture, including Dostoevsky's infamous dislike of Jews. It is in this novel that Dostovesky's favorite hero, Alesha Karamazov, does not defend Jews from slanderous accusations.[29] Such allusions serve both as a reminder and as a warning about the stability and longevity of racial stereotypes in a given culture. As a cultural production Gorovetz's film also reminds its audience of the role that high culture plays in the dissemination of stereotypes that breed hatred and intolerance. Starting their lives on the pages of literature or other texts, in real life such stereotypes can be used to justify genocide — hence Gorovetz's coded call for both artist and art to exercise responsibility.

Gorovetz's film explores the psychological underpinnings of anti-semitism and he chooses the sphere of sexuality to play out this theme. Thus, the Ukrainian collaborator is physically attracted to a Jewish woman — the beautiful daughter of the ladies' tailor. Probably impotent — his wife is childless — the Ukrainian man finds sexual gratification in peeping at the Jewess. Both characters stand as a trope for the inverted binarisms that form the basis of the Jewish stereotype: the Jewish woman is physically strong (significantly she is played by a Jewish actress), but the Ukrainian man is puny. She oozes health but he is sickly: bony, yellow in complexion with receding hair, he is hardly the epitome of the Ukrainian machismo of the Zaporozhian Cossacks. When he propositions the Jewish woman, whose husband is away, she humorously rejects him, so showing that he would not be able to satisfy her physically. This sexual desire of a handsome, healthy Jewish woman for her presumably virile Jewish husband, and not for the puny Christian man, inverts the trope of antisemitism that is based on the idea that a Jewish woman can not be satisfied by her Jewish partner. The possible impotency of the Ukrainian man functions as a reference to the psychology of antisemitism. The reader will recall that Freud identified the fear of castration as the main psychological current feeding the antisemitism of non-Jewish men in Europe.[30] Christian men think that the sexuality of Jewish men is impaired because of their "castrated" penis and, according to Sigmund Freud and Otto Weininger, loathe them in a paradoxical mixture of superiority and fear of becoming like them if castrated.[31] In the film, the man who lusts for a Jewish woman is impotent. He derives satisfaction by verbally abusing her. But while he calls her a *zhidovka*, a *kike,* at the same time he mellows in her presence in a perverted sense of gratification from the abuse. It can be argued that he compensates for his lack of virility and physical strength by transferring those powers to the Germans — in their collective physical abuse of Jewish women they satisfy his personal sadistic fantasies that he himself is too weak to perform. His epileptic fit can be seen as compensation for the sexual act which he would like to perform on a Jewish woman, even if it amounted to rape. The fit can thus be interpreted as a violent act of self-destruction as compensation for — and as a substitute for — an aggressive act which he wants to commit on the Jewish woman but cannot because of his physical disabilities. In the film, the desire for what one cannot have seems to be one of the psychological components of antisemitism.

The sexual aspects of the Jew's body are reflected in a number of scenes in the film. In one particularly striking act a Jewish teenage girl is taking a bath when she has her first period. Her mother, the tailor's daughter, is helping to wash her when she discovers the menstrual blood in the bath. This theme of blood is highly symbolic: the girl takes a bath before going on a "journey" which, as we know, becomes the journey to the Babi Yar massacre. This scene is emblematic of a sexual maturity and potential motherhood which will never be fulfilled. The menstrual blood becomes the powerful symbol of the victimization of Jewish women. The girl's mother's reaction to her daughter's first menstruation suggests a culturally significant event. Speaking in Yiddish she expresses joy at her daughter's sexual maturation, thus emphasizing the celebration of life and procreation.

The link between Jewish cultural practices and sexuality is also conveyed by the way the camera focuses on the Jewish boy's body. It centers on his penis, thus exposing the fact that the boy is not circumcised (his mother is from Lithuania and probably Christian).[32] But the tailor's intense gaze is also often fixed on the naked boy's penis. This prompts the viewer to associate the image of the vulnerable naked baby boy, exposed to the viewer for observation, with the images of the exposed body of Christ in a telling symbol of future crucifixion. It also encourages viewers to consider the Old Testament story of the boy Isaac, who was saved from sacrifice by God but who, if he was living in Europe in the twentieth century, would become a victim of Nazi racist genocide. The penis of a Jewish boy is the locus of the covenant between God and His chosen people, and the bond that ostensibly makes the Jews into a clan is based on "blood" ties. Can a Jew escape his own race? Can a Jew be a Jew without belonging to the clan by "blood"? These questions had a clear answer in Russian intellectual religious thought as articulated by Rozanov, Vladimir Soloviev, and Pavel Florensky. In the case of the little boy, not being Jewish in Halachic law does not prevent him from being considered a Jew in the eyes of Nazi law. And indeed, in the film the baby boy meets his end at Babi Yar with the rest of the Jews, part-Jews and even non-Jews. The boy's Russian nanny, the childless wife of the epileptic collaborator, is emotionally attached to him. She offers to keep the boy in the safety of her house and to return him to the mother after the "relocation," once the family settles down. But she too meets her end at the massacre of Babi Yar, joining the victims through bonds of love that transcend race and ethnicity. As a true Christian, she mystically feels that there is indeed another Christ in the body of the little Jewish boy. The story of the baby boy's naked body thus becomes the story of the eternally resurrected body of the male Jew who comes to this world in order to be massacred by the world. There is no hope for the messiah, Jewish or Christian in this world. For Gorovetz, the Jew and the Christian are synthesized in the image of the Jewish/Christian boy's body.[33]

Ehrenburg's image of the Jew-boy being eternally sacrificed by "Christians" as seen by Julio Jurenito is brought once more to realization in Gorovetz's film. The reader will remember that Ehrenburg did not want his novel about the Jewish tailor Lazik to be published in the Soviet Union after the Shoah because of the danger that his depiction of Lazik would feed into the stereotype of the Jew and also because of the lack of acknowledgment of Jewish victimization. Gorovetz similarly found it possible to make a serious film about a Jewish tailor only after the collapse of the Soviet Union in 1990–1991. He immigrated to Israel in the same year and thus joined the artistic community of the Russian Jewish "Diaspora." The next two chapters will be devoted to the topic of the negotiation of the Jewish body by two important writers: Dina Rubina and Alexander Goldstein, who approach the issue of their Jewish "Diasporic" selves through the concept of Jewish corporeality.

Notes

1   Sigmund Freud. Analysis of a Phobia in a Five-Year-Old Boy. *The Standard Edition of the Complete Psychological Works of Sigmund Freud,* Ed. J. Strachey, trans. J. Strachey with Anna Freud. London: Hogarth Press. 1955–1974. Vol. 10. 5–49. 36.

Chapter 7

2   See Mark Lipovetskii. Rastratnye strategii ili metamorfozy 'chernukhi'. *Novyi mir.* No. 11. 1999. 193–210.

3   See Ed. Dennis Ioffe. *Diskursy telesnosti i erotizma v literature i kul'ture.* Moscow: Ladomir. 2008.

4   See the ongoing discussion on http://www.interkavkaz.info/index.php?showtopic=1293&st=60

5   See Alice Nakhimovsky. Review on Jakub Blum and Vera Rich. *The Image of the Jew in Soviet Literature: The Post-Stalin Period. Russian Review.* Vol. 45. No 4. 1985. 437–438.

6   *Ivan Vasilievich meniaet professiiu.* Dir. Leonid Gaidai. Mosfilm. 1973.

7   Vasilii Belov. *Vse vperedi.* Moscow: Sovetskii pisatel'. 1987. In English: Vassily Belov. *The Best Is Yet To Come.* Trans. by P. O. Gromm. Moscow: Raduga Publishers. 1989. *Damskii portnoi.* Dir. Leonid Gorovetz. 1990.

8   Kathleen Parthé. *The Russian Village Prose: The Radiant Past.* Princeton, NJ: Princeton University Press. 1992.

9   On Russian nationalism in literature and culture from the end of the 1980s to 2006 see Rosalind Marsh. *Literature, History and Identity in Post-Soviet Russia, 1991–2006.* Oxford, Bern: Peter Lang. 2007.

10   See the extracts from the interview that Belov gave before the XXVII Congress of the Communist Party of the Soviet Union on the back of the front page in Vasilii Belov. *Vse vperedi.* Moscow: Sovetskii pisatel'. 1987.

11   For a humorous summary of the novel's plot see Arnold Macmillin. Chekhov and the Soviet Village Prose Writers: Affinities of Fact and Fiction. *Modern Languages Review.* Vol. 93. No. 3. 1998. 754–761.

12   Medved' comprises of two roots: med — honey and ved — to know. Medved' is thus someone who knows where the honey is.

13   For a discussion of the "village prose" writers' nativist ideas see Kathleen Parthé. *Russia's Dangerous Texts: Politics Between The Lines.* New Haven, CT: Yale University Press. 2004.

14   For a short overview of homosexual subculture in Russia see Leslie Feinberg. Roots of Russian "homosexual subculture." *Workers World Newspaper.* July 15, 2004.

15   In high culture it was epitomized in the much-quoted poem by Fyodor Tiutchev, the poet of Slavophile orientation.

16   Houston Stuart Chamberlain. *Foundations of the Nineteenth Century.* Trans. John Lees. Introd. By George L. Mosse. New York: Howard Fertig. 1977.

17   Vasily Rozanov. Byl li Khristos evreem po plemeni? *Okolo narodnoi dushi.* Moscow: Respublika. 2003. 60 –67. V. V. Rozanov. Eshche raz o neevreistve Khrista. *Okolo narodnoi dushi.* Moscow: Respublika. 2003. 68–71.

18   See Christine Worobec. *Possessed: Women, Witches and Demons in Imperial Russia.* De Kalb: Northern Ilinois University Press. 2001 and Henrietta Mondry. *Pure, Strong and Sexless: The Peasant Woman's Body and Gleb Uspensky.* Amsterdam: Rodopi. 2006.

19   This image is widely known in Russia due to its prominence in Bulgakov's novel *Master and Margarita.* See David Bethea. *The Shape of Apocalypse in Modern Russian Fiction.* Princeton: Princeton University Press. 1989.

20   See Mary Douglas. *Purity and Danger. An Analysis of Concepts of Pollution and Taboo.* London: Routledge. 1984.

21   Translator's name is P. O. Gromm.

22   The first Russian edition came out in 1987 with 100,000 copies, the second in 1987 came out with 200 000 copies. The 1989 edition in the English translation came out with 6,350 copies.

23   See Segei Iurskii. *Igra v zhizn'.* Moscow: Vagrius. 2007.

24   Of relevance is the fact that Smoktunovsky played a Jewish character Moisei Moiseevich from Chekhov's story *Steppe* in a film adaptation of this story, *Step'* (1974).

25   Gabriella Safran. Dancing with Death and Salvaging Jewish Culture in *Austeria* and *The Dybbuk. Slavic Review.* Vol. 59. No. 4. 2000. 761–781.

26   Elena Katz. *Nether With Them Nor Without: The Russian Writer and the Jew in the Age of Realism*. Syracuse: Syracuse University Press. 2008.

27   See Judith Deutsch Kornblatt. *Ladies' Tailor* and the End of Soviet Jewry. *Jewish Social Studies*. Vol. 5. No. 3. 1999. 180–195.

28   Rosalind Marsh. *History and Literature in Contemporary Russia*. London: Macmillan. 1995.

29   See David Goldstein. *Dostoevsky and the Jews*. Austin: University of Texas Press. 1981.

30   Sigmund Freud. Analysis of a Phobia in a Five-Year-Old Boy. *The Standard Edition of the Complete Psychological Works of Sigmund Freud*, Ed. J. Strachey, Trans. J. Strachey with Anna Freud. London: Hogarth Press. 1955–74. Vol. 10. 5–49. 36.

31   See Sander Gilman. *Freud, Race and Gender* Princeton: Princeton University Press. 1993 on the link which Sigmund Freud and Otto Weininger made between Christian antisemitism and the Christian male's fear of castration and the belief that circumcision is a form of castration.

32   Judith Deutsch Kornblatt suggests that the uncircumcised child is symbolic of the end of Soviet Jewry. Op. cit.

33   Gorovetz immigrated to Israel shortly after he shot this film. See an interview in *Kino-Glaz*. No. 1. 1994. 20.

Chapter 8

The Repatriated Body: A Russian Jewish Woman Writer in Israel, or the Corporeal Fantasy of Dina Rubina, 1990s to the Present

> "We are willing to accept a Spaniard with the name Jaime [pronounced Haim in Russian], but grimace when pronouncing the word Haim"
> V. Ze'ev Jabotinsky. 1903.[1]

The travel sketches and stories of the highly successful contemporary Russian Jewish émigré writer living in Israel, Dina Rubina (b. 1953) provides an excellent case study of the construction of an alternative corporeal gendered Self.[2] As a Russian language author writing about Jewishness, and as an Israeli author whose books continue to be published in Russia, Rubina is an important cultural phenomenon.[3] What makes her of particular interest, however, is that, since her arrival in Israel, she has increasingly identified Spain as her historic homeland, and the Spanish body as a fantasized corporeal Self.[4] Such acts of re-creation reveal how processes of racial identification and fluidity of identity are informed by stereotypes of the ethnic body as fostered by high and popular culture. An exploration of these processes reveals the diachronic construction of corporeal Self through the intersection of three fundamental states: homeland/Diaspora (Soviet Union, Russia), repatriation/immigration to historic homeland (Israel) and imagined historic homeland/Diaspora (Spain).

This chapter examines the extent to which Rubina's fantasized corporeal Self is informed and influenced by what Edward Said refers to as "textual attitudes" (92), consisting of a vision of the world as seen through the lens of inter-referential texts, as well as by her native experiences as an ethnic Other in the hostile culture of the Soviet Union and in post-Soviet Russia where antisemitic stereotypes of the Jewish body are, as we have already seen, one of the most stable discursive formations.[5] The inter-referential texts that Rubina recycles include both hostile and/or Russian sources as well as congenial and/or foreign texts, including the work of German Jewish novelist Lion Feuchtwanger (1884–1956).[6] An exploration of the motives behind Rubina's invention of an alternative ethnic Self provides an overview of notions of ethnic and racial Otherness, mimicry, introjection and identification,[7] including her reaction to — and acceptance of — the perceived ethnic Jewish body in Israel and the construction of her ethnic and cultural identity as a Russian Jewish woman writer in search of her fantasized corporeal Self. Well aware of which features of the Jew's body were caricatured by hostile cultures, in real life and in fiction, Rubina chose to create an alternative body, one more palatable to the surrounding Russian/ Soviet culture. This involved finding a body with an alternative ethnicity, one whose external, physical characteristics would be more acceptable to a hostile culture. As a young girl in the Soviet Union and as a mature woman in Russia and Israel, Rubina claimed the Spanish body as the one with which she was most comfortable.

Above all, Rubina is a writer, and as such she is linked to Russian and Western writers as an admiring reader and pupil and as their professional peer. Her writings reveal a woman who, in order to become acceptable to herself, had to ensure that her body conformed to the vision of the "Jewess's" body as created by Russian and Western literature and culture.[8] As evident from her sketches, her body is acceptable to her only if it converges with the image created by the literary and artistic imagination and, as writers who created this image are male, it is this body as a male construct that becomes acceptable to the woman writer herself. A Russian Jewess had to become a Spanish (Jewess) in order to play out this fantasy in the flesh.

Rubina's Russian Jewish Self in Israel

Most of Rubina's stories written after her immigration to Israel in 1990 describe her newly discovered community of kin and attest to her astute interest in the racial and ethnic markers of Jewishness. Rubina acknowledges that, since her arrival in Israel, people whom she meets, works with and befriends have become the subjects of her work: Jews have become the material she observes, studies, and distills into refined Russian prose. Jewry thus becomes a site for the expression and self-expression of Rubina's ethnicity and hybridity. A close reading of her work also reveals that she is well aware of various manifestations of prejudice against, and persecution of, Jews in Russia. Her autobiographical narrator makes it clear in numerous stories that her decision to leave for Israel was motivated by antisemitism, as well as by the desire to give herself and her family an opportunity to live in their historical homeland.

Although this opportunity includes the acquisition of the native Hebrew language, Rubina herself continues to write only in Russian, holding such a fine stylist of the Russian language as Anton Chekhov to be her teacher and model.[9] This language preference is a focus of both pride and anxiety. As much as she is in love with the sound and structure of Hebrew, she has not succeeded in learning this language to perfection; she is, she confesses, illiterate in Hebrew, making mistakes in both speaking and writing. This theme of language has connotations specific to the history of the Jewish people, in particular to Russian Jewish writers. As is demonstrated by Sander Gilman, the Jewish accent has been viewed not only as a marker of ethnicity and linguistic limitation, but also as a sign of physical pathology, a manifestation of abnormality in the throat and mouth apparatus.[10] In response to Russian Jewish writers in turn-of-the-century Russia, some literary critics maintained that Jews could not master the Russian language.[11]

Rubina also reveals her understanding of racial difference in the distinction she draws between Jews who come from Islamic countries and those who come mainly from Christian lands as manifested in their differing attitudes to work, with Ashkenazi Jews epitomizing self-discipline and self-control whereas Jews from Islamic lands reveal a more relaxed attitude toward all spheres of life (her narrator makes it clear that a hard-working writer like Rubina herself belongs to the first category, constantly reminding readers that she is used to discipline, and that discipline has become her second nature). She also reveals her assumptions of racial difference as manifested in appearance, with dress and shoes becoming semiotic expressions of disparity. One of Rubina's most memorable descriptions of the Israeli nation is that of a "people who walk around town in house slippers" (24)[12] — this image is anthropologically symbolic as "house slippers" contrast with the tight shoes that constrict the feet, covering a part of the body which, in Eastern and North African cultures, is exhibited for erotic purposes. Uncovered feet are widely considered erotic in Middle Eastern cultures, and tight shoes stand as an emblem of Western civilization's self-discipline and restraint.

Thus it is the Jewish body to which Rubina returns as the primary object of her anthropological project. Her evaluating gaze views this body with all the criteria learned from her home country. The following description of a Jewish body by Rubina's autobiographical persona Zyama in her novella "Vot idet messiia!" ("Here Comes the Messiah!" [1999]) illustrates the extent to which she has internalized the stereotype of Jewish physical features:

He was of small stature, puny, and not just ugly, but exquisitely, cinematically, grotesquely ugly. Judging by what he was wearing, he was more than thirteen years old (thirteen marking one's coming of age): a black frock-coat, black trousers and, most strikingly, a broad-brimmed black hat—the young man was a student at one of those ultra-religious yeshivas.

So then, he was fantastically ugly.

Before her departure from Moscow all the trolley-bus stops in the district where Zyama's family lived had been plastered over with leaflets from some patriotic society. One of the leaflets showed Satan in the guise of a Jewish youth wearing clothes peculiar to the time of the Pale of Settlement... On the leaflet one of the young man's feet, clad in a black boot, was thrust forward, the other one he had furtively put away behind him and — oh horrors! — it was the devil's hairy hoof. The artist had put the principal charge of his passionate and sincere hatred into the way he had depicted a typically Jewish physiognomy as he understood it: long hooked nose, sloping brow, chin cut short, small squinting eyes... in a word, a character from a funny anecdote.

So then, a young man, wearing precisely the same clothes, with precisely the same face — an ugly freak from an antisemitic anecdote — was sitting opposite Zyama on a number 36 Jerusalem bus on the Ramot-City Center route. She even took a quick glance under his seat to see whether he had a hoof or not. She didn't detect a hoof, but a foot wearing an orphanage-style black boot, disproportionately large, squashed like a peasant's bast shoe, which he had crossed over his other foot and was weightily swinging. On his lap lay open a pocket prayer book and the young man was muttering a prayer, his hat rocking in time with the movement of the bus.

This ugly, clownish, puny individual was so filled with calm, all his gestures breathing the virtue of serenity — the movements of someone unfamiliar with humiliation — that at that moment Zyama even felt her heart muscle contract as strongly as if she had been struck. Genuine happiness at the thought that this young man had been born here and was living here. (230–231)

In this description the ambivalence of Rubina's attitude toward the Jewish male body becomes clear: on the one hand, as a sophisticated and well-educated person, she is fully aware of the history of antisemitic stereotypes that build on religious imagery and associations of Jews with the Devil; on the other, she accepts the very concept of typical Jewish features.[13] She thus confirms her belief in the visible physical features of the Jew and betrays her anxiety about this very physicality. Although she is relieved that the boy was born in Israel, thus escaping the aggressive antisemitism of Russia, she nevertheless passes a negative aesthetic judgment on his appearance and lists all the features that in her mind constitute this particular form of Jewish ugliness.

There is, however, an invisible line that divides Rubina's own body from the body of this Jewish boy, based on the implication that her own body does not share his physical characteristics. As encoded in the expression "cinematically ugly" Rubina clearly regards herself as a spectator, the Jew's body as the exhibit. There is thus a separating screen of Otherness between her own body and that of the Jewish boy. From her description of this episode the reader presumes that the narrator herself is not identified as a Jew by the Russian crowd, because she does not have those Jewish features that make the Jew visible. Rubina thus comforts herself with her assumption that her body is not physically marked as that of a Jew, especially a female Jew.

It is evident from Rubina's texts that in Israel she never did find a Jewish subject with whom she would like to identify — not among her expatriates, the Russian Jews with whom she was associated in Russia, not among the European Ashkenazi Jews, and certainly not among those Arab-Jews, the *mizrahi* who, as we learn in her stories, she despises as part of the "house slipper-wearing" nation (24). (She provides the word *mizrahi* with an ethnographic note for her Russian readers: "a derogatory nickname for an Eastern/Asiatic Jew" [23].) Israel, as exotic and as Oriental as it is, somehow did not satisfy Rubina's search for her ethnic roots. Both the country and the society turned out to be too "Levantine" (23) for the Jewish, Russian-speaking writer who had internalized many Jewish stereotypes, both male and female.

And indeed, as fantastic and nonsensical as these stereotypes may be, not all of them are negative — some gendered stereotypes might even appeal to the narcissistic ego of a Jewish woman. Certainly it was often the body of the Jewess which, in the tradition of Walter Scott, Western writers chose as a locus for their erotic masculine fantasies. Among those stereotypes that appeal to the quest for the exotic is the fantasy of the beautiful Jewess, immortalized in Lion Feuchtwanger's famous novel *The Jewess from Toledo* or *A Spanish Ballad* (*Die Judin von Toledo* or *Spanische Ballade* [1955]). This novel tells the story of the love between a Castilian king and a beautiful Jewess — and indeed, it is often in Spain where the tradition of the "textual attitude" in classical literary texts locates beautiful Jewesses.[14] In Russia Vasily Botkin in his well-known travel notes *Letters from Spain* (1857) claimed that Jewesses of Spain were extremely beautiful and that they constituted a different "type" (130*)* from their European counterparts. He stressed their likeness to the "antique statues of Egyptian women" (131).[15] Thus a Jewess can be beautiful by proxy, via the link with the imagined Orient, as Spain stands as a substitute for the fantasized Middle East of antiquity.

In her travel sketches Rubina searches for a Jewish location outside the Middle East — in Spain, the country with the possible remains of the special, highly valued "type" of Jewish ethnicity that has been marked by writers as different from that of the Jews of Russia. By searching for a Jewess in Spain Rubina acts as a Russian writer well aware of the literary tradition to which she belongs. But she is also a Jewish writer who understands her Jewishness as a racial, ethnic and cultural category, and it is in this guise that she conducts part of the search for her ethnic roots in Spain, among Spanish women. Her male predecessors chose Spain as the locale for the search for an exotic female Other, but in the case of Rubina it is the search for the exotic body of the Self that takes her to this country. Her writing reveals that she has problems with accepting her own Self as a Russian Jewish woman both in Russia and in Israel.

Rubina's Spanish Self in Spain

In real life Rubina shares the fate of Jewish people in Israel, and many of her stories are devoted to the theme of the continuous physical destruction of Jews even in their own country. In her stories, Israel is a homeland, not the exotic land of the exotic body of the Other — her stories are filled with the mutilated bodies of fellow Jews who have been severely injured by shells and grenades thrown in terrorist attacks and on battlefields, or mutilated when taken hostage during the wars. In one story Rubina describes the asymmetrical face of an Israeli soldier, one side of which remains as handsome as the face of Adonis but the other side has been completely wiped off by a grenade. One does not have to go to the exotic Orient to look for monsters when your own people suffer such grotesque injuries. When it comes to the collective body of the nation, Rubina expresses her respect for it and solidarity with it. But when it comes to individual identification, she is unable to satisfy the requirements of the fantasy of her own exotic body in the country that has become her own. In its harsh reality the Israel of today does not provide acceptable ground for the romantic fantasy of the exotic body of a Jewish woman, the kind of body that would satisfy Rubina's needs. Hence the trip to Spain.

Rubina's travel sketch "Voskresnaia messa v Toledo. Putevye zapiski" ("Sunday Mass in Toledo, Travel Notes" [2001]) describes her tour of Spain, a trip inspired originally by her interest in the Jewish history of this country as well as by the hypothesis of the Jewish roots of Columbus and the nature of his project.[16] Rubina quotes liberally from Simon Wiesenthal's *Sails of Hope: The Secret Mission of Christopher Columbus* (1973), and by doing so she displays textual attitudes toward Spain and the Jewish Diaspora. Although it was Israel and the United States that became the primary countries for the relocation of Russian and Soviet Jewry (or, as it was described by one turn-of-the-nineteenth-century commentator, for the relocation of "part of the collective Jewish body"[17]), Rubina chooses Spain as the location in which to undertake her search for the remaining bodies that survived the Spanish Inquisition, the pogroms and the Holocaust. It is here, she believes, that the genetic markers of Jewishness can be traced and observed.[18]

This travel sketch has two epigraphs: a short poem written by Rubina in her childhood, and a lengthy quotation from the *History of the Spanish Inquisition*[19] on the expulsion of Jews from Spain in 1492. Both epigraphs encapsulate the spirit of Rubina's project: they demonstrate a personal preoccupation with Spain already evident in her childhood, and her identification with the collective fate of the Jewish people. The sketch is built on the intertwining of two lines: family history and the history of the Jewish nation. The persecution of Jews in Spain has been well documented, however, Rubina's family history is more complicated. The "document" bearing the family tree (and showing where the Rubin family branched out from a Spanish family) was allegedly lost during their evacuation from western Russia to Tashkent during World War II. Although there is something comic in Rubina's father's claim that the family tree contained the name of Baruch Spinoza, the famous Dutch philosopher of Spanish Jewish origin, the ambiguity surrounding the lost document does not undermine the reality of its existence. And indeed, this document can be seen to serve as a metaphor for those many documents lost by Jewish families during the time of the Holocaust and displacement.

Rubina starts this sketch with a description of Spanish women's bodies:

The majority of Spanish women have a pair of splendidly formed buttocks.
A Spanish woman may have elegant feet and palms of her hands, a thin waist, fragile shoulders, ordinary breasts, but her hips are always there, and let me assure you — these hips are truly full! They are not some kind of poles with the help of which models move along catwalks, they are a real woman's body. Look at the work of Velasquez.
For two weeks we loafed about various provinces of Spain — Seville, Cordoba, Granada, Castile and Catalan — and during all this time, on the streets, in pubs and bars, bus stations, in hotel corridors, in front of our eyes walked by, swam by, trotted rumps of various sizes but always of the definite proportions of thoroughbred Andalusian mares.
There is nothing offensive in this description. I myself have the same croup, because my ancestors come from Spain, and I myself look like all Spanish women put together. (294–295)

This powerful introduction contains a thoroughly calculated challenge, and is subversive on a number of levels. The woman's body is depicted as akin to that of an animal, but the normally derogatory comparison of a woman with a mare in terms of the taxonomies embodied in the binary opposition of man-logos to woman-animal is here turned upside down and evaluated as a compliment. This comparison breaks the binary between the animal and the human body and subverts the hierarchies imposed by Western Christian tradition in which animals are treated as inferior others.[20] At the same time, the glorification of the physicality of a "real" woman's body is an attack on the cult of anorexic bodies of fashion models and celebrities as presented and revered by contemporary popular culture. Yet even this attack has a hidden ethnic subtext, as the bodies on the catwalks that Rubina refers to are not of Spanish origin: if all Spanish women had broad hips and big buttocks, one would not to find them among the models. Although critical of pop culture's perception and representation of a woman's body, Rubina subscribes to the ethnic stereotype manifested and exploited by this culture at the same time: it is enough to mention Jennifer Lopez and her much advertised buttocks to see how the Spanish/Latino body that Rubina wants to adopt as her own has, in fact, been appropriated by a highly commercialized pop culture. Rubina's task here, however, is to elevate aesthetically the much-ridiculed Jewish body.

Her reference to the representation of the body in high culture, as in Velasquez's paintings, shows that she accepts the aesthetic ideals as constructed by high culture which creates both ethnic and gender stereotypes through showing "Spanish" women's bodies as broad-hipped with well-developed buttocks.[21] Here ethnicity and gender are conflated and Rubina accepts this stereotype. It should be noted that the size and the shape of the pelvis has been used in racist science as a marker of both gender and racial differences. Jewish men and women have often been used as examples of an artificially constructed anatomical anomaly, including the claim that Jewish women have narrow pelvises, whereas men have broad ones, (e.g. the opposite of the body structure of Europeans).[22] Such a feature renders the body of a "European" Jewess both aesthetically ugly and anatomically anomalous. See, for instance, this description given of the size of the pelvis by a professor of anthropology at Vienna University in 1920:

The biological (or ontological) difference of the Jew is the source of his feminized nature... among the Jews the physical marks of distinction between the sexes are expressed only weakly. Among them, women are often found to have a relatively narrow pelvis and relatively broad shoulders and men to have broad hips and narrow shoulders. (162)[23]

Rubina's description of the horses as thoroughbred ("pure-blooded" in Russian), serves to rehabilitate her own Jewish body by making it that of a Spanish woman. The reader knows that Jews in racist discourses have been viewed as people of mixed blood, and the notion of "pure-bloodedness" can be assigned to Spanish, but not Jewish women.

This difference between the hybridity of the Jew and the purity of the Spanish body becomes particularly clear in Rubina's description of an Israeli woman's body in her story "Vo vratakh tvoikh" ("Within Your Gates" [2005])[24]:

> The pregnant secretary Naomi looked simultaneously like the Spanish King Philip IV in Velasquez's portrait, and like a mare in foal with a heavy backside. So by a stretch of the imagination Naomi could be taken for a Habsburg on top of a mare in foal. (345)

The reductionist connotations of this representation of the Israeli Jewish woman's physical body are all too well evident and in stark contrast to the celebrated buttocks of Spanish women. Clearly Rubina does not want to represent a Jewish woman's body as aesthetically appealing according to the standards of high culture. With the head of a male and the lower body of a woman, this Jewish centaur looks like a monster, and comes close to the imagined bodies of the exotic compound and composite creatures encountered in the "Orient".[25] Only the head is regarded as a representation from high culture, through its similarity to a painting by Velasquez, whereas the lower body belongs to the domain of a procreating female animal. Such a grotesque body is a caricature and, even if we attempt to view it in terms of Bakhtinian carnivalesque, it still carries reductionist connotations.[26] In Bakhtinian terms the grotesque body is a liberating body; here, in the geographic space of Israel, such a body can be viewed as liberated from the hostile gaze of a dominant culture. Yet Rubina's Russian-speaking readers in Russia and elsewhere include those very members of the hostile group who will regard her stereotypes of Jew/ess's bodies as a contribution to antisemitic discourse.

That Rubina has a need to be accepted aesthetically by dominant/Christian culture, high and low, becomes further evident in an episode concerning her husband, Boria. Rubina uses a story as told by a Russian acquaintance of Boria during his Russian days. This Russian woman, who lived in Spain with her husband, allegedly describes Spanish men and women thus:

> [Rosa] once spoke very enthusiastically about Spain. Women there, she said, are very beautiful.
> —And what about men? — Boria asked in surprise.
> —Men are not — said Rosa. Men, well, they look like you (296).

This passage expresses more than the vanity of Rubina the narrator, who chose to include it as yet another flattering compliment to her appearance: if she looks like "all Spanish women," and Spanish women are beautiful, then she is clearly beautiful. On a deeper level Rosa's evaluation of Spanish women as beautiful makes it possible for Rubina to view herself as aesthetically acceptable to the common Russian, to the mob — a very telling bid for approval in view of the history of anti-Jewish violence in the country of Rubina's birth. Her aesthetic appeal can be regarded as illustrative of the principle encapsulated in the Russian proverb about Jews being beaten according to their mugs, not according to their passports — a statement that confirms the Jew as racially Other, and one that implies that the obvious racial differences of Jewish facial features are so unattractive that they can provoke violence.

Rosa's story also encapsulates the essence of the stereotype of the male Jew versus the Jewess. As was mentioned in the Introduction, this view was nurtured by European and Russian romanticism, with the male Jew depicted as physically repulsive and the female as attractive and worthy only of the love of Christian heroes with whom the romantic writers eagerly associated themselves.[27] But in Rubina's story, as told by her female narrator, the attractive Jewess first of all satisfies her own narcissistic demands, and the Jewess is attractive not because she looks like a Jew, but because she looks Spanish. Not only is she attractive to representatives of high culture, her male colleagues from the Christian world, but also to the simple average Soviet citizen.

In Spain, Rubina can wear her Spanish body, and what better proof of its authenticity can there be than being taken by a Spanish tour guide for one of his own? Rubina confesses that she takes obvious pleasure in being able to dissolve into the crowd, not to stand out as an Other, even though the official motive for her travel project is to feel what it was like for her ancestors to be Jews in Spain and she fills her sketch with documented historical information on the persecution of Jews during the Spanish Inquisition. This information is given in the form of direct quotations or as retold narrative. The historical information is presented as based on secondary sources, but Rubina personally relives the history of the Jewish people, beyond the limitations of academic knowledge and the new visual information which she encounters during her travels.

The Jewish past also has a mystical presence in her mind, as we learn that since childhood she has had a recurring dream of walking barefoot on the cobbled street of a medieval city. Rubina's childhood was spent in Tashkent, a city in central Asia, and the streets of this city had no traces of

Gothic architecture. This dream has puzzled and haunted her, but she has not been able to recognize the special layout of the pebbles in any Western cities in Germany or France. This is not surprising in view of the fact that Rubina's alleged family chronicle tells of Spanish roots and, as an impressionable girl, she was overwhelmed by this exciting information. But this is not how she views the dream. For her, the dream has nothing to do with contemporary reality; rather, it is a recollection of her real historical past, of the time when she lived in Spain in body and soul. Rubina does finally recognize the ornamentation on the pavement from her dream in the last city she visits in Spain — Toledo.

Her search for the "right" kind of pavement creates suspense in the sketch, which is structured around visits to various Spanish cities: Barcelona, Seville, Cordoba, Granada and, eventually, Toledo. The dénouement of the sketch, occurring on the very last page, occurs when Rubina finally recognizes the design on the pavement as the same design she saw in her dream. Indeed, for her there is nothing left to see in Spain, as she came here to find her own body, even if this body could have been burned on the fires of *auto-da-fé* some five hundred years previously:

> From the dark... of the Cathedral we came out into a warm street paved with dark pebbles, and sat on the bench.
> —The trip is over, I said... Took off the sandal from my right foot and with the sole of my foot I sensed the cool "right kind of ornament of the pebbled surface." And I shuddered, waking up from my dream, which now reached me in reality.
> —I was running here barefoot... Along this market place... in a different childhood... Maybe I was being chased to the bonfire... (346).

In the geographic location of the mass murder of Jews the neutral dream of walking on the pebbled pavement is realized as a nightmare. There is no other discussion of reincarnation in this text, no discourse on Jewish mysticism. The ethnic body is understood to be a part of the collective body that survives through generations. The family tree in the lost "document" has many branches, and Rubina is one of them, the motif of the dream functioning as a sign of her belonging to the persecuted people of Israel. With her own family evacuated from western Russia to central Asia during World War II, the theme of the Holocaust could not have been woven into her personal history, but in Rubina's view to belong to the Jewish people is to share their tragic history, and she chooses the tragic time of the Spanish Inquisition as a moment in history where she can face the fate of the collective Jewish body.

The Textual Body: Rubina as
a Feuchtwangerian Jewess

If it is clear by now why Rubina chose Spain as a destination to find her own exotic body, why did she find it in Toledo? Why not in Granada or Seville? The first of the two epigraphs to her sketch provides a hint. It reads:

> It happened in Seville / But maybe in Toledo / Where Spanish men live and Spanish women / Where already in the morning dances start / — unidentified verse from the scatterings of my childhood in Tashkent (294).

Although she conceals the source of her inspiration for the Spanish theme, the answer lies in Rubina's childhood. As mentioned earlier, Feuchtwanger's novel *The Jewess from Toledo* had romanticized the love between a king, Alfonso VIII, and the Jewess Rachel. The novel was translated into Russian as *A Spanish Ballad* and published in 1969.[28] As with all of Feuchtwanger's historical novels, it uses history as a parable for contemporary politics. Feuchtwanger, who was forced to flee Nazi Germany, presents the tragic story of the love between the Christian king and a Jewess as a parable of the fate of Jewish people in Christian Europe in the 1930s-1940s.[29] King Alfonso uses the beauty of Rachel, the young Jewess from a noble Jewish family, to satisfy his egotistic needs, but fails to protect her from a violent mob. Similar to this is the fate of Rachel's father, an important merchant from the Islamic kingdom of Seville who is invited to Castile by Alfonso to rebuild an economy devastated by feudal wars and crusades. He makes his kingdom very prosperous but his peacekeeping policy makes him an archenemy of the warlords who treacherously kill him and his daughter. King Alfonso betrays both of them by failing to protect them.

The publication in Russia of Feuchtwanger's historical novel provided the Soviet Jewish reader with a rare opportunity to gain knowledge of Jewish history.[30] Although this history was distilled through the prism of Feuchtwanger's artistic and subjective interpretation, his novels were viewed as reliable texts documenting fragments of Jewish history. The educational value of this novel cannot be overestimated in a country in which only a few universities in Moscow and Leningrad had the subject of Semitic studies on their academic curricula, and even they were severely limited by censorship imposed on the subject. Feuchtwanger's historical novels, such as his famous trilogy on Josephus Flavius's *The Judaic War* (1932–1942) and *Jew Süss* (1926), became a valuable source of information on Jewish history for millions of Soviet readers. For impressionable young minds in the 1960s both the informative content and the spirit of Feuchtwanger's novels were of tremendous value. An escapee from Nazi Germany in the United States, Feuchtwanger used his art as a platform to express patriotic Jewish pride in the history of his people and provided spiritual support for Soviet Jews stripped of their historical past and cultural present. In the 1960s Soviet Jewish teenagers learned about the history of the Jewish people, albeit through the romanticized lens of Feuchtwanger's writing. They were provided with noble heroes of their own, and could use this knowledge to counter antisemitic stereotypes and to build their own national identity. The publication of *A Spanish Ballad* in 1969 coincided with the height of the anti-Zionist campaign in the Soviet press that followed the Six-Day Arab-Israel War. This campaign, as we have seen, saw racially loaded anti-Jewish caricatures filling the pages of newspapers and magazines. Feuchtwanger's novel was read as an allegory for the indestructibility of Judeophobia and helped Soviet Jews to put their current experience into the context of the history of their people.

Apart from providing spiritual support for Jewish girls, the novel had an additional value — it has as its heroine the beautiful young Jewish woman, Rachel, nicknamed "Formosa" in Spanish on account of her beauty. This young Jewess from Toledo has all the characteristics a teenage girl would desire: she is beautiful, intelligent, and rich; refined by Moorish and Jewish cultures, she arouses the passion of a Christian king. This "Spanish ballad" satisfied the fantasy of what Said calls *latent* Orientalism, which he identifies as a process of learning, discovery and practice. It also developed into a *practicing* form, as it became a site for dreams, images, fantasies, myths, even obsessions.[31] Feuchtwanger's novel created a unified erotic continuum of refined Islamic and Jewish civilizations in twelfth-century Spain, subsequently feeding the fantasies of Jewish teenage girls in the Diaspora such as the young Dina Rubina. Melanie Klein describes this process of identification as first going through the stage of introjection[32] and the Feuchtwangerian "Spanish ballade" undoubtedly served as one of the elements of introjection for a teenage girl in Tashkent — a girl involved in the project of inventing an alternative ethnicity through reinscribing her body in the process of becoming Spanish. Even the topography of Rubina's childhood verses, which she used as an epigraph to her travel sketch, coincides with that of the geography of Feuchtwanger's heroine — from Seville to Toledo. But the process of introjection is one part of the dynamics of identification, followed by projection. In Rubina's case negative stereotypes of the Jewish body become projected.

Rubina's Secret "Self" and Spanish Jews in Israel

Although Rubina's fantasy of the Spanish body is realized in this travel sketch, her approach to the "real" bodies of Spanish Jews in Israel is markedly different. And, what is even more important for the purpose of this investigation, Rubina's positioning of her own body vis-à-vis Spanish bodies in Spain on the one hand and those of Spanish Jews in Israel on the other, is also different. Her novella "Poslednii kaban iz lesov Pontevedra: Ispanskaia siuita" ("The Last Wild Boar from the Pontevedra Forests: A Spanish Suite" [2001]) describes a passionate and tragic love story in which four ex-Spanish Jews — two couples — live and act out a relationship of treachery and infidelity, ending in the murder of one of the men.[33] The complicated love ties that connect the four characters consist of a number of transgressions, including not only adultery, but also brother-sister incest. But, in spite of the Orientalist components of this story (lust, incest, treachery, murder of a love rival), Rubina maintains an authorial distance from her Spanish heroes. She remains an observer while her protagonists act out — literally act out in the form of dance or a play staged during the Purim festival — their relationship. Rubina's physical space always remains demarcated and separated vis-à-vis that of the four Spaniards; her gaze follows their acts even as she involuntarily becomes a voyeur of sexual encounters in various combinations between the people involved in the relationship. Although in this story her autobiographical heroine is a professional pianist, she does not share the physical space on the stage with the four acting Spaniards, remaining instead a member of the audience rather than a performing participant. The dénouement takes place during the *Purimshpiel*, a play performed during the festival based on the Biblical story of Esther, a patriotic Jewish woman, who saves her people by convincing her husband, the powerful Persian king, to kill the archenemy of the Jews, Haman. This story, which in European culture has served as a source of various Orientalist fantasies, is further Orientalized by Rubina.[34] Her Orientalization, however, is also subversive. She draws parallels between the brother–sister incestuous relationship between the two Spanish characters and the love between Esther and the Jewish leader Mordecai. Rubina refers to one of the apocryphal versions of the story according to which Esther and Mordecai were related. Rubina thus parodies the traditional story by adhering to the profane version, while also valorizing the idea of the congenital continuity between ancient Jewish bodies and their contemporary descendants: relatives having carnal relationships both then and now. In this way Rubina adapts the Old Testament story and creates a phylogenetic argument for the exotic Jewish body. As a transgressive body it is anomalous and pathological — as we have seen a predisposition to incest has been viewed as a marker of Jewish pathology both by medical scientists and by theologians. Just as Rubina maintains the distance between her own body and that of her four Spanish Jewish protagonists, there is also a marked refusal to draw similarities between her appearance and that of the Spanish women in this story. Indeed, there is also not a single line describing her own appearance — a curious absence given her constant preoccupation with her Spanish looks as expressed in other work.

What is the reason for such a conspicuous absence? A key is to be found in the description of her Spanish Jewish heroines with their thin bodies (149) and their pallid yellow complexions and protruding eyes (*"vypuklye glaza"* [72]). Here we find a combination of signifiers that conform to the stereotype of the unattractive appearance of Jewish women.[35] But there is also a curious void, a notable absence of description that would make the reader imagine the corporeal characteristics of their bodies. There is nothing of the vividness of the images of the Spanish women's bodies that appear in her travel sketch. One woman, Bruria, is described as thin. Another, Lucia, is also described as small with a face resembling a wooden carving of the Virgin Mary — it is quite clear that Rubina encounters difficulties in the representation of these Jewish women's bodies. She is gripped by the constraining force of stereotypes even as she tries to be subversive: she describes the face of Lucia as that of a carving of Mary with a "lustful smile" (171), thus introducing the profane into the domain of the sacred. The irony of this image is manifested itself in the paradox that Christian culture appropriated and construed the visual image of an ideal woman by inscribing its ideals and tastes onto the face of the Jewish woman who gave birth to Christ. By adding a lustful smile to the face of St. Mary, Rubina subverts the Christian cultural mythology of immaculate conception while at the same time enlisting the anti-Jewish stereotype of the oversexed Jewess. As a marker of this oversexed Jewish woman, the "lustful smile" has become a staple of the Jewish stereotype in contemporary popular culture, and in Russian literary culture it was well explored by Rubina's favorite writer, Chekhov.[36] As discussed earlier, Chekhov's character Susanna from "The Mire" is oversexed and immoral; she has no qualms about seducing a Russian officer at the same time that she is having an affair with his brother, thus dragging them into an incestual relationship. Similarly, in Ivanov's *The Yellow Metal* an oversexed Brodkina is involved in the quasi-incestual relationship with Trusengeld. In Rubina's work we can see how she has internalized the stereotype of a young (oversexed) Jewish woman and then projected it. As a writer who identifies herself with male representatives and representations of high culture, she introjects the ideal female characters created by male writers such as Chekhov, and these ideal women keep their sexuality firmly under control. Internalized, this stereotype became the basis for "identification" in Kleinian terms. The negative stereotype became projected onto Jewish objects, "projection" being a stage in the process of object relations.

But it is a different matter altogether for the bodies of Spanish women — those that have been ennobled by the purifying brush of such artists as Velasquez and Goya. To resemble these bodies means to fall into the mold defined by the refined taste of the European canon: it is better to have your Spanish buttocks protrude rather than your bulging Jewish eyes; it is self-comforting to look Spanish rather than Jewish in the milieu of Western culture, but it is quite safe to look like a Russian Jewess in Israel. This is how mimicry works in nature, and this is how it works in the case of Dina Rubina and her autobiographical heroines. In numerous interviews, as well as in her stories, she compares life to a carnival, and maintains that donning numerous masks is as natural for her as it is for a participant in a Venetian carnival or for any creative personality, especially a writer.[37]

A Jewish Woman's Body in the Hierarchy of Soviet Nations

A Jewess from (Soviet) Russia of Rubina's generation had many reasons to resort to mimicry. She was informed by the (visual) ideals generated by the local dominant culture which were further distilled through the subjectivity of her personal fantasy. Lacan stresses that "the effect of mimicry is camouflage, in the strictly technical sense. It is not a question of harmonizing with the background but, against a mottled background, of becoming mottled — exactly like the technique of camouflage practiced in human warfare" (99).[38] By becoming Spanish in Russia and Jewish in Spain, by "passing" for Spanish in Spain but being Russian Jewish in Israel, Rubina shows this form of Lacanian "mottledness." In her case this kind of mimicry/camouflage is culture-specific; it is based on the paradox of rejection and the internalization of an oppressive dominant culture, and on the replacement of this culture with an alternative, foreign one — one that historically and geographically provided an oasis of religious and cultural tolerance. In Jewish history such a culture and place was Moorish Spain. This mimicry finds its expression in the economy of the quasi-orientalist discourse of a woman writer, a discourse that articulates the racial/cultural/historical Otherness of its subject and the quest for belonging. She rejoices when she dissolves in the crowd of Spanish people in Spain, thus confirming her need for the mechanism of the mimicry. By doing this she paradoxically proves that there is no such a thing as a "Jew's body," the body which she nevertheless desperately tries to shake off.

In regard to mimicry, this case study answers a number of questions. To what extent did the mechanism of mimicry work for Jews in Russia? To what extent are the racial characteristics of a Jew a cultural construct? Are there biological characteristics that betray "the race" of a Jew in northern countries? What are the chances of a teenage Jewish girl with dark hair and olive skin being taken for... a Russian — the master people in the Soviet hierarchy of nationalities?

The reader knows that in Russia, with its strong antisemitic tradition, the stereotype of the Jew's body has been well established, with darkness of skin and hair, and the shape and color of the eyes, as its stable characteristics.[39] But Jews are not the only people who are marked by such "characteristics" — Mediterranean people have similar features, as do Romany Gypsies, Armenians and Georgians, among other nations of the former Russian and Soviet empires. In terms of stereotypes, it is easier for a Jew to "pass" for one of these people.[40] So the teenage girl who wants to be accepted by her friends has to invent a more acceptable ethnicity. In the antisemitic environment of the Soviet Union in the 1950s and 1960s when Rubina was growing up, looking Spanish was clearly a better option than looking Jewish. Joshua Singer described the scene he encountered in post-revolutionary Russia when Jews pretended to be Romany Gypsies in order to survive.[41] Jews were at the very bottom of the list of nations. As extra-territorial people they did not have the privilege of cultural or religious self-expression: there was no Jewish art in the 1960s. How could one identify oneself with a people that did not have any material culture to be proud of, a people never to be seen among the family of nations who paraded themselves on the Kremlin stage adorned in colorful ethnic costumes, a people whose only pictorial representations were the antisemitic caricatures masquerading as anti-Zionist cartoons in Soviet newspapers? One "knew" from posters, sculptures, paintings, theatre and film what a Russian proletarian woman's body or a Ukrainian peasant woman's body looked like.[42] One "knew" what a delicate prima ballerina looked like and a sophisticated actress, but were there Jewish women who looked like any of these prototypes, especially those a teenage girl would like to adopt as a model of imitation? What kind of bodies did they have? There were in fact Jewish women in stardom both in the ballet and in the cinema — Maya Plisetskaya and Elina Bystritskaya. Both of them occupied top places in Soviet ballet and cinema, but their Jewish origins were thoroughly concealed from the public, and they passed for beautiful "Russian" women.[43]

How did one fill the gap between the caricature (the Brodkins and the Meilinsons with their "protruding eyes") and the void? The Lacanian projective gaze works in the symbolic field of vision, and in a situation like this invents what it is to look Jewish along the patterns established by the dominant culture in its written and visual manifestations. When there is no chance of passing for a native (a Slav), one attempts to be second best, which in the hierarchy of Soviet nations meant being non-Slavic. One learns to identify oneself with what is nearest in appearance, to approximate the image constructed on the basis of scattered knowledge.

Scholars of the body constructs in the Diaspora noted that human bodies embody difference because they refuse homogenization — they define the "normal" (white, blond, Slav) against which difference is measured — but such differences are culturally learned and only then naturalized as essence.[44] In Rubina's case, this learned construct serves to satisfy the aesthetic need of both a young person and an adult woman writer to accept her own body. For her, it is the "Spanish" body: a conglomerate of family history, literature, scatterings of academic knowledge and adolescent fantasies and trauma. The paradox is that "the Spanish body" Rubina created could not have been possible if she did not believe in the phenomenon of the Jewish body.

Notes

[1] Vladimir Zhabotinskii. Toska o patriotizme. *Ezhenedel'nyi zhurnal*. 1903. 16.05. No. 17. 3.

[2] On the overview of Russian Jewish literature after Glasnost see Mikhail Krutikov. Constructing Jewish Identity in Contemporary Russian Fiction. Eds. Zvi Gitelman, Musya Glants and Marshall I. Goldman. *Jewish Life after the USSR*. Bloomington: Indiana University Press. 2003. 252–274.

[3] Rubina's interest in themes of ethnicity has been noticed by commentators. See Elionora Shafranskaia. *Mifopoetika 'inoetnokul'turnogo teksta' v russkoi proze Diny Rubinoi*. Moscow: LKI. 2007.

[4] Rubina's work is translated into a number of European languages, and she is a recipient of two important literary awards.

[5] Edward Said. *Orientalism: Western Representations of the Orient*. New York: Vintage Books. 1979.

[6] This approach is not inter-textual.

[7] I used these notions as they entered academic discourse on identity based on the work of such theorists as Edward Said and Melanie Klein. Klein's notion of the dynamics of introjection

and projection is especially relevant to Rubina's case because of Klein's personal negotiation of her own Jewishness. Melanie Klein. *The Psychoanalysis of Children*. New York: Delacourt Press. 1975.

8   See Nadia Valman. *The Jewess in Nineteenth Century British Literary Culture*. Cambridge, UK: Cambridge University Press. 2007.

9   See "Interv'iu Diny Rubonoi". Ioanna Mianovska. *Dina Rubina vchera i segodnia*. Torun': Adam Marszalek. 2003.

10   Sander Gilman. *Difference and Pathology: Stereotypes of Sexuality, Race and Madness*. Ithaca: Cornell University Press. 1985.

11   V. V. Rozanov. Evrei v russkoi literature. *Novoe vremia*. 06.05. 1912. 3–4.

12   Dina Rubina. 'Vot idet Messiia!' *Nash kitaiskii biznes*. Moscow: Eksmo. 2004.

13   See Joshua Trachtenberg. *The Devil and the Jews: The Medieval Conception of the Jews and its Relation to Modern Anti-Semitism*. Philadelphia. The Jewish Publication Society. 1983.

14   Mikhail Lermontov wrote his first play on the topic of a tragic and quasi-incestual love of a beautiful Spanish Jewess set during the time of the Inquisition in fifteenth-century Spain. M. Lermontov. *Ispantsy*. Sobranie sochinenii. Moscow: Akademiia Nauk. Vol. 3. 1961. 10–168.

15   V. P. Botkin. *Pis'ma ob Ispanii*. Leningrad: Nauka. 1976. There is an irony in Botkin's description of various ethnic types because his contemporaries claimed that he borrowed them from existing travel literature. Botkin thus was engaged in the project of "textual attitudes" himself. On the image of a beautiful Jewess in Russian culture see: Mikhail Vaiskopf. Sem'ia bez uroda. Obraz evreia v literature russkogo romantizma. *Novoe literaturnoe obozrenie*. No. 27. 1997. 76–99. L. Z. Feldman et al. *"Prekrasnaia evreika" v Rossii XVII–XIX vekov*. Moscow: Drevlekhranilishche. 2007.

16   Dina Rubina. Voskresnaia messa v Toledo. *Vysokaia voda venetsiantsev*. Moscow: Vagrius. 2005. 294–346.

17   V. Tan. Evrei i literatura. *Svobodnye mysli*. 18.02. 1908. 1–9.

18   On challenges to the representation of Jews and Jewishness in American culture see Ed. Norman Kleeblatt. *Too Jewish? Challenging Traditional Identities*. New York: The Jewish Museum and Rutgers University Press. 1996.

19   By H. Lorente.

20   On taxonomies in the representations of woman/animal bodies see Nigel Rothfels. *Representing Animals*. Bloomington: Indiana University Press. 2002.

21   Rubina often refers to the art of painting in her work. She explains her knowledge of this material due to the fact that both her father and her husband are artists.

22   Sander Gilman. *Sexuality: An Illustrated History*. New York: John Wiley and Sons. 1989.

23   Quoted in Sander Gilman. *Freud, Race and Gender*. Princeton: Princeton University Press. 1993. 162.

24   Dina Rubina. Vo vratakh tvoikh. *Voskresnaia messa v Toledo*. Moscow: Vagrius. 2005. 313–384.

25   See Said. Chapter "Imaginative Geography and its Representations." Op. cit. 49–73.

26   M. M. Bakhtin. *Rabelais and Hid World*. Bloomington: Indiana University Press. 1984.

27   See Eds. Monika Greenleaf and Stephen Moeller-Sally. *Russian Subjects: Empire, Nation and the Culture of the Golden Age*. Evanston IL: Northwestern University Press. 1998.

28   Lion Feuchtwanger. *Ispanskaia ballada*. Polnoe sobranie sochinenii. Vol. 13. Moscow: Khudozhestvennaia literatura. 1969. 365–808.

29   On the Spanish interpretation of the historic Raquel see Martin Largo, Ramon Jose. *La judia de Toledo: desde Lope de Vega hasta Franz Grillparzer*. Madrid: Auryn. 2000.

30   The publication of Feuchtwanger's work in the Soviet Union became possible as a result of his positive comments on the country during his visit in 1936. He had a number of meetings with Stalin which he described in his book *Moscow 1937*. It was translated into Russian but banned soon after by Stalin himself. However, due to his general left-wing politics, Feuchtwanger's work was allowed to be published in the USSR. See V. A. Torchikov, *Vokrug Stalina*. St. Petersburg. 2000.

31 Edward Said. *Orientalism*. New York: Vintage Books. 1979.
32 Melanie Klein. *The Psychoanalysis of Children*. New York: Delacorte Press. 1975.
33 Dina Rubina. Poslednii kaban iz lesov Pondevedra. *Voskresnaia messa v Toledo*. Moscow: Vagrius. 2005. 6–178.
34 Racine's *Esther* (1689) is one such example. On the Jewish identity of Esther see Eve Kosofsky Sedgwick. *Epistemology of the Closet*. New York: Harvester Wheatsheaf. 1990.
35 Rubina also uses "protruding eyes" as a marker of the Jewish body also in her story "Kamera naezzhaet". This stable racial marker of Jews in antisemitic discourse was used controversially in Jean-Paul Sartre's *Anti-Semite and Jew*. On this issue see Jon Stratton. *Coming Out Jewish*. London: Routledge. 2000.
36 On contemporary popular culture and Jewish women's sexuality see Jon Stratton. *Coming Out Jewish*. On this issue in historical perspective see Linda Nochlin. Starting with the Self: Jewish Identity and Its Representation. Ed. Linda Nochlin and Tamar Garb. *The Jew in the Text*. London: Thames and Hudson. 1995. 7–20.
37 Ella Mitina. "Maska, ia tebia znaiu". 15 April 2006. http://www.peoples.ru/art/literature/prose/belletristika/rubina/
38 Jacques Lacan. The line and light. *Four Fundamental Concepts of Psycho-Analysis*. London: Penguin Books. 1994. 67–123.
39 O. V. Belova. *Etnokul'turnye stereotipy v slavianskoi narodnoi traditsii*. Moscow: Indris. 2005.
40 Another contemporary Russian Jewish writer, Ulitskaia, works with the theme of physical similarity and psychological likeness between women of these nationalities. See Liudmila Ulitskaia. *Medeia i ee deti.* Moscow: Vagrius. 2002.
41 Joseph Sherman and Henrietta Mondry. Russian Dogs and Jewish Russians: Reading Israel Joshua Singer's 'Liuk' in a Russian Literary Context. *Prooftexts: A Journal of Jewish Literary History.* Vol. 20. No. 3. 2000. 191–317.
42 Elizabeth Waters. Female Form in Soviet Political Iconography. Ed. Barbara Evans Clements ed. *Russia's Women: Accommodation, Resistance, Transformation*. Berkeley: University of California Press. 1991. 225–242.
43 See their memoirs: Maia Plisetskaia. *Ia — Maiia Plisetskaia*. Moscow: Novosti. 1994 and Elina Bystritskaia. *Vstrechi pod zvezdoi nadezhdy*. Moscow: Vagrius. 2008.
44 Smadar Lavie and Ted Swedenburg. Introduction. Ed. Smadar Lavie and Ted Swedenburg. *Displacement, Diaspora, and Geographies of Identity*. Durham: Duke University Press. 1996. 1–25.

Chapter 9

The Jewish Patient: Alexander Goldstein and the Postmodern Russian Jewish Body in Israel, 2000s

> "Arabs proudly smell of themselves, Jews already lost their smell in contrast to their olive-skinned neighbors, they are ashamed of their formerly strong sweat glands and hope to become similar to other nations sunk in sterility"
>
> Alexander Goldstein. 2001.[1]

Alexander Goldstein (Aleksandr Gol'dshtein) (1957–2006) is writer of complex postmodernist prose that appeals to a high-brow Russian-speaking readership both in Russia and in the Diaspora. He won major literary prizes — the Antibooker and Malyi Booker in 1997 and the prestigious Andrei Belyi award in 2001. As a representative of the younger generation of Russian Jewish writers, he belongs to the group of the Russian intellectuals of Jewish descent who did not have a particular interest in Jewish antiquities or in aspects of Yiddishkeit.

Goldstein was born in Tallin, the capital of Estonia. He lived for thirty years in Baku, Azerbaijan, where he attended school and graduated from university.[2] In 1990 he immigrated to Israel as a consequence of the political instability and ethnic tensions brought about by the disintegration of the Soviet Union.[3] He died in Tel Aviv from lung cancer. Goldstein's fragile health was part of his construct of the self-reflecting authorial subject of his two important books: *Rasstavanie s Nartsissom* (*Parting with Narcissus* [1997]) and *Aspekty dukhovnogo braka* (*Aspects of Spiritual Marriage* [2001])[4] for which he won the Andrei Belyi award.[5] This award is given specifically to achievements in Russian prose, and in developing and advancing the potential of the Russian literary language. The essays in *Aspects of Spiritual Marriage* attest to his interest in Roman and Greek antiquity, Egyptology, intellectual history, and the history of philosophy and religion from Kundera, Lacan and Confucius to Catholicism, Hinduism, and Buddhism. This scope and breadth of knowledge is typical of a Russian (Jewish) representative of his generation and attests to the quest to embrace foreign cultures intellectually. This quest was how his generation compensated for their lack of ability to travel outside the Soviet Union as the country's borders were sealed for the majority of the intelligentsia, especially for those of Jewish descent. The desire to embrace knowledge about all that was non-Russian or non-Slavic was also a result of an aversion to the Russocentrism of the monocultural package of information parceled out by official Soviet culture.

Despite the openly antisemitic policy of this official Soviet culture, there is no evidence in Goldstein's essays of a desire to acquire knowledge about Jewish culture during his years in the Soviet Union, and the Jewish theme is not present at all in his work during this pre-emigration period. With his arrival in Israel and his exposure to a different form of Jewish life as represented there he began to experience a new interest in things Jewish. Goldstein's work provides an interesting insight into the construction of one's own identity on the basis of a postmodernist assemblage of various pieces of academic, anthropological, and linguistic knowledge relating to aspects of Jewishness. There are no allusions to religious Jewish sources in Goldstein's works written in Israel, no academically catalogued cultural practices or linguistic associations. Although his postmodernist prose is saturated with literary quotations without quotation marks (clearly aimed at the sophisticated reader), allusions, and cross-references to a wide range of multicultural sources, this rich fabric of references tellingly neglects any important mention of Jewish history and culture. It is precisely this lack that provokes interest, and in what follows presents an attempt to identify those points, topics and issues that Goldstein problematizes in order to construct his own multilayered identity in Israel. While maintaining the focus of this investigation — the theme of the Jew's body — the present chapter will demonstrate Goldstein's choice of topics that helped him to create boundaries between his own physical and ontological body and the bodies of various ethnic, class, and gender Others that he refers to in his essays.

In the essay "1990," included in *Aspects of Spiritual Marriage*, Goldstein is explicit about why he left Russia: ethnic tensions between Azeris and Armenians caused many people of other ethnicities, including Jews, to fear for their safety. Jews know from their historical experience and collective memories that any form of violence can grow into anti-Jewish pogroms, hence his friends' and his own decision to leave for Israel. In another essay, "On Literary Immigration," Goldstein writes about the need to acknowledge a new cultural phenomenon in recent Russian literary culture — the emergence of a literature that is written in the Russian language yet is not Russian literature as such. He refers to the development of English-language literature written by Indians, which is viewed as a separate brand of literature. He maintains that this new literature, written in Russian but in places geographically and territorially outside Russia, can only enrich Russian literature. Coming from a writer who writes in Russian and who receives Russian literary awards but who lives in Israel, this suggestion testifies to the realization of a new phenomenon taking place globally and from which Russian culture is not immune. In this way Goldstein declares himself an author whose new linguistic and geo-political experiences link him with various international authors writing in the language of the former Soviet Empire, but having a more complicated national identity. It can be argued that this identity is formed by "blending" — a concept advanced by the cognitivists Gilles Fauconnier and Mark Turner — and Goldstein's work can be viewed as an example of this phenomenon, characterized by its authors as a marker of our times.[6] Fauconnier and Turner write about "conceptual blending," the merging of episodes taken from any historical moment in time, any geographical locus in space, any personality, real or dreamed, contemporary or belonging to past epochs, and it is the merging of these various components that forms the individual identities of our contemporaries. It is from this breadth of topics, changes of times and locations and diversities of cultural paradigms that Goldstein weaves his narratives, thereby testifying to the viability of the concept of blending in the formation of contemporary identities. Certainly in Goldstein's essays the main subject is his own self-referential authorial persona. His first main work has a telling title — *Rasstavanie s Nartsissom* (*Parting with Narcissus*) — and clearly reveals the main object of the writer's interest as his own Self. Goldstein freely takes material from the historical past of any nation or culture that may help him to express his thoughts at any given moment. He then combines these fragments with any aspect of his own current experience. From this combination there emerges the construct of his own identity. For this construct, the concept of the Jew's body is a building block.

The title of Goldstein's second book, *Aspects of Spiritual Marriage*, attests to the author's confidence that "aspects" are more tangible than the whole, and it is on the aspects of the Jew's body that the present chapter will concentrate. In the case of Goldstein, his own Jewish body stands as an example of the concept of blending as a way of constructing identity. Psychological introjection, identification with people and what Foucannier and Turner call "non-people" — imaginary people, including real historical figures whom the subject did not know personally, literary characters and characters taken from folk wisdom — are all blended to produce this body.

What is particularly interesting in the case of Goldstein's construction and self-perception of his own body is its metathetical mode. He endows himself with various features of the Jew's body that have been created by various hostile cultures, and reverses the evaluation of this body. The physical, physiological and psychological features of his body become the object of his narcissistic pride. He constructs a special kind of Self, different from the class and racial Other and uses his body as the site of this difference. If, as seen in most of the works analyzed so far, being small, and sickly, and having a low libido and indefinite gender characteristics are regarded as negative and derogative markers of the Jewish male, then, in the case of Goldstein, all these features become positive attributes of his special Self. They become aspects of the body that the author exhibits to his reader, who is then prompted to admire it on the basis of its well-calculated and deliberately selected representation. His texts demonstrate that Goldstein calculatingly chose the most flattering light in which to exhibit his own body — he is both a stage director and a voyeur, a photographer and a writer, making sure that the advertised model leaves the best impression on the reader/viewer. It is no accident that the cover of *Aspects of Spiritual Marriage* features the picture of an eye — the author is a voyeur of his own body, as is the reader, and the descriptions of scenes from the writer's own sexual life that are scattered through the book only affirm that the reader will be made party to various physiological and psychological aspects of the life of the author's body. If, when choosing the image for the book cover, Goldstein tried to create an intertextual connection with Georges Bataille's proto-pornographic novel *Story of the Eye*, then he was also revealing postmodernist authorial irony toward the French author: like Bataille, he too needs to engage in non-normative sexual practices to achieve sexual satisfaction.[7] In addition and in parallel to Bataille's work, Goldstein appears to derive pleasure from the act of describing his (probably fantasized) experiences, and in exposing himself to the inevitably voyeuristic gaze of the reader.

Goldstein's body is thus one with sexual fluids, and as a writer who spends most of his life reading, he constructs his body by "blending" aspects of material from which literary sexed male bodies have been made. In a charming poem which is a translation of an English nursery rhyme by the Russian children's poet of Jewish origin, Samuil Marshak, the narrator asks the question: *"Iz chego sdelany mal'chiki?"* ("What are little boys made of?").[8] Goldstein often reflects on his own Self as a child, and his narcissism undoubtedly has its roots in an infantile stage of development. In a way, his book can be regarded as giving answers to Marshak's question, but with one modifier: the question he poses is, "What are *Jewish* boys made of?" or, to be more accurate, "What is a special Russian Jewish boy like me made of?" Answers to these questions are provided in the text and although they are not given in full, they come in the form of various "aspects," or fragments of existence.

In his book Goldstein confesses that his major fear when he arrived in Israel was that, because of the poverty inherent in emigration, "an anthropological transformation" (130) of his Self would take place. His text shows his preoccupation with two main anthropological areas: the sphere of sexuality and genealogy, and that of food. As the reader may recall, both have been identified by the anthropologist Mary Douglas in her classic monograph *Purity and Danger* as concepts with symbolic significance, the aim of which is to guard and protect the boundaries of a clan or ethnic grouping.

The Sexual Fluids of the Jewish Client

The meaning of the concept of "spiritual marriage" that Goldstein puts into his title is revealed almost at the end of the book, in his essay "Dom v pereulke" ("The House in the Lane"). There are forty essays in the book, of which this one is number thirty-seven. The house in the lane is a house with a peep show, where male clients are allowed to touch the female strip-tease artist. The experience combines both voyeuristic and tactile pleasure — it does not include genital sex. Men achieve orgasm by means of masturbation, although for extra pay girls can help their clients to achieve orgasm by touching their penises with their own hands. Goldstein explains the reasons for starting to visit the "House." These explanations reveal quasi-scientific theories about the healthy male body, and especially the necessity to have a regular discharge of seminal fluid for maintaining physical and mental health. One of the main taboos that post-Soviet Russian prose broke was that of human sexuality, and discussions and descriptions of these themes have long since lost their sensational character. Goldstein realizes that it is difficult to shock the reader in the same way that, for example, Viktor Erofeev's novel *The Russian Beauty* did, and his description of the reasons for his visits to the whorehouse has a rather matter-of-fact, mundane character. His common-law wife leaves him, citing as one of the reasons his inadequate sexual performance. Significantly for the purpose of this investigation, Goldstein admits that her evaluation of his libidinal drive as "modest potency" (279) is true. Nevertheless, the biological formation of semen in his body continues to take place, leading to his need for regular discharge of the accumulated seminal fluids. As a direct result of his upbringing Goldstein has an aversion to the masturbation that he is forced to resort to, albeit with the help of paid sex-workers. These explanations demonstrate that Goldstein is theorizing his own sexual behavior, inserting quasi-medical and historical subtexts into his own writing.

To admit one's own modest sex drive in the context of Israeli macho culture means to position oneself as an Other. To celebrate one's own low physical potency for a male Jew in Israel means to juxtapose oneself to the physically strong "Mediterranean Jews" — those who were born in the region and to whom popular culture assigns the sexual passions and heightened libidos of "Alpha males."[9] Goldstein, who was born in Northern Europe, uses references to folk wisdom and old scientific beliefs based on analogies between climate, temperament and the character of the people inhabiting these regions. As was mentioned in the first chapter, nineteenth-century "sciences" such as history and anthropology created direct connections between the character of peoples and the territory they occupied: Russians were supposed to have a melancholic character because of the cold climate and the flat landscape of the Russian plains, whereas Jews and Arabs were viewed as having fiery temperaments because of the hot climate of the Middle East. In this continuum Goldstein positions himself as a man with a cold temperament, somebody who is indeed an outsider among the population of the land of Israel, thus creating for himself a minoritarian locus. He subverts the notion of the high sexual potency of Israeli males while at the same time privileging his own body against those of Israeli males or other physically potent men living in Israel. As a self-positioned minoritarian character he is playing with the notion of binarisms, in this particular case with the opposition between physical strength and intellectual abilities. His position presents a calculated challenge to contemporary Israeli society because he exposes this society as privileging physical force over intellectual values. This theme of Israel as a country that betrayed what Goldstein views as Jewish culture resonates strongly in the many essays in his book, and will be referred to later. What is important here is that Goldstein treats sexuality as one of the aspects of the idea of a Jew's body within the broader context of Jewish cultural values and traditions. By making himself into an Other in Israel in relation to males, he paradoxically positions himself as a "proper Jew," even though this is a personal construct based on the values of the societal micro-culture, the "substrata" ("1990," [232]) to which his family belonged.

Goldstein's expressed aversion to masturbation, which he describes as deriving from his teenage years, is also highly significant within the theme of a male Jew's body. In this instance the body is a site on which culture and society inscribe meaning: as a boy from a privileged and educated family he was taught certain standards, and abstention from masturbation was one such marker of being a man of culture. Indeed, to suppress the instincts and the impulses of the physical body is the main task of culture. As an extremely well-informed writer, Goldstein must be familiar with the work of Foucault, his *The History of Sexuality* in particular, and be acquainted with medical discourses on sexual behavior in general and on masturbation in particular. In this context Goldstein's "conservative" approach to masturbation has to be viewed as a calculated strategy, the aim of which is to challenge the privileging of nature over nurture and to declare his position of privileging discipline over relaxation. It is also a manifestation of the desire to privilege spirit over matter. Indeed, if the "matter" — the physiological organism — needs to be attended to, then that process has to be undertaken methodically. Thus, Goldstein needs to visit the "House" twice a week in order to evacuate the spermal fluids from his body. His descriptions of the sperm-collecting organs show his desire to see the process as the mechanical workings of a biological organism. He likens his body to a plumbing system that gets clogged, his penis to a tap from which flows fluid — the lexis and imagery are thus constructed on an analogy with machinery. Whereas the regularity with which the buildup of sperm occurs is presented as a normal part of nature, his refusal to masturbate is presented as a carefully calculated sign of cultured restraint.

These descriptions also have a peculiar similarity to various medical theories of humors and fluids that dominated pre-modern medicine as built on the Hippocratic-Galenic tradition. The regular discharge of fluids was considered to be paramount for the physical well-being of an organism and, in the same way that menstruation was viewed as part of the natural healing process of the body, the regular discharge of semen was also construed as a necessity. The notions of blocked arteries and the harm that could be done to the body through an excess of coagulated blood or semen — the tenets of Hippocratic-Galenic medicine — are clearly analogous to Goldstein's quasi-medical reasoning concerning the need for the regular discharge of sexual fluids. Scholars have noted that:

> In popular culture as well as in learned medicine, the healing power of nature was thus *facultas expultrix*, the "expelling faculty" of the body. This notion was basic in the Hippocratic-Galenic concept of "crisis." The crisis (a positive

turning point in the course of disease) was usually identified with some form of bodily discharge (138).[10]

Goldstein's regular visits to the "House" are necessary as part of this evacuation process, and it is implied that the body, otherwise in a state of crisis, needs to be thus relieved.

The medicalization of the process of semen emission found in Goldstein's text is also symptomatic of a particular view of the male sexed body which was widely spread in late nineteenth-century Europe. Characteristic for the upper middle classes, the view that the regular discharge of sperm was necessary for the healthy male body made visits to brothels almost a medical exercise. This practice was famously challenged by Leo Tolstoy in *The Kreutzer Sonata*, in which he attacked medical doctors for a number of practices relating to human sexuality, including the belief in the necessity of sexual intercourse for young men before marriage. Ironically, Tolstoy, who tried to suppress his own libido, fathered a child after he wrote *The Kreutzer Sonata* and, as a result of this, his intellectual arguments were seen to be undermined by the biological requirements of the male body.[11] Goldstein's postmodernist authorial "I" is informed by numerous concepts and views taken from various times and space, but his belief and practices in relation to the health of a sexed male body are provocatively anachronistic. It is quite clear that Goldstein views his visits to the "House" as part of a healthy routine, and the "House" becomes the equivalent of a health clinic with the writer himself as patient.

Another important layer in the theme of masturbation is related to religion, particularly Christianity with its cult of celibacy. Goldstein ends his essay by declaring his intention to read the hagiography of the monk St. Seraphim, who abstained from sex. Reference to Father Seraphim is ironic in relation to Russian literature in the context of Tolstoy's advocacy of the suppression of the male libido as expressed in a number of his stories written after *The Kreutzer Sonata*, notably *The Devil* and *Father Sergius*.

But if Goldstein visits the medicalized "House" as a patient, who are the "healers"? Are they depicted as quasi-health practitioners? What is their ethnic and class background? This level of Goldstein's narrative incorporates the story of the ethnic and racial Other, as most sex workers are imported from Eastern Europe and are of Slavic origin. Other male clients in the "House" masturbate while looking at the strip-tease act, but Goldstein waits for the women to perform the act on him. He becomes attached to one particular Russian woman, Alla, because he derives a special enjoyment from the way she caresses his penis. Alla becomes Goldstein's favorite, not only because she has a special touch, but also because, he maintains, she puts her heart into the exercise. The author starts frequenting the "House," and even brings special gastronomic treats for Alla. During those eating sessions he indulges in monologues on intellectual themes. He calls this sexual relationship a "spiritual marriage," meaning a sexual relationship without penetration or inter-genital stimulation. Alla's magic hands do the job, and Goldstein's mind is freed from the burden of a body clogged by fluids. The euphemisms that he finds for his sexual fluids are telling — "milk" and "honey" presumably stand for sperm and semen (as well as the obvious allusion to the promised land). The link between sperm and milk is based on similarities in color and consistency, which is reflected in the folk word for sperm — "*molof'ia*," phonetically linked to "*moloko*" (milk). "Honey" has obvious narcissistic connotations, but also reveals Goldstein's academic knowledge of Russian sexual discourse: Rozanov shocked his contemporaries when he maintained that ambrosia and nectar, the food of the gods on Mount Olympus in Ancient Greek mythology, was nothing but genital secretions. In Rozanov's case the erotic fixation was on the vagina; in the case of the Russian Jewish Narcissus the nectar is produced by his own body.

Why does Goldstein "not rub his genitals against" (295) those of Alla, the woman with whom he is seemingly falling in love? He claims that his attraction to Alla became quite overwhelming, and that he started anticipating scenes of marital bliss. Although those scenes are depicted as obscenely trite — there is even a domestic cat in the cozy family, the archetypal image of kitsch — it is quite clear that in his loneliness and nostalgia for Russia, Goldstein allows the fantasy of this marriage to have the potential to develop into reality.

The fantasy and anticipation of a fully developed relationship is brought to an abrupt stop by Alla's sudden and unexpected disappearance. She returns to Russia, with her son and a man, without saying goodbye to Goldstein. This departure serves as a rude awakening for Goldstein, and puts him into the position of a naïve dupe taken for a ride by a cheap prostitute. In a comment on this episode one critic called Goldstein a *schlimazel*, and indeed he spends more money on Alla than he can afford, eventually being forced to take on extra work but still ending up in debt.[12]

But there is a symbolic level to this story of the betrayal of a Russian Jewish male by a Russian woman. Alla epitomizes the "motherland" that betrayed her Jewish suitors no matter how generous and dedicated they had been toward her. Goldstein's "spiritual marriage" to a Russian woman has connotations of a post-oedipal love of a man toward his mother, thus explaining the notion of "spiritual marriage" on a psychological level. It is quite uncanny that Goldstein received the Andrei Belyi prize for this novel as there is a connection between the love of an intellectual for a Russian peasant woman as depicted in Belyi's novel *Serebrianyi golub'* (*Silver Dove*) and Goldstein's attraction for Alla. This link is made evident in Goldstein's statement that, "Men are in love with buxom and plump Russian women; they fight for the right to patronize them" (297).[13]

Yet, there is another aspect of a "spiritual marriage" that explains Goldstein's abstention from genital contact with Alla, that has to do with the boundaries of the body. Goldstein protects his body not only because of narcissism and his fear of contracting venereal disease or AIDS — he uses condoms even when women perform manual sex on him. He is actually protecting the ethnic boundaries of his racial body, a Jewish body that he does not want to be contaminated by the fluids of a non-Jewish woman. This can be viewed as the main reason for his peculiar behavior. This guarding of the racial body, although not apparent in the essay "The House in the Lane," becomes the theme of another essay, "Nashestvie" ("An Invasion") which will be analyzed further on in this chapter. Despite Goldstein's cultural and linguistic affiliations with Russia, and despite his isolation and cultural loneliness in Israel, he perceives himself as racially Jewish. In order to remain a Jew, he has to guard the boundaries of his body in terms of genealogy and conception. His guarding of his racial purity is akin to the protection of a purebred male dog whose pedigree could be destroyed by coitus with a stray bitch, and the Slavic women who come to work as sexual workers are conceived as such stray females. Russian thinkers of the turn of the century — Vladimir Soloviev, Rozanov and Florensky — were preoccupied with the concept of the preservation of racially pure bodies by Jews. Their interest in this topic related to the concept of a special metaphysical nature of the physical Jewish body and the implications of this body for Christianity. Irrespective of their Judeophilia or Judeophobia, they recognized the fact that Jews were regarded as the chosen people. The eschatological implications of this belief was that Christians could be saved only through Jews, whose resurrection was guaranteed. An intellectual like Goldstein was well aware of the "privilege" of being a Jew, and he probably introduced a special irony into the trope of avoiding sexual contact with non-Jewish Russian women: in Russian culture Jews have been demonized through their association with dark forces and the Devil, and treated with disgust and repulsion out of fear of contamination. Goldstein can now derive a certain pleasure from reversing the positioning of the oppressor and the victim and erecting boundaries between his privileged Jewish body and that of a non-Jewish female. In the dynamics of the preservation of "pure" bodies, identified by Mary Douglas as "purity and danger," Goldstein has once more used his metathetic strategy of reversal, and it is his male Jewish body that he guards from contamination by the impure fluids of a racial Other. After all, the events take place in Israel, where he is master in his own home and where any Russian woman is an outsider.

Food as a Marker of Racial Differences

Sexual fluids and the avoidance of sexual contact are not the only ways culture erects boundaries between racial bodies. Food is another important anthropological area of racial difference, and the laws of kashrut as identified in Leviticus are the archetypal example of this form of guarding the Jewish nation from the Other. As Michael Satlow has amply demonstrated in his *Tasting the Dish: Rabbinic Rhetorics of Sexuality,* sexual transgressions as well as eating pork are the tropes that separate the nation from the "evil Gentile" (65).[14]

In Marshak's famous children's poem quoted earlier, in relation to the question "What are boys made of?" there is another question: "What are girls made of?" (*"Iz chego sdelany devochki?"*). Although the answer to the first question includes sports and military toys, girls are made from sweets and creamed pastries, slices of cakes and chocolates. Goldstein's description of Alla's favorite food with which he supplies her has a highly symbolic significance:

> She liked minced beefsteaks covered in fried onions, bought in the Ukrainian shop, ham with a thick layer of fat, salami rich in calories, the wormy softness of Roquefort cheese, rich sweet cakes with butter cream, rum puff tops adorned with a mountain of whipped cream, the bitter thickness of coffee, tea as strong as a narcotic, liqueurs of monastery origins, brandy, Finnish vodka, Carmel wines, "Davidoff" and "Yves Saint Laurent" brands of cigarettes as well as the soldiers' favorite brand — "Camel" cigarettes without a filter. (293)

What strikes the contemporary reader in this list of food and drink is their unfashionable quality: they are no longer part of the culinary discourse of the contemporary Western gastronomic canon established by food gurus. The abundance of fat and sugar not only bespeaks this sort of food's unhealthy quality, it also reveals it as hopelessly plebeian. This food's old-fashioned status, which dates back to the post-World War II era, can have an appeal only to those less fortunate representatives of Third World nations who associate wealth with food rich in calories.[15] For Alla, who comes from Russia, the food from a Ukrainian shop, desirable to the women of her mother's generation because of its richness and abundance, provides the gratification of which she has been deprived of in her own country. Certainly culinary books of the 1950s are full of recipes based on butter and sugar, and illustrations of creamy pastries, cakes with thick layers of cream, and numerous salamis, sausages and cold meats. Indicative of the change of fashion in body shape and beauty, the Twiggy type of body that emerged in the 1960s brought with it a new type of diet. Carbohydrates became labeled as fatty food, and high-fat protein food was rendered undesirable by the new cultural discourse in the West. Soviet women were famously ridiculed in the West for being fat and shapeless and their diet exemplified the political flabbiness of the Soviet regime and the inadequacy of the socialist economy from the 1960s to the 1980s.

Mikhail Kozakov, the famous Russian Jewish actor and film star who immigrated to Israel roughly at the same time as Goldstein, describes this wave of emigration in his memoirs as "kolbasnaia" ("cold sausage meat").[16] This term is anthropologically significant: in the 1980s Russians associated real food with meat products, and it was the lack and subsequent high cost of this food, as a result of the Socialist state's economic collapse and the discontinuation of state subsidies of food, that caused the mass emigration from the former Soviet Union. So the average Russified member of the Jewish intelligentsia had the same cultural preferences for food as his less fortunate counterparts who could not immigrate to Israel. Not being Jewish, Alla belongs to that less fortunate group that could not leave Russia when the Soviet Union fell apart, and she is hungry for the kind of food that others have learned to treat critically. But Goldstein presents her choice of particular food as a marker of her Otherness. Alla is an "essential" Other because she *likes* the food which Goldstein does not touch.

Apart for marking Alla's provinciality and class, the food has another symbolic meaning. Pork as ham and salami, as well as the mixing of dairy products with meat, represent two transgressions of the laws of kashrut. And, although there is no evidence that Goldstein himself kept kosher, there is also no evidence that he consumed any of these food items. He makes a point of describing his verbosity during these sessions: while Alla eats, he is talking about intellectual matters:

> During those eating sessions I engaged in rhetoric, spoke excitedly and poetically on topics of literature and aesthetics. It was of interest to Allochka who was free of any intellectual preferences and who, while eating cake, drinking liqueur and smoking tobacco, absorbed with seeming sympathy everything I pontificated about: be it the messianic feminism of Sofia Olsen and Regina Kuen, the

language of emancipatory movements, the Maghribian brotherhood "Statue in the Desert," the gnoseology of chess (the depth of my understanding of the game did not coincide with my practical skills) or about the text, which you hopefully did not omit while leafing through this book (295).

Despite the authorial self-irony, the image of the Self that Goldstein constructs is superior to that of Allochka. He is all words while she is silent, he is theorizing while she is devouring, he is an erudite while she is *a tabula rasa* who, ironically, is ignorant even of issues of such relevance to her sex and gender as the feminist movement. Of particular importance is the fact that Goldstein does not provide any evidence that he eats the same food as Alla.

In his essay "Pis'mo" ("A Letter") we learn about the kind of food which Goldstein used to eat — food that is in stark contrast to that favored by Alla.

> A hot bun which has been taken out of the oven with a melting piece of butter and a not-too-thick layer of caviar, an almost transparent slice of pastrami with Dijon mustard—almost a daily treat for tea, then the summery softness of avocado, a kiwi fruit, papaya, a four dollar rum baba from the French bakery of Sylvie Manor (132).

The food a successful writer can afford to eat is chosen in accordance with his exquisite taste — food that is both elegant and aristocratic in its lightness and volume. The blend of French and Russian delicacies in combination with subtropical fruit could be matched only by the stock of London's Harrods or the Eliseevsky shops in pre-Revolutionary Moscow and St. Petersburg. Indulging in this luxury is a reward Goldstein reaps as a successful writer — as we have seen, he is the recipient of a number of literary prizes and his books sell well during his lifetime. This diet supports his self-fantasy as an aristocrat, a fantasy further revealed by his purchase of eighteenth-century prints of paintings of European aristocrats. His imaginary interlocutor is the Russian empress Elizabeth [Petrovna]. The fact that he is a Jewish writer who lives in Israel and writes in the Russian language, and that he is awarded prestigious literary prizes in Russia, creates a typically postmodernist paradox based on the gratification of the body in an admittedly imagined style of royalty. Goldstein's decision to allude to an Empress rather than to an Emperor is puzzling, and may be viewed as a strategy to valorize the affectation of his posturing. His choice of prints makes evident his love of baroque and rococo, and his playful effeminateness is a strategy to valorize the extravagance of his tastes. For a refined Jewish male to have a Russian male Emperor in military uniform to play out his royal fantasy would be grotesque, distasteful, and out of place in the frame of Goldstein's texts.

When Goldstein can afford to live the way he wants, or at least to eat (and dress) the way he wants, he demonstrates refined taste. This taste shows that he treats his body with respect, and also that the very essence of his body is refined. This notion of refinement is constructed as effeminate, and in this interpretation Goldstein constructs the image of the Self by challenging gender stereotypes. Being effeminate means being in stark contrast with the macho male figure, and these males are depicted as racial and social Others not only through their sexual vigor but also through their diets. When reflecting on the fantasy of "spiritual marriage" with Alla, he positions himself as sexually different vis-à-vis other males. In his descriptions of Alla's body he creates a physiological link between food and sexuality: Alla's body becomes more corpulent "from pork, sweets and pastries" (296) and her "sensuality, made of meat, pastry dough and alcohol, resented pressures of abstention" (297). In this description of Alla's body there is a two-way causal connection between sexuality and food: she is sensual because of the kind of food she eats, and she prefers certain kinds of food because she is sensual. She is thus a product of nature and nurture and, unlike Goldstein, she cannot regulate her Self through self-discipline. As such, this female body attracts certain kind of men against whom Goldstein positions himself as the Other. Significantly, he calls them "real men":

> Real men: a car, a credit card, a mobile phone, beer, football, *shashlyk* at the seaside, three children, an Alsatian dog and a house (297).

This description is given at the end of the essay "The House in the Lane" which rhetorically delineates its significance. It highlights "aspects" of food, gender and sexuality as notions that inform the idea of the identities of the Self and the Other. Goldstein prefers not to be like the others in order to be the Self. His own body, which is not like that of "real men," celebrates marginality, and this marginality is self-invented and self-styled against the stereotype of the male Jew's body as invented by the dominant culture.

In his chapter-essay "Nashestvie" ("Invasion") Goldstein reflects on the class and ethnic differences between the Self and those numerous underprivileged people who came to Israel as *gastarbeiter* in search of work and income. His Self in Israel is that of an *ole hadash* and a citizen who enjoys all the financial privileges that the state gives to Jewish newcomers. He notes that, as a Russian writer and essayist in Israel, his income is small, compared to the wages of foreign workers. In his commentaries he problematizes class differences between himself and the working class *gastarbeiter* from Eastern

Europe, and constructs a dividing line out of the anthropological areas of food and ethnos as manifested in physical appearance. The lexis in which he formulates this class difference is ambivalent: "...the unbridgeability of the differences between myself and the lower classes" (21). The expression "lower classes" in application to *gastarbeiten* is intentionally risqué, connoting racial, and not only class, differences. Goldstein's reflections on this theme are interspersed with reminiscences of how he was fed as a child. It is clear that the formative years of the construction of his identity belong to his childhood when his (Jewish) parents gave him special treatment due to his poor health. As a young boy he was prone to respiratory infections and later in his short life he was afflicted with lung cancer. As a sickly child he was given special kinds of food, including the proverbial "*gogol-mogol*" — beaten egg yolks with sugar — that doting Russian parents of the privileged classes gave their children as a remedy when they were ill with colds:

> When in my childhood I was ill from respiratory problems, I was given to eat *gogol-mogol* which I stirred with a silver plated spoon adorned by a little monkey, who helped my parents to tell stories about various animals (how can I forget the fear which my parents experienced when I ran a temperature)... (21)

And:

> It is truly surprising how many people come from European countries — judging by the map they belong to Europe — and when they were children their doting parents did not feed them with *gogol-mogol* (22).

"*Gogol-mogol*" is fetishized by Goldstein, who is framing his Self as a product of love in which privilege is linked with physical weakness. The rough and rude, physically big and healthy Ukrainians and Romanians earn the same amount of money that he does, but being plebian they do not spend their money on food: "They are used to eating gruel and will never spend money on elegant food" (20). His own diet, even before literary success made him relatively well off, is, as seen in "The House in the Lane," tellingly elegant, despite his "meager income" as "a paper industry employee" (21):

> I like to treat myself to cheese with big holes, half a dozen thin slices of salmon, some honey, a few pieces of dried pineapple, other little luxury items (22).

Characteristics that Goldstein gives to central Europeans are evidence of his treatment of them as ethnic, or racial Others, as opposed to "class" Others. In fact, his characterization of outsiders in Israel demonstrates that, for him, class is identical with race and ethnicity, and it is the upper-class Jew such as himself that emerges superior to the outsiders:

> What is there to say about the Romanians, the faded rags of these humble
> slaves-builders, these unshaven faces, their barbaric speech with meaningless
> Latin structures (20).

It is clear that these Romanians and Ukrainians, who eat floury soups and coarse gruels, will never rise to the level of civilized Europeans like Goldstein himself. Goldstein thus displaces the evaluative center of the binarism of the Jew and the Christian, and uses the symbolic meaning of food as a mechanism for creating this boundary. The irony of this mechanism lies in the history of the reception of the Jew as an outsider in Europe on the basis of dietary difference: Jews were frequently humiliated for not eating pork. The demonization of Jews on the basis of accusations of a ritual attitude toward human blood is an example of this metathesis: one of the kosher laws is not to consume blood — the notion of the blood libel is based on the opposite of this dietary prohibition. In Israel Goldstein grants himself the freedom of applying the same method to Christians, and positions his Jewish Self in stark contrast to the "barbarian" (20) non-Jewish Other.

In addition, the unmistakably medicinal and dietary qualities of his food make him into a Jewish patient not only in matters of sex therapy, but also in his diet. He celebrates his sickly and physically weak body as part of his superior Self. He creates a special, chosen and highly exclusive body, a body constructed out of various aspects of what he believes to be the Ashkenazi Diasporic male body and the bodies of those famous intellectuals who, like the consumptive Franz Kafka or the sickly Marcel Proust, became giants of thought and gurus of style, not in spite of but because of their physical handicaps. Goldstein views intellectualism as a marker of the Jewish male: he often writes about chess, which he characterizes as a Jewish game. Goldstein's favorite chess guru is the chessmaster Mikhail Tal'. There is a telling description of his physical features in the essay-chapter "Ob odnoi vstreche" ("About a certain meeting") which testifies to Goldstein's preference in Jewish male appearance:

> I was looking closely at a picture of Mikhail Tal' on the cover of the book.
> There are almost no faces like his in Israel. As a result of the extermination
> of Jews in the remaining part of the nation there disappeared a dream about
> an unknown future which had put a special spiritual aura on the collective
> physical appearance of the nation... but Tal's physical features came from that
> past, before the destruction, and had an imprint of sickly refinement from the
> old époque (205–206).

Mikhail Tal' had a physical handicap — two fingers on his right hand were fused. For Goldstein this is a marker of *"otmechennost'"* (206), of being marked or chosen. This description reveals a great deal about the psychological underpinnings of Goldstein's construction of the (Jewish) Self.

Daniel Boyarin, in his important *Unheroic Conduct: The Rise of Heterosexuality and the Invention of the Jewish Man* (1997), took a similar authorial position regarding the question of gender stereotypes of "real" men. He states that as a young man he liked ballet and not body-building. He chose to be viewed as a "sissy" by his surrounding (Gentile) peers because those very attributes that made him appear as a "sissy" were what made him a Jew: "Rather than producing in me a desire to 'pass' and to become a 'man,' this sensibility resulted in my desire to remain a Jew, where being a sissy was all right" (xiii).[17] It is this culture, in which it "is all right" to be sickly and effeminate, that Goldstein tries to preserve and which, like Boyarin, he declares as his own. It is a conscious political decision in terms of body politics.

Constructing an Ashkenazi Male Body

With regard to issues of race and ethnicity Goldstein's essays present a challenge to the assumptions of "political correctness" in Israel. His position is openly provocative toward matters of cultural and ethnic diversity in that country. He positions himself as a representative of European Jewry and takes a pro-Ashkenazi stance. He maintains that Ashkenazi Jews surrendered their cultural heritage under the pressure of such political correctness. In the same way that ethnic Romanians are presented as barbarians, remnants of the Roman Empire as made evident now only through their language, all non-European ethnicities in Israel, are depicted as a threat to Ashkenazi culture. The target of Goldstein's discourse on contemporary Israel is the racial impurity of its society. The provocative title of his essay, "Invasion," near the beginning of his book, attests to his uncompromising attitude towards the body politics of Israel. For him, Jews are synonymous with European Jewry, and he openly glorifies this ethnic identity. His conceptualization of European Jewry is noteworthy:

> The Jewish character of Israel, an axiom in no need of proof when considered outside the borders of this country, when considered inside the country becomes a theorem which needs to be proven. When talking about Jews I naturally mean the Ashkenazim. In their far distant origins it is of Eastern character, but in the last two thousand years it has become European in character... in Israel it

has returned to the Hanaanic womb, broken by the noisy bazaar, Levantine laziness, and by the heat (25).

What is striking in this passage is the non-critical use of the concept of national character. The notion of *"evreiskii kharakter"* ("Jewish character") is a calque from the notion of *"natsional'nyi kharakter"* (national character), a nineteenth-century concept that was loved by Russian conservative thinkers and has been appropriated by nationalists in the post-Soviet Russia of the present day. When Goldstein writes about the axiomatic existence of "the Jewish character" of Israel, he has in mind the fact that Israel is perceived by the rest of the world as a mono-ethnic Jewish state. At the same time, however, he slips into using the phrase as a concept with definite historic and political meaning. His uncritical treatment of the notion of the Jewish character attests to his acceptance of the racial stereotypes that are part of this concept. And indeed, he believes that European Jewry is a community defined not only by culture and religion, but also by race and ethnicity.

In this passage an erudite reader will recognize echoes of Rozanov's views on Jewish refinement in contrast with the barbarity of Europe when they arrived there two thousand years ago: "The Jews are the most refined people of Europe" (34), he wrote, and, "They cleaned the snot from the notorious Europeans and put a prayer book into their hands... What would have come of us, what kind of savages would we have been, were it not for the Jews?" (35).[18] Goldstein's echo of such sentiments epitomizes the way he uses aspects in his construction of his postmodernist texts: his blending of thoughts and concepts from a vast cultural heritage of discourses allegedly produces new meanings and effects. But there is also an alarming side to this playful and somewhat uncritical employment of concepts of nineteenth-century biological and ontological discourse. The irony and sarcasm of his discursive strategies create an ambiguity of meaning that in turn creates uncertainty and inexact perceptions. In this way Goldstein's texts contribute to the promulgation of racial and ethnic stereotypes in spite of his playful intentions as a postmodernist author not to take himself too seriously. It is easy to take such fragments out of context, because the context itself is so unclear, and to use those fragments as building blocks for the construction and perpetuation of stereotypes of gender, sex, race and ethnicity.

Goldstein's conceptualization of food as a marker of racial and ethnic identity for the Jewish population of Israel is made into one that divides the Ashkenazi Jews from the "Eastern" Asiatic Jews from Arabic countries:

The Jewish essence here is cheaply given away, it lowers itself for the sake of things which should be treated as a bogey but which here have become an ideal. Sweet and sour meet stews, gefilte fish, chopped herring with boiled egg and onions, honey biscuits, the conciliators (the majority of the Israeli-born Ashkenazim) gave preference to the Maghrib pita dough which bloats stomachs with its rough filling made of chickpeas; these collaborators like football and beer (25).

As a result of Goldstein's narrative strategy the very Jewishness of the non-Ashkenazim, "their essence" (25), becomes questionable: the flat pita bread that they eat, for example, is described as Arabic, not Jewish. Their simple plebeian tastes lead to the trivialization of a nation that plays football and *shich-besh* instead of chess. Men "love female flesh thoughtlessly, while the law requires them to remove the blanket with thoughtful tenderness" (26). Goldstein fears the loss of a national identity which, for him, is synonymous with ethnicity and race. The body that he guards is a body with boundaries, and the loss of form of the body is analogous to the death of the nation: "Soon our own mother will not be able to separate us from the landscape" (26).

In his diatribes against dog-eating Thai and Chinese *gastarbeiter* in Israel, and against Africans from sub-Saharan Africa, Goldstein is provocatively and outrageously racist, rebelling against norms of political correctness in order to define his independent Self which he regards as a biological body. His body is privileged because it is the product of a culture he considers to be refined (in this way Goldstein can be seen to be guarding the biological boundaries of the collective Jewish body). And it is his biological body, one of the few pure bodies in a nation that has failed to preserve its racial purity, which he guards from contamination.

That Goldstein's postmodernist work presents a self-referential racial body that is informed by the knowledge of the history of body discourse becomes apparent in his invocation of Rozanov in his *Parting with Narcissus*. Goldstein tells the story of his Platonic relationship with a Russian woman from St. Petersburg on her occasional visits to Israel. This intercontinental relationship is devoid of any bodily contact — the woman does not want to have any sexual contact by penetration. She does, however, perform an act of manual sex on Goldstein in response to his sudden erection in the midst of a crowd of Israelis celebrating Hannukkah on the streets of the religious neighborhood of Mea Shearim. This is the very neighborhood which, in his essay in *Aspects of Spiritual Marriage,* he describes as inhabited by Jews who still smell of themselves unlike the rest of the Jews in Israel — as seen in the passage used as an epigraph to this chapter. He uses the idea of the smell of a Jew's body as a subtle allusion to Rozanov's characterization of the Jews (found throughout Rozanov's writings). In *Parting with Narcissus* he makes Rozanov's typology more clear: this very same crowd of Jews celebrating

Hannukkah in Mea Shearim is characterized this time by his Russian woman partner as a living illustration of what she terms "Rozanov's Judaism" (388). Goldstein's erection and the Russian woman's help in ridding him of the excesses of sexual fluids that this erection produces follow on from the identification of the crowd of Jews as one big family related to one another by blood ("*krovorodstvennye*" [388]). Rozanov's fantasy of Judaism created an image of the Jewish family in which an individual body is linked to a collective body that culminates in an orgiastic ecstasy, as was demonstrated earlier in Chapter Three. But Rozanov also maintained that onanism was a marker of genius, and among the men of genius that he mentioned were a number of great men of Russian literature. When Goldstein "tells the story" of his own erection *à la Rozanov* ("I felt as if I was on the verge of sinful incest [*krovosmesheniia*]" [388]), and even when he describes the quasi-onanistic spilling of his semen on the street from the hand of his partner, he is clearly playing with the notion of a raced body in a manner which satisfies his own narcissistic, this time Jewish, Self.

The mythology of the Jew's special body with a special type of sexuality has thus been reconfigured by Goldstein into a positive sign, into a rhetorical gratification of his own literary and physical ego. Although he maintains that his Russian girlfriend avoided genital contact with him because she came to the Holy Land to get rid of earthly sins, it is possible that Goldstein's narcissistic body guards itself from contact with the Russian woman in the same way that she erects a border between her Russian body and the Jewish body of Goldstein. This is indeed in accordance with Rozanov's paradoxical and schizophrenic desire to connect, and yet not to connect, with the Jewish body. If this body is special in the Biblical sense, then the salvation of all non-Jews will come through it, so it is in the interests of Christians to keep it racially pure, uncontaminated by non-Jewish blood and semen. At the same time, would it not be good to have some of this Jewish blood running in one's veins? Having solved the paradox of Rozanov's politics of the Jewish body, Goldstein protects his Jewish Self in the manner suggested by Rozanov. In addition, through this chain of literary associations and cultural typology, Goldstein's narcissistic ego finds a strategy to protect itself from the paranoid suspicion that his Russian "girlfriend" might find him physically unattractive as a man, or indeed as a Jew.

The extent to which Goldstein feels free to play with the stereotypes of a Jew's body when living and writing in Israel can be illustrated by another fascinating example of his glorification of the alleged unique smell, the *foetor Judaicus,* of the Jew's body. Although *foetor Judaicus* is seen as a stable marker of the Jewish body, Goldstein applies the notion of this special smell to Israeli women (one recalls the distinctive odor of Chekhov's character Susanna in *Tina*). In his *Parting with Narcissus*, Goldstein describes the physical appearance of Israeli women, emphasizing their difference from Jewish women in the Diaspora, including in Russia.[19] He insists that Israeli women are all of strong build ("*krupnye*") and that, despite taking showers every day and wearing clean underwear, they emit a special smell related to genitalia. This smell is described as stupendous ("*oduriaiushchii*") and has an arousing effect on Goldstein-the-male. This construct of a Jewish woman's body in Israel contains the counterimage of the small and degenerate Jew's body of the Diaspora, hence their alleged height and strong build that make them more akin to Aryan women and Russian peasant women as they have been conceived historically by Russian high culture and in official Soviet discourse. But this construct also has a positive meaning in a Rozanovian sense: despite the influences of culture, the Jewish woman's body still behaves as part of nature. One of the essays in *Parting with Narcissus* is devoted to the theme of the body in contemporary photography, and refers to Camille Paglia's book *Sex, Art and the American Culture* (1992). Goldstein names this feminist critic as the "Rozanov of today" (144), and quotes her comparison of certain body images in contemporary art with the evil flowers ("Les Fleurs du Mal") from the fields of Baudelaire's poetry. In this context Israeli women's genitalia are depicted by Goldstein as a part of nature, with he himself occupying a similar position to that of Rozanov. If Paglia speaks openly on topics such as genitalia, about which Rozanov only "whispered into his interlocutor's ears" (144), then Goldstein at the turn of the new century, can write openly about subjects that shocked the public at the turn of the last century. The irony is that Goldstein's implied courage in dealing with the sexed body carries racial and ethnic material: he is bold enough to publicize his views on the genital smells of Israeli women but at the same time he sanitizes the odors of Jewish women in the Diaspora, who supposedly do not smell. Why do they not emit a smell? One easy answer is that the Jew's body becomes liberated only in Israel and so, in the same way that Jewish men re-forged their puny Diasporic bodies into the iron bodies of Israeli soldiers, Jewish women blossomed in Israel into bodies liberated from the constraints of (European) civilization. But this notion of a woman's body is gendered: it places Jewish women on the level of nature, and although they blossom in the place where the Garden of Eden once was, they become equated with their primordial grandmother Eve.[20] The irony is that feminists have long maintained that for women, going back to Eden means just that: becoming equated with nature. So the Israeli woman's body in Goldstein is a doubly-prejudiced one: both in terms of race and gender. But the authorial

Self, the Narcissus in Goldstein, is gratified by the alleged erections that he experiences while being part of the Jewish collective in Israel. Significantly, however, there is no evidence of sexual contact by penetration with Jewish or Israeli women in Goldstein's texts, an absence that makes questionable his claim to belong to the collective Jewish body. His preference for a body that does not smell is indicative of the strength of the cultural construct of a raced, gendered, and ultimately alien body against which the Narcissus defines the Self against the Other.

A contemporary of Goldstein, scholar Denis Ioffe, who called Goldstein a *schlimazel,* also described him as a "Person of Moonlight" (2002), alluding to Rozanov's tract on sexual pathology, *People of Moonlight* (1909/1911).[21] This description is significant in the context of the present investigation. Like Ilya Ehrenburg's Lazik Roitschwantz, Goldstein was buried in the Holy Land. Like Lazik, he had reservations about his historical homeland. But Lazik's trip to Israel took place before the Holocaust, when the *entire* country was called Palestine, and Lazik did not like the way Arabs treated him. In spite of some fifty years' difference between the two trips to the Holy Land, both "heroes" dreamed of returning to their home country, Russia, yet both died in Israel and did not take this controversial step. Their anticipation of the return to the place where the Jew's body has been treated with such disgust is telling evidence of the complexity of the Diasporic Jewish identity which is negotiated through the construct of the body. It is a manifestation of the ethnic and cultural estrangement of the Russian Ashkenazi Jews from the current Israeli ethos and ethnic identity. A Russian male Jew is a *schlimazel* in any time and space. The fact that Ioffe, albeit ironically, chose as a weapon for his polemics against Goldstein the Rozanovian notion of a non-normative sexuality is a valuable example of how a Jew's sexuality and gender are unavoidably linked to his racial roots. The Russian cultural archetype has thus come full circle, reasserting in the twenty-first century the fin-de-siècle notion of a link between Jewish race and sexuality. The fact that the critic who used this notion is himself a Jewish male and a professional *literator* of Russian origins who has lived in Israel reaffirms the longevity of the psychological introjection of anti-Jewish stereotypes by Jewish intellectuals. Alexander Goldstein can be viewed as a present-day Russian Kafka and a Russian Otto Weininger and in a postmodernist mold. It was this Viennese Jew who in his famous *Sex and Character* (1903) articulated a "blend" of race and gender in application to a Jewish male, and who turned this construction into a weapon against himself before it was turned against others: he committed suicide. In this guise he was well known to Goldstein, who mentions him in his *Parting with Narcissus*. This weapon is still used today both by Jewish intellectuals and their enemies in reference to the Jew's body.

Notes

¹   Aleksandr Gol'dshtein. *Aspekty dukhovnogo braka.* Moscow: Novoe literaturnoe obozrenie. 2001. 9.

²   See In Memorium. *Novoe literaturnoe obozrenie.* Vol. 81. No. 5. 2006. 234–257.

³   On fears of pogroms among the Jewish population of Baku in 1990 see Mark Kharitinov. *Dnevnik ianvaria 1990 goda. Novoe literaturnoe obozrenie.* Vol. 84. No. 2. 2007. 665–675.

⁴   Aleksandr Gol'dshtein. *Rasstavanie s Nartsissom: Opyty pominal'noi ritoriki.* Moscow: Novoe literaturnoe obozrenie. 1997.

⁵   Aleksandr Gol'dshtein. *Aspekty dukhovnogo braka.* Moscow: Novoe literaturnoe obozrenie. 2001.

⁶   Gilles Fauconnier and Mark Turner. *Conceptual Blending and the Mind's Hidden Complexities.* New York: Basic Books. 2002.

⁷   Georges Bataille. *Story of the Eye.* Tran. Joachim Neugroschel. San Francisco: City Lights Books. 1987.

⁸   Samuil Marshak. Iz chego sdelany mal'chiki i devochki. *Detskie pesni.* TATSEL. RU, accessed February 19, 2008.

⁹   As a contemporary critique of the Israeli male machismo see the film *Walk on Water.* Dir. Eytan Fox. 2004. See an anonymous review of this film that discusses the issue of the "Israeli macho man" in *Jewish Week, Washington.* March 24, 2005.

¹⁰ Gianna Pomata. Menstruating Men: Similarity and Difference of the Sexes in Early Modern Medicine. Ed. Valeria Finucci and Kevin Brownlee. *Generation and Degeneration: Tropes of Reproduction in Literature and History from Antiquity to Early Modern Europe.* Durham, NC: Duke University Press. 109–152. 138

¹¹ Peter Ulf Moller. *Postlude to The Kreutzer Sonata: Tolstoj and the Debate on Sexual Morality in Russian Literature in the 1890s.* Leiden: E. J. Brill. 1988.

¹² Denis Ioffe. Anosios Gamos. Opyt vkhozhdeniia v chuzhuiu tonal'nost'. *Topos.* http://www.topos.ru/article/344.

¹³ Goldstein evokes the notion of separation from the love object. On Bely see Aleksandr Etkind. *Khlyst: Sekty, literatura i revolutsiia.* Moscow: Novoe Literaturnoe Obozrenie. 1998.

¹⁴ Michael Satlow. *Tasting the Dish: Rabbinic Rhetorics of Sexuality.* Atlanta: Scholars Press. 1996.

¹⁵ See the famous book of the Stalin era *Kniga o vkusnoi i zdorovoi pishche.* Ed. Prof. O. P. Molchanov et al. Moscow: Pishchepromizdat. 1952. On food in Russian culture see *Food in Russian History and Culture.* Ed. Musya Glants. Bloomington: Indiana University Press. 1997.

¹⁶ Mikhail Kozakov. *Akterskaia kniga.* Moscow: Vagrius. 1997.

¹⁷ Daniel Boyarin. *Unheroic Conduct: The Rise of Heterosexuality and the Invention of the Jewish Man.* Berkeley: California University Press. 1997.

¹⁸ A polemical Jewish response to the notions of the smell of the Jew's body in the Russian Silver Age culture is found in Osip Mandelstam's famous trope "the musk of Judaism." See Leonid Katsis. *Osip Mandel'shtam: Muskus Iudeistva.* Moscow: Mosty kul'tury. 2002.

¹⁹ V. V. Rozanov. *Apokalipsis nashego vremeni.* Moscow: Respublika. 2000.

[20] See Elizabeth Grosz. *Volatile Bodies: Towards a Corporeal Feminism*. Bloomington: Indiana University Press. 1994.

[21] Denis Ioffe. Anosios Gamos. Opyt vkhozhdeniia v chuzhuiu tonal'nost'. *Topos (Literaturno-filosofskii zhurnal).* http://www.topos.ru/article/344. Accessed January 22, 2009.

Chapter 10

The "Real" Jewish Bodies of Oligarchs: Important Jewish Personalities and Post-Soviet Corporophobia

> "Parasitic ethnicity is like a vampire. It sucks the drive out of the ethnic environment and shows the pulse-rate of ethnogenesis"
>
> Lev Gumilev. 1993.[1]
>
> "Their inborn skin color is virtually jaundiced and seems to manifest a continuous separation of the bile that enters the blood"
>
> Immanuel Kant. 1775.[2]

This chapter concentrates on those Jewish males who, unlike Goldstein, did not emigrate in the 1990s but rather remained in Russia in the last decade of the twentieth century and who, having made their fortunes out of the collapse of the Soviet Union, became victims of political changes in Putin's Russia in the present. The freedom of expression in the 1990s has taken its toll on the representation of both fictional and real Jews in post-Soviet Russia, as is evident in the construct of the Jew's body. Alongside the unprecedented rise to political and economic prominence of Jewish businessmen during the 1990s there arose fears about the subjugation of Russia by Jews.[3] The change of presidency from Boris Yeltsin to Vladimir Putin saw the demise of a number of political powerbrokers, or "oligarchs," of the 1990s, including the two most prominent — Vladimir Gusinsky and Boris Berezovsky.[4] As well as their fabulous wealth, both these men had considerable influence on the Russian mass media in the 1990s, including the ownership of central TV stations, radio stations and the print media. Since they both went into exile, after having escaped imprisonment on charges of corruption in 2000, the Russian media has gradually changed as it has become increasingly gripped by the strong hand of the State apparatus which was only too anxious to regain control.[5] Putin was unwilling to tolerate the oligarchs' involvement in Russian politics, nor was he prepared to put up with their criticism of his own actions.[6] Pressure to oust Berezovsky from the Duma came from various conservative and nationalistic circles, including members of the so-called military-industrial complex and various publishers, writers, and journalists. One such figure was Alexander Prokhanov, editor-in-chief of the extreme right-wing newspaper *Zavtra* and a writer of patriotic fiction with a strong nostalgia for Stalinist times. In 2002 he published a novel, *Gospodin Geksogen* (*Mr. Hexogen*), which contained damning images of the Jewish oligarchs and an overt attack on Gusinsky and Berezovsky.[7] The novel contains thinly veiled caricatures of the two men who are portrayed as destroyers of Russia whose goals were foiled thanks to the cunning plan of a group of true Russian patriots, the army and secret services generals who lured the two Jewish oligarchs into a trap. A new leader, who has all the physical characteristics of Putin, has been promoted by this group and he saves Russia from imminent destruction at the hands of the two oligarchs and international Jewry. Prokhanov depicts Berezovsky and Gusinsky in the guise of two quasi-fictional characters, Zaretskii and Astros, and these representations provide a striking example of contemporary Russian culture's mode of depicting Jews via the construct of their bodies. The representation of Jews' bodies in Prokhanov's novel is particularly interesting as it depicts real historic personalities whose visibility in the 1990s and the present decade in the Russian media was prominent due to their numerous appearances on TV and in the press. What physical features and mannerisms does Prokhanov assign his characters to make them resemble the real Berezovsky and Gusinsky? What are those features that make them typically Jewish in the eyes of Prokhanov and his audience? How does the writer achieve the transformation of the personal and unique features of an individual into "typical" features that are supposed to represent race?

For Prokhanov, whose novel represents an example of Russian pulp fiction that has acquired considerable importance in modern Russia,[8] the battle between Russia and the two Jewish oligarchs is the battle between Russians and Jews. He openly conducts this battle on the territory of race, physiology and the hereditary. In this book, Russia has to fight a conspiracy led by the Jews whose alleged aim is the extermination of Russian ethnicity. Here we can see a thematic continuation from the conspiracy theory expounded by Belov in his infamous novel of Glasnost times to the revisionist plot of Prokhanov's novel. With the oligarchs either in exile or, in Khodorkovsky's case, in prison, and with Yeltsin's inner circle ousted from power, Prokhanov feels free to express openly anti-Jewish feelings that appear in the form of "biological" antisemitism.

The plot of Prohaknov's novel is based on the notion of taking revenge for the deeds of the oligarchs by using their own strategies and the tactics they allegedly used against the Russian people. And as the alleged goal of the Jewish oligarchs was the annihilation of the Russians as an ethnic collective, Prokhanov feels free to unleash the language of racial hatred. In this novel the Jews, represented by Zaretskii, openly speak about the annihilation of the Russian nation. If, in Belov's novel *The Best is Yet to Come,* Misha Brish speaks sarcastically about Russian women refusing to give birth, then in Prokhanov's novel Zaretskii has a more open and aggressive plan for the demographic decline of the Russian nation:

> The Russian people as a nation are dead, they are no longer a nation, but a quickly disappearing sum of species, and we supervise this population and we regulate the numbers... We have torn out the will of the people, torn out their tongue, cut off their testicles (78–79).
> If they start procreating we will forbid their women to bear children (80).

In this novel, media magnate Astros (Gusinsky) develops a whole laboratory as a base for his biological experiments. He employs not only scientists but also a mysterious midget who is an alchemist and a sorcerer. This little man is a personification of the eternal Jew with demonic powers, and he conducts his experiments by consulting a book with writing that suspiciously resembles Hebrew. Some of the experiments in the laboratory are devoted to the sexual behavior of Russian women, who are encouraged to engage in auto-sexual gratification and so do away with their need for men. The danger of this auto-eroticism is in line with the warnings issued in Belov's novel about the new trends in sexual behavior, with women being encouraged to seek pleasure from sex rather than to have sex for the purpose of procreation. In Prokhanov's novel the Jewish media magnate has the power to disseminate his experiments to hundreds of millions of viewers, thus controlling the demography of the Russian people.

Another branch of this laboratory is named "the laboratory of anthropological improvements" (167). The experiments here are directed toward creating a certain anthropological type based on models of famous Jews. Because Astros owns a TV channel he can use the medium of television to promote one racial type and to annihilate another. Thus, a Russian is made to look like a degenerate specimen with mental deficiencies as represented in his physical appearance: blond hair, a face manipulated to have a narrow forehead, yellow teeth. This "animal-like" (169) man is dressed in a "northern" style shirt that is supposed to serve as an additional marker of the recognizability of the Slavic Nordic anthropological being who is presented as a degenerate type in need of correction. The laboratory's aim is to "form reality" (170) and it uses the Jewish anthropological type as a model for this change. Thus, the laboratory aims to create a composite ideal based on well-known Jewish personalities, including Albert Einstein.

Of importance is Prokhanov's description of the physical form of Jews, and his description of Einstein, whose photographs are well known to contemporary audiences, represents the strategy with which he approaches the depiction of a "real" Jew's body:

On the screen appeared the portrait of Albert Einstein, thoughtful, calm with deep eternal sadness in his kind and slightly narrowed eyes. Einstein disappeared and was replaced by a famous comedian from Odessa, plump and cute; he leaned his head slightly towards one side, his cherry-like eyes sent out rays and he attracted involuntary sympathy by having some resemblance to the famous physicist, perhaps in the shape of his ears. His image was followed by that of a young handsome man, a right-wing politician who not long ago dreamt about becoming Russia's president. He was replaced by a famous actor-puppeteer with an ascetic face, hooked nose and an old wrinkled mouth, but with very kind, but sad eyes.[9] Then again appeared Einstein, stressing the family resemblance with the former figures — the same noble mustache and sad gaze directed into non-Euclidian space, and the love for everything living and not living. From this etalon constantly repeating yet changing image there began to appear a similar-looking type (168).

The function of this composite type is to make acceptable the very same features that serve as indicators of typically Jewish features, consisting as they do of such stable clichés as sad eyes and an intelligent gaze. The individual faces also include those features that have been marked by the Russian culture as ugly: hooked nose and unusually shaped ears. Astros, in his construction of the etalon, has his own "Jewish" perception of "Jewish" features, which he perceives as pleasant and appealing, but the Russian narrator and his Russian protagonist have a different one. The flattering Jewish figure created by Jews turns out to be repulsive to the Russian viewer. Certainly the main protagonist Beloseltsev (a name meaning "white village") experiences a physical aversion to this construct. As his surname attests, Beloseltsev represents a warrior of the Russian people and an upholder of Russian nativist values. For him, the Jewish faces, as well as the simulated and artificially created ideal based on these faces, prompt a strong sense of repulsion. Astros's own face is presented as dominated by one aspect of his features — the shape of his eyes. Although blue in color, they are not to be confused with the blue eyes of a Slav because of their "bulging shape" (114) — the reader will recognize the stable stereotype of Jewish physiognomy in antisemitic discourse.

Zaretskii's Body

The idea of race and biology is further reinforced by the physical body of the oligarchs. Zaretskii's complexion is depicted as a sickly yellow — yellow being a marker of race (referring to Jews' Asiatic origins) and denoting the diseased nature of a Jew's body. The reader will remember that the color of a Jew's skin was used as a marker of both race and the physically sick body in the medical literature at the turn of the nineteenth century.[10] Because yellow skin was considered to be a sign of jaundice, it was used to signify the diseased nature of the Jew's body. In Prokhanov's novel these markers become constant characteristics of Zaretskii's Jewish physique:

> Zarestkii put his malaria-like yellow hand on to the plump white hand of the president's daughter (78).
> He laughed, baring his yellowish teeth (78).
> His yellow hepatitis-like color was matched by his sarcasm and irony (78).
> Zaretskii's sickly yellowish face (267).
> A tormenting thought wrinkled his yellow forehead (271).
> The skin on his face, on his bald head and his hairy hand rapidly yellowed, became filled with some mysterious pigment, as if he was a chameleon and changed his coloring in line with his changing emotions (80).

Prokhanov obviously is not concerned about confusing medical diagnoses of malaria and hepatitis; indeed, this is quite acceptable to him as his aim is to depict the grotesque, race-formed body that is plagued by evils and sicknesses and marked by color. In line with the stable trope of the mutability of the Jew's body, Prokhanov makes Zaretskii change color. Not only is he likened to a chameleon, but his mutating abilities go beyond the identification with a single species: he "started losing outline, became devoid of shape and color, became runny like a jelly, floated like an enormous medusa" (80).

Prokhanov wrote his novel in the early 2000s and is clearly eager to introduce aspects of virtual reality into his narrative, as seen in his use of fantasy elements in the style of the genre of *The Lord of the Rings* to depict the Jew's body: "In [Zaretskii's] transparent bluish depth, in the layers of tissue, there was a faintly darkened smoky center, a mysterious hole, which linked this reality with the other, outer reality, from which a mysterious bubble flowed out, only to flow back and be sucked in again" (80).

Having paid his tribute to popular culture, Prokhanov creates a collage made up of the stable features of the Jew's body and new clichés concerning the depiction of repulsive physical monsters from outer space. The body is both super-human and non-human; it is out of bounds. Its primitive amoeba-like structure reaffirms the notion of the rudimentary nature of a Jew's body with a new twist: this monster survives due to its mutability based not only on earthly elements but also on a virtual, fantasy reality. Such physical characteristics make the creature a difficult target to eliminate.

Among the staple stereotypes of the Jew's body with which Zaretskii is aligned is the Jew as a devil, a sadistic and bloodthirsty being:

> Zaretskii rubbed his dry hands. He looked like a devil who was looking at victims suffering in hell, throwing wood into fire (218).
> You did it out of pure sadism!.. You pervert, tormentor!.. You like peoples' sufferings!..You like Sheptun's head which had been cut off! (217).
> It is with good reason that the red-browns [fascists and communists] make drawings which depict you with an axe covered with blood! (218).

Prokhanov implicates Zaretskii in the assassination of a Russian general by Chechen rebels, thus inviting the reader to identify him as Berezovsky. Of importance here is the introduction of the stable cultural markers of the Jew in Russia which materialize in pictorial images of a bloodthirsty vampire who is driven by pathological impulses and instincts. A severed head stands as an allegory for the story of John the Baptist, whose head was demanded by Herod's stepdaughter, Salome, as described in Matthew 14:8 and Mark 6:25 — the beheading and the presentation of the severed head are frequently used in Christian art.[11] This story from the Scriptures has been interpreted in Christian tradition as a sign of Jewish tribalism, treachery and vengefulness, as well as bloodthirstiness.[12]

Russian Body Politics of Jewish Powerbrokers and Eurasianism

Both oligarchs are viewed as representatives of the same tribe, a tribe led by a hereditary "ancient instinct" (270) which makes "their psyche" (270) behave in a predetermined manner. The narrator claims that the predictability of Jewish behavior makes it easy for Russians to manipulate them. Their primeval ("*reliktovyi*" [270]) instinct, he argues, leads Jews to panic, making them more vulnerable. Prokhanov's strategy here is quite clear: to turn the tide of opinion against Jews and to rid the Russian people of the Jewish presence. He justifies this strategy through an alleged Jewish conspiracy to both outsmart the Russians and to change them genetically. This conspiracy gives Prokhanov's Russian heroes the moral authority to adopt what they see as the techniques of their enemy to rid the Russian soil of the Jewish presence by employing methods of biological warfare. Those who want to genetically re-engineer Russians through their scientific experiments become the objects of Russian psychobiological expertise and manipulation. The following extract reveals how the Russian conspirators against Zaretskii use biological and psychological data on the body as ammunition in their overtly genetic warfare:

> We know his habits, one of which is to get locked in the bathroom and to masturbate there in the froth of a bubble bath surrounded by mirrors... We have the full medical history of all his illnesses starting from his early childhood, including psychopathic breakdowns and venereal diseases. We have his fingerprints, wax imprints of his teeth, chest x-rays, hair samples, his genetic code (58).

This forensic description of a Jewish oligarch's body is quite astounding and serves as a powerful reminder of the dominant culture's obsession with the Jew's body. In the novel's plot the conspirators want to annihilate Zaretskii, and intend to use this information in their hunt for him when and if he goes into exile. The tragic example of the death of the former Russian agent in Britain, Alexander Litvinenko who was poisoned by plutonium in 2007, makes a current reading of this novel a chilling experience. It also suggests that the link between Russian literature and Russian politics is as strong as it has traditionally been in modern Russian history.[13]

Prokhanov's overt battle against Jewish powerbrokers and dignitaries is based on the notion of a Jewish conspiracy in which the whole of international Jewry is seen as part of the same political group, but Prokhanov appropriates this very notion of conspiracy for his fight against Jews. The tribal unity of the Jewish group is believed to be secured by blood ties which are viewed as the driving force of every individual member of the group. As a counter to this conspiracy, Prokhanov creates a Russian conspiracy also based on blood ties, this time among those of Russian blood. There is a haunting scene in the novel in which all the Russian participants are linked in a disturbing ritual involving the communal drinking of the warm blood of a killed animal. This initiation ceremony stands as an allegory for a pagan rite in which members of a Russian group participate in both the ritual slaughter and the consumption of an animal. This ritual serves as a parallel to what antisemitic myths attribute to Jewish rites at their core: the ritual intake of blood. It also serves as a powerful reminder of the centrality of the mechanism of psychological projection and the introjection of the racial Other. Christians make Jews take blood because they themselves have made a symbol from this act and because they have projected this belief in the mystical power of blood onto Jews.[14] In a second step, having imagined that Jews have unique powers due to their "special attitude towards blood" (Rozanov), they then appropriate this belief and try to become as "powerful" as Jews, hence the "ritual" blood-taking by the Christians and Russian warriors in Prokhanov's novel. Central to this pattern of behavior is their fear and jealousy of what they consider to be the special knowledge and power of Jews.[15]

In the novel the Russian protagonist Beloseltsev enters into an agreement with a Chechen Muslim warrior in order to create an alliance against Jewish domination. The Oxford-educated Chechen bases this political alliance on racial grounds, with his hatred of Jews serving as a uniting force between his people and the Russians. He repeats verbatim the idea of the demographic decline of the Russian nation which becomes almost a refrain in the novel: "Russians have astonishingly weakened as a nation. They have lost the will to govern. Men do not want to fight, women do not want to bear children" (183). Whereas the Chechen is slender and handsome, the Jew is described as aesthetically ugly with a physically and psychologically sick body. Prokhanov romanticizes the Islamic design of the interior of the Chechen's apartment, but he creates a Frankenstein-like experimental laboratory for Astros and an ultra-modern, sterile and plastic environment for Zaretskii. The Chechen powerbroker is thus clearly a friend, the Jewish powerbrokers are enemies.

The political map in the novel is divided into two main spheres of influence: Western civilization with America and Jews at its center, and Russia with its Asiatic satellites. Like his alter ego Beloseltsev, Prokhanov is by profession a specialist on Asia and Africa. He is also an important figure in the contemporary political movement of Eurasianism, and serves as editor-in-chief of the newspaper *Zavtra*, a mouthpiece for the Eurasianist movement. Eurasianism, is a popular belief system in Russia, with a significant number of politically influential followers.[16] It advocates the division of the world into different civilizations based on mentality and race: the Atlantic nations are represented by America, the United Kingdom, and Israel, and so-called Eurasia is represented by Russia and its imagined satellites from the East. Most of these Eastern nations are Islamic and non-Christian; they are viewed as having a different mentality and a different set of values, as they have not been influenced by the rationalism and materialism of Judaism. This theory works in opposition to globalization and "melting pot" societies; it rejects notions of "universal values" and "the new world order."

Prokhanov's characters base their political actions on these tenets of Eurasianism (the alliance that his literary alter ego Beloseltsev makes with the "good" Chechen is a micro-model of this theory), and their fight against Jewish domination presupposes an alliance with the Islamic nations of the Russian Federation, as well as with the new states of the former Soviet Union and other Asian nations. At its core this political alliance is nostalgic, structured around the desire to resurrect the spheres of the former political influence of the Soviet Union. Israel and the United States become the enemy of Russia, with Arab and Islamic nations once more becoming Russia's friends. If in the days of the Soviet Union the dominant rhetoric in international affairs was based on the concepts of imperialist exploitation and class differences, then in Russia today the Eurasianist rhetoric is overtly biology-based. Supported by the terminology of Lev Gumilev's (1912–1992) Eurasianist theories on the "complementarity" of various ethnic identities and the lack of compatibility among other ethnic groups, this theory isolates Jews as the ultimate Others. Gumilev considers the ethnicity of the Turkic and Ugro-Finnic peoples to be compatible with that of Russia, whereas Semitic ethnicity belongs to a group outside the Slavonic and Turkic peoples. His discourse is quasi-scientific, based as it is on concepts of biology:

> The super-ethnic system... is closely connected with the nature of its region. Each of its constituent parts and subsystems finds an ecological niche for itself... But if a new foreign ethnic entity invaded this system and could not find a safe ecological niche for itself, it would be forced to live at the expense of the inhabitants of the territory, not at the expense of the territory itself... In zoology the combination of an animal and a tapeworm in the intestines is called a chimerical construction... Living in the host's body the parasite takes a part in its life cycle, dictating a heightened need for food and altering the organism's biochemistry by its own hormones forcibly secreted into the blood or bile of the host (302).[17]

There is a striking similiarity between Gumilev's discourse and Hitler's *Mein Kampf* in which Jews were called vermin and parasites not only as a rhetorical device, but also to give the author respectability through his use of quasi-scientific terminology. In Gumilev's writing the same ideas are couched in scientific terminology to add a degree of scientific respectability to the views expressed. Hitler used terms like "toxins remain in the national body" (212) and "harmful poisons" (212) in reference to the Jewish presence within the collective body of the German nation.[18] Gumilev's theory is a surreptitious restatement of the Nazi theory of racial purity, updated to include the terminology of hormones, genes, and the conflation of notions of ethnicity and race. His main work, *Ancient Russia and the Great Steppe,* was dedicated to the history of the interaction between the state of Khazaria and Old Rus' in the eighth and ninth centuries.[19] In the works of Gumilev and other Eurasianists, Khazaria, whose rulers and nobility accepted Judaism as its state religion, serves as an example of a state hostile to the Russian and Slavic people. When in Prokhanov's novel Astros leads a project under the name of "New Khazaria," he evokes this link with Eurasianism as professed by its main ideologue, Alexander Dugin.[20]

Prokhanov has Astros identify the aim of the "New Khazaria" project as an attempt to move the center of Jewish civilization into Russia. According to Eurasianist ideology, such an alliance would be destructive for Russia because of the very antagonistic nature of the two types of civilizations. In line with Eurasianist teachings, Prokhanov's novel celebrates the ethnic alliance between the Russians and the Chechens, and demarcates the place for Jews outside this group. The Jews' collective body is thus presented as incompatible with the body of Russia and that of its old imperial subjects on the oil-rich periphery of the Russian empire.

In Prokhanov's novel's pseudo-apocalyptic imagery, Russia's body is compared to that of a woman who is trying to give birth and yet cannot rid herself of the burden of the uterus.[21] As a body it is physically tortured, its convulsions the result of unhealthy mistreatment, stimulation and sadistic torture inflicted by Jews and other dark-colored Others. Jews encourage traitors to use the Kremlin as a center for their conspiracy and from there, from the office formerly occupied by Leon Trotsky, they send torturing waves and signals:

> Using the method of acupuncture, exciting and suppressing at the same time, they held the country in total obedience, and the country, like a woman who was left without strength and suffering from illness, lay under the light of surgical lamps and could not give birth. People in masks injected chemicals into her enormous stomach in which an invisible child rolled in it in painful convulsions. (259)

This bizarre imagery is a quasi-postmodernist caricature of multiculturalism and globalization with acupuncture and chemical induction as a collage of Asian and Jewish alterities. These foreign methods are presented as endangering the body of the Russian woman in the same way that globalization and postmodernist cultural eclecticism endanger Russia's biological and cultural identity. The fact that foreign conspirators try to interfere with the fetus at its uterine stage stands as a metaphor for the interference in the biological integrity and genetic purity of the Russian racial and ethnic body. In Prokhanov's world, the battle is thus fought on the level of body politics. Various people of "Caucasian nationality"[22], such as the Azeries, are attacked for their involvement in child prostitution and child molestation, and are put under scrutiny for their part in the abuse of the (sexed) bodies of Russian children and teenagers. The very demographic future of Russia is presented as being under threat from these ethnically foreign people who infect Russian children with AIDS and make them dependent on drugs. In Prokhanov's novel the fear of degeneration of the nation runs as high at the turn of the new century as it did during the fin-de-siècle period, and Jews and other racial Others, represented through the recycled apocalyptic imagery of pulp fiction, are viewed as the main destroyers of the Russian nation. The novel won the National Best-seller title in the year of its publication.

Notes

[1] Lev Gumilev. *Tysiacheletie: vokrug Kaspiia*. Moscow. 1993. 41.

[2] Kant's explanation of the yellow skin color of Asian-Indians. See Immanuel Kant. Of the Different Human Races. Eds. Robert Benasconi and Tommy L. Lott. *The Idea of Race*. Indianapolis/Cambridge: Hackett Publishing Company. 2000. 8–23.

[3] See Marshall I. Goldman. Russian Jews in Business. Eds. Zvi Gitelman, Musya Glants and Marshall I. Goldman. *Jewish Life after the USSR*. Bloomington: Indiana University Press. 2003. 76–99.

[4] For a good exposé on Berezovsky and Khodorkovsky see the BBC TV documentary "Russia's Godfathers". 2005.

[5] Rosalind Marsh. *Literature, History and Identity in Post-Soviet Russia, 1991–2006*. Bern: Peter Lang. 2007.

[6] On Putin's and the Russian government's position vis-à-vis Jewish prominence in the Russian society today see Robert J. Brym. Russian Anisemitism, 1996–2000. Eds. Zvi Gitelman, Musya Glants and Marshall I. Goldman. *Jewish Life After the USSR*. Bloomington: Indiana University Press. 2003. 99–117.

[7] On Prokhanov's Stalinist nostalgia see his comments in Elizabeth Rich, Ed. *Russian Literature after Perestroika, South-Central Review*. Special issue. Vol. 12. No. 3/4. Fall/Winter. 1995. 22–25. On Prokhanov and the right-wing writers see Rosalind Marsh. *Literature, History and Identity in Post-Soviet Russia, 1991–2006*. Bern: Peter Lang. 2007.

[8] See Stephen Lovell and Birgit Menzel, Eds. *Reading for Entertainment in Contemporary Russia: Post-Soviet Popular Literature in Historical Perspective*. Munich: Sagner. 2005.

[9] These descriptions probably refer to Zhvanetskii, Yavlinskii and Obraztsov.

[10] Gilman writes about the "image of a diseased and 'yellow' Jew": "One needs only to remember *The Yellow Book* whose color evoked the very spirit of fin-de-siécle self-conscious

degeneracy" (114). See Sander Gilman. Salome, Syphilis, Sarah Bernhardt and the Modern Jewess. *The Jew in the Text: Modernity and the Construction of Identity*. Eds. Linda Nohlin and Tamar Garb. London: Thames and Hudson. 1995. 97–121.

[11] On the reception of Salome and John the Baptist story in Russian turn-of-the-century culture see Olga Matich. *Erotic Utopia: The Decadent Imagination in Russia's Fin De Siècle*. Madison: Wisconsin University Press. 2005. In the broader European context see Sander Gilman. Salome, Syphilis, Sarah Bernhardt and Modern Jewess. *The Jew in the Text: Modernity and the Construction of Identity*. Eds. Linda Nohlin and Tamar Garb. London: Thames and Hudson. 1995. 97–121.

[12] Robert J. Brym states that in 2000 a poll run by a popular Russian television anchor asked if the viewers believed Jews used Christian blood to make *matzot* during Passover—about half the respondents said yes. Russian Anisemitism, 1996–2000. Eds. Zvi Gitelman, Musya Glants and Marshall I. Goldman. *Jewish Life After the USSR*. Bloomington: Indiana University Press. 2003. 99–117.

[13] Rosalind Marsh. *Literature, History and Identity in Post-Soviet Russia, 1991–2006*. Bern: Peter Lang. 2007.

[14] Alan Dundes. *The Blood Libel Legend: A Casebook of Anti-Semitic Folklore*. Madison: University of Wisconsin Press. 1991.

[15] On the psychology of fear in modern societies in application to the Vampire myth see Franco Moretti. The Dialectic of Fear. *New Left Review*. Vol. 1. No. 136. 1982. 67-85.

[16] For a detailed discussion of Eurasianism see Vadim Rossman. *Russian Intellectual Antisemitism in the Post-Communist Era*. Lincoln: University of Nebraska Press. 2002.

[17] Lev Gumilev. *Etnogenez i biosfera Zemli*. Leningrad. 1989. 302.

[18] Adolf Hitler. *Mein Kampf*. Introduction by D. C. Watt. Trans. by Ralph Manheim. London: Hutchinson of London. 1969.

[19] Lev Gumilev. *Drevniaia Rus' i velikaia step'*. Moscow: Tov-vo Klyshnikov. 1992.

[20] On Aleksandr Dugin see Rossman. Op. cit.

[21] See Marina Aptekman. Kabbalah, Judeo-Masonic Myth, and Post-Soviet Literary Discourse: From Political Tool to Virtual Parody. *The Russian Review*. Vol. 64. No. 4. 2006. 657–681.

[22] For a response to this stereotype see the documentary *Litso Kavkazskoi Natsional'nosti* (2001). Dir. Georgii Gabelia.

Chapter 11

The Post-Soviet Assault on the Jew's Body: the New Racial Science

> "Mr. Foster was so struck with the general appearance of the Cashmereans as to be almost inclined to imagine that he had been suddenly transported among the nation of Jews"
>
> John Bigland. 1816.[1]

This chapter examines the presence of the Jew's racialized body in the quasi-scientific writing of post-Soviet period. It examines the work of two racially aggressive authors, Grigory Klimov (1918–2007) and Vladimir Avdeev (b. 1962), whose pseudo-scientific assumptions are presented as respectable social theories.[2] Avdeev and Klimov are popular not only inside Russia and the former Soviet Union, but also among the Russian Diaspora around the globe. Klimov had an Internet site, and received letters from followers from various parts of the world, including such "remote places" as Australia and New Zealand.[3] He died in the United States in December 2007.

Psychopathology of Race: Klimov's "Advanced Sociology"

The most extreme manifestation in Russian discourse of the political exploita-tion of linking race and psychopathology, including sexual perverseness, is found in the work of the contemporary author Grigory Klimov. Klimov's appeal to the post-Soviet Russian reader is explained by the fact that, due to his unusual biography, he himself falls into the category of "returned" authors.[4] Klimov defected to the West after World War II and, according to the information on his website, was employed by US intelligence organizations as an expert on communist societies.[5] His popularity in post-Soviet Russia is explained by the aura of authority that surrounds him as a person and his rare insight not only into the workings of communist governments, but also into the secrets of major institutions within the United States. The fact that his works were banned from publication in the Soviet Union puts him on a par with authors such as Vasily Rozanov and other representatives of conservative and ultra-conservative Russian thought. His advanced age gave him an additional status of respectability and wisdom.

After the fall of the Soviet Union Klimov became a member of the Russian Writers' Union. He is the author of openly antisemitic books with such provocative titles as *Bozhii narod* (*God's Chosen People* [1989]), *Protokoly sovetskikh mudretsov* (*Protocols of the Elders of the Soviets* [1981]) (the title echoes *Protocols of the Elders of Zion*), and *Krasnaia kabala* (*The Red Kabala* [1987]), all of which are available in various bookshops and can be downloaded from Internet sites. His work promotes the idea of the existence of a Jewish conspiracy, a theory based on the biological nature of the Jewish race. Klimov uses a number of quasi-scientific terms, such as "bionegativity" and "degeneracy." His scientific method is termed "Degeneralogiia" ("Degenerology") and the branch of science he has developed is known as "Vysshaia Sotsiologiia" ("Advanced Sociology").

Klimov's work is focused almost exclusively on the pathology of the Jewish race, which for him is the prime example of degeneration and psychopathology. Every political problem that Russian society has faced over the last two centuries is regarded as the result of the activities of Jews. The main postulate of Klimov's theory is that all Jews are degenerates, and that all degenerates are either Jews or have an admixture of Jewish blood. Once Jewish blood enters the genetic pool of the nation, this nation becomes poisoned, damaged by agents of destruction that cannot be identified as Jewish because their physical appearance has been altered. Klimov's method of application of such theories is simple: he postulates an admixture of Jewish blood in all prominent and important political personalities in the history of Russia and the Soviet Union, explaining their destructive role by their psychopathological drive to dominate the political life of the country. He terms such a drive the "complex of power." The following passage from an interview entitled "Sut' problemy" ("The Core of the Problem"), which Klimov gave in 2001,[6] demonstrates his methodology, approach and use of terminology:

> When close relatives marry each other, then children from such a union will be degenerates. This is an old and well-known fact. This is why the Christian

Church forbids marriage between relatives up to six generations.
If a group of religious leaders does the opposite and ENCOURAGES such marriages and even FORBIDS marriages outside the sect, then this sect will be full of degenerates in four to five generations.
Do you know such a sect, which forbids mixed marriages and which continues marriages between relatives as it has done for a several thousand years?
Yes, we know such a sect.
Many degenerates have strange characteristics, such as the insatiable desire to dominate, and an abnormal, pathological desire always to be on top. Many of them have an insatiable power mania.
These degenerates feel that they are the "chosen people," an "élite group" (superiority mania), and at the same time they feel that they are being "persecuted" and "chased away" (persecution mania). But superiority mania and persecution mania are siblings (1).

This is one of Klimov's most diplomatic and cryptic descriptions of a degenerative group, in which the reader nevertheless easily identifies Jews. His book *Bozhii narod* (*God's Chosen People*) is structured as a series of lectures, and consists of thirteen chapters in which he concentrates entirely on Jews as a prime example of a degenerate nation. Here, in this interview, Klimov explains the difference between his approach and racism, maintaining that any body politic that advocates the racial purity of blood is itself a source of degeneracy. Jews and Judaism are identified not only as degenerate, but also as racist; such is the double-edged sword of Klimov's methodology in application to Jews.

Klimov divides degeneracy into three stages: 1/ sexual perversions; 2/ psychological illnesses; 3/ inborn defects. These categories allow Klimov to include homosexuals and lesbians in the category of degenerates, and to create a link between race and gender. The main aim of Klimov's diagnosis of groups of people as degenerates is to expose them as a destructive force in the political, economic and cultural life of contemporary societies, and Russia in particular. In fact, he describes degenerates as "weapons of mass destruction" (1).

Sexual Degeneracy

In his "advanced sociology," Klimov focuses on a number of features, including sexual transgressions and Jewish pathology, as a political weapon against enemies/Jews.[7] His self-proclaimed mission is to save the Russian nation from pollution by Jewish blood and it comes as no surprise that he refers to Rozanov in his work, albeit with an ironic mistrust of this writer's sanity:

> Here is an example. There is a rather famous writer in the history of Russian literature –Vasily Vasilievich Rozanov. In an article entitled "Jehovah's Angel and the Jews" Rozanov wrote about the attitude of Jews towards *goyim*: "He (the *goy*) can be made even more ill when he is sick, or be given medicine which does not work. It is possible to spoil the *goyim's* literature. It is possible to damage and destroy their trade and industry."
>
> One has to say that V. V. Rozanov himself was a very ambivalent person, e. g. from the viewpoint of advanced sociology he was a degenerate and psychologically sick. I think that sexually he was also not normal. At the age of twenty he married a forty-year-old woman, something which a normal man would not do. He explained the reason for his marriage in this way: this forty-year-old woman used to be Dostoevsky's mistress and out of respect for Dostoevsky he married her. The marriage was short, this psychopathic woman left him.
>
> In the article "Jehovah's Angel and the Jews" V. Rozanov acted as an antisemite, but soon he started to flirt with Jews—he was a terrible chameleon (6).[8]

In this attack on Rozanov there are echoes of Rozanov's own practice of accusing his enemies of sexual perversions. In Klimov's case Rozanov becomes the object of such a "methodology." Klimov accuses both Rozanov and his partner Apollinariia Suslova of being psychopaths in a move that is symptomatic of his tactic of damning sexual deviants: in his work even divorced women fall into the category of degenerates.[9] Even writers like Rozanov and Dostoevsky, who made negative pronouncements about Jews, fall into the category of degenerates, sexual deviants, or biologically flawed individuals ("bionegatives").

This, however, does not mean that Klimov is less manipulative than Rozanov in his mission. Indeed, various personalities become objects of Klimov's manipulation by means of his interpretation of their sexualities.

Dostoevsky, His Own Pathologies and His "Crypto-Jews"

Klimov uses Dostoevsky as he uses Rozanov, as an expert on Jews, while at the same time being an object of Klimov's study of psychopathology. The alliances Klimov forges with Rozanov and Dostoevsky, however, are only partial.[10] Klimov does not hesitate to use isolated fragments of texts and biographical information, including the behavioral or psychological characteristics of a given personality, if they suit his arguments. He uses Dostoevsky as an authoritative figure to fight the enemy, while at the same time implicating him as a suspect personality. In the following example, Klimov uses this method twice:

> In this lecture series we shall address the problem dubbed "The Jewish Question." This is a very difficult problem for an objective investigation. Even such an important specialist as F. M. Dostoevsky, writing about the Jewish Question in his *Diary of a Writer,* warned that he "is not in a position to shed light on this fundamental problem of humankind" and that he "does not feel that he has enough strength in him"...
>
> For instance, in the original draft of *The Brothers Karamazov* there was a mention of the true reason for Smerdiakov's murder of his own father, F. P. Karamazov. He killed his father because he regularly sodomized and raped him when Smerdiakov was a child. And the original manuscript of the novel *The Possessed* contained Stavrogin's confession of his rape of a nine-year-old girl who hanged herself out of despair.
>
> All this Dostoevsky removed from the final version of his novel, and the sin of patricide is thus presented as a result of the abstract ruminations of the atheist Ivan, and the arrogant and criminal character of Stavrogin remains unexplained.
>
> Why has Dostoevsky done this? This is what we are going to talk about...
>
> So, in our lecture series we shall spell out everything that F. M. Dostoevsky could not spell out himself. Why could he not say it? Of course Fedor Mikhailovich knew all this, but because he was a biologically negative person, he simply could not afford to spell it out. If he had started unveiling ALL the secrets of the "chosen people," then he would have had to uncover his own secrets. And people like him cannot afford to do that (1).[11]

There is no further explanation as to why Dostoevsky could not unveil his own secrets, but it is implied that the reader should be able to decipher the message with the help of his or her knowledge of Dostoevsky's epilepsy. An even more learned reader would be aware of the rumor spread by Dostoevsky's friend and publisher, Nikolai Strakhov, that the unpublished first edition of Chapter Nine, which includes Stavrogin's confession of his sexual abuse of a young girl, was autobiographical. Strakhov spread the rumor that Dostoevsky conveyed to him his own experiences of seducing a teenage girl.[12] This chapter, "At Tikhon's," is included in the full edition of *The Possessed,* in the version that Dostoevsky himself prepared for publication in *Russkii vestnik.*[13]

Klimov's strategy here is based on the idea that understanding itself constitutes a committed act. According to him, Dostoevsky revealed in a highly cryptic form various Jewish sexual pathologies. Out of fear of Jews, or self-censorship, he made his characters the Karamazovs not to be Jews, but crypto-Jews. He used this technique as a way of showing his readers that he knew the secrets of the Jews and understood the danger Jews posed for the Russian people. In this way Dostoevsky, the great Russian classic writer, remains a revered figure. However, according to Klimov, because Dostoevsky was an epileptic, he himself was touched by degeneracy, and if he showed any of the pathologies of a quasi-Jew it is because he was a psychopath himself and did not want to admit it. This is why he did not make his characters Jews. Both Rozanov and Dostoevsky in Klimov's purist universe are themselves suspects. Here Klimov shows consistency in his body politics which can be paralleled to Nazi body politics: Jews, sexual perverts, and epileptics fall into one category — that marked for extermination.

The Jewish Origins of Soviet Leadership

One of the crudest and yet most stable and effective methods of political damage and discreditation is to expose somebody's Jewish roots. This strategy has been a trademark of the Russian right wing press since the 1870s and has been a feature in Russian discourse since the Glasnost reforms.[14]

With the fall of censorship controls during Glasnost in the 1980s and in post-Soviet Russia, searching for and exposing information on the Jewish roots of important political personalities from Russia's present and past has become a favorite weapon in the fight against the "enemy" on the pages of the free press. Information suppressed during the Soviet era on the ethnic origins of various leaders has become a great novelty for the masses who do not have specialized knowledge about the background of such historical personalities, especially the iconic ones of the caliber of Karl Marx and Vladimir Lenin. Nothing had a more sensational effect on the masses during Glasnost than the exposure of Marx's Jewish roots or the revelation that Vladimir Lenin's grandfather was a converted Jew.[15] The exposure of the Jewish origins of important left-wing political leaders is based on the assumption that Jews are enemies of the Russian people in the same way that they are enemies of all Christian people. The well-documented Nazi propaganda that equated Jews in occupied territories with Bolsheviks/communists was repeated by Russian political personalities amidst the upheavals of Russian society during the Perestroika years. This mode of dealing with political opponents clearly has not disappeared from Russian political culture.[16] The phenomenal success that Klimov's books continue to enjoy in the twenty-first century attests to the longevity and indestructibility of the myth of Jewish evil and the need by Russian culture to view the Jew as an archetypal Other. Here is an example of one of his arguments that appears to have an unfailing appeal to a certain portion of the Russian reading public:

> For us Russians this Jewish question is of special importance because Jews were the main driving force of the two "Russian" revolutions. The communist theory, as everybody knows, was invented by Karl Marx (maiden name [sic] Mordecai Levi) — a Jew, whom Jews themselves call an antisemite. If you will open any Jewish encyclopedia, there you will find that Karl Marx was an antisemite. But why was he an antisemite? It remains a mystery...
> So, Mordecai Levi (Karl Marx) invented communist theory. The whole of history linked to the two revolutions in Russia is also linked to the Jews. The leader of the February Revolution, Kerensky, was a half Jew. Here we strike another mystery: all capitalist sources in the West and all the communist sources in the Soviet Union are silent about it. For some reason to talk about Jews in relation to the Russian Revolution is forbidden, this theme is TABOO (1).[17]

The general reader does not usually have access to a Jewish encyclopedia, and therefore is likely to treat Klimov's work as an authoritative source. Klimov avoids a discussion of Jewish self-hatred not because he is naïve himself, but because he aims at a naïve reader who is driven by the logic that if Marx the Jew hated Jews, he had good reason to do so. Klimov exploits the trust of his reader when he presents information on the alleged Jewishness of revolutionary figures. His tactics are two-fold: to expose the Jewish origins of important historical personalities and to invent Jewish origins for important personalities. In this regard his tactics are identical to those of Rozanov in his struggle against political opponents: Rozanov invented the Jewishness of such writers as Vladimir Korolenko and Dmitry Merezhkovsky, and exposed the Jewishness of his Jewish opponents.[18] Klimov invents Jewishness in Kerensky, Stalin — whom he presents as "a half Jew from the Caucasus"("*kavkazskii poluevrei*" [13, Ch. 2]) — and even Hitler, who is also presented as half-Jewish.[19]

Communists Equal Jews, Homosexuals, and Other Sexual Perverts

Of special importance in the context of this work is Klimov's decision to describe Marx's Jewish surname as "a maiden name" ("*v devichestve*"

[1]). This expression is chosen with the specific aim of attributing to Marx ambivalent sexuality. And it comes as no surprise that later in the book Klimov advances the idea of the psychopathy of communist leaders, and accuses Marx and Engels of having a homosexual relationship. Klimov diagnoses Lenin, who is said to be half Jewish from his mother's side, as a homosexual and a pederast (7, Ch. 1). Here is Klimov's depiction of the suspect friendships between the male revolutionaries:

> Karl Marx was practically kept by Friedrich Engels, who was quite well off, and as is customary in such relationships Engels spent a fortune on the object of his passion — Karl Marx. Similar relationships existed between Herzen and Ogarev. All these professional revolutionaries, as a rule, are homosexuals of various kinds. But these facts become known only much later, when it is already too late, after these scumbags already have caused so much evil to humankind (12, Ch. 8).

Soviet leader Leonid Brezhnev is described as a sexual pervert because he was allegedly married to a Jewish woman. According to Klimov the result of this relationship is a psychopathic daughter who was in an incestuous relationship with her father:

> There were rumors spread in Moscow that Brezhnev slept with his daughter. This is why she turned out to be so out of control.
> I also know about these rumors. Because Brezhnev's wife was Jewish, their children could not have been normal. Besides, Brezhnev's brother was an alcoholic, and if one or the other sibling is not normal, the second one will have some sort of sexual pathology. This is possibly why Brezhnev married a Jewish woman. It is quite possible that Brezhnev himself was a touch Jewish. It happens often that men who are a quarter Jewish marry Jewish women. Their children will almost always be degenerates or, in order not to use such a strong word, bionegative, psychonegative. (2, Ch. 2)

Klimov's strategy for dealing with Jews and homosexuals is based on creating an equation between the two groups. The cause and effect between Jewishness and homosexuality are interchangeable: most Jews are homosexuals because most Jews are psychopaths, and most homosexuals are Jews because they, too, are psychopaths. Klimov diagnoses the mania that both Jews and homosexuals share as "superiority mania" — he maintains that both Jews and homosexuals consider themselves to be special, "chosen people" (3, Ch. 9). It is clear that Klimov is enraged by the advances made by various racial and sexual minorities in post-Soviet society, and he uses his attacks against Jews and homosexuals as a double-edged sword, exploiting prejudices against race and gender to ignite hatred in his readers who were brought up in a society in which homosexuality was a criminal offense. Here is a sample:

> Psychiatrists say that most homosexuals consider themselves to be chosen people and an elite. Is this not why Jews regard themselves as chosen people? But who put this idea into their heads? The rabbis. Jewish rabbis introduced the idea of the "chosen, God's people" and hammered it into the heads of the Jews. Here we have the roots of all this. According to the bitter-sweet formula of Professor Lombroso, who was one of the most prominent psychiatrists of his time and a descendant of rabbis and Talmudists, there are six times more madmen and psychopaths among Jews than among non-Jews. And this means that there are six times more homosexuals (3, Ch. 9).

Klimov is aware that, in terms of cause and effect, his argument stands on slippery ground, and he resorts to the tactic of referring to scientific authorities. In the case of Cesare Lombroso, Klimov has an especially effective figure of authority: not only was Lombroso a medical scientist, he was also a Jew. Lombroso's views are not presented in any articulate manner, it being part of Klimov's tactics to hide behind the authority of a name, while leaving the actual facts as vague as possible. Auguste Forel is another nineteenth-century sexologist to whom Klimov refers as part of his tactic of using a scientific basis for his argument that sexual perversions and political deviance are linked. In the following example Forel is quoted to advance the idea of the similarities between Jews and masons, both of whom are accused of sharing the same psychotic patterns of behavior, which are in turn seen as the results of their sexual perversions:

> Here on my bookshelf I have a book by the famous nineteenth-century psychiatrist Auguste Forel, *The Sexual Question*. Forel was the leading psychiatrist well before Freud. He was in charge of the psychiatric hospital in Zurich, Switzerland, and gained a number of prestigious awards. The book was published in New York in 1924 by the Medical Publishing House. The first edition came out in German in 1906.
> I have to say that this is a very open and honest book. In it Auguste Forel discusses sexual instinct not only as a medic and psychiatrist, but also as a sociologist and simply as a healthy person. So in this authoritative book, on page 243, he writes that masons are homosexuals, and that homosexuals are inclined to create secret societies and clandestine brotherhoods of the masonry type. On page 244 he once more addresses this topic, and writes that when homosexuals find out about a secret society, they are compelled to join it (3, Ch. 9).

Klimov emphasizes the dangers of secret societies, such as those formed by masons and homosexuals, stressing that masons are always Judeomasons, and that this broad, all-encompassing explanation, whereby Jews and masons conquered the Western world and imposed their power over Russia, can be applied to the whole of modern Western and Russian history. Crude as it might seem, this simple formula works astonishingly well in terms of the reception that Klimov's work receives by Russian-speaking readers in Russia and the former Soviet Republics, as well in the Russian Diaspora abroad. In fact, the simpler the idea the better. Any reference to scientific sources published before the Russian Revolution serves merely as a safety device. Klimov might have a book by Forel on his bookshelf, but his readers most certainly do not, nor are they likely to go and look for one in a library, which in any probability does not have a copy of it anyway. And how many readers have access to a specialized scientific library that might have a copy of Forel's book in Russian?

Klimov's use of these specific nineteenth-century sexologists and biological scientists is highly symptomatic: their work makes moral judgments on the basis of people's sexual behavior. Klimov uses the same sources that inspired Western and Russian turn-of-the-century antisemitic discourse, first as a tool to create and define the Other, and then as a weapon to fight this archetypal Other, the Jew.

The Old Testament as Source and Evidence of Sexual Perversions

Klimov uses the Old Testament to support his portrayal of Jews as a sexually perverse and degenerate race. Incest, homosexuality and sadism are all presented as typical of Jewish ethnicity since ancient times. Authors like Rozanov and Kychko similarly based their accusations of sexual perversions among contemporary Jews on the stories in the Old Testament. However, when Rozanov argued that open discussions on various sexual deviations was a positive step for educational purposes, he referred to the Old Testament as a laudable example of a culture that does not place a taboo on issues of human sexuality.

In accusing Jews of degeneracy, Klimov uses the Old Testament as evidence of the pathological sexuality of the whole of the Jewish people, suggesting that these stories have to be exposed as proof of Jewish degeneracy and pathology:

Jews used degeneracy from Biblical times. In the Bible there are many examples.
The Bible consists of two parts: the Old Testament and the New Testament.
Many people say, "Listen, these are such abominable matters... Well, the New
Testament is a good thing, but why is this disgusting Judaic Old Testament put
with the New Testament into the one holy Bible?.."
I think that putting the two books together is a good thing. So that people can
see in contrast what kind of filthy and abominable deeds took place in the Old
Testament. Then everyone will be convinced of the necessity for the publication
of the New Testament.
The forefather Abraham, from whom the Jews allegedly descend, put his wife
Sarah into the Pharaoh's bed. Then he does the same trick with another ruler,
some Avimelech. Both of these rulers Sarah infected with syphilis... This is the
first example of immorality in the Old Testament. (5, Ch. 8)

Fear of Crypto- and Hidden Jews and
the Essence of Body Politics

It is quite clear that Klimov's mission, the aim of his so-called Advanced
Sociology or Degenerology, is to save Russians from the admixture of
Jewish blood — to stop them from becoming polluted by blood that will
bastardize Russians and make degenerates of them. This fear is akin to the
fear of contamination by syphilis in the nineteenth century which, as has been
demonstrated, was a way of concealing fear of physical contact with Jews. It
was Jews who were believed to be diseased, and the Jew's body that was seen
as the source of syphilitic illness. In Klimov's case we have a contemporary
equivalent of such a fear of contamination. He presents degeneracy as a
disease that is as concealed as any other one spread through sexual contact,
and that contaminates the healthy bodies of gentiles for many generations to
come. For this reason Klimov is fixated not so much on pure Jews — those
who are identified as Jews and who do not hide their Jewishness — but on
crypto-Jews, those who either hide their Jewishness or who do not know
that they have the (genetic) "virus" of Jewishness. In an extended metaphor
Jewishness here is likened to venereal disease: it is not the victim of full-
blown syphilis with all the markers of the diseased body that is dangerous,
but the unsuspected patient in whose body the virus exists in its nascent
form. This line of reasoning is apparent in the following statement:

What is the relationship between the two million Jews [in Russia] and the twenty-three million of those with Jewish blood (*s prozhid'iu*) or the crypto-Jews as they are called? Which of them is better, which is worse?

According to Doctor Alfred Kinsey's statistics, 4 percent of open and honest homosexuals do not present as great a danger as the 33 percent of semi-homosexuals. This is because there are ten times more hidden homosexuals than there are open ones. By analogy, I maintain that two million open Jews are a lesser evil than twenty-three million part-Jews. The majority of those part-Jews have Russian surnames.

The products of the majority of mixed marriages are a mixture of Satan and Antichrist. This is because, as a rule, degenerates from the local community enter into mixed marriages with Jews (9, Ch. 10).[20]

Klimov thus relies on the "common sense" of the Russian people, assuming that they will not want to enter into sexual contact and marriage with a Jew, in the same way that a healthy person would not want to have sexual contact with somebody with venereal disease. He maintains that only delinquents from the local population can be attracted to Jews who, apart from being shown to be biologically flawed, are also depicted as dark, demonic forces. Klimov is quite happy to support his "scientific facts" with arguments from the religious antisemitic repertory, reminding his readers about the Satanic nature of Jews. The biological underpinning of Klimov's argument is not lost on his readers, as may be seen from the following statement by his anonymous interlocutor:

So do you mean that, when entering into marriage, together with the test of syphilis, it is necessary to introduce a compulsory test of degeneracy, e.g. Jewishness? And to warn both sides of the consequences? (9, Ch. 10)

In his attempt to define and preserve the Russian nation as a racial entity, Klimov thus reinvents the degeneration theory that was so popular at the dawn of the new century at the time of the political disintegration of the Russian state. He bases his arguments on the fear of contamination, of contracting "Jewishness" as an illness. For Klimov, Jewishness is a characteristic of Satan, and an eschatological ticket for eternal damnation.

The following exchange of opinions between the Russian journalist and Klimov illustrates to what extent he deems it convenient and necessary to maintain the belief in the invincible hereditary strength of Jewish blood. Jewishness becomes a biological hazard, even when its presence in the human body is reduced to minute quantities, and the person who has even the smallest admixture of Jewish blood is biologically predetermined to be the enemy of the Russian people. Klimov operates on the level of the discourse of biological contamination, comparing the hereditary transmission of Jewish blood with the spreading of the AIDS virus. Jews, like AIDS-infected people, form a category of "bionegative people" whose genes will forever have a negative impact on future generations. When asked whether Russia's problems will be solved when all Jews finally leave the country, Klimov replied:

> No, this is not so. Do not forget that that some seventeen million part-Jews, so called Jewish "mixlings," will remain behind in Russia. And this leaves us with the same problem. I think that this problem will never have a final solution, but it is possible to keep it under control. (19, Ch. 3)

If Klimov does not call for a final solution, or for making Russia *Judenfrei*, it is only because he understands the political advantages and the unifying power of having a common enemy.

The Raceology of Vladimir Avdeev

Another author to make a major contribution to the proliferation of the racial literature of the past and to invent his own biological theory of race is Vladimir Avdeev. Avdeev publishes anthologies, which include the writings of Russian racial scientists from the turn of the century, as well as his own solo-authored monographs. His anthology *Russkaia rasovaia teoriia do 1917 goda* (*Russian Racial Theory before 1917* [2004])[21] includes Ivan Sikorsky's medical opinion on the Beilis murder trial which gives ample "evidence" of the existence of a blood libel among Jews and their predisposition to sadistic and murderous acts. Needless to say, Sikorsky's piece "Ekspertiza po delu ob ubiistve Andriushi Iushchinskogo" ("Expert Opinion on the Andriusha Iushchinskii Murder Case"), which was published in 1913 as a separate brochure, is printed in the anthology as an example of an authoritative scientific opinion from a learned academic. The anthology is richly illustrated with pictures and drawings of phrenological and craniological skull measuring instruments, as well as with images of human faces that show likenesses with various animals, thus promoting the "science" of physiognomy. In his preface Avdeev argues for the urgent need to rediscover the work of the Russian racial scientists of the past in order to use their theories as ammunition in the struggle against the non-Russian ethnic and racial members of post-Soviet Russian society:

> The Soviet State, which is the successor state to the Russian Empire, fell apart exactly at that stage when its Russian population fell in numbers and became less than a half of the total population. A similar fate is awaiting the United States of America where the white part of the population is already almost in the minority. (25)

It was noted in the first chapter that in his monograph *Rasologiia* (*Raceology*) Avdeev admits using Jews as a litmus paper test for his methodology on racial politics.[22] His interest in Jews is based on the same political motivations as was that of Rozanov — that is, fear of the political and "anthropological collapse" of the Russian state. Like Rozanov, whose fear of Jews reached its apogee at the time of Russia's political crises, Avdeev maintains that it is the non-Russian and non-European members of society who are responsible for the fall of the Soviet Union, which he regards as an anthropological, racial and cultural equivalent of the Russian Empire. In a sense, Avdeev is a witness to Rozanov's "prophecy" — he is alive to witness the alleged collapse of the Russian state, destroyed by racially alien and hostile elements as predicted by Rozanov. Although Rozanov's views on this issue were more complex, when taken to the extreme, stripped of their literary sophistication and translated into the language of bombastic propaganda and political slogans, the simplified message is heard loud and clear: racial Others have destroyed the Russian/Soviet Empire.

In the case of Avdeev, racial themes and stereotypes always privilege the Russians as Aryans, while vilifying the Other as non-Aryans. These stereotypes are presented as proven fact, confirmed by the whole community of biological scientists and thinkers. Avdeev quotes numerous historical figures who made their contribution to racist science such as Joseph Arthur Gobineau, Houston Stewart Chamberlain, Paolo Mantegazza, Havelock Ellis and numerous German scientists at the turn of the century.

Jewish Smell and Olfaction

One stable and "proven" marker of racial difference that finds its way into Avdeev's reworking of racist views is the phenomenon of smell — the belief that inferior races emit peculiar smells that are offensive to white people. Chekhov used it as a marker of the Jewish body, albeit as a satirical device. Rozanov used this idea of the peculiar smell of Jews as part of an anthropological dyad incorporating smell and olfactory capacities, and in his work Jews are characterized both by their smell and by their attitude toward smell — not only do they emit primordial odors but they also preserve the archaic capacity to enjoy various aromas in their own peculiar way. He argued that this enhanced sense of smell exists in parallel with their heightened olfactory ability, with both these features serving as markers of their physiological and ontological difference. This difference, in turn, was marked positively or negatively, depending on the target of Rozanov's polemics — indeed, the aromatics of bodily smells could be extolled by Rozanov whose mission was to rehabilitate the physical body with its sexual and procreative functions.

In Avdeev's *Raceology* the idea that different races are characterized by different bodily smells is presented as a scientific fact. Explained as a "biochemical racial difference" (145), bodily smells of non-whites are presented as offensive: "Ancient travelers noted that the Chinese smell of musk, and a Roman historian of the fourth century a.d., Ammianus Marcellinus, maintained that Jews smell of garlic" (145). On this basis Avdeev issues the following warning to his contemporary Russian reader:

> In line with the aforesaid we do not recommend using gastronomic and cosmetic products manufactured by other races. Healing mud from the shores of the Dead Sea, which is advertised on our TV, must be used by Semites, not by Russian beauties (145).

In the chapter entitled "Racial smells and preferences of cannibals" (244) Avdeev once more turns to the subject of the smell of the Jews. This time, however, he also elaborates on the subject of olfaction. This dyad, as used by Rozanov in his *The Olfactory and Tactile Attitude of the Jews to Blood*, and the link between the two physiological phenomena, made also by Avdeev, is highly indicative of the strength and longevity of racial stereotypes in a given culture. Avdeev maintains that the idea of the "particular racial smell" (244) has been in circulation from the times of antiquity, and that it was further confirmed by European scientists in the nineteenth century. Avdeev informs his readers that, "Medieval missionaries spoke of the 'Judaic stench,'" (244) and that one of the founding fathers of anthropology, Johann Blumenbach, wrote of the "ethnic characteristics of skin," and the Russian anthropologist Anatoly Bogdanov, in the 1860s, observed that, "Some nations emit peculiar smells; for instance, it is well known that hunting dogs used to detect runaway slaves by distinguishing between the smell of a black Negro and of an American Indian" (245).

This information is adapted to Avdeev's own diagnosis of the peculiarities of Jewish smells and olfaction:

> Among the race-specific features one should mention the shape of the *olfactory bulb* among the Jews [emphasis in the original text]. It has been known from ancient times that various races and tribes have their own specific smell, which originated in prehistoric times. The specific parts of the brain responsible for olfaction have, from an evolutionary point of view, the most ancient origins, and their development preceded other forms of psychological activity. There is no need to elaborate on the importance of smell in the animal world. It is striking that in the human world too this is important, although this is not always appreciated. *The perfumes, lotions, fragrances of various peoples also have differences, because their purpose is to embellish the natural smell of their owners* [emphasis in the original text]. The spicy perfumes of the Mediterranean people are repulsive to the representatives of Nordic races, and this example is an excellent illustration of the biology of humanity's cultural and historical genesis. Karl Voight stated: "The smell of a nation is a part of its historical make up" (245).

Avdeev uses Jews as an example of the link between smell and olfaction. In his view, the whole concept of the atavistic cells of the Jewish body is in itself indicative of the stability of this stereotype of the Jew's body. Avdeev accords this viewpoint the status of scientific fact. Although examples taken from "scientific literature" relate to the sense of smell emitted by a particular body, rather than to olfaction, in the case of Jews Avdeev creates a nexus between the two. In describing the Jews' heightened sense of smell in a subchapter on cannibals, Avdeev presents Jews as an atavistic people driven by archaic instincts such as the propensity to cannibalism. Avdeev manipulates his text in such a way that it implicates Jews even in the act of murder. What lurks behind the text is the mythology of ritual killings and blood libel among Jews.

Sadistic Jews, Bolsheviks and Chechen Women

It comes as no surprise that in his racial theories, Avdeev emphasizes the special sadistic nature of Jews. Moreover, he makes a connection between this sadism and Jewish political behavior. Riding the favorite horse of anti-Jewish propaganda in post-Soviet Russia, Avdeev promotes the view that the majority of the Bolshevik élite were Jews (a view exploited by the

White Army and Hitler's propaganda machines). In contemporary Russian political reality, the racial stereotype of the aggressive and sadistic enemy of the Russian people is also applied to Chechens. Avdeev supports this stereotype with another "scientific explanation," claiming that the degree of aggressiveness varies from one race to another, and can been measured by the special index "Th":

> The "Th" index is an index of the special configuration of the first finger and the palm of the hand, and is one of the most important dermatoglyphic parameters used for some ten years in the statistic analysis of various races and ethnicities...
> In Ashkenazi Jews, from Russia, this index reaches 21–5, which explains the Bolsheviks' atrocities during the time of the Civil War, since most of the Red Army commissars were Ashkenazi Jews.
> But the most aggressive in the whole world are women from the Chechen region of Urus-Martan, the ones who acted as suicide bombers in a great number of terrorist attacks on Russian territory. It is important to note that the very name Urus-Martan in Chechen means "dead Russian's head" (435).

Sexual Anomalies

The reader will recall that the sexual pathology of the racial Other has been a powerful polemical device throughout the centuries, and various Russian and Soviet authors have used the Old Testament as a source to confirm the existence of sexual anomalies among Jews. Avdeev uses the Old Testament as a text rich with stories of sexual transgressions, and so draws his conclusion on the predisposition of Jews to sexual perversions:

> V. P. Osipov [an important Russian psychologist] devotes a few chapters of his wonderful book [*General Textbook on Mental Illnesses*] to the description of all kinds of sexual perversions which were flourishing in Biblical times. On this evidence it becomes conclusively clear that in order to understand the "spiritual beauty" of the Old Testament one has to get hold of a textbook on *sexual criminology* [emphasis in the original text]." (422)

Avdeev juxtaposes stories of sexual transgressions found in the Old Testament with Indo-European folklore, maintaining that, in Russian folk and fairy tales, there is not a hint to be found of sexual perversions. When it suited him, Rozanov praised the Old Testament for its honesty in addressing topics of sexuality and "transgressions," and criticized Russian and Christian culture for hypocrisy and a conspiracy of silence. Avdeev maintains that the absence of such topics from Russian writings points to the lack of the phenomenon in real life.

Avdeev supports his arguments concerning the propensity of Jews to sexual perversions with quotations from V. P. Osipov's *General Textbook on Mental Illnesses* (1923), alleging a racial basis of sexual anomalies among people from the Middle East. He concludes by warning of the dangers of racial hybridity, as the etiology of sexual perversions, he believes, results from the mixing of bloods between races:

> V. P. Osipov in his fundamental *General Textbook on Mental Illnesses* based his conclusions on data taken from comparative psychiatry and psycho-reflexology which proved that mass homosexuality and pederasty originate from the East, from those geographic regions where major races came into contact with each other and where the mixing of bloods resulted in the predominance of the most unnatural forms of behavior, including sexual behavior. *The mixing of bloods leads to confusion of values with an unavoidable erasure of moral values* [emphasis in the original text] (421).

It is clear that Avdeev is using "scientific" opinions on the dangers of hybridization to promote the idea of the necessity of preserving the purity of Russian ethnicity. Although the idea of Eurasianism, which advocates the complementarity of Turkic and Slavic people in the territory of the Russian empire, has gained momentum in post-Soviet political discourse, Avdeev does not support this fashionable ethnic theory. He opposes any form of hybridity, and maintains that Russian ethnicity is based on Nordic connections. In opposing Eurasianism, he demonstrates consistency with the turn-of-the-century's staple racial prejudice against the "Yellow Races." For Avdeev, Turkic and Mongol people are part of the "colored races" (423), and he attacks the followers of the Eurasian theory on the basis of the scientific evidence of biological differences between Russian and Asiatic peoples.

The Psychopathology of Monotheism

In Wagnerian fashion, as followed by the Nazi fascists in Germany, Avdeev privileges the indigenous, polytheistic beliefs of pre-Christian Russian tribes over the monotheist religion that came from the Middle

East. In a subchapter entitled "The psychopathology of monotheism" (443), he unleashes his biologically based attack on Judaism and Christianity, proclaiming that monotheism is nothing more than a product of a psychotic and delusionary mind:

> It is stated practically in every psychiatry textbook that the main symptom of epilepsy is monomania... According to the opinions of many independent commentators on the Old Testament, Moses was an epileptic. In Exodus he writes about himself, saying, "It is difficult for me to speak and I am slow of tongue."
> Our contemporary Russian historian S. N. Plekhanov writes: "Monotheism emerged not from a higher way of understanding reality, but it reflects the deficiency of the world which gave birth to it. The primitive nomadic tribes which were led by Moses, this run-away priest from Memphis, for ten years saw in front of them only homogenous nature; so it is out of this situation the idea was born that life is ruled by only one powerful force" (443).

Avdeev juxtaposes the Hebrew God Jehovah to the polytheism of "Ancient Germanic, Slavic and Celtic tribes" (443) and this list is symptomatic of the goal of Avdeev's racial politics — to elevate Slavs to the level of Aryan people through the classification system of racial science. Avdeev rejects Christianity as yet another "Semitic religion" (444) and, as such, classifies it as "obviously pathological" (444). Slavs are put in line with Germanic and Celtic tribes, whereas Christ is put alongside the Prophet Mohammed and the apostle Paul. All three are declared to be epileptics, thus sharing the same marker of supposed psychopathology with which Moses was said to be afflicted.

Avdeev's conclusion is aphoristic in its brevity, and it is formulated as a political slogan: "The problem of Aryan polytheism and Semitic monotheism is not a problem of the freedom of religious choice, but is first and foremost a problem of the racial-archetypal brain structure"(445).

Dangers of Degeneration: A Survival Kit for the Russian Nation

The main goal of Avdeev's mission is the preservation and extension of the life of the Russian people. The resurrection of racial arguments is not an aim in itself, but a way of preserving Russian ethnicity which, he believes, is in great danger of extinction. Avdeev argues that "races and nations have their biological clocks, which secure their maximal longevity, strength and expansion" (486). He maintains that the whole of human history consists of "occult wars" which have as their aim the imposition of one nation's model onto another in order to extend its own life and which have a negative effect on the biological life of different races. Among such alien cultural models are "calendar systems, sacral geographies, archetypal symbolism, fashions, 'methods of time adjustment'" (486). Avdeev translates this esoteric list into concrete historical facts and events, and among the threats to the Russian people he includes a number of foreign and allegedly Jewish phenomena. His conclusion on the threat to Russian ethnicity is categorical and clear:

> A great number of patriotically minded sociologists and political scientists complain that the biological mass of the Russian people is shrinking, and they offer a number of recipes for the recovery of the nation without understanding the very mechanism of its degeneration. For as long as the Russian people live in accordance to the Christian calendar and pray to the East, and will visit Lenin's Mausoleum, and follow foreign fashions, there can be no chance for recovery. For as long as we continue to use foreign goods and to view them as an emblem of perfection, the biological mass, potency and expansion of our nation will not be possible (486).

Like the Silver Age thinkers, Rozanov and Pavel Florensky, Avdeev believes that Jews have a secret and a key to the biological survival of their own ethnicity. This is evidenced from his ideas on the need to use an authentic system of chronology for a nation's survival: he cites the Jewish state of Israel's use of the Hebrew calendar as a prime example of the success of such a method for the longevity of an ethnic group. Eschatological rivalry was a driving force in Rozanov's (and Florensky's) obsession with the Jews, and toward the end of his life (in his letters before his death) Rozanov admitted that he would like Jews to teach the Russians their survival skills. The preservation of the Russian nation as an anthropological entity was the aim of his constant attention to matters related to Jewish life. From the vantage point of the new millennium, Russian patriots are still trying to preserve the Russian racial state, and their Judeophobia shows similar signs of "envy," which appear to be an integral part of the psychology of phobias and "philias," including Judeophilia.[23]

Left and Right Brain Hemispheres and Politically Left and Right Races

Avdeev also gives a racial and biological underpinning to the political forces that put the Russian state and the Russian racial entity under the threat of extinction at the beginning of the twentieth century. He divides nations into politically left and right categories in line with their biological predisposition. Russians, who are classified as Aryans, are included in the group of people who have a similar "racial brain structure" (448) as Aryans; this is characterized by the preference for the right spatial model in the system of right-left binarisms. Chinese, Jews and Arabs are classified as "left" preferring races. Chinese Taoism teaches its adherents to prefer left over right, as illustrated by their allocation of seating or décor arrangements that favor the left in times of peace and celebration and the right in times of war and mourning. The preference of Jews and Arabs for the left is symbolized by their system of writing — from right to left, or anti-clockwise. Avdeev regards the Jewish influence on the development of modern Europe as of primary importance, and it is the biological preference of left over right that characterizes Jews as an "archetype"(448) of left "bio-politics" (449):

> Scattered all over the world, Jews began to exert a growing influence on the cultural, political and economic life of Europe. In modern times this influence reached its apogee during the bourgeois revolutions, especially during the French Revolution. Jews were granted emancipation in the realia of this new socio-political formation. No longer confined to the enclaves of a Diaspora, and having acquired equal rights, they became integrated into European society. But having acquired a European appearance, they nevertheless brought into the surrounding culture peculiarities of their own racial mentality. The word "revolution" which denoted the radical destruction of the domineering patriarchal and conservative value system, started to be associated with the left side of the political spectrum.
> Words such as left, humanitarian and progressive gradually became synonyms, while right became synonymous with the conservative and the reactionary. Unnatural Egyptian-Chaldeic-Judaic systems of spatial orientation blossomed among white European nations, which had been brought up in the racial system of the ancient Aryans. And with the accession of the dominance of the ideas of Karl Marx, a rabbi's grandson, communism came to be identified as an ideology of the left. It was proclaimed as the hope for the whole of humankind, and all those who opposed it were proclaimed obscurantists or fascists. This is how the archetype of the white race has been deformed and desecrated (449).

From Avdeev's "theorizing" we can extrapolate a variation of a number of themes and approaches explored by Russian thinkers at the turn of the nineteenth century: Berdiaev's attack on the Judaic roots of Marxism, Soloviev's allegations regarding the corporeality of the Jewish mentality on the basis of the Jewish alphabet with its accent on consonants and omitted "spiritual" vowels, and Rozanov's fantasy of a single geopolitical and biological continuum of Ancient Middle Eastern peoples — the Egyptians, Israelites and Mesopotamians. The strategy of blurring the boundaries between Semitic people and their neighbors in the political reality of Russia today results in the creation of a unified Other to whose numbers any quasi-Eastern nation can be added; this is demonstrated by Avdeev's inclusion of Chechens into the group of people with a biological predisposition to aggression. Russians as Aryans are put into the same category as Aryan fascists in an open declaration of a political alliance based on the affinity of shared racial theories. What lurks behind this proclamation is the theme of the Jewish conspiracy — if fascists are the victims of Jews, then all allegations against fascists, including the Holocaust, are also a Jewish invention. Paranoid fears of the Jewish ability to pass for Aryans through their mutability and their ability to acquire a European appearance is part of the repertory of turn-of-the-century racial science which is incapable of resolving the paradox between the mutability of Jews and their racial stability.

Racial Ecology

Avdeev also gives a "scientific" underpinning to one of the most stable antisemitic stereotypes in Russian culture, a stereotype recently explored again in Alexander Solzhenitsyn's *Two Hundred Years Together*.[24] This stereotype depicts Jews as greedy and exploitative, and has been a staple image of anti-Jewish folk beliefs in a peasant culture that privileges agricultural and menial labor over trade and commerce. These beliefs can best be described as "ecological fears":

> The Semitic philosophy of life results in the depletion of rich soil and turning it into desert, and the sands of the desert encroach onto fertile land, threatening to devour it and destroy its future. The Aryan philosophy is the total opposite to this philosophy, and is as follows: plow the land with a plow, and cross the sea with a boat, and then, one day, learn to ignore the rational side of life, create paradise here on earth and at the end of your days descend into it (the soil) (402).

This bizarre statement can be deciphered as an accusation directed against the excessive rationality of the Jews combined with their economic greed, as opposed to the supposed wisdom of Aryans who know when to stop in their earthly pursuits. Aryans create paradise on earth, and their descent into the earth, rather than into heaven, marks the difference between the eschatological beliefs of monotheist Semitic religions such as Judaism, Christianity and Islam on the one hand, and polytheists on the other. To the God of Semitic monotheistic religions Avdeev juxtaposes the indigenous gods of Aryan people and Nordic races, of whom Russians form an integral part, as seen in the following examples:

> For the first time our Gods have given us a chance to change the destiny of our race for the better. Already today we have the ability to create an ideal Nordic human being to live at the time of the expansion of the North into the limitless spaces of Asia (294).
> And what is the scientific method to model such a race? Genetic therapy, purification of the genes of the white people, and "cleansing" of the genes which cause "race pollution" (295).
> And with the help of human cloning it will be possible to increase the number of cleansed, more valuable peoples into the millions, and this becomes possible in the lifetime of one generation (295).

In Avdeev's racialized scientific project we can detect echoes of the turn-of-the-nineteenth-century's preoccupation with the purity of blood. In Avdeev's case, however, science is divorced from Christian theology. If Rozanov wanted the Jewish body to be preserved for the fulfillment of the eschatological promises of the Old Testament, and if Father Pavel Florensky quantified the admixture of Jewish blood in future generations while nevertheless admitting that only the Jews had been promised resurrection, then in the contemporary obsession with the Jew's body fears are centered around the question of physical survival in the reality of the present-day world. In this contemporary project the notion of blood is given a strictly biological meaning, and is used in combination with another biological component of the human body — genes. In Avdeev's reasoning, there is no need for competition between Christian and Judaic concepts of the afterlife and resurrection, because the immortality of the body is taken out of the domain of monotheistic religions, and the notion of "soul" is made obsolete. The afterlife is understood as a physical return to the mother-wet-soil, a pagan symbol from Russian folklore. At the core of Avdeev's project is the real physical survival of the white Aryan race, free from all degenerate elements of Semitic and other non-white genes.

This project is designed to appeal to a post-Soviet generation that has been brought up in an atheist and technocratic state that places the future firmly in the hands of scientific achievement. In Avdeev's reckoning, if science is permitted to become powerful, it will help people to achieve immortality, but it will be the immortality of a new race that has completed the process of genetic cleansing through the correction of genes. If there is going to be paradise on earth, it will be made with the help of science at the hands of the pure race which deserves to survive, while an end will be put to the existence of all the degenerate races. The new message is encoded in a new form of human genetic engineering:

> Every citizen's work towards the well-being of his race will become a guarantee of immortality which he/she will achieve in his/her progeny. Individual immortality lies in the immortality of the race. What other moral imperative can be compared to this one for its simplicity and power? (296)

In this new project Jews and other colored people will become a conquered disease of the past, like the plague. The total eradication of degenerate races, the dream of the author of *Mein Kampf*, thus becomes possible at the hands of contemporary Russian racial "scientists."

Fear of Russophobia and Racial Engineering in Russian Body Politics Today

How representative are Avdeev's ideas? This may be deduced from the fact that the preface to *Raceology* was written by a member of the Russian Duma, A. N. Savel'ev, holder of a Ph.D. degree in political science.[25] This demonstrates how widely spread racist ideology is among influential members of Russian society, including those directly involved in policymaking. Clearly, we are no longer in the fictional world of Prokhanov's novel with leading politicians as heroes. Savel'ev welcomes Avdeev's work as an example of a genuinely scientific approach to the danger of the Russian nation becoming obsolete. He accepts Avdeev's conclusion that, "Russians are a racially pure nation; homogenous and mainly of Nordic European origin" (7):

> The nation has to be protected against the movement of migrants into the larger Russian cities. Apart from the purely biological consequences of such a migration (the disappearance of genes which help to withstand AIDS, for example), the mass migration of various alien racial types into Russian territory destabilizes cultural patterns and creates a life style which threatens social stability. Racio-demographics and culturological investigations in this field are highly necessary in order to ensure that the necessary steps are taken to maintain Russia's national security (7).

Savel'ev maintains that this approach has nothing in common with the ideology of fascism and Nazism that originated and flourished in Western Europe.[26] Russian racial science, he argues, will help to secure the survival not only of the Russian nation, but also of Russia's ethnic minorities. This last point, which maintains that ethnic minorities need to be prevented from mixing with the Russian ethnos for their own health and good, is, in fact, the premise of the ideology of apartheid, yet Savel'ev pretends to be oblivious to this. Or, as he puts it, all current anti-racist discourses and views are the legacy of communist propaganda, and his reader should automatically classify attacks on the ideology of apartheid as a part of communist propaganda which needs to be reevaluated. Racial science has been discredited both by Western powers and by the communists in Russia, and the reason for this is clear — both the Western élite and communist leadership were infiltrated by non-white personalities, and subsequently tricked and deceived by those elements. Such is the thrust of the arguments of contemporary raceologists.

Does such writing have an impact on public opinion in Russia today? The answer is yes — some Russian and Western readers perceive it as a serious contribution to science[27], especially in the context of discussions on Russia's demography. Demography was the subject of a 2006 annual presidential address to the nation, which identified declining birth rates among the Russian population as a priority for action, and proposed a number of financial schemes to help boost population growth. At the same time, because of economic problems caused by demographic crises, there is also a need to import immigrant labor. Such immigrants come from Russia's close neighbors — the fifteen former Soviet republics whose people speak Russian as a second language. The majority of those people are non-Slavs and non-Caucasians; they are of Turkic and Mongol ethnicity and most are Muslim. In this situation not only are Chechens viewed as hostile to Russia, but all "non-whites" are treated with suspicion as either terrorists or supporters of terrorism. Whereas the extreme reaction of groups such as the skinheads results in beatings and even murders of such "darkies," the more moderate reaction of the Russian public still expresses itself in sympathy and support for the racist discourse propagated by Avdeev, Savel'ev, Klimov, Prokhanov and numerous other authors from various groups in Russian society today.[28] In post-Soviet Russia at the beginning of the new millennium fears that the Russian ethnos may be doomed to extinction are viewed in the context of anthropological "science" and (pseudo-)genetics, and in many ways these fears correspond to the paranoia of some Russian thinkers from the pre-Soviet era. One can say with confidence that the Soviet experiment did not succeed in destroying these fears of extinction, even if, ironically and paradoxically, "the race" they want to preserve has almost been destroyed by the Soviet experiment.[29] The Russian national identity today is constructed on the basis of ethnicity, and this essentialization of Russianness functions as part of the binarism of the Russian "Self" and the ethnic and racial Other."[30] "The Jew" is seen as the archetypal enemy of the Russian ethnos and the stereotype of the Jew is based on the concept of the unchangeability of his/her biological essence. The image of an enemy coming from new "hostile" ethnic minorities such as the Chechens is constructed on the basis of the well-established stereotype of the Jew as the racial Other. In this way the stereotype of the Jew's body functions on the level of crypto-Jews and quasi-Jews, and is recycled by Russian culture as one of its most stable constructs.

Notes

[1] John Bigland. An Historical Display of the Effects of Physical and Moral Causes on the Character and Circumstances of the Ancients and Moderns in Regards to their Intellectual and Social State. Ed. H. F. Augstein. *Race: The Origins of an Idea, 1760–1850*. Bristol UK: Thoemmes Press. 1996. 68–80. 73.

[2] Avdeev's *Rasologiia* has been discovered by the sympathizers of racial theories in the USA. See review on the second edition (2007) of *Rasologiia*: "Vladimir Avdeyev: Race Scientist" in *American Renaissance*. http://www.amren.com/mtnews/archives/2007/12/vladimir avdeye. php. Accessed August 8, 2008.

[3] I came across his writing on the recommendation of a member of the Russian Diaspora in New Zealand.

[4] See A. Kuzmin. Khazarskie stradaniia. *Molodaia gvardiia*. No. 6. 1993. 245–250.

[5] http://www.klimov.kiev.ua/Books/Common/Essence.htm.

[6] Sut' problemy. Interv'iu Grigoriia Petrovicha Klimova po sluchaiu ego 80-letiia. http://www. klimov.kiev.ua/Books/Common/Essence.htm. Updated June 10, 2001. Accessed February 5, 2006. Also see the interview taken by the Russian writer Iaroslav Mogutin in *Mitin Zhurnal*, http://www.mitin.com/people/mogutin/klimov.shtml. Accessed July 1, 2009.

[7] On the Jewish scholarly perspective on the rhetoric of sexual perversions see Michael L. Satlow. *Tasting the Dish: Rabbinic Rhetorics of Sexuality*. Atlanta, GA: Scholars Press. 1996.

[8] G. Klimov. Bozhii narod. www.klimov.kiev.ua.Books/Bn04.htm. p. 6. Accessed February 5, 2006.

[9] Apollinariia Suslova (1838–1919) was Dostoevsky's mistress who later became Rozanov's wife. See Mark Slonim. *Tri liubvi Dostoevskogo*. Moscow: Imidzh. 1991.

[10] This approach is well established in Russian discourse. Plekhanov's formula "*otsiuda i dosiuda*" ("from here up to here"), an attempt to define a new revolutionary attitude to the cultural heritage of the past, was applied in Soviet Russia to works of literature as a method of censorship. This censorship was achieved by selecting only those works or parts of those works that could contribute to the formation of the official discourse of the state, leaving out everything that was potentially controversial and could challenge the foundations of Marxist-Leninist philosophy. G.V. Plekhanov. Zametki publitsista. *Sbornik statei*. Moscow: Ogoniok. 1949.

Chapter 11

[11] "Chosen people" is a euphemism for Jews. G. Klimov. *Bozhii narod.* Chapter "Angely sveta". http://www.klimov.kiev.ua/Books/Bnar/Bn01.htm. p.1. Accessed February 5, 2006.

[12] This information was made public in 1970 as a result of the publication of Bursov's monograph on Dostoevsky. B. Bursov. *Lichnost' Dostoevskogo.* Leningrad: Sovetskii pisatel'. 1974. On the negative reception of this information in Soviet Dostoevsky scholarship see Henrietta Mondry [G. Mondri]. *Otsenka vospriiatiia F. M. Dostoevskogo v Sovetskom literaturovedenii 1970–1980-ykh gg.* Ph. D. Thesis. Johannesburg: University of the Witwatersrand. 1984.

[13] F. M. Dostoevskii. *Besy.* Polnoe sobranie sochinenii v tridtsati tomakh. Leningrad: Nauka. Vol. 11. 1974.

[14] Aleksandr Ianov. *Russkaia ideia i 2000-yi god.* New York: Liberty Publishing House. 1988.

[15] See Yuri Slezkine. *The Jewish Century.* Princeton: Princeton University Press. 2004.

[16] Mordekhai Altshuler. The Unique Features of the Holocaust in the Soviet Union. Ed. Yaacov Ro'i. *Jews and Jewish Life in Russia and the Soviet Union.* London: Routlege. 1995. 171–189.

[17] G. Klimov. *Bozhii narod.* Chapter Angely sveta. http://www.klimov.kiev.ua/Books/Bnar/Bn 01.htm. p.1. Accessed 2/05/2006.

[18] Henrietta Mondry [G. Mondri]. *Pisateli-narodniki i evrei.* St. Petersburg: Akademicheskii proekt. 2005.

[19] Stalin, Iosif Dzhugashvili, was a native of Ossetia, an ethnic enclave in Georgia. Klimov's canard about Hitler's part-Jewish origins was used by Apollon Kuzmin, a representative of National Bolshevism, who wrote: "It was perfectly demonstrated by Grigorii Klimov, when he described 'Hitler's Political Bureau,' in which everybody was either of mixed origins, or converted to Christianity, or had Jewish wives." (235). See A. Kuzmin. Khazarskie stradaniia. *Molodaia Gvardiia.* No. 6. 1993. 245–250.

[20] G. Klimov. *Bozhii narod.* Chapter Angely sveta. http://www.klimov.kiev.ua/Books/Bnar/Bn 01.htm. p.9. Accessed February 5, 2006.

[21] V. Avdeev. *Russkaia rasovaia teoriia do 1917 goda.* Biblioteka rasovoi mysli. Moscow: Feri. 2004.

[22] V. Avdeev. *Rasologiia.* Biblioteka rasovoi mysli. Moscow: Belye al'vy. 2005.

[23] On "inverted world of Judeophilia" see Laura Engelstein. *The Keys to Happiness.* Ithaca: Cornell University Press. 1992.

[24] See Ksenia Polouektova. *Alexander Solzhenitsyn's 200 Years Together and the "Jewish Question."* ACTA No. 31. The Hebrew University of Jerusalem. 2008.

[25] A. N. Savel'ev. Predislovie. In V. Avdeev. *Rasologiia.* Biblioteka rasovoi mysli. Moscow: Belye al'vy. 2005. 1–7.

[26] In post-Soviet Russia and the post-Soviet Republics the Holocaust is still not acknowledged fully. See Stefan Rohdewald. Post-Soviet Remembrance of the Holocaust and National Memories of the Second World War in Russia, Ukraine and Lithuania. *Forum for Modern Languages Studies.* Special issue: *Representations of the Past in European Memorials.* Vol. 44. No. 2. 2008. 173–184.

[27] Eugene Avrutin in his article published in a scholarly journal dubs Avdeev as a historian and a representative of "recent scholarship" on race (16). See Eugene Avrutin. Racial Categories and the Politics of (Jewish) Difference in Late Imperial Russia. *Kritika: Explorations in Russian and Eurasian History* 8. Vol. 1. 2007. 13–40. 16.

[28] Andreas Umland, Toward an Uncivil Society? Contextualising the Recent Decline of Extremely Right-Wing Parties in Russia, Cambridge, MA: The Weatherhead Center for International Affairs, 2003, Working paper No. 02–03, on line, iii, 43.

[29] This is the view of Alexander Solzhenitsyn. See Dorothy G. Atkinson. Solzhenitsyn's Heroes as Russian Historical Types. *The Russian Review.* Vol. 30. No. 1. 1971. 1–16.

[30] On the Russian national identity in post-Putin Russia see Karl C. Schaffenburg. Russkiy and Rossiiskiy: Russian National Identity After Putin. *Orbis.* Vol. 51. No. 4. 2007. 75–737.

Conclusion

Assembling the Jew's Body: Continuity, Recycling, Change

The twenty-first-century continuity of the construct of the Jewish body in Russian culture has to be seen as part of Russia's recent political and cultural history, involving as it does a special interest in formerly and formally forbidden topics from the Soviet era. The revival of interest in racist theories in post-Soviet Russia goes hand in hand with the rise of Russian self-assertiveness.[1] In nationalistic and patriotic circles at the present time, interest in the work of pre-Soviet conservative thinkers like Vasily Rozanov is high,[2] and may be explained by the search undertaken by the extreme political Right for authoritative substantiation of their racist views by thinkers of the past. Russian political parties today lay considerable stress on the importance of Russian unity, and influential political figures, such as Alexander Prokhanov, define this unity as a unity of blood. Philosophers of the Russian Silver Age offer further appeal to this new Russian Right and the general public at large as a consequence of the intense religious renaissance in post-Soviet Russia.[3] Derived from the work of various turn-of-the-nineteenth-century thinkers, who, like Rozanov, incorporated contemporary racist views into the wider debate on the differences between Christianity and Judaism, a revival of racial arguments is taking place today as part of the focus on Russian religious and national identity.[4] In this search for a new identity, post-Soviet Russia relies heavily on the resurrection of pre-Revolutionary ideas and ideologies of nationhood, and on the unity of blood ties as a cornerstone for such an identity. The writings of early twentieth-century pre-Revolutionary racist scientists and thinkers are now being published alongside works previously banned in the Soviet Union. In the cases of Klimov and Avdeev, the degree of biased selectivity applied by the contemporary political Right to interpretations of the ideas of thinkers and scientists of the past as a way of exposing the supposed vices of Jews and Judaism and the innate goodness of the Russian people is all too clear.

The prestigious literary Ivan Bunin Award in 2009 went to Alexander Prokhanov. The bitter irony of this event is encapsulated in the very description of the prize which defines its aim as "the revival of the best traditions of Russian national literature". In this context Prokhanov's writing was described by one commentator as "a mixture of the pre-revolutionary Black Hundred rhetoric and *Pravda* editorials".[5]

Throughout its existence, Russian literature has served both as a source of national pride and as an inexhaustible reservoir of ideas, and it remains one of the major components in the formation of Russian national identity today.[6] Any representation of Jewish characters in the work of the nineteenth-century classics, such as that of Anton Chekhov, will continue to be used as a reliable repository of ethnic and racial stereotypes. Russian literature made an important contribution to the construct of the Jewish body and it became an essential medium for the dissemination of this construct. As a formative element in the phenomenon of textual attitudes, identified by Said as a significant component in the construction of the racial and ethnic Other, it made an impact on non-Jewish and Jewish readers and writers alike. The Russian Jewish writers Ilya Ehrenburg, Dina Rubina and Alexander Goldstein have all distilled in their writings both learned "textual attitudes" and their personal experiences of being a Jew in Russia and abroad. Russian Jewish writers and film directors inevitably define their Jewish Self against the cultural construct of the Jewish body.

Russian culture continues to define and represent Jews as members of a Race Apart, classifying Jewish biology and pathology as inherited characteristics. As a criminal fraudster, former oligarch Mikhail Khodorkovsky stands as an illustration of the phylogenetic belief that Jews are prone to committing fraud. This view was articulated in scientific literature well into the twentieth century, as seen in the 1930 volume of *Problems of the Biology and Pathology of Jews,* which was based on pseudo-scientific and anachronistic statistics from the 1900s. The culture continues to recycle this view, and a link is made between the Rottenbergs, the Pinyas, the Brodkins and the Russian Jewish oligarchs on the level of the biological script. When Khodorkovsky was put on trial in 2005, he was kept inside a barred cage.[7] This is emblematic of the way Russian culture constructs the Jew: inside a cage, Khodorkovsky was made to look not merely like someone guilty of company fraud, but like a hardened criminal. When the Russian serial murderer Andrei Chikatilo, who was accused of cannibalizing his victims, was brought to trial in 1992, he was kept inside a cage identical to

Khodorkovsky's, both to protect him from public attack and to demonstrate that cannibalism is regarded as a non-human condition. When somebody like Khodorkovsky is put into a cage, the intention is not only to humiliate him for his political ambitions, but also to signify that a Jew is an exhibit, his body exposed for observation both as a sight and a site onto which the viewer can inscribe hostile meanings. Furthermore it carries an allusion to the international Jewish conspiracy: he is kept in a cage because the Jewish commandoes might somehow engineer his escape.

The most stable construct linked to the Jewish biological body, which Russian culture continues to recycle, is that of a sadistic Jew, driven by instinct to harm Christians. The actions of Jews are often regarded as based on the "secret" Jewish practice of using Christian blood for ritual purposes. This attitude is illustrated in the case of the Russian priest, Alexander Men' (1935–1990), who was born into a Jewish family but baptized by his mother when he was only seven months old.[8] The special issue of the journal *Chernaia Sotnia* (*Black Hundred*) in 1995, entitled "Aleksandr Men' i delo Beilisa" ("Alexander Men' and the Beilis Affair"), clearly demonstrates that, even as a Christian priest and theologian, a Jew is still treated as a member of the Jewish race. Men' was most likely murdered by a group of antisemitic fanatics, but his murderers have never been found. The author of the article, Dr. Lanin, "proves" that Beilis committed the ritual murder of the Christian boy Iushchinskii, and uses as evidence Vasily Rozanov's *The Olfactory and Tactile Attitude of the Jews to Blood*. But he also accuses Father Alexander Men' of concealing and denying the Judaic practice of using Christian blood for *matzot* and other ritual purposes. He chooses Father Men' because Men' was born Jewish, and his "racial" origins serve as proof of his concealed empathy for Jews. What is clear from the case of Father Men' is that, in the perception of Russians, a Jew remains a Jew even when he or she is converted to Christianity. Like the Marranos, forced converts to Catholicism in Spain under the Inquisition, Jews in Russia today continue to be defined by their "race."[9]

There is yet another example that epitomizes the continuity of the construct of the sadistic, bloodthirsty Jew who is also the enemy of the Russian people and their culture. This is the accusation leveled against Jews for the murder of the Russian poet Sergei Esenin. It relates to the idea of a conspiracy involving Trotsky and Jewish revolutionaries. Esenin (1895–1925) has been made into a cult figure by Russian patriots because of his peasant origins and his special love for rural Russia, both of which are seen as forms of true patriotism, as opposed to the Bolshevik vision of planning and creating an industrialized Russia. Since the Chernobyl disaster, industrialization has come to be viewed in a largely negative light, while the veneration of the countryside has grown into an important aspect of this new form of Russian patriotism.[10] Within this myth-building of Russianness, a special place has been found for Esenin's famous good looks, viewed as a typical example of the native Russian ideal of beauty. Blonde and blue-eyed, Esenin was also famous for his drunken brawls. This sort of behavior is perceived and portrayed as positive, as a form of Russian boisterousness and honest self-expression that makes this type of masculinity. In 1925 Esenin hanged himself in a drunken stupor in a Petrograd hotel, but, especially since Glasnost and the renewed expression of Russian nationalism, Russian culture has been keen to find martyrs who perished at the hands of the Bolshevik leaders, many of whom have now for the first time been openly identified as Jews. In the late 1980s a rumor surfaced alleging that Esenin was murdered by agents of Trotsky, who made the murder look like suicide.[11] This conspiracy myth identified Trotsky and the Bolshevik Jews as bloodthirsty sadists. One detail in particular was picked up and emphasized by the conspiracy mythmakers: Esenin cut his wrist before he hanged himself and used his own blood to write his suicide note. This detail helped trigger a particular murder theory: it provided an association between blood-letting and Jews — a stable element of blood libel. The fact that there is evidence that Esenin was psychotic in the last three years of his life, and that he attempted to commit suicide on a number on occasions, has been ignored or dismissed by the fabricators of the murder theory.[12] In order to support the ritual murder theory, images of Esenin's body revealing signs of abuse had to be provided. This resulted in fabricated photographs that were shown as "documentary material" in the recent TV drama *Esenin* (2005).[13] Directed by Igor Zaitsev, this eleven-episode drama was based on the novel of the same name by Vitaly Bezrukov, who in turn based his work on theories provided by various articles in literary and popular magazines of the late 1980s.[14] The message of the myth built around Esenin's "murder" is clear: Trotsky and his Jewish minions sadistically murdered the "last poet of the [Russian] village" (this is the title Esenin gave himself during his lifetime), the "golden-haired Russian poet," (256) as he is lovingly called by Russian patriots.[15]

The case of Esenin's alleged murder by the Bolshevik Jews under Trotsky's leadership encapsulates all the aspects of the pathological, naturally criminal Jew as depicted in the novels of Ivanov and Shevtsov, and has overtones of the Beilis Affair. The logic of the argument is circular: Jews are pathological because of their special racial difference, and they are different because they are anomalous by nature.

The scale of the dissemination of this kind of material on the TV screen is enormous.[16] In 2006 Putin expressed his opinion that film is the most powerful medium in Russia today and therefore must make a constructive contribution to the building of the nation.[17] He also stressed that an important task for all the media is to foster patriotic feelings among the Russian people.

In December 2008 the results of the national project "Imia 'Rossiia'" (The Name "Russia"), conducted by the TV channel "Russia," the Fund of the Public Opinion and the Institute of Russian History were announced. These results consisted of a list of three historic personalities chosen by Russian voters to carry the "Name 'Russia.'" These were: the medieval prince Alexander Nevsky, the Prime Minister Pyotr Stolypin and Joseph Stalin. This list is highly illustrative of the self-assertiveness and nationalism of new Russia. When asked to comment on the result of this poll, the representative of the opposition party Drugaia Rossiia (Alternative Russia), Alexander Ryklin, made it quite clear that the people voted for Alexander Nevsky because the TV program organizing the poll emphasized his patriotic struggle against the foreign invaders, such as Swedes and Germans. He made a link between contemporary xenophobia nurtured by the Putin government and the choice to vote for the medieval Russian warrior prince who defeated foreigners. When the representative of the Communist Party in the Duma, Nikolai Kharitonov, was asked to comment on the choice made by the Russian people he explained that the Prime Minister Stolypin deserves to carry the honor of the "Name 'Russia'" because of his intended agricultural reforms and because he was assassinated by the "Jew terrorist Bogrov."[18] It was said that Stalin, in turn, deserves the honor because he had made Russia into a superpower. Both the list and the comments of the member of the Duma illustrate the continuity in anti-Jewish stereotypes, based on the notion of the sadistic treacherous Jew who is an enemy of the Russian nation. The reader will recall that Stolypin's murder in 1911 took place during the Beilis Affair, and that Vasily Rozanov started his campaign against Jews as a consequence of the link he made between the two acts. It was stated in the Introduction that it was in Stalin's Russia that Russianness was essentialized as a biological category. In new Russia today this trend continues as Russianness is being constructed as a biological classification. The Russian nation continues to define itself against the hostile Other, and, as the Other, the Jewish body continues to be the site onto which a hostile culture inscribes negative images. At the height of the popularity of eugenics in Russia in the 1920s the Jewish body was defined as "an exemplary organism" because it exhibited paradoxical features both of pathology and strength. Its perceived strengths remain a source of fear for many Russians, and its imagined pathologies are used as the motivation for continuing to exclude it from the collective body of the Russian nation. As long as the Jewish body remains the archetypal body of the Other to all things Russian, the Russian culture will continue to look for, to invent and to reinvent, signs and markers of its recognizability.

Notes

1   On the history of Black Hundred see Walter Laqueur. *Black Hundred: The Rise of the Extreme Right in Russia*. New York: Harper Collins. 1993.

2   See James Scanlan. Ed. *Russian Thought after Communism: The Recovery of a Philosophical Heritage*. New York: M. E. Sharpe. 1994.

3   See John Garrard and Carol Garrard. *Russian Orthodoxy Resurgent Faith and Power in the New Russia*. Princeton: Princeton University Press. 2008.

4   Ian Lilly and Henrietta Mondry. Eds. *Russian Literature in Transition*. Nottingham UK: Astra Press. 1999.

5   See Krutoi imperets. *Kommersant*. No. 199. 24. 10. 2009. 5. Members of the 2009 jury included prominent academics: the President of the State Institute of Russian Language and the Vice-Chancellor of the M. Gorkii Literature Institute, among others.

6   Vera Tolz. *Russia: Inventing the Nation*. London: Arnold. 2001.

7   See the picture in Claire Bigg. Russia: After Khodorkovskii, What Next For Oligarchs? Radio Free Europe / Radio Liberty. www.rgerl.org/feature article/2005/06.

8   On Alexander Men' see Judith Deutsch Kornblatt. *Doubly Chosen: Jewish Identity, the Soviet Intelligentsia, and the Russian Orthodox Church*. Madison: University of Wisconsin Press. 2004.

9   Marvin Perry and Frederick M. Schweitzer. *Antisemitism: Myth and Hate from Antiquity to the Present*. New York: Palgrave. 2002.

10 Vasily Belov is a typical representative of this discource.

11 See Henrietta Mondry. Who Killed the Russian Poet Esenin? Antisemitism in Soviet Literary Criticism under Glasnost. *Jewish Affairs*. Vol. 46. No. 2. 1991. 25–35.

12 Esenin's friend, poet Anatolii Mariengof, maintained that Esenin suffered from hallucinations and depression from 1922. See his *Roman bez vran'ia*. Moscow: Vagrius. 2006.

13 *Esenin*. PRO — Cinema Production. Director Igor Zaitsev. 2005.

14 See Eduard Khlystalov. Taina gostinitsy Angliter. Istoriia odnogo chastnogo rassledovaniia. *Moskva*. No. 7. 1989. 112–200. Ivan Lystsov. Ubiistvo Esenina. *Molodaia Gvardiia*. No. 10. 1990. 245–260.

15 Ivan Lystsov. Ubiistvo Esenina. *Molodaia Gvardiia*. No. 10. 1990. 245–260.

16 Rosalind Marsh. *Literature, History and Identity in Post-Soviet Russia, 1991–2006*. Bern: Peter Lang. 2007.

17 Ibid.

18 See http://news:bbc.co.uk/hi/russian/news/default.stm. Accessed December 29, 2008. Alexander Nevsky received 525, 575 votes, Pyotr Stolypin received 523, 766 votes, and Stalin received 519, 071 votes.

Bibliography

Primary Sources

Avdeev, V. *Rasologiia: nauka o nasledtvennykh kachestvakh liudei.* Biblioteka rasovoi mysli. Moscow: Belye Al'vy. 2005.

----------. Ed. *Russkaia rasovaia teoriia do 1917 goda.* Biblioteka rasovoi mysli. Moscow: Feri. 2004.

Belov, Vasilii. *Vse vperedi.* Moscow: Sovetskii pisatel'. 1987. In English: Vassily Belov. *The Best Is Yet To Come.* Trans. P. O. Gromm. Moscow: Raduga Publishers. 1989.

Belyi, Andrei. Shtempelevannaia kul'tura. *Evrei i zhidy.* Ed. G. S. Zelenina. Moscow and Jerusalem: Mosty kul'tury, Gesharim. 2005. 365–376.

Binshtok V. I., Bramson M., Dembo G. I., Gran M. M., Eds. *Voprosy biologii i patologii evreev.* Vol. 3. No. 2. Leningrad: Izd-vo Evreiskogo Istoriko-Etnograficheskogo Obshchestva. 1930.

Binshtok, V. I. and Novosel'skii, S. A. Evrei v Leningrade 1900–1924 gg. *Voprosy biologii i patologii evreev.* Eds. Dr. V. I. Binshtok, Dr. A. M. Bramson, Prof. M. M. Gran, Prof. G. I. Dembo. Leningrad: Prakticheskaia meditsina. 1926. 30–64.

Binshtok, V. I. O zadachakh nauchnykh sbornikov "Voprosy biologii i patologii evreev". *Voprosy biologii i patologii evreev.* Eds. Dr. V. I. Binshtok, Dr. A. M. Bramson, Prof. G. I. Dembo and Prof. M. M. Gran. Leningrad: Prakticheskaia meditsina. 1926. 3–6.

Bogdanov, A. P. Antropologicheskaia fizionomika. *Russkaia rasovaia teoriia do 1917 goda.* Ed. V. B. Avdeev. Moscow: Feri-V. 2004. 111–144.

Botkin, V. P. *Pis'ma ob Ispanii.* Leningrad: Nauka. 1976.

Bystritskaia, Elina. *Vstrechi pod zvezdoi nadezhdy.* Moscow: Vagrius. 2008.

Chekhov, A. P. A. S. Suvorinu. 16 August 1892. *Sobranie sochinenii v dvenadtsati tomakh.* Vol. 11. Moscow: Khudozhestvennaia literatura. 1956. 586–590.

----------. A. S. Suvorinu. 17 January 1897. *Sobranie sochinenii v dvenadtsati tomakh.* Vol. 12. Moscow: Khudozhestvennaia literatura. 1956. 140–141.

----------. A. S. Suvorinu. 27 March 1894. *Sobranie sochinenii v dvenadtsati tomakh.* Vol. 12. Moscow: Khudozhestvennaia literatura. 1956. 49–50.

----------. A. S. Suvorinu. 7 May 1889. *Sobranie sochinenii v dvenadtsati tomakh.* Vol. 11. Moscow: Khudozhestvennaia literatura. 1956. 356–358.

----------. D. V. Grigorovichu. 5 February 1888. *Sobranie sochinenii v dvenadtsati tomakh.* Vol. 11. Moscow: Khudozhestvennaia literatura. 1956. 193–195.

----------. Dama s sobachkoi. *Sobranie sochinenii v dvenadtsati tomakh.* Vol. 8. Moscow: Khudozhestvennaia literatura. 1956. 394–411.

Bibliography

----------. E. M. Sharovoi. 28 February 1895. *Sobranie sochinenii v dvenadtsati tomakh*. Vol. 12. Moscow: Khudozhestvennaia literatura. 1956. 73–75.

----------. Ivanov. *Sobranie sochinenii v dvenadtsati tomakh*. Vol. 9. Moscow: Khudozhestvennaia literatura. 1956. 19–86.

----------. P. F. Iordanovu. 24 November 1896. *Sobranie sochinenii v dvenadtsati tomakh*. Moscow: Khudozhestvennaia literatura. Vol. 12. 1956. 123–126.

----------. P. S. Kramarevu. 8 May 1881. *Sobranie sochinenii v dvenadtsati tomakh*. Vol. 10. Moscow: Izd-vo Pravda. 1985. 10–11.

----------. Ryb'ia liubov'. *Sobranie sochinenii v dvenadtsati tomakh*. Vol. 7. Moscow: Khudozhestvennaia literatura. 1956. 99–101.

----------. Perekati-pole. *Sobranie sochinenii v dvenadtsati tomakh*. Vol. 5. Moscow: Khudozhestvennaia literatura. 1955. 275–291.

----------. Step'. *Sobranie sochinenii v dvenadtsati tomakh*. Vol. 6. Moscow: Khudozhestvennaia literatura. 1955. 16–112.

----------. Tina. *Sobranie sochinenii v dvenadtsati tomakh*. Vol. 4. Moscow: Khudozhestvennaia literatura. 1955. 474–492.

Chernyshevskii, N. G. Pis'mo 8 marta 1878 goda. *Polnoe sobranie sochinenii v piatnadtsati tomakh*. Vol. 15. Moscow. 1939–1953. 193.

Dikhtar, S. R. Deklassirovannoe evreistvo g. Minska. *Voprosy biologii i patologii evreev*. Vol. 3. No. 2. Eds. Dr. V. I. Binshtok, Dr. A. M. Bramson, Prof. G. I. Dembo and Prof. M. M. Gran. Leningrad: Izd-vo Evreiskogo Istoriko-Etnograficheskogo Obshchestva. 1930. 3–60.

Dostoevskii, F. M. *Besy. Polnoe sobranie sochinenii v tridtsati tomakh*. Leningrad: Nauka. Vol. 11. 1974.

Ehrenburg, Ilya and Grosssman, Vasily. *The Complete Black Book of Russian Jewry.* Trans. and ed. David Patterson. New Brunswick NJ: Transaction Publishers. 2003.

Erenburg, I. Burnaia zhizn' Lazika Roitshvanetsa. *Neobychainye pokhozhdeniia*. St. Petersburg: Kristall. 2001. 931–1127.

----------. Neobychhainye pokhozhdeniia Khulio Khurenito i ego uchenikov. *Neobychainye pokhozhdeniia*. St. Petersburg: Kristall. 2001. 33–256.

Erenburg, Il'ia. *Liudi, gody, zhizn'*. Books five and six. Moscow: Sovetskii pisatel'. 1966.

Eshevskii, S. V. O znachenii ras v istorii. *Russkaia rasovaia teoriia do 1917 goda*. Ed. V. B. Avdeev. Moscow: Feri-V. 2004. 55–110.

Fet A. A. *Vospominaniia.* Moscow: Pravda. 1983.

Feuchtwanger, Lion. *Ispanskaia ballada*. Polnoe sobranie sochinenii. Vol. 13. Moscow: Khudozhestvennaia literatura. 1969. 365–808.

Florenskii, Pavel. Evrei i sud'ba khristian (Pis'mo V. V. Rozanovu). V. V. Rozanov. *Sakharna. Sobranie sochinenii*. Ed. A. Nikoliukin. Moscow: Respublika. 1998. 361–368.

Frug, S. G. V korchme i v buduare. *Voskhod*. October 1889. 21–37.

Gol'dshtein, Aleksandr. *Aspekty dukhovnogo braka*. Moscow: Novoe literaturnoe obozrenie. 2001.

----------. *Rasstavanie s Nartsissom: Opyty pominal'noi ritoriki*. Moscow: Novoe literaturnoe obozrenie. 1997.

Goncharov, I. "Khristos v pustyne": Kartina g. Kramskogo. *Sobranie sochinenii*. Vol. 8. Moscow: Izd-vo Pravda, biblioteka Ogoniok. 1952. 220–231.

Bibliography

Gumilev, Lev. *Drevniaia Rus'i velikaia step'*. Moscow: Tov-vo Klyshnikov. 1992.
----------. *Etnogenez i biosfera zemli*. Leningrad. 1989.
----------. *Tysiacheletie vokrug Kaspiia*. Moscow. 1993.

Ivanov, Valentin. *Zheltyi metall*. Moscow: Molodaia Gvardiia. 1956.

Karabchievskii, Yurii. *Zhizn'Aleksandra Zilbera*. *Druzhba narodov*. No. 7. 1990. 97–146.
Karaev, N. I. Rasy i natsional'nosti s psikhologicheskoi tochki zreniia. *Russkaia rasovaia teoriia do 1917 goda*. Ed. V. B. Avdeev. Moscow: Feri-V. 2004. 207–218.
Kharitinov, Mark. Dnevnik ianvaria 1990 goda. *Novoe literaturnoe obozrenie*. Vol. 84. No. 2. 2007. 665–675.
Klimov, G. *Bozhii narod*. www.klimov.kiev.ua.Books/Bn04.htm. p. 6. Accessed February 5, 2006.
------------. Interv'iu s Grigoriem Petrovichem Klimovym. Iaroslav Mogutin. *Mitin Zhurnal* http://www.mitin.com/people/mogutin/klimov.shtml. Accessed July 1, 2009.
Korolenko, Vladimir. O pogromnykh delakh. *Polnoe sobranie sochinenii*. Vol. 9. Petrograd. 1914. 281–297.
Kozakov, Mikhail. *Akterskaia kniga*. Moscow: Vagrius. 1997.
Kychko, T. K. *Iudaizm bez prikras*. (In Ukrainian). Kiev: Vidavnitstvo Akademii nauk USSR. 1963.

Lermontov, M. Ispantsy. *Sobranie sochinenii*. Vol. 3. Moscow: Akademiia Nauk. 1961. 10–168.

Melikhov, Aleksandr. *Ispoved'evreia*. Moscow and St. Petersburg: Limbus Press. 2004.
Minakov, P. A. Znachenie antropologii v meditsine. *Russkaia rasovaia teoriia do 1917 goda*. Ed. V. B. Avdeev. Moscow: Feri-V. 2004. 373–384.

Plekhanov, G. V. Zametki publitsista (otsiuda i dosiuda). *Sbornik statei*. Moscow: izd-vo Pravda, biblioteka Ogoniok. 1949. 23–47.
Plisetskaia, Maia. *Ia-Maia Plisetskaia*. Moscow: Novosti. 1994.

Remizov, Aleksei. *Vzvikhrennaia Rus'*. St. Petersburg: Akademiia Nauk. 2003.
Rozanov, V. V. *Apokalipsis nashego vremeni*. *Sobranie sochinenii*. Ed. A. Nikoliukin. Moscow: Respublika. 2000.
----------. *Apokalipticheskaia sekta (Khlysty i skoptsy)*. St. Petersburg. 1914.
----------. Brak i khristianstvo. *V mire neiasnogo i nereshennogo. Sobranie sochinenii*. Ed. A. Nikoliukin. Moscow: Respublika. 1995. 107– 339.
----------. Dary Tsertsery (Shekhiny). *Vo dvore iazychnikov. Sobranie sochinenii*. Ed. A. Nikoliukin. Moscow: Respublika. 1999. 254–264.
----------. Evrei v russkoi literature. *Novoe vremia*. 06.05. 1912. 3–4.
----------. Iudaizm. *Taina Izrailia*. St. Petersburg: Sofiia. 1993. 105–227.
----------. K prekrashcheniiu ritual'nogo uboia skota. *Sakharna. Sobranie sochinenii*. Ed. A. Nikoliukin. Moscow: Respublika. 1998. 307–309.
----------. *Mimoletnoe. Sobranie sochinenii*. Ed. A. Nikoliukin. Moscow: Respublika. 1997.
----------. Novoe issledovanie o Fete. *O pisatel'stve i pisateliakh. Sobranie sochinenii*. Ed. A. Nikoliukin. Moscow: Respublika. 1995. 614–619.
----------. Oboniatel'noe i osiazatel'noe otnoshenie evreev k krovi. *Sakharna. Sobranie sochinenii*. Ed. A. Nikoliukin. Moscow: Respublika. 1998. 276–413.
----------. *Opavshie list'ia*. Munich: Neimanis. 1970.

Bibliography

----------. Pis'ma 1917–1919 godov. *Literaturnaia ucheba.* No. 1. 1990. 70–88.

----------. Pis'ma k E. Gollerbakhu. *Izbrannoe* . Munich: A. Neimanis. 1970. 515–564.

----------. *Poslednie list'ia. Sobranie sochinenni.* Ed. A. Nikoliukin. Moscow: Respublika. 2000.

----------. *Sakharna. Sobranie sochinenii.* Ed. A. Nikoliukin. Moscow: Respublika. 1998.

----------. *Uedinennoe.* Moscow: Sovremennik. 1991.

----------. Literaturnye novinki. *O pisatel'stve i pisateliakh. Sobranie sochinenii.* Ed. A. Nikoliukin. Moscow: Respublika. 1995. 166–175.

----------. Magicheskaia stranitsa u Gogolia. *O pisatel'stve i pisateliakh. Sobranie sochinenii.* Ed. A. Nikoliukin. Moscow: Respublika. 1995. 383–421.

----------. V chem raznitsa drevnego i novogo mirov. *Vo dvore iazychnikov. Sobranie sochinenii.* Ed. A. Nikoliukin. Moscow: Respublika. 1999. 231–236.

----------. Byl li Khristos evreem po plemeni? *Okolo narodnoi dushi. Sobranie sochinenii.* Ed. A. Nikoliukin. Moscow: Respublika. 2003. 60 –67.

----------. Eshche raz o neevreistve Khrista. *Okolo narodnoi dushi. Sobranie sochinenii.* Ed. A. Nikoliukin. Moscow: Respublika. 2003. 68–71.

Rozanov, V. V. and Gershenzon, M. O. Perepiska V. V. Rozanova i M. O. Gershenzona, 1908–1918. *Novyi Mir.* No. 3. 1991. 215–242.

Rubina, Dina. 'Vot idet Messiia !' *Nash kitaiskii biznes.* Moscow: Eksmo. 2004.

----------. Poslednii kaban iz lesov Pondevedra. *Voskresnaia messa v Toledo.* Moscow: Vagrius. 2005. 6–178.

----------. Vo vratakh tvoikh. *Voskresnaia messa v Toledo.* Moscow: Vagrius. 2005. 313–384.

----------. Voskresnaia messa v Toledo. *Vysokaia voda venetsiantsev.* Moscow: Vagrius. 2005. 294–346.

Shevtsov, Ivan. *Liubov' i nenavist'.* Moscow: Voennoe izd-vo Ministerstva oborony SSSR. 1970.

----------. *V bor'be s D'iavolom.* Moscow: Pravoslavnoe izd-vo Entsiklopediia Russkoi tsivilizatsii. 2003.

----------. *Vo imia otsa i syna.* Moscow: Moskovskii rabochii. 1970.

Sikorskii, I. A. Dannye iz antropologii. *Russkaia rasovaia teoriia do 1917 goda.* Ed. V. B. Avdeev. Moscow: Feri-V. 2004. 229–266.

Sholom Aleikhem [Aleichem]. Iosele-Solovei. *Sobranie sochinenii v shesti tomakh.* Ed. M. S. Belen'kii, S. Z. Galkin et al. Vol. 1. Moscow: Khudozhesvennaia literatura. 1959. 149–330.

----------. Tev'e-Molochnik. *Sobranie sochinenii v shesti tomakh.* Eds. M. S. Belen'kii, S. Z. Galkin et. al. Vol. 1. Moscow: Khudozhesvennaia literatura. 1959. 467–620.

Soloviev, V. S. *Pis'ma Vl. S. Solovieva.* Vol. 1. St. Petersburg. 1908.

----------. Evreistvo i khristianskii vopros. *Taina Izrailia.* St. Petersburg: Sofiia. 1993. 31–79.

Solzhenitsyn, Aleksandr. *Dvesti let vmeste (1795–1995).* Vol.1. Moscow: Russkii put'. 2001.

Trivus, S. A. Massovye psikhozy v evreiskoi istorii. — Sabbatianstvo. *Voskhod.* Vol. 7. 1900. 79–101.

Turgenev, I. S. Pis'mo Ia. P. Polonskomu 1872 goda. *Polnoe sobranie sochinenii i pisem v dvatsati vos'mi tomakh.* Moscow and Leningrad: Nauka. Vol. 9. 1960–1968. 236.

Ulitskaia, Liudmila. *Medeia i ee deti.* Moscow: Vagrius. 2002.

Zhabotinskii, Vladimir. Toska o patriotizme. *Ezhenedel'nyi zhurnal.* 1903. 16.05. No. 17. 1–5.

Zoshchenko, Mikhail. *Istoriia odnoi perekovki. Belomorsko-Baltiiskii Kanal imeni Stalina. Istoriia stroitel'stva 1931–1934 gg.* Eds. M. Gorkii, L. Averbakh, S. Firin. Moscow: OGIZ. Gosudarstvennoe izdatel'stvo "Istoriia fabrik i zavodov". 1934. Reprint edition of 1998. 493–527.

----------. Iz dnevnika. *Neizdannyi Zoshchenko.* Ed. Vera von Wiren. Ann Arbor: Ardis. 1976. 93–94.

----------. Vozvrashchennaia molodost'. *Sobranie sochinenii v trekh tomakh.* Vol. 3. Leningrad: Khudozhestvennaia Literatura. 1987. 5–161.

Films

Damskii portnoi. Directed by Leonid Gorovetz. For a-Film Studio. Kiev and Moscow. 1990.

Esenin. Directed by Igor' Zaitsev. PRO – Cinema Production. 2005.

Iskateli schast'ia. Directed by Vladimir Korsh-Sablin. Sovetskaia Belarus' Studio. Leningrad. 1936.

Ivan Vasilievich meniaet professiiu. Directed by Leonid Gaidai. Mosfilm. 1973.

Moskva slezam ne verit. Directed by Vladimir Menshov. Mosfilm. 1979.

Secondary Sources

Adams, Mark B. Eugenics in Russia, 1900–1940. *The Wellborn Science: Eugenics in Germany, France, Brazil and Russia.* Ed. Mark B. Adams. Oxford: Oxford University Press. 1990. 160–187.

Ainsztein, Reuben. The end of Marxism-Leninism. *New Statement.* London. December 15. 1978. 94–98.

Aitken-Sawn, Jean and Baird, D. Circumcision and the cancer of the cervix. *British Journal of Cancer.* Vol. 19. No. 2. 1965. 217–226.

Altshuler, Mordekhai. The Unique Features of the Holocaust in the Soviet Union. *Jews and Jewish Life in Russia and the Soviet Union.* Ed. Yaacov Ro'i. London: Routlege. 1995. 171–189.

Andrew, Joe. *Narrative and Desire in Russian Literature, 1822–49.* New York: St Martin's Press. 1993.

----------. *Narrative, Space and Gender in Russian Fiction: 1846–1903.* Amsterdam: Rodopi. 2007.

Aptekman, Marina. Kabbalah, Judeo-Masonic Myth, and Post-Soviet Literary Discourse: From Political Tool to Virtual Parody. *The Russian Review.* Vol. 64. No. 4. 2006. 657–681.

Aronson, Gregor and Frumkin, Jacob, Eds. *Russian Jewry 1917–196.* New York. 1969.

Assaf, David, Ed. and introd. *Journey to a Nineteenth-Century Schtetl: The Memoirs of Yekhezekel Kotik.* Detroit: Wayne State University Press. 2002.

Bibliography

Atkinson, Dorothy G. Solzhenitsyn's Heroes as Russian Historical Types. *The Russian Review*. Vol. 30. No. 1. 1971. 1–16.

Augstein, H. E. Ed. and introd. *Race: the Origins of An Idea, 1760–1850*. Bristol: Thoemess Press. 1996.

Avrutin, Eugene. Racial Categories and the Politics of (Jewish) Difference in Late Imperial Russia. *Kritika: Explorations in Russian and Eurasian History* 8. No. 1. 2007. 13–40.

Balukhatyi, S. D. Rannii Chekhov. *A. P. Chekhov. Sbornik statei i materialov*. Vol. 1. Literaturnyi muzei Chekhova. Rostov-on-Don: Rostovskoe knizhnoe izdatel'stvo. 1959. 3–95.

Bakhtin. M. M. *Rabelais and His World*. Trans. H. Iswolsky. Bloomington: Indiana University Press. 1965.

Barringer, Tim. *Reading The Pre-Raphaelites*. New Haven: Yale University Press. 1999.

Bataille, Georges. *Story of the Eye*. Trans. Joachim Neugroschel. San Francisco: City Lights Books. 1987.

Belova, Olga. *Etnokul'turnye stereotipy v slavianskoi narodnoi traditsii*. Moscow: Indrik. 2005.

ben Shimon Halevi, Z'ev. *Kabbalah: Tradition of Hidden Knowledge*. London: Thames and Hudson. 1991.

Benua, Aleksandr. Religiozno-filosofskoe obshchestvo. *V. V. Rozanov. Pro et Contra*. Vol. 1. Ed. D. K. Burlaka. St. Petersburg: Izdatel'stvo Russkogo Khristianskogo gumanitarnogo instituta [RKhGI]. 1995. 132–142.

Berdiaev, Nikolai. *Mirosozertsanie Dostoevskogo*. Paris: YMCA-Press. 1968.

Bethea, David. *The Shape of Apocalypse in Modern Russian Fiction*. Princeton , NJ: Princeton University Press. 1989.

Bezrodnyi, Mikhail. O 'iudoboiazni' Andreia Belogo. *Novoe literaturnoe obozrenie*. No. 28. 1997. 100–125.

Bigland, John. An Historical Display of the Effects of Physical and Moral Causes on the Character and Circumstances of the Ancients and Moderns in Regards to their Intellectual and Social state. Ed. H. F. Augstein. *Race: The Origins of an Idea, 1760–1850*. Bristol, UK: Thoemmes Press. 1996. 68–80.

Bland, Kalman. *The Artless Jew: Medieval and Modern Affirmations and Denials of the Visual*. Princeton NJ: Princeton University Press. 2000.

Blum, Arlen. *Evreiskii vopros pod sovetskoi tsenzuroi. 1917–1991*. St. Petersburg: Peterburgskii evreiskii universitet. 1996.

Blum, Jakub and Rich, Vera. *The Image of the Jew in Soviet Literature: The Post-Stalin Period*. London: Institute for Jewish Affairs. 1984.

Blumenau, L. B. Nravstvennaia evoluitsia i vyrozhdenie. *Vestnik psihopatologii, kriminologii i gipnotizma*. St. Petersburg. January 1904.

Boyarin, Daniel. *Unheroic Conduct: The Rise of Heterosexuality and the Invention of the Jewish Man*. Berkeley: University of California Press. 1997.

Brudny, Yitzhak M. *Reinventing Russia: Russian Nationalism and the Soviet State, 1953–1991*. Cambridge, MA: Harvard University Press. 2000.

Brym, Robert J. Russian Anisemitism, 1996–2000. Eds. Zvi Gitelman, Musya Glants and Marshall I. Goldman. *Jewish Life After the USSR*. Bloomington: Indiana University Press. 2003. 99–117.

Bukhshtab, Boris Ia. *A. A. Fet. Ocherk zhizni i tvorchestva*. Leningrad: Nauka. 1990.

Bursov, B. *Lichnost' Dostoevskogo*. Leningrad: Sovetskii pisatel'. 1974.

Bibliography

Carlson, Maria. Fashionable Occultism: Spiritualism, Theosophy, Freemasonry, and Hermeticism in Fin-de-Siecle Russia. *The Occult in Russian and Soviet Culture*. Ed. Bernice Glatzer Rosenthal. Ithaca: Cornell University Press. 1997. 135–152.

Chamberlain, Houston Stuart. *Foundations of the Nineteenth Century*. Trans. John Lees. Introd. George L. Mosse. New York: Howard Fertig. 1977.

Chekhov, M. P. *Vokrug Chekhova*. Leningrad: Academia. 1933.

Chekin, Leonid. The Godless Ishmaelites: The Image of the Steppe in Eleventh-Thirteenth-Century Rus'. *Russian History*. Vol. 19. Nos. 1–4. 1992. 9–28.

Chernenko, Miron. *Kinematograficheskaia istoriia Sovetskogo evreistva 1934–1941*. Moscow: Evreiskoe nasledie. 2001.

Chernyi, Boris. Tema izgnaniia i iskhoda u Chekhova. *Russko-evreiskaia kul'tura*. Ed. Oleg Budnitskii. Moscow: Rosspen. 2006. 191–216.

Cohen, Jeremy and Rosman, Moshe, Eds. *Rethinking European Jewish History*. Oxford: The Littman Library of Jewish Civilization. 2008.

Comas, Juan. *Race and Science*. New York: Columbia University Press. 1961.

Cooper, J. C. *Symbolic and Mythological Animals*. London: The Aquarian Press. 1992.

Darskii, D. O Fete. *Russkaia mysl'*. No. 8. 1915.

de Gobineau, Arthur. The Inequality of Human Races. *The Idea of Race*. Ed. and introd. Robert Bernasconi and Tommy L Lott. Indianapolis: Hackett Publishing Company. 2000. 45–54.

Deutsch Kornblatt, Judith. *Doubly Chosen: Jewish Identity, the Soviet Intelligentsia, and the Russian Orthodox Church*. Madison: University of Wisconsin Press. 2004.

----------. *Ladies' Tailor* and the End of Soviet Jewry. *Jewish Social Studies*. Vol. 5. No. 3. 1999. 180–195.

Douglas, Mary. *Purity and Danger. An Analysis of Concepts of Pollution and Taboo*. London: Routledge. 1984.

Dreizin, Felix. *The Russian Soul and the Jew: Essays in Literaty Ethocriticism*. Ed. D. Guaspari. Washington, DC: University Press of America. 1990.

Druzhnikov, Yury. *Informer 001: The Myth of Pavlik Morozov*. Transaction Publishers. 1996.

Dundes, Alan. *The Blood Libel Legend: A Case Book in Anti-Semitic Folklore*. Madison: University of Wisconsin Press. 1991.

Eco, Umberto, Ed. *On Ugliness*. London: Harvill Secker. 2007.

Edel'shtein, Mikhail. Istoriia odnogo stereotipa. *Evrei i zhidy v russkoi klassike*. Ed. G. S. Zelenina. Moscow and Jerusalem: Mosty kul'tury. Gesharim. 2005. 384–391.

Efron, John. *Defenders of the Race: Jewish Doctors and Race Science in Fin-de-siecle Europe*. New Haven: Yale University Press. 1994.

Eilberg-Schwartz, Howard. *God's Phallus: And Other Problems for Men and Monotheism*. Boston: Beacon Press. 1994.

----------. *People of the Body: Jews and Judaism From an Embodied Perspective*. Albany: SUNY Press. 1992.

Engelstein, Laura. *The Keys to Happiness: Sex and the Search for Modernity in Fin-de-Siecle Russia*. Ithaca, New York: Cornell University Press. 1992.

Epshtein, Mikhail. Malen'kii chelovek v futliare: sindrom Bashmachkina i Belikova. *Voprosy literatury*. No. 6. 2005. 193–203.

Etinger, Iakov. The Doctors' Plot: Stalin's Solution to the Jewish Question. *Jews and Jewish Life in Russia and the Soviet Union*. Ed. Yaacov Ro'i. London: Routledge. 1995. 103–127.

Etkind, Aleksandr. *Khlyst: sekty, literatura i revoliutsiia*. Moscow: Novoe literaturnoe obozrenie. 1998.

Bibliography

Fauconnier, Gilles and Turner, Mark. *Conceptual Blending and the Mind's Hidden Complexities*. New York: Basic Books. 2002.

Fedina, V. S. *A. A. Fet (Shenshin): Materialy k kharakteristike*. Petrograd. 1915.

Feinberg, Leslie. Roots of Russian "homosexual subculture." *Workers World Newspaper*. July 15. 2004.

Feldman, L. Z. et al. *"Prekrasnaia evreika" v Rossii XVII–XIX vekov*. Moscow: Drevlekhranilishche. 2007.

Finucci, Valeria and Brownlee, Kevin, Eds. *Generation and Degeneration: Tropes of Reproduction in Literature and History from Antiquity to Early Modern Europe*. Durham: Duke University Press.

Fowkes, Ben. *The Disintegration of the Soviet Union: A Study In The Rise And Triumph Of Nationalism*. New York: St. Martin's Press. 1997.

Frankel, Jonathan. *The Damascus Affair: 'Ritual Murder,' Politics and the Jews in 1840*. New York: Cambridge University Press. 1997.

Freedman, Jonathan. Henry James and the Discourses of Antisemitism. *Between "Race" and Culture: Representations of "the Jews" in English and American Literature*. Ed. Bryan Cheyette. Stanford: Stanford University Press. 1996. 62–83.

Freud, Sigmund. Instincts and Their Vicissitudes. *On Metapsychology: The Theory of Psychoanalysis*. The Penguin Freud library. Vol. 11. London: Penguin books. 1991. 105–138.

----------. Analysis of a Phobia in a Five-Year-Old Boy. *The Standard Edition of the Complete Psychological Works of Sigmund Freud*. Vol. 10. Ed. J. Strachey, trans. J. Strachey with Anna Freud. London: Hogarth Press. 1955–74. 5–49.

----------. *Introductory Lectures on Psychoanalysis*. The Penguin Freud Library. Vol. 1. London: Penguin books. 1991.

----------. On the Mechanism of Paranoia. *The Standard Edition of the Complete Psychological Works of Sigmund Freud*. Vol. 12. Trans. James Strachey. London: The Hogarth Press. 1958. 59–80.

----------. *New Introductory Lectures on Psychoanalysis*. The Penguin Freud library. Vol. 2. London: Penguin books. 1991.

----------. *The Interpretation of Dreams*. Trans. and ed. James Strachey. New York: Avon Books. 1998.

----------. Three Essays on the Theory of Sexuality. *On Sexuality*. The Penguin Freud Library. Vol. 7. London: Penguin books. 1991. 33–155.

Frezinskii, B. Fenomen Il'i Erenburga (tysiacha deviat'sot dvadtsatye gody). Il'ia Erenburg. *Neobychainye pokhozhdeniia*. St. Petersburg: Kristall. 2001. 5–33.

Garrard, John and Garrard, Carol. *Russian Orthodoxy Resurgent Faith and Power in the New Russia*. Princeton: Princeton University Press. 2008.

Geizer, I. M. *Chekhov i meditsina*. Moscow: Medgiz. 1954.

Geller, Jay. The Aromatics of Jewish Difference; or Benjamin's Allegory of Aura. *Jews and Other Differences*. Ed. Jonathan and Daniel Boyarin. Minneapolis: University of Minnesota Press. 1997. 203–256.

Gilman, Sander L. *Freud, Race and Gender*. Princeton: Princeton University Press. 1993.

----------. Freud and the Sexologists: A Second Reading. *Reading Freud's Readings*. Ed. Sander L. Gilman et al. New York: SUNY Press. 1994. 47–76.

----------. *Difference and Pathology: Stereotypes of Sexuality, Race and Madness*. Ithaca: Cornell University Press. 1985.

-----------. *The Visibility of the Jew in the Diaspora: Body Imagery and its Cultural Context.* Syracuse, New York: Syracuse University Press. 1992.

-----------. *The Jew's Body.* London: Routledge. 1991.

-----------. *The Case of Sigmund Freud: Medicine and Identity at the Fin de Siècle.* Baltimore: The Johns Hopkins University Press. 1993.

-----------. Salome, Syphilis, Sarah Bernhardt and the Modern Jewess. *The Jew in the Text: Modernity and the Construction of Identity.* Ed. Linda Nohlin and Tamar Garb. London: Thames and Hudson. 1995. 97–121.

Gippius, Zinaida. Zadumchivyi strannik. *V. V. Rozanov: Pro et Contra.* Vol. 2. Ed. D. K. Burlaka. St. Petersburg: RKhGI. 1995. 143–185.

Gitelman, Zvi, Ed. *Bitter Legacy: Confronting the Holocaust in the USSR.* Bloomington: Indiana University Press. 1997.

Goldberg, Anatol. *Ilya Ehrenburg: Revolutionary, Novelist, Poet, War Correspondent, Propagandist: The Extraordinary Epic of a Russian Survivor.* New York: Viking. 1984.

Goldman, Marshall. Russian Jews in Business. Glants, Musya and Goldman, Marshall I., Eds. *Jewish Life After the USSR.* Bloomington: Indiana University Press. 2003. 76–99.

Goldstein, David. *Dostoevsky and the Jews.* Austin: University of Texas Press. 1981.

Golomshtok, Igor. *Totalitarian Art in the Soviet Union, the Third Reich, Fascist Italy and the People's Republic of China.* London: Collins Harvill. 1990.

Greenleaf, Monika and Moeller-Sally, Stephen, Eds. *Russian Subjects: Empire, Nation and the Culture of the Golden Age.* Evanston IL: Northwestern University Press. 1998.

Grossman, Leonid. Naturalizm Chekhova. *Vestnik Evropy.* No. 7. 1914. 218–247.

Grosz, Elizabeth. *Volatile Bodies: Towards a Corporeal Feminism.* Bloomington: Indiana University Press. 1994.

Gulyga, Arsenii. Razum pobezhdaet (O nauchno-khudozhestvennykh povestiakh Mikhaila Zoshchenko). *Sobranie sochinenii v trekh tomakh.* Vol. 3. Leningrad: Khudozhestvennaia Literatura. 1987. 694–710.

Hake, Egmont. *Regeneration: A Reply to Max Nordau.* Westminster: Archibald Constable. 1895.

Hamilton, Susan, Ed. *Animal Welfare and Anti-Vivisection 1870–1910: Nineteenth-Century Women's Mission.* London: Routledge. 2004.

Hellebust, Rolf. *Flesh to Metal: Soviet Literature and the Alchemy of Revolution.* Ithaca: Cornell University Press. 2003.

Heritier, Francoise. *Two Sisters and Their Mother. An Anthropology of Incest.* Trans. Jeanine Herman. New York: Zone Books. 1999.

Hoffmann, David L. and Kotsonis, Yanni, Eds. *Russian Modernity: Politics, Knowledge, Practices.* New York: St. Martin's Press. 2000.

Hutchings, Stephen C. *Russian Modernism: The Transfiguration of the Everyday.* Cambridge UK: Cambridge University Press. 1997.

Ianov, Aleksandr. *Russkaia ideia i 2000-yi god.* New York: Liberty Publishing House. 1988.

Ioffe, Denis. Anosios Gamos. Opyt vkhozhdeniia v chuzhuiu tonal'nost'. *Topos.* http:// www.topos.ru/article/344. Accessed January 22, 2009.

----------. Ed. *Diskursy telesnosti i erotizma v literature i kul'ture.* Moscow: Ladomir. 2008.

Iurskii, Segei. *Igra v zhizn'.* Moscow: Vagrius. 2007.

Ivanov, Yurii. *Ostorozhno, sionizm! Ocherki po ideologii, organizatsii i praktike sionizma.* Moscow: Politizdat. 1969.

Bibliography

Ivanovskii, A. A. Opyt antropologicheskoi klassifikatsii naseleniia Rossii. *Russkii antropologicheskii zhurnal*. No. 3/4. 1903. 103–115.

Izmozik, Vladlen. Jews in 19th and 20th Century Russian History Textbooks. *Jews in Eastern Europe*. No. 38. Spring and Fall. 1999. 45–73.

Kaganovsky, Lilya. *How the Soviet Man Was Unmade: Cultural Fantasy and Male Subjectivity Under Stalin*. Pittsburg: University of Pittsburg Press. 2008.

Kalmanskii, E. Paradoksy peresechenii: evrei v proizvedeniiakh A. P. Chekhova. *Evrei v Rossii: Istoriia i kul'tura*. Vol. 3. St. Petersburg: Peterburgskii evreiskii universitet. Trudy po iudaike. 1995. 171–186.

Kamenetskii, I. V. *Prirodnye bogatstva Evreiskoi avtonomnoi oblasti*. Moscow: Der Emes. 1936.

Kantor, V. Metafizika evreiskogo 'net' v romane Il'i Erenburga "Khulio Khurenito." Ed. Oleg Budnitskii et al. *Russko-evreiskaia kul'tura*. Vol. 2. Moscow: Rosspen. 2006. 345–372.

Karasova, T. A. Ed. *Sionizm v sisteme imperializma: ocherki istorii i sovremennost'*. Moscow: Nauka. 1988.

Karlinsky, Simon. *The Sexual Labyrinth of Nikolai Gogol*. Cambridge, MA: Harvard University Press. 1976.

Katsis, Leonid. *Osip Mandel'shtam: Muskus Iudeistva*. Moscow: Mosty kul'tury. 2002.

Katz, Elena. *Neither With Them Nor Without Them: The Russian Writer and the Jew in the Age of Realism*. Syracuse: Syracuse University Press. 2008.

Kelly, Catriona. *Comrade Pavlik: The Rise and Fall of a Soviet Boy Hero*. Granta Books. 2005.

Khlystalov, Eduard. Taina gostinitsy Angliter. Istoriia odnogo chastnogo rassledovaniia. *Moskva*. No. 7. 1989. 112–200.

Kleeblatt, Norman, Ed. *Too Jewish? Challenging Traditional Identities*. New York: The Jewish Museum and Rutgers University Press. 1996.

Klein, Melanie. *The Psychoanalysis of Children*. New York: Delacorte Press. 1975.

Kleiton, Daglas. Ulybka Konstantina: k probleme poeticheskogo iazyka Chekhova. *Avtor i tekst*. Eds. V. M. Markovich and Vol'f Shmid. St. Petersburg: St. Petersburg University Press. 1996. 341–354.

Klier, John D. Outline of Jewish-Russian History: 1954–2001. *An Anthology of Jewish-Russian Literature: Two Centuries of Dual Identity in Prose and Poetry*. Vol. 2. Ed. Maxim Shrayer. New York: M. E. Sharpe. 2007. 1199–1206.

----------. *Imperial Russia's Jewish Question, 1855–1881*. Cambridge UK: Cambridge University Press. 1995.

----------. *Russia Gathers Her Jews: The Origins of the "Jewish Question" in Russia, 1772–1825*. DeKalb: Northern Illinois University Press. 1986.

----------. Traditional Russian Religious Antisemitism: A Useful Concept or a Barrier to Understanding? *Jewish Quaterly* No. 174. Summer 1999. 29–34.

Klier, John D. and Lambroza, Shlomo, Eds. *Pogroms: Anti-Jewish Violence in Modern Russian History*. Cambridge UK: Cambridge University Press. 1993.

Kol'tsov, N. K. *Uluchshenie chelovecheskoi prirody*. Petrograd: izd-vo Vremia. 1923.

Korneev, L. A. *Sionizm — vrag mira i progressa: Material v pomoshch lektoru*. Moscow: Znanie. 1978.

Kosofsky Sedgwick, Eve. *Epistemology of the Closet*. New York: Harvester Wheatsheaf. 1990.

Krutikov, Mikhail. Constructing Jewish Identity in Contemporary Russian Fiction. *Jewish*

Bibliography

Life after the USSR. Eds. Zvi Gitelman, Musya Glants and Marshall I. Goldman. Bloomington: Indiana University Press. 2003. 252–274.

Kunitz, Joshua. *Russian Literature and the Jew*. New York: Columbia University Press: 1929.

Kurganov, E. and Mondry, H. [G. Mondri]. *Vasilii Rozanov i evrei*. St. Petersburg: Akademicheskii proekt. 2000.

Kuzmin, A. Khazarskie stradaniia. *Molodaia gvardiia*. No. 6. 1993. 245–250.

Lacan, Jacques. *The Four Fundamental Concepts of Psycho-Analysis*. Ed. Jacques -Alain Miller, trans. Alan Sheridan. New York: W. W. Norton. 1978.

Lafont, Maria. *Soviet Posters. The Sergo Grigorian Collection*. London: Prestel. 2007.

Lanin, P. Aleksandr Men' i delo Beilisa, *Chernaia sotnia*. No. 9/11. 1995.

Laqueur, Walter. *Black Hundred: The Rise of the Extreme Right in Russia*. New York: Harper Collins. 1993.

Largo, Martin and Jose, Ramon. *La judia de Toledo: desde Lope de Vega hasta Franz Grillparzer*. Madrid: Auryn. 2000.

Lavie, Smadar and Swedenburg, Ted. Introduction. *Displacement, Diaspora, and Geographies of Identity*. Ed. Smadar Lavie and Ted Swedenburg. Durham: Duke University Press. 1996. 1–25.

Layton, Susan. "A Hidden Polemic with Leo Tolstoy: Afanasy Fet's Lyric 'Mine was the madness he wanted...'". *The Russian Review* Vol. 66. April 2007. 220–237.

Ledger, Sally and Lukhurst, Roger, Eds. *The Fin De Siècle: A Reader in Cultural History, c. 1880–1900*. Oxford: Oxford University Press. 2000.

Leibler, Isi. *Soviet Jewry and Human Rights*. A Human Rights Research Publication. 10/6. Melbourne: Human Rights Publications. 1965.

Leontiev, Konstantin. *Analiz, stil' i veianie. O romanakh gr. L. N.Tolstogo*. (Reprint) Providence: Brown University Press. 1968.

Lerman, D. *Promyshlennost' Evreiskoi avtonomnoi oblasti*. B.m: TsS OZET. 1936.

Letopis' zhizni i tvorchetsva A. P. Chekhova. 1860–1888. Vol. 1. Moscow: Nasledie. 2000.

Levin, A. Kh. and Chervakov, V. Kh. *Abrazan'e u asviatlen'ni navukovai ekspertizy*. Minsk. 1932.

Levin, Michael. *Why Race Matters. Race Differences and What They Mean*. Westport, CT: Praeger. 1997.

Lieberman, George. The Jewish Experience in Russian Literature as Reflected in the Writings of Leo Tolstoy. *Proceedings of the 8th World Congress of Jewish Studies*. Jerusalem: World Union of Jewish Studies. 1982. 135–140.

Lilly, Ian and Mondry, Henrietta, Eds. *Russian Literature in Transition*. Nottingham UK: Astra Press. 1999.

Lipovetskii, Mark. Rastratnye strategii ili metamorfozy 'chernukhi'. *Novyi mir*. No. 11. 1999. 193–210.

Livers, Keith A. *Constructing the Stalinist Body: Fictional Representations of Corporeality in the Stalinist 1930s*. Lanham: Lexington Books. 2004.

Lovell, Stephen and Menzel, Birgit, Eds. *Reading for Entertainment in Contemporary Russia: Post-Soviet Popular Literature in Historical Perspective*. Munich: Sagner. 2005.

Lystsov, Ivan. Ubiistvo Esenina. *Molodaia Gvardiia*. No. 10. 1990. 245–260.

Macmillin, Arnold. Chekhov and the Soviet Village Prose Writers: Affinities of Fact and Fiction. *Modern Languages Review*. Vol. 93. No. 3. 1998. 754–761.

Bibliography

Markovich V. M. and Shmid, Vol'f, Eds. *Avtor i tekst.* St. Petersburg: St. Petersburg University Press. 1996.

Marks, Steven G. *How Russia Shaped the Modern World: From Art to Anti-Semitism, Ballet to Bolshevism.* Princeton: Princeton University Press. 2003.

Marsh, Rosalind. *History and Literature in Contemporary Russia.* London: Macmillan. 1995.

----------. *Literature, History and Identity in Post-Soviet Russia, 1991–2006.* Oxford, Bern: Peter Lang. 2007.

Masing-Delic, Irene. *Abolishing Death: A Salvation Myth of Russian Twentieth-Century Literature.* Stanford: Stanford University Press. 1992.

Matich, Olga. *Erotic Utopia: The Decadent Imagination in Russia's Fin De Siècle.* Madison: Wisconsin University Press. 2005.

Mianovska, Ioanna. *Dina Rubina vchera i segodnia.* Torun': Adam Marszalek. 2003.

Mirskii, M. B. *Doktor Chekhov.* Moscow: Nauka. 2003.

Mitrokhin, Nikolai. Evrei, gruziny, kulaki i zoloto Strany Sovetov. *Novoe literaturnoe obozrenie.* No. 80/4. 2007. 195–220.

Mochulsky, Konstantin. *Dostoevsky: His Life and Works.* Princeton: Princeton University Press. 1971.

Modzhorian, L. A. *Sionizm kak forma rasizma i rasovoi diskriminatsii.* Moscow: Mezhdunarodnye otnosheniia. 1979.

Mogil'ner, Marina. Evreiskaia antropologiia v Rossii v kontekste evropeiskikh rasovykh issledovanii (XIX–XX vv). *Istoriia i kul'tura rossiiskogo i vostochnoevropeiskogo evreistva: Novye istochniki, novye podkhody.* Ed. Oleg Budnitskii. Moscow: Dom evreiskoi knigi. 2004. 116–137.

Moller, Peter Ulf. *Postlude to The Kreutzer Sonata: Tolstoj and the Debate on Sexual Morality in Russian Literature in the 1890s.* Leiden: E. J. Brill. 1988.

Mondry, Henrietta [G. Mondri]. *Otsenka vospriiatiia F. M. Dostoevskogo v Sovetskom literaturovedenii 1970–1980-ykh gg.* Ph D Thesis. Johannesburg: University of the Witwatersrand. 1984.

----------. *Pisateli-narodniki i evrei.* St. Petersburg: Akademicheskii proekt. 2005.

----------. *Rozanov i evrei.* St. Petersburg: Akademicheskii proekt. 2000.

----------. Beyond the Boundary: Vasilii Rozanov and the Animal Body. *Slavic and East European Journal.* Vol. 43. No. 4. 1999. 651–674.

----------. Ob odnom kripto-evree u A. Chekhova. *New Zealand Slavonic Journal.* Vol. 41. 2007. 43–55.

----------. *Pure, Strong and Sexless: The Peasant Woman's Body and Gleb Uspensky.* Amsterdam: Rodopi. 2006.

----------. Vasily Rozanov and Sexual Anomalies of Gogol and the Jews. *Wiener Slawistischer Almanach.* No. 48. 2001. 53–77.

----------. Who Killed the Russian Poet Esenin? Antisemitism in Soviet Literary Criticism under Glasnost. *Jewish Affairs.* Vol. 46. No. 2. 1991. 25–35.

Moretti, Franco. The Dialectic of Fear. *New Left Review.* Vol. 1. No. 136. 1982. 67–85.

Mosse, George. *Nationalism and Sexuality: Respectability and Abnormal Sexuality in Modern Europe.* New York: Howard Fertig. 1985.

Murav, Harriet. *Identity Theft: The Jew in Russia and the Case of Avraam Uri Kovner.* Stanford: Stanford University Press. 2003.

----------. The Beilis Murder Trial and the Culture of Apocalypse. *Cardozo Studies in Law and Literature.* Vol. 12. No. 2. 2000. 243–263.

Bibliography

Naiman, Eric. *Sex in Public: The Incarnation of Early Soviet Ideology.* Princeton: Princeton University Press. 1997.

Nakhimovsky, Alice. Review on Jakub Blum and Vera Rich. *The Image of the Jew in Soviet Literature: The Post-Stalin Period. The Russian Review.* Vol. 45. No. 4. 1986. 437–438.

-----------. *Russian Jewish Literature and Identity: Jabotinsky, Babel, Grossman, Galich, Roziner, Markish.* Baltimore: The Johns Hopkins University Press. 1992.

Nathans, Benjamin. *Beyond the Pale: The Jewish Encounter with Late Imperial Russia.* Berkeley: University of California Press. 2002.

Nikitin, N. Vskormlennye iadom sionizma. *Krasnaia zvezda.* May 23. 1970.

Nikitina, I. Il'e Erenburgu. 27 iulia 1962. *Sovetskie evrei pishut Il'e Erenburgu, 1943–1966.* Ed. Mordekhai Altshuler et. al. Jerusalem: The Centre for Research and Documentation of East-European Jewry. The Hebrew University of Jerusalem. 1993. 431–435.

Nochlin, Linda. Starting with the Self: Jewish Identity and Its Representation. *The Jew in the Text.* Eds. Linda Nochlin and Tamar Garb. London: Thames and Hudson. 1995. 7–20.

Nordau, Max. Degeneration. *The Fin de Siècle: A Reader in Cultural History c. 1880–1990.* Ed. Sally Ledger and Roger Luckhurst. Oxford: Oxford University Press. 2000. 13–17.

Paperna, A. I. Iz Nikolaevskoi epokhi. *Evrei v Rossii: XIX vek.* Ed. V. E. Kel'ner. Moscow: Novoe literaturnoe obozrenie. 2000. 27–177.

Paperno, Irina. *Chernyshevsky and the Age of Realism.* Stanford, CA: Stanford University Press. 1988.

Paramonov, Boris. *Portret evreia.* St. Petersburg: Izd-vo Grzhebina. 1993.

Parker, Alexander A. *Literature and the Delinquent: The Picaresque Novel in Spain and Europe, 1599–1753.* Edinburgh: Edinburgh University Press. 1967.

Parthé, Kathleen. *Russia's Dangerous Texts: Politics Between The Lines.* New Haven, CT: Yale University Press. 2004.

-----------. *The Russian Village Prose: The Radiant Past.* Princeton, NJ: Princeton University Press. 1992.

Patai, Raphael and Patai Wing, Jennifer. *The Myth of the Jewish Race.* New York: Charles Scribner's Sons. 1975.

Pereira N. G. O. Negative Images of Jews in Recent Russian Literature. *Canadian Slavonic Papers.* Vol. 48. Nos. 1–2. 2006. 47–64.

Perry, Marvin and Schweitzer, Frederick M. *Antisemitism: Myth and Hate from Antiquity to the Present.* New York: Palgrave. 2002.

Petrovskii-Shtern, Iokhanan. *Evrei v Russkoi armii, 1827–1914.* Moscow: Novoe literaturnoe obozrenie. 2003.

Polouektova, Ksenia. *Alexander Solzhenitsyn's 200 Years Together and the "Jewish Question."* ACTA No. 31. The Hebrew University of Jerusalem. 2008.

Pomata, Gianna. Menstruating Men: Similarity and Difference of the Sexes in Early Modern Medicine. *Generation and Degeneration: Tropes of Reproduction in Literature and History from Antiquity to Early Modern Europe.* Ed. Valeria Finucci and Kevin Brownlee. Durham, NC: Duke University Press. 109–152.

Radzinsky, Edvard. *Rasputin: The Last Word.* St. Leonard: Allen and Unwin. 2000.

Rancour-Laferrière, Daniel. *Out from under Gogol's Overcoat: a Psychoanalytic Study.* Ann Arbor: Ardis. 1982.

Rank, Otto. *Art and Artist: Creative Urge and Personality Development.* New York: W. W. Norton. 1989.

Bibliography

-----------. *The Incest Theme in Literature and Legend (Fundamentals of the Psychology of Literary Creations)*. Trans. Gregory C. Richter. Baltimore: The Johns Hopkins University Press. 1992.

-----------. *The Trauma of Birth*. New York: Dover Publications. 1993.

Rayfield, Donald. *Anton Chekhov: A Life*. New York: Henry Holt and Co. 1997.

Rich, Elizabeth, Ed. *Russian Literature after Perestroika, South-Central Review*. Special issue. Vol. 12. No. 3/4. Fall/Winter. 1995.

Ro'i, Yaacov. *The Struggle for the Soviet Jewish Emigration, 1948–1967*. Cambridge UK: Cambridge University Press. 1991.

Rohdewald, Stefan. Post-Soviet Remembrance of the Holocaust and National Memories of the Second World War in Russia, Ukraine and Lithuania. *Forum for Modern Languages Studies*. Special issue: *Representations of the Past in European Memorials*. Vol. 44. No. 2. 2008. 173–184.

Roll-Hansen, Nils and Broberg, Gunnar. *Eugenics and the Welfare State: Sterilization Policy in Demark, Sweden, Norway, and Finland*. Uppsala Studies in History of Science. Uppsala: Uppsala University Press. 2005.

Romanenko, V. *Chekhov i nauka*. Khar'kov: Khar'kovskoe knizhnoe izdatel'stvo. 1962.

Rossman, Vadim. *Jewish Conspiracy and Yellow Peril: Antisemitism and Sinophobia in the Nineteenth Century*. Jerusalem: The Vidal Sassoon International Centre for the Study of Antisemitism. The Hebrew University of Jerusalem. 2004.

-----------. *Russian Intellectual Antisemitism in the Post-Communist Era*. Lincoln: University of Nebraska Press. 2002.

Rothfels, Nigel. *Representing Animals*. Bloomington: Indiana University Press. 2002.

Rubenstein, Joshua and Altman, Ilya, Eds. *The Unknown Black Book: The Holocaust in The German Occupied Territories*. Bloomington: Indiana University Press. 2008.

Rubenstein, Joshua. *Tangled Loyalties: The Life and Times of Ilya Ehrenburg*. New York: Basic Books. 1996.

Ruder, Cynthia A. *Making History for Stalin: The Story of the Belomor Canal*. Gainesville: Florida University Press. 1998.

Rutberg, N. I. and Pidevich, I. N. *Evrei i evreiskii vopros v literature sovetskogo perioda*. Moscow: Grant. 2000.

Safran, Gabriella. Dancing with Death and Salvaging Jewish Culture in *Austeria* and *The Dybbuk*. *Slavic Review*. Vol. 59. No. 4. 2000. 761–781.

----------. *Rewriting the Jew: Assimilation Narratives in the Russian Empire*. Stanford: Stanford University Press. 2000.

Said, Edward. *Orientalism: Western Representations of the Orient*. New York: Vintage Books. 1979.

Satlow, Michael L. *Tasting the Dish: Rabbinic Rhetorics of Sexuality*. Atlanta, GA: Scholars Press. 1996.

Savel'ev, A. N. Predislovie. V. Avdeev. *Rasologiia*. Biblioteka rasovoi mysli. Moscow: Belye al'vy. 2005. 1–7.

Scanlan, James, Ed. *Russian Thought after Communism: The Recovery of a Philosophical Heritage*. New York: M. E. Sharp. 1994.

Schaffenburg, Karl C. Russkiy and Rossiiskiy: Russian National Identity After Putin. *Orbis*. Vol. 51. No. 4. 2007. 75–737.

Segall, Helen. Il'ia Grigor'evich Erenburg. *Russian Prose Writers Between the World Wars*. Dictionary of Literary Biography. 2003. Detroit: Thompson, Gale. 56–77.

Bibliography

Semanova, M. Chekhov i Gleb Uspenskii. (K voprosu o tvorchestve Chekhova vos'midesiatykh godov). *Uchenye Zapiski*. Leningrad: Leningradskii Gosudarstvennyi Pedagogicheskii institut. 1959. 3–63.

Senderovich, Savelii. O chekhovskoi glubine, ili Iudofobskii rasskaz Chekhova v svete iudaisticheskoi ekzegezy. *Avtor i tekst*. Eds. V. M. Markovich and Vol'f Shmid. St. Petersburg: St. Petersburg University Press. 1996. 306–340.

Shafranskaia, Elionora. *Mifopoetika 'inoetnokul'turnogo teksta' v russkoi proze Diny Rubinoi*. Moscow: URSS. 2007.

Sherman, Joseph and Mondry, Henrietta. Russian Dogs and Jewish Russians: Reading Israel Joshua Singer's 'Liuk' in a Russian Literary Context. *Prooftexts: A Journal of Jewish Literary History* Vol. 20. No. 3. 2000. 191–317.

Shrayer, Maxim. *An Anthology of Jewish-Russian Literature: Two Centuries of Dual Identity in Prose and Poetry*. 2 Vols. New York: M. E. Sharpe. 2007.

Shternshis, Anna. *Soviet and Kosher: Jewish Popular Culture in the Soviet Union, 1923–1939*. Bloomington: Indiana University Press. 2006.

Sicher, Efraim. *Jews in Russian Literature After the October Revolution*. Cambridge: Cambridge University Press. 1995.

Siniavskii, Andrei. *"Opavshie list'ia" Vasiliia Vasilievicha Rozanova*. Moscow: Zakharov. 1999.

Sionizm-otravlennoe oruzhie imperializma. Dokumenty i materially. [sbornik] Moscow: Politizdat. 1970.

Sirotkina, Irina. *Diagnosing Literary Genius: A Cultural History of Psychiatry in Russia, 1880–1930*. Baltimore: The Johns Hopkins University Press. 2002.

Slezkine, Yuri. *The Jewish Century*. Princeton: Princeton University Press. 2004.

Slonim, Mark. *Tri liubvi Dostoevskogo*. Moscow: Imidzh. 1991.

Smedley, Audrey and Smedley, Brian. Race as Biology is Fiction, Racism as a Social Problem is Real. (Anthropological and Historical Perspectives on the Social Construction of Race). *American Psychologist*. Vol. 60. No 1. 2005. 16–26.

Soboleva. Evrei. *Narody Rossii: etnograficheskie ocherki*. St. Petersburg: Obshchestvennaia pol'za. 1878–1880. Vol. 1. 391–392.

Soifer, Valerii. *Vlast' i nauka: istoriia razgroma genetiki v SSSR*. New Jersy: Tenafly. 1989.

Sovetskie evrei pishut Il'e Erenburgu. 1943–1966. Ed. Mordekhai Altshuler et. al. The Centre for Research and Documentation of East European Jewry. Jerusalem: The Hebrew University of Jerusalem. 1993.

Stratton, Jon. *Coming Out Jewish*. London: Routledge. 2000.

Swift, Mark. Chekhov's 'Ariadna': A Portrait of Psychopathy and Sin. *Slavonic and East European Review*. Vol. 86. No. 1. 2008. 26–57.

Tager, A. *Delo Beilisa i tsarskaia Rossiia*. Moscow: Reprint edition. 1995.

Tan, V. Evrei i literatura. *Svobodnye mysli*. 18.02. 1908. 1–9.

Todorov, Tzvetan. *Nous et les autres: La reflexion française sur la diversité humaine*. Paris. Seuil. 1989.

Tolstoy, Helena. From Susanna to Sarra: Chekhov in 1886–1887. *Slavic Review*. Vol. 50. No. 3. 1991. 590–600.

Tolz, Vera. *Russia: Inventing the Nation*. London: Arnold. 2001.

Torchikov, V. A. *Vokrug Stalina*. St. Petersburg. 2000.

Trachtenberg, Joshua. *The Devil and the Jews: The Medieval Conception of the Jews and its Relation to Modern Anti-Semitism*. Philadelphia. The Jewish Publication Society. 1983.

Bibliography

Umland, Andreas. Toward an Uncivil Society? Contextualising the Recent Decline of Extremely Right-Wing Parties in Russia. Cambridge, MA: The Weatherhead Center for International Affairs. 2003. Working paper no. 02–03.

Unander, D. *Shattering the Myth of Race: Genetic Realities and Biblical Truth.* Valley Forge, PA: Judson Press. 2000.

Vaiskopf, Mikhail. Sem'ia bez uroda. Obraz evreia v literature russkogo romantizma. *Novoe literaturnoe obozrenie.* No. 27. 1997. 76–99.

Valman, Nadia. *The Jewess in Nineteenth Century British Literary Culture.* Cambridge, UK: Cambridge University Press. 2007.

Vasilenko, G. S. Predislovie. R. Krafft-Ebing. *Polovaia psikhopatiia.* Moscow: Respublika. 1996. 3–7.

Vermel', Solomon. *V. G. Korolenko i evrei. (Vospominaniia, pis'ma).* Moscow. 1924.

Voprosy biologii i patologii evreev. Eds. Dr. V. I. Binshtok, Dr. A. M. Bramson, Prof. G. I. Dembo and Prof. M. M. Gran. Leningrad: Prakticheskaia meditsina. 1926.

Walker Bynum, Caroline. *Theology and Practice in Late Medieval Northern Germany and Beyond.* Philadelphia: University of Pennsylvania Press. 2007.

Waters, Elizabeth. Female Form in Soviet Political Iconography. *Russia's Women: Accommodation, Resistance, Transformation.* Ed. Barbara Evans Clements. Berkeley: University of California Press. 1991. 225–242.

Weinberg, Robert. Jews into Peasants? Solving the Jewish Question in Birobidzhan. *Jews and Jewish Life in Russia and the Soviet Union.* Ed. Yaacov Ro'i. London and New York: Routledge. 1995. 87–103.

Weinerman, Eli. Racism, Racial Prejudice, and the Jews in Late Imperial Russia. *Ethnic Racial Studies.* Vol. 17. No. 3. 1994. 442–495.

Weitz, Eric. Racial Politics without the Concept of Race: Reevaluating Soviet Ethnic and National Purges. *Slavic Review.* Vol. 61. No. 1. Spring 2002. 1–29.

Westermarck, Edward. *The History of Human Marriage.* 5th Ed., 3 Vols. London: Macmillan and Co. 1925.

Wheen, Francis. *Karl Marx: A Life.* London: Fourth Estate. 1999.

Worobec, Christine. *Possessed: Women, Witches and Demons in Imperial Russia.* De Kalb: Northern Ilinois University Press. 2001.

Yerushalmi, Yosef Hayim. *Freud's Moses: Judaism Terminable and Interminable.* New Haven: Yale University Press. 1991.

Index of Names

Index of Names

Index of Names

Index of Subjects

LaVergne, TN USA
07 January 2010
169152LV00002BA/1/P